Law and the Brain

Law and the Brain

Edited by

S ZEKI
AND
O GOODENOUGH

Originating from a Theme Issue first published in Philosophical
Transactions of the Royal Society B: Biological Sciences

OXFORD
UNIVERSITY PRESS

OXFORD

UNIVERSITY PRESS

Great Clarendon Street, Oxford OX2 6DP

Oxford University Press is a department of the University of Oxford.
It furthers the University's objective of excellence in research, scholarship,
and education by publishing worldwide in

Oxford New York

Auckland Cape Town Dar es Salaam Hong Kong Karachi
Kuala Lumpur Madrid Melbourne Mexico City Nairobi
New Delhi Shanghai Taipei Toronto

With offices in

Argentina Austria Brazil Chile Czech Republic France Greece
Guatemala Hungary Italy Japan Poland Portugal Singapore
South Korea Switzerland Thailand Turkey Ukraine Vietnam

Oxford is a registered trade mark of Oxford University Press
in the UK and in certain other countries

Published in the United States
by Oxford University Press Inc., New York

British Library Cataloguing in Publication Data

Data available

Library of Congress Cataloging in Publication Data
Law and the brain / edited by O. Goodenough and S. Zeki.—1st ed.
p. cm.
Includes bibliographical references and index.
1. Law—Psychological aspects.   2. Cognitive neuroscience.
3. Neurosciences—Social aspects.
4. Neurobehavioral disorders—Law and legislation.
I. Goodenough, Oliver R.   II. Zeki, Semir
K346.L379 2006   340′.1′9—dc22   2005023085

Typeset by Newgen Imaging Systems (P) Ltd., Chennai, India
Printed in Great Britain
on acid-free paper by
Biddles Ltd., King's Lynn, Norfolk

ISBN 0–19–857011–2 (Pbk.)   978–0–19–857011–0
ISBN 0–19–857010–4 (Hbk.)   978–0–19–857010–3

1 3 5 7 9 10 8 6 4 2

Preface

The legal process is often invoked to resolve scientific or economic problems such as may arise when a bridge collapses, or an aeroplane crashes, or a ship sinks; or when a mishap occurs on the operating table; or when patent protection is sought for an invention claimed to be novel; or when it is necessary to assess the effect of a commercial practice on competition in a market; or when a baby dies, for no apparent reason, in its cot; or when it is sought to identify a fingerprint on a murder weapon.

Problems of this kind may be very difficult and very important. Much may turn on their accurate resolution. But they are not the kind of problem to which the articles in this special review are directed, which are of a much more fundamental nature, concerned with the motivation of individual human beings to act in the way they do.

Legal rules do not exist for their own sake. They exist because they are thought to be necessary or desirable to curb excesses of anti-social behaviour, to encourage responsible government, to protect individual freedom and autonomy, to promote beneficial forms of economic activity, to encourage socially desirable patterns of behaviour, and so on. All these purposes (and the list could of course be extended almost indefinitely) depend on collective judgements about human motivation, the factors that influence human beings to think, decide and act as they do.

In the past, the law has tended to base its approach to such questions on a series of rather crude working assumptions: adults of competent mental capacity are free to choose whether they will act in one way or another; they are presumed to act rationally, and in what they conceive to be their own best interests; they are credited with such foresight of the consequences of their actions as reasonable people in their position could ordinarily be expected to have; they are generally taken to mean what they say.

Whatever the merits or demerits of working assumptions such as these in the ordinary range of cases, it is evident that they do not provide a uniformly accurate guide to human behaviour. A decision may be guided by reason, but it may be guided by emotion, intuition or some other influence altogether. Why else does a claimant, having received an apology, disdain an offer of compensation? Why else do normal people confess to crimes they have not committed? Even if it is accepted that the will of all human beings is free, the choices open to some are, in practice, constrained in a way that those of others are not. It seems that foresight is somewhat randomly distributed among human beings, like oil in the crust of the Earth.

As the articles in this themed issue cogently show, our endeavour to resolve problems of this kind are greatly assisted by what Goodenough & Prehn (2004) call 'an approach that seeks to integrate into the study of human thought our rapidly emerging knowledge about the structure and functions of the brain and about the formal properties of agents and decision-making processes'. It is surely true, as O'Hara (2004) suggests, 'that our brains are the product of evolutionary forces and that our brain structures influence our thought, feelings and actions'. If so, one must agree with Chorvat & McCabe (2004) that

'By studying precisely how these mechanisms function, as well as other decision making mechanisms operate, we can better understand the limits and proper scope of law'.

The content of these articles must be of profound interest to any open-minded lawyer. For, as Goodenough (2004) puts it, 'the discoveries of cognitive neuroscience are rapidly expanding our understanding of the workings of the human brain' and Goodenough & Prehn (2004) 'Law is, in its own way, an investigative science, a learned and academic discipline which probes into the nature of human thought. . . . The classic legal process of seeking to articulate the mental landscape on issues of right and wrong into word-based rules is a rigorous intellectual exercise, relentlessly tested back against reality in hundreds and thousands of *in vivo* experiments: actual human disputes . . .'.

As the same authors graphically suggest, one may advance explanations about the science of automobiles without ever opening up the bonnet of a car: 'With the engine exposed, a much more complete explanation is possible'.

August 2004   Tom Bingham
House of Lords, London SW1A 0PW, UK

References

Chorvat, T. & McCabe, K. 2004 The brain and the law. *Phil. Trans. R. Soc. B* **359**, 1727–1736. (doi:10.1098/rstb.2004.1545)

Goodenough, O. R. 2004 Responsibility and punishment: whose mind? A response. *Phil. Trans. R. Soc. B* **359**, 1805–1809. (doi:10.1098/rstb.2004.1548)

Goodenough, O. R. & Prehn, K. 2004 A neuroscientific approach to normative judgment in law and justice. *Phil. Trans. R. Soc. B* **359**, 1709–1726. (doi:10.1098/rstb. 2004.1552)

O'Hara, E. A. 2004 How neuroscience might advance the law. *Phil. Trans. R. Soc. B* **359**, 1677–1684. (doi:10.1098/rstb.2004.1541)

Contents

CRIMINAL RESPONSIBILITY AND PUNISHMENT

This book was originally published as an issue of the Philosophical Transactions of the Royal Society B: Biological Sciences (Volume 359; Number 1451/November 29, 2004) but has been materially changed and updated.

List of Contributors

Abigail A. Baird Department of Psychological and Brain Sciences, Dartmouth College, Hanover, NH 03755, USA (Abigail.baird@dartmouth.edu)

Lord Tom Bingham House of Lords, London, SW1A 0PW, UK

Terrence Chorvat School of Law, George Mason University, 3301 North Fairfax Drive, Arlington, VA 22201, USA (tchorvat@gmu.edu)

Jonathan Cohen Department of Psychology, Center for the Study of Brain, Mind, and Behavior, Princeton University, Princeton, NJ 08544, USA

Kevin N. Dunbar Department of Psychological and Brain Sciences, Dartmouth College, Hanover, NH 03755, USA

Tom F.D. Farrow Department of Academic Clinical Psychiatry, Division of Genomic Medicine, University of Sheffield, The Longley Centre, Norwood Grange Drive, Sheffield, S5 7JT, UK

Jonathan A. Fugelsang Department of Psychology, University of Waterloo, 200 University Avenue West, Waterloo, Ontario, N2L 3G1, Canada (jafugels@uwaterloo.ca)

Venkatasubramanian Ganesan Department of Academic Clinical Psychiatry, Division of Genomic Medicine, University of Sheffield, The Longley Centre, Norwood Grange Drive, Sheffield, S5 7JT, UK

Russell D. Green Department of Academic Clinical Psychiatry, Division of Genomic Medicine, University of Sheffield, The Longley Centre, Norwood Grange Drive, Sheffield, S5 7JT, UK

Joshua Greene Department of Psychology, Center for the Study of Brain, Mind, and Behavior, Princeton University, Princeton, NJ 08544, USA (jdgreene@princeton.edu)

Oliver R. Goodenough Vermont Law School, Chelsea Street, South Royalton, VT 05091, USA (ogoodenough@vermontlaw.edu)

Robert A. Hinde St John's College, University of Cambridge, St John's Street, Cambridge CB2 1TP, UK (rah15@cam.ac.uk)

Hon. Morris B. Hoffman Second Judicial District (Denver), State of Colorado, 1437 Bannock Street, Courtroom 9, Denver, CO 80202, USA (morris.hoffman@judicial.state.co.us)

Catherine J. Hughes Department of Academic Clinical Psychiatry, Division of Genomic Medicine, University of Sheffield, The Longley Centre, Norwood Grange Drive, Sheffield, S5 7JT, UK

Mike D. Hunter Department of Academic Clinical Psychiatry, Division of Genomic Medicine, University of Sheffield, The Longley Centre, Norwood Grange Drive, Sheffield, S5 7JT, UK

Owen D. Jones Vanderbilt University Law School and Department of Biological Sciences, 131 21st Avenue South, Nashville, TN 37203–1181, USA (owen.jones@vanderbilt.edu)

David H. Leung Department of Academic Clinical Psychiatry, Division of Genomic Medicine, University of Sheffield, The Longley Centre, Norwood Grange Drive, Sheffield, S5 7JT, UK

Kevin McCabe Department of Economics, George Mason University, 4400 University Drive, Fairfax, VA 22030, USA and School of Law, George Mason University, 3301 North Fairfax Drive, Arlington, VA 22201, USA

Erin Ann O'Hara Vanderbilt University Law School, 131 21st Avenue, South Nashville, TN 372–3–1181, USA (erin.ohara@law.vanderbilt.edu)

Kristin Prehn Berlin Neuroimaging Center, Department of Neurology, Charité University Medicine, Berlin Campus Mitte, Schumann-Strasse 20/21, 10117 Berlin, Germany

Robert M. Sapolsky Department of Biological Sciences, and Department of Neurology and Neurological Sciences, Stanford University School of Medicine, Gilbert Laboratory, MC 5020, Stanford CA 94305–5020, USA (sapolsky@stanford.edu)

Sean A. Spence Department of Academic Clinical Psychiatry, Division of Genomic Medicine, University of Sheffield, The Longley Centre, Norwood Grange Drive, Sheffield, S5 7JT, UK (s.a.spence@sheffield.ac.uk)

Jeffrey Evans Stake Indiana University School of Law-Bloomington, 211 South Indiana Avenue, Bloomington, IN 47405, USA (stake@indiana.edu)

Paul J. Zak Center for Neuroeconomics Studies, Claremont Graduate University, 150 East Tenth Street, Claremont, CA 91711, USA (paul@pauljzak.com)

Semir Zeki Laboratory of Neurobiology, Department of Anatomy and Wellcome Department of Imaging Neuroscience, University College London, Gower Street, London, WC1E 6BT, UK

Law and the brain: introduction

Combining law and the brain as a matter for study requires not just the integration of two apparently remote fields of study but also of two profoundly different orientations towards research and study. We believe that, in spite of the difficulties, such a combination, perhaps even emerging in a new specialized discipline in the future, will not only enrich both fields but is the ineluctable consequence of the current assault on the secrets of the brain. The effort to bring the fields together is therefore a worthy task, and this issue is the first systematic effort to test this expectation.

1. New possibilities from science

It was not very many years ago that neurobiology, devoted largely to studying the structure and functioning of the brain, would have considered the law quite remote from its field of enquiry; anyone attempting to connect the two would have been the subject of ridicule. It is a measure of the advances made in neurobiology over the past 20 years that the connection between the two no longer seems tenuous and that eminent neurobiologists should address questions and use language that would have seemed more suited to a court of law or to a department of academic jurisprudence. This enlargement of the province of neurobiology is not restricted to law; indeed the latter may even be considered to be a relative newcomer. Aesthetics, morality, emotional states and decision-making processes are all topics that neurobiologists are currently engaged in actively researching. Yet these areas of interdisciplinary study can still be, to a large degree, pursued with a comfortable level of academic detachment. Law is potentially different—it has immediate practical applications with social and political consequences.

The factors that have brought this radical change in research strategy can be pinpointed with some precision. They can be traced to two advances, one technical and the other conceptual. The technical advance is the development of methods for studying human brain activity. The primary impetus for developing such techniques may have been medical (for example to determine the size and extent of injuries to the brain or the spread of cancers), but they have been modified substantially to make a very considerable impact in studying brain *activity* as well as *anatomy*. There is every sign that the technology associated with such studies will develop and that present-day techniques will soon be outmoded, being replaced by ones that are capable of giving us even more intimate details of the workings of the brain. This technology has recently seen prodigious use by cognitive neuroscience, which relates brain activity to human thought and behaviour, creating a working model of the brain and mind.

The conceptual advance is even more dramatic. It rests on the realization that subjective mental states—the feeling of love, the appreciation of beauty, the desire to cheat, the effort to read the mind of others and much else besides—have particular neural correlates that can be studied with such precision as modern-day technology affords, and which future technology will improve upon. Previously, the study of subjective mental states would have been considered by many to be an unscientific pastime, because it was not objectively verifiable. However, modern-day technology has modified all that, by showing that subjective mental states usually correlate with specific kinds of neural activity across different brains. This has introduced a new framework of enquiry that is bound to have profound effects in many areas of human endeavour, including the law.

2. New opportunities for law

Nor is the scepticism about combining law and the brain limited to neuroscience. Although few would dispute that making, considering and enforcing law are all mental activities, the application of a biological understanding about thought and behaviour to problems in the law has, until recently, been slow to gain acceptance (see O'Hara 2004; Kuklin 2004). Even today, legal scholarship often focuses on the somewhat technical issues of drafting, interpretation and application, as much a field of literary study as a science of behaviour. Over the past century, significant steps have been made in looking beyond these internal concerns, and the academic study of law has expanded to include approaches informed by a variety of other disciplines, in particular the social sciences.

The law has long scavenged other fields for its theoretical underpinnings, and during the twentieth century the most popular targets for incorporation shifted from theology and philosophy to economics and sociology. In this, law was no better or worse than public discourse more generally. Incorporating biology into legal doctrine is of course more problematic. To the extent that biological approaches had been included in the great arguments of the twentieth century between fascism, communism, capitalism, socialism, dictatorship and liberal democracy, they often wore a distorted and appropriately discredited aspect that had more to do with political expediency than with any accurate application of the admittedly limited science of the times. But that biology should have been thus misused in the past is not a good reason for not taking account of its findings in the future, always of course with appropriate safeguards.

There has been a persistent, if perhaps secondary, tradition for applying the insights of psychology to problems of law, a tradition that has illuminated a number of questions (see, generally, *Psychology, Public Policy and Law*). The new neuroscience has the potential to put a biologically informed psychology front and centre in jurisprudential study. In part, this is a second-hand insight, scavenged once again from the impact that neurobiology is having on such traditional sources of legal borrowing as economics and even philosophy. The impact that behavioural economics, experimental economics and, now, neuroeconomics are having on the mother discipline is beginning to percolate into the study of law (e.g. Goodenough & Prehn 2004; Hoffman 2004; Zak 2004). However, the step from the law to cognitive neuroscience is likely to become more and more a direct one.

3. Putting law and the brain together

This issue constitutes the first serious attempt by a major scientific journal to address questions of law as reflecting brain activity and, conversely, to emphasize that it is the organization and functioning of the brain that determines how we enact and obey laws.

This neurological link is not unique to law; indeed, it may be said that all human activity is a product of the organization and functioning of the brain, and reflects that activity, fortified by the demands of evolution of which the brain is the most exquisite product. Some aspects of the brain are widely shared across the human species; others are subject to individual variation. The 'bread and butter' of evolution is rooted in variability, which endows individuals with different aptitudes and potentials, on which selective processes can act in the golden and amoral pursuit of shaping the content of the next generation and thus ensuring the survival of the species. Yet variability, while being one of the engines of evolution, is also the source of a problem for the legal system, for in the interests of the common good it cannot allow unchecked expression of that variability. The legal system, not unlike the religious system with which it has been traditionally connected and from which it has often derived inspiration, may therefore be considered at one level to be a struggle against biology, but a struggle that is also ultimately rooted in biology and dictated by the evolutionary biological imperative of maximizing the replicative success of its human participants.

This much belongs perhaps to the relatively safe domain of academic jurisprudence. But there are real issues that the legal system will face as neurobiological studies continue relentlessly to probe the human mind, the motives for our actions, our decision-making processes, aesthetic judgements, and such issues as free will and responsibility. This pursuit will not be a one-way process. The legal profession is at least two millennia older than the neurobiological profession, which is not much more than 150 years old at best, and in its current state of probing the mind of man and his subjective states is far younger than that. The design of paradigms to study brain activity in relation to such topics as the sense of justice, the weighing of probabilities, concepts of ownership and other factors that are important in law, will be not only aided by legal theory and practice, but, indeed, derived from them to a large extent. Yet, as the articles in this issue show, neurobiology has already raised issues that are fundamental to the legal system, and not just in an academic sense but in a practical sense too.

Of the practical ones, the simplest example is the use of modern technology as an improvement and eventual replacement of older, unreliable and controversial techniques. It is quite possible that, in the very near future, brain-imaging techniques will replace finger-printing and lie detector tests as reliable indices of identity and of the truthfulness of a witness's statement (see Spence *et al.* 2004). This in itself will have repercussions that will probably provoke changes in the law. For example, whereas fingerprinting merely reveals the pattern on fingers and has been used—controversially in some cases—as a means of identification, a functional brain scan will be capable of revealing much more. In this, scanning is not unlike DNA analysis, which can be used in establishing identity and, by extension, parenthood, but which also carries much more information about the individual and has raised troubling issues of privacy and fairness in the law.

Perhaps more problematic for the legal system will be a determination, through the use of modern brain technology, of the extent to which individuals are responsible for their actions. There are naturally states—for example, acute damage, malfunctioning or underdevelopment of the frontal lobe—in which individuals may have lost all sense of morality or propriety as society defines it, with the consequence that they may be held with biological justice not to be responsible for their actions or their consequences (Sapolsky 2004). The more we probe into the brain, and especially the emotional brain and the reasoning brain, the more we are likely to be confronted with mitigating neurological reasons with reason for weighing carefully the type and degree of punishment (Greene & Cohen 2004). The law has, as a general approach and without a detailed knowledge of the brain and its mechanisms, recognized limitations on responsibility in doctrines such as the famous *crimes passionelles* of the French and other legal systems. The linked problems of free will, the degree to which the legal system may assume that the actions of any individual, whether criminal or not, are determined by a free will and, interestingly, the extent to which those dispensing punishment may so interpret the mind and brain of the offender, together take a prominent place in this themed issue. These problems are, of course, unlikely to be resolved easily, but there seems little doubt that the accretion of neurobiological evidence will have a determining influence in the very near future on decisions of the criminal law.

While current and future brain studies are thus likely to be of particular interest in criminal law, it is also likely that other branches of law will come under the spell of new discoveries. The law of property and possession, contract, trust, inheritance, marriage, evidence and many of the other sub-branches of the legal system will all receive detailed scrutiny as neurobiology begins to probe the determining way in which the human brain organizes its decisions and preferences. Above all, perhaps, the law itself will come under more intense scrutiny when neurobiologists begin to probe the brain's sense of justice. Theoretically, it would be difficult for any legal system to enact laws and dispense judgements that most citizens in society can be demonstrated by objective neurobiological evidence to consider unjust. It is indeed possible that, in a 'millennial' future, perhaps only decades away, a good knowledge of the brain's system of justice and of how the brain reacts to conflicts may provide critical tools in resolving international political and economic conflicts.

In his influential *Lectures on jurisprudence*, John Austin (1873), a disciple of Jeremy Bentham and J. S. Mill, tried to promote the notion that jurisprudence should study law as it is, not as it should be, describing and analysing it without reference to whether it is good or bad. The articles in the present themed issue and in future issues of other learned journals, influenced by the developing discipline of neurobiology as applied to jurisprudence, are perhaps more concerned with law as it should be once the characteristics of the organ that ultimately provides all laws will be known. That is a millennial future that all those interested in both branches can begin to look forward to.

4. The special challenges of combining science and policy

In addition to the general problems of interdisciplinary study, the combination of law and neurobiology faces the special challenges inherent in combining science with questions of policy and its application in law. In part, this arises from a divergence in basic orientation. As Sapolsky (2004) notes in this issue, good science often moves forward by holding questions open, by entertaining a number of possible hypotheses, by recognizing the contingent nature of scientific truth. The law, by contrast, has to close questions out, providing yes or no answers in a short period of time based on limited information. The cultivated uncertainty that is a scientific virtue is anathema to legal decision-making. Scientists frustrate lawyers, and lawyers make scientists nervous. Good work at the law/brain interface requires a cross-cultural understanding as well as an interdisciplinary one.

Another obstacle arises from the problem that scientists have in understanding the utility of counterfactual myths as foundations for effective legal regimes. For instance, in a literal sense, human equality is a myth. Variation ensures that each of us has our own package of strengths and weaknesses. Neither of us, Zeki or Goodenough, has the ability to paint respectably, write good detective fiction, compose songs or play sweeper for even a middling kind of football team. Yet, as a legal matter, the democratic societies in which we live treat us as the equal of those who can do these things. This equality myth is a key element in the maintenance of a particularly admirable kind of social order, a counterfactual that pays dividends in fairness and stability. Proving the law wrong in its declared assumptions may not actually affect the utility of those assumptions (e.g. Goodenough 2004).

An involvement in questions of social application can expose scientists and their research programmes to the vicissitudes of politics. Even in a settled democracy, politics is a rough-and-tumble arena, a wrestling ring where conflicting interests and beliefs square off with lots of broken limbs and bruises. Grants, appointments and laboratory access are tricky enough to obtain on the basis of scientific merit, without also putting them at risk in that wrestling ring. However, it is a risk that we think more scientists should be willing to take. The problems facing us as individuals, members of societies and inhabitants of an increasingly endangered ecosystem all have scientific components. We need the knowledge and insights that scientists can provide, whether about global warming, genetically engineered foods, the spread of disease or the decision-making processes of adolescents (Baird & Fugelsang 2004). Our politics can be only as good as all branches of society help to make them.

Finally, there are particular inhibitions and taboos about the biology of moral judgement that grow from the deployment, in past years, of cartoons of this kind of science as window-dressing for ideas, some of them quite hideous, that had their source in other passions. Currently, these inhibitions about using biological knowledge to inform policy in the moral realm are most frequently linked with left-leaning political concerns. Certainly biological explanations of morality have had a chequered past in the hands of Spencer and his successors, but biology has been called upon to support the excesses of the left as well as of the right (e.g. Goodenough 1997; Singer 2000; Greene 2003; Kuklin 2004). Ironically, on questions such as stem cell research, it is the right that is resisting the uses of biology. In a model of moral judgement discussed by many of the authors in this themed issue, Haidt (2001) suggests that the rational explanation of a moral choice follows an intuitive judgement. A similar process probably also applies to these cartoon uses of science in politics. Generally, the excesses of both the right and the left have had limited causal connection with the pieces of scientific camouflage that have been commandeered to give them respectability. Rather than being linked to repressive approaches, Greene (2003) argues that a scientific understanding of the nature of moral judgement should help promote tolerance and peace.

We believe that the antidotes to the ignorant use of bad science in law and policy are better science, not less science, and a better understanding of what the science means, rather than greater ignorance. We hope that the work presented in this themed issue will promote these goals. They do not shy away from making their political starting and ending points known, and there is enough of a spread from left to right in the positions taken in this issue to suggest that the insights coming from neurobiology, honestly interpreted, will confirm, confound, challenge and surprise all parts of the political spectrum.

The insights may even throw light on the difficult choices between conflicting social goods that underlie many of our most intractable legal and political dilemmas.

5. This issue

The essays in this issue cover a range of topics at the intersection of law and neurobiology. Their organization here is not random. Taken in order, they are intended to provide a loose progression for the reader. The Preface by Lord Bingham, Britain's senior law lord, together with this Introduction by us are intended to set the stage. The first two essays, 'The neuroeconomic path of the law' by Judge Morris Hoffman (Colorado) and 'How neuroscience might advance the law' by Erin O'Hara (Law, Vanderbilt), put the combination of law and the brain into its context in jurisprudence and the legal academy, both intellectually and politically. The next two essays, 'Law and the sources of morality' by Robert Hinde (Zoology, Cambridge) and 'Law, evolution and the brain' by Owen Jones (Law and Biology, Vanderbilt), examine the underlying principles of evolutionary biology that provide a foundation for the proximate brain mechanisms involved in morality and law. In the final introductory article, Oliver Goodenough and Kristin Prehn (Psychology, Humboldt) describe 'A neuroscientific approach to normative judgement in law and justice', reviewing the state of research into normative judgement, making the link between law and cognitive neuroscience, and providing, along the way, an introduction to the methods of cognitive neuroscience for the lay reader.

The next pair of articles, 'The brain and the law' by Terrence Chorvath (Law, George Mason) and Kevin McCabe (Economics and Law, George Mason) and 'Neuroeconomics' by Paul Zak (Economics, Claremont Graduate University) provide complementary reviews of exciting developments in economics growing out of the new neuroscience. Both also suggest potential applications of these developments to legal concerns, particularly in the realms of economic exchange and institution building. Although non-lawyers often think first of criminal law when they consider the legal system, creating structures for reliable economic activity is one of law's most important functions. Zak's essay also includes an introduction to brain anatomy for non-specialists.

Moving to more specific legal problems, the issue next presents a pair of articles on courtroom concerns: 'A cognitive neuroscience framework for understanding causal reasoning and the law' by Jonathan Fugelsang (Psychological and Brain Sciences, Dartmouth) and Kevin Dunbar (Psychological and Brain Sciences and Education, Dartmouth), and 'Scanning the deceiving brain' by Sean A. Spence, and his colleagues (Psychiatry, Sheffield). A better understanding of how people evaluate evidence as they come to decisions and of the neurological processes of deception should be of particular interest to judges and courtroom advocates. The next article, Jeffrey Stake's treatment of 'The property' 'instinct', posits a neurobiological logic for this important human—and perhaps animal—institution.

The themed issue closes with a group of four articles that revolve around the conundrum of criminal responsibility. In 'For the law, neuroscience changes nothing and everything' Joshua Greene (Psychology, Princeton) and Jonathan Cohen (Psychology, Princeton), advance a forceful attack on the idea of free will generally and on the patterns of criminal punishment that flow from a starting point of volition and blame. Robert Sapolsky (Biology and Neurology, Stanford) offers a further critique of the law of criminal responsibility, making the explicit connection between 'The frontal cortex and the criminal justice system'. In 'The emergence of consequential thought: evidence from neuroscience', Abigail Baird (Psychological and Brain Sciences, Dartmouth) and Jonathan Fugelsang review the emerging understanding of the physiology of brain maturation in adolescents and draw conclusions about the ability of this group to reason effectively about the consequences of their actions. Finally, Oliver Goodenough poses the countervailing question: 'Responsibility and punishment: whose mind?' He suggests that the psychology of punishment may have more to do with the legal tests of competency than the psychology of the offender.

We believe that this issue can be read not only for its specific articles but also as an interrelated whole. As editors, we have been challenged, educated and provoked to further thought by the contributions to this themed issue. Whether you are a specialist in law, psychology or neurobiology, or are simply a reader with a lively interest in recent developments in subjects of critical importance for humanity, we hope that you, too, will find the articles that follow exceptionally stimulating reading.

References

Austin, J. 1873 *Lectures on jurisprudence, or the philosophy of positive law*, 4th edn. (ed. R. Campbell). London: John Murray

Baird, A. A. & Fugelsang, J. A. 2004 The emergence of consequential thought: evidence from neuroscience. *Phil. Trans. R. Soc. B* **359**, 1797–1804. (doi:10.1098/rstb.2004.1549)

Chorvat, T. & McCabe, K. 2004 The brain and the law. *Phil. Trans. R. Soc. B* **359**, 1727–1736. (doi:10.1098/rstb.2004.1545)

Fugelsang, J. A. & Dunbar, K. N. 2004 A cognitive neuroscience framework for understanding causal reasoning and the law. *Phil. Trans. R. Soc. B* **359**, 1749–1754. (doi:10.1098/rstb.2004.1550)

Goodenough, O. R. 1997 Biology, behavior, and criminal law: seeking a responsible approach to an inevitable interchange. *Vermont Law Rev.* **22**, 263–294.

Goodenough, O. R. 2004 Responsibility and punishment: whose mind? A response. *Phil. Trans. R. Soc. B* **359**, 1805–1809. (doi:10.1098/rstb.2004.1548)

Goodenough, O. R. & Prehn, K. 2004 A neuroscientific approach to normative judgment in law and justice. *Phil. Trans. R. Soc. B* **359**, 1709–1726. (doi:10.1098/rstb. 2004.1552)

Greene, J. 2003 From neural 'is' to moral 'ought': what are the moral implications of neuroscientific moral psychology? *Nature Rev. Neurosci.* **4**, 847–849.

Greene, J. & Cohen, J. 2004 For the law, neuroscience changes nothing and everything. *Phil. Trans. R. Soc. B* **359**, 1775–1785. (doi:10.1098/rstb.2004.1546)

Haidt, J. 2001 The emotional dog and its rational tail: a social intuitionist approach to moral judgment. *Psychol. Rev.* **108**, 814–834.

Hinde, R. A. 2004 Law and the sources of morality. *Phil. Trans. R. Soc. B* **359**, 1685–1695. (doi:10.1098/rstb.2004.1542)

Hoffman, M. 2004 The neuroeconomic path of the law. *Phil. Trans. R. Soc. B* **359**, 1667–1676. (doi:10.1098/ rstb.2004.1545)

Jones, O. D. 2004 Law, evolution and the brain: applications and open questions. *Phil. Trans. R. Soc. B* **359**, 1697–1707. (doi:10.1098/rstb.2004.1543)

Kuklin, B. H. 2004 Evolution, politics and law. *Valparaiso University Law Review* **38**, 1129–1248.

O'Hara, E. A. 2004 How neuroscience might advance the law. *Phil. Trans. R. Soc. B* **359**, 1677–1684. (doi:10.1098/rstb.2004.1541)

Sapolsky, R. M. 2004 The frontal cortex and the criminal justice system. *Phil. Trans. R. Soc. B* **359**, 1787–1796. (doi:10.1098/rstb.2004.1547)

Singer, P. 2000 A *Darwinian left*. New Haven, CT: Yale University Press.
Spence, S. A., Hunter, M. D., Farrow, T. F. D., Green, R. D., Leung, D. H., Hughes C. J. & Ganesan, V. 2004 A cognitive neurobiological account of deception: evidence from functional neuroimaging. *Phil. Trans. R. Soc. B* **359**, 1755–1762. (doi:10.1098/rstb.2004.1555)
Stake, J. E. 2004 The property 'instinct'. *Phil. Trans. R. Soc. B* **359**, 1763–1774. (doi:10.1098/rstb.2004.1551)
Zak, P. J. 2004 Neuroeconomics. *Phil. Trans. R. Soc. B* **359**, 1737–1748. (doi:10.1098/rstb.2004.1544)

Introductory essays

1

The neuroeconomic path of the law

Morris B. Hoffman

Advances in evolutionary biology, experimental economics and neuroscience are shedding new light on age-old questions about right and wrong, justice, freedom, the rule of law and the relationship between the individual and the state. Evidence is beginning to accumulate suggesting that humans evolved certain fundamental behavioural predispositions grounded in our intense social natures, that those predispositions are encoded in our brains as a distribution of probable behaviours, and therefore that there may be a core of universal human law.

Keywords: neuroeconomics; law; human evolution; behaviour; brain

1.1 Introduction

Developments at the intersection of evolutionary biology and neuroscience are beginning to approach a powerful resonance with the foundations of law. In this essay, I argue that significant advances in our understanding of evolution, the brain and behaviour presage a similar revolution in our understanding of the roots of law. The old paradigm of law as a purely cultural construct to repress our natural aggressions is giving way to a deeper understanding of the law's adaptive value and its role as an institutional expression of evolved social behaviours.

It is becoming clearer, with each advance in evolutionary biology, that the distinctions between animal morphology and animal behaviour are arbitrary, and that evolution is a powerful tool to explain aspects of both. At the same time, advances in neuroscience are suggesting a brain-to-behaviour mechanism that may supply what has been the missing link in the notion that complex behaviours have a significant evolutionary component. Together, these disciplines are not only completing evolution's tale, they are also shedding significant light on the age-old question of human nature, and therefore on the foundations of human nature's institutional analogue, the law.

1.2 The Darwinian pragmatism of Holmes

Law's first significant and quite unsatisfactory encounter with evolutionary biology began in the late 1800s as a kind of legal version of Social Darwinism. Its champion, Oliver Wendell Holmes Jr, constructed an elegant foundation built on what, at that time, was thought to be evolution's relentless drive towards self-interest through aggression.

In 1897, Holmes published a law review article in the *Harvard Law Review* called 'The path of the law' (Holmes 1897). It was profoundly influential, and set the stage for a revolution in twentieth century jurisprudence. Richard Posner has called it 'the best article-length work on law ever written' (Posner 1992, p. x). The revolution it began, and the one in whose midst we still find ourselves today, has had enormous consequences, both good and bad.

Holmes's jurisprudential model was based on a rather startling (for its time) synthesis of law and biology. The core idea, which Holmes first published 16 years earlier in his small book *The common law* (Holmes 1881), was that the march of the common law is like the march of evolution—not guided by any external goals (i.e. 'natural law') but rather shaped by the interaction of individual judges' proximate decisions and the ultimate judgement of precedent. Judges push the boundaries of the law just enough to accommodate what their experience tells them should be an acceptable result in a single case. Rules that work (that is, rules that are accepted over time) survive as precedent. Rules that do not work, die.

In 'The path of the law', Holmes (1897) polished and tightened these insights into four forceful and striking axioms, which he argued completely described and informed all of jurisprudence.

(i) If you want to know the law and nothing else, you must look at it as a bad man, who cares only for the material consequences which such knowledge enables him to predict . . . . (p. 459).
(ii) The prophecies of what courts will in fact do, and nothing more pretentious, are what I mean by the law (p. 461).
(iii) The duty to keep a contract at common law means a prediction that you must pay damages if you do not keep it—and nothing else (p. 462).
(iv) [I]t would . . . be a gain if every word of moral significance could be banished from the law altogether (p. 464).

These insights were a breath of fresh air to a jurisprudence suffocating from a stilted kind of formalism, in which legal thinking was almost entirely limited to the mundane acts of identifying, classifying and labelling legal principles. In a very real sense, Holmes had begun to do for jurisprudence what Darwin had done for biology: insights untethered to any grand external assumptions were making it possible to see both disciplines on a very large scale, and therefore to see deep connections between what had before seemed to be isolated observations.

But Holmes's insights came at a heavy price, in part because they were based on a primitive understanding of evolution, not unlike Herbert Spencer's primitive understanding. The revolution Holmes began was not just a revolution against legal formalism; it was, as Professor Albert Alschuler has so aptly described it, a revolution against the very idea of right and wrong (Alschuler 2000, p. 10). In the law, as in the natural world, Holmes insisted that there is no right or wrong, only a relentless struggle for survival.

As Professor Alschuler also recognized, Holmes's valueless philosophy is the grandfather of the principal school of modern American jurisprudence: law and economics (Alschuler 2000, pp. 2–8). Although the law and economics movement has contributed greatly to a deep understanding of the law and its applications (e.g. Posner 1983), it has its limitations, especially to those of us who suspect that there may be more to the rule of law than setting arbitrarily deterrent levels of game theoretic payoffs. Classical economics can predict certain human behaviours and can also tell us whether behaviours are efficient or inefficient, but it cannot tell us whether behaviours are right or wrong.

To a great extent, the law and economics vision sees law simply as the expression of a relentlessly hedonistic, and therefore quite mutable, marketplace. In Posner's extreme world, we do not ask whether it is right or wrong for one person to torture another, we insist only that the torturing decision be made in a free market; that is, no one can be physically forced to submit, and the torturer and the tortured must be free to agree to a price that reflects the intersection of their mutual preferences. Because most people prefer not to be tortured, the price for torture will skyrocket, and torturing behaviours will be driven out by a price that reflects most people's disinclination to be tortured (and their disinclination to pay high prices to torture), not by laws prohibiting the torture itself (Posner 1983, p. 82). According to this view, our traditional labelling of torture as 'wrong' is an unnecessarily normative-laden synonym for 'unpopular'.

This analysis can be quite enlightening, especially to those of us with libertarian inclinations, but it is far from a complete description of the foundations of law. As I will discuss in more detail below, biology is now making it clear that humans are not relentlessly hedonistic, at least not in the classic economic sense. Moreover, just like Holmes's model, the assumptions of law and economics beg the deepest questions of all: *why* do people have the preferences they have, and should they really be free to express any preference as long as the marketplace can absorb it? In fact, Holmes himself expressed exasperation about universal preferences he recognized but could not explain, calling them 'can't helps' (Alschuler 2000, p. 24).

Other attempts to describe the axioms of law—by legal philosophers such as John Rawls (1971) and Robert Nozick (1974)—are also incomplete for the same reason: they presuppose that people, and therefore the law, must act in certain ways. For example, Nozick posits three sets of rules from which he argues all our notions of distributive justice emanate: (i) rules governing how un-owned property is acquired; (ii) rules governing how owned property may be transferred; and (iii) rules governing how violations of the acquisition and transfer rules should be rectified (Nozick 1974, pp. 150–153). But why must we have rules governing the acquisition and transfer of property, and what should those rules say? Why must we have rules to rectify violations of the acquisition and transfer rules, and how exactly should those violations be rectified?

At the bottom of all these taxonomies in the legal sub-floor lies the real foundation: why do people behave the way they do, and how should society react to those behaviours?

1.3 The ancient debate about justice

Of course, the debate about human nature, and therefore about justice, has been going on since the dawn of the human race. The Greek version of the debate, as retold by Plato, pitted Thrasymachus ('Justice is nothing else than the interest of the stronger') (Plato *ca*. 360 B.C., 1901 edition, p. 19) against Socrates ('Justice is the excellence of the soul', p. 43). Hobbes and Locke tangled over the same question. Indeed, the Enlightenment debate about the essence of human nature was very much a part of the compromises that made up the American constitution (McGinnis 1996).

All of these efforts to describe and justify the rule of law—Socrates's, Locke's and Jefferson's divine man, Thrasymachus's, Hobbes's, Alexander Hamilton's and Spencer's selfish man, Holmes's bad man, Posner's rational man and Nozick's free man—depend on unstated assumptions about why people behave the way they do. Those assumptions tend to coalesce around two quite unsatisfactory poles. The Socratic side of the debate generally attributes its assumptions about why people behave the way they do, and especially why people *should* behave in particular ways, to the divine, and for that reason the Socratic approach has, quite unfortunately, gone out of favour in our post-modern world.

The Holmesian side of the debate, buoyed by its misinterpretation of Darwin, assumes that all behaviours are ultimately expressions of raw self-interest.

David Hume added an important ingredient to the debate—and the twinkle of a synthesis—by recognizing the emotional component to human behaviour. He was among the first post-Renaissance philosophers to observe that humans do not always act 'rationally' in the sense of making conscious, calculated choices. Instead, our behaviours are often driven by emotion, and our sense of deliberation is often a mere artefact of conflicting emotions. Hume also recognized, long before Darwin, that some aspects of our emotion-driven behaviours—both for good and evil—seem to be 'kneaded into our frames' (Hume 1748, p. 271).[1]

Research in evolutionary biology and neuroeconomics is suggesting that Socrates and Hume may have had it right all along, if we replace Socrates's 'divine' with 'evolved reciprocity', and Hume's 'kneaded into our frames' with 'inherited'. It appears the Holmesian assumptions about why people behave the way they do are not at all accurate, and may be misinterpretations of even deeper truths about human behaviour, truths that much more completely describe, and may even justify, the rule of law. When we add evolutionary and neuroeconomic insights to the way we frame these foundational questions, and specifically the insight that we are often driven by our evolved neuroarchitectures to act in a very complicated, yet often predictable, kind of socially modulated self-interest, a case can be made, and I will try to make it here, that there is indeed a relatively fixed and immutable set of right and wrong human behaviours. In this neuroeconomic model, the law is neither an inexplicable divine good, nor a cultural veneer against inexplicable original sin, nor a mere lubricant for arbitrary market preferences. It is an expression of our evolved natures as a profoundly social species.[2]

Before I expand on neuroeconomics and its effects on the foundations of law, let me refer to some more general observations about the relationship between evolution and behaviour.

1.4 Evolution and behaviour

Evolutionary biology has undergone a revolution of Copernican proportions since Darwin's and Holmes's time, and may be about to undergo another. The first revolution was about evolutionary morphology: how exactly do genes express themselves in physical traits? The rediscovery of Mendel, integrated with the discovery of DNA and the mechanics of replication and protein production, began to create a powerful picture of exactly how genetic information is transmitted across generations, how mutations can arise in that transmitted information, how, once transmitted, the genetic information is expressed in physical traits, and how an individual animal's interaction with its environment can make an inherited trait more, or less, likely to appear in subsequent generations. Adding game theory into the mix has given evolutionary biologists a powerful insight into the ways adaptation works within and between populations.

A similar synthesis is now taking place with respect to evolved *behaviours*. Anthropologists, biologists, economists and linguists are coming to understand that the evolutionary forces that shaped all animal bodies, including ours, have also shaped the menu of behaviours that animals, including us, entertain in response to certain stimuli, as well as the probabilities associated with each particular choice in that menu (see Wilson 1975;

Dawkins 1989). Indeed, because natural selection is the evolutionary motor, it is incorrect to think of morphology and behaviour as separate animal functions; everything an animal is—the package it comes in and the way that package interacts with its environment—is the ultimate, though of course not proximate, product of evolutionary pressures. That is, opposable thumbs make evolutionary sense only because they came with the behaviours to use them. Function and form—and therefore behaviour and morphology—are inseparable in evolution's long march (see Dawkins 1999).

E. O. Wilson has even suggested that this evolutionary synthesis between mind and body presages a fusion between the social and natural sciences (Wilson 1998). But even on a less grand scale, the idea that complex animal behaviours, and especially human behaviours, might have a significant evolutionary component has been the object of intense criticism. There have been two primary challenges: (i) the puzzle of altruism; and (ii) the question of how it is that genes act on brains to produce behaviours that can be inherited.

1.5 Altruism

The initial reaction, by biologists and social scientists alike, to the realization that Earth's creatures are the product of an evolutionary process that naturally weeds out the weak and infertile, was the assumption that every animal would therefore tend to become, as one modern philosopher of science has put it, a 'powerful loner, who knows when to cheat and can do it well; he is a kind of Nietzschean *übermensch* who breaks the conventions of sociability and morality with one powerful swipe of his well-oiled and bloodied fighting appendage' (Casebeer 2003). Indeed, Spencer's social philosophy and Holmes's legal philosophy are rather straightforward extensions of this primitive view of evolution.

It turns out, of course, that nature herself is much more complex. We have known for some time that individuals across animal populations do not exhibit anything like the uniform level of self-interested sexual and male–male aggression that natural selection seems to predict. In social and not-so-social species alike, even the most aggressive individuals seldom behave like Nietzschean über-animals, practising instead all kinds of more modulated behaviours. *Displays* of aggression, for example, often substitute for actual aggression. Cooperation, not competition, seems to rule. In fact, at the extreme end of this selfish/selfless continuum of behaviour, individual animals have been known to sacrifice their own fitness, even their own lives, for the benefit of other related and even non-related individuals. How can this kind of altruistic behaviour be explained by natural selection?

The puzzle was neatly solved in its weakest form (kin altruism) by W. D. Hamilton, who demonstrated that seemingly altruistic behaviours between related individuals make perfect evolutionary sense if we refocus the fitness inquiry from individual animal fitness to individual gene fitness (Hamilton 1964). From the gene's point of view, parents should always sacrifice themselves for three or more children (or five or more grandchildren) since, on average each child carries one-half of the parent's genes (and one-quarter of the grandparent's genes). Parental sacrifice is not about an individual acting altruistically; it is about parental genes acting quite selfishly.

But how does evolution explain altruistic behaviours between non-related individuals? One explanation is that natural selection simply is not perfect, and behaviours that are adaptive on average can go terribly wrong on occasion in individual circumstances. That is, we all have powerful and perfectly adaptive urges to save our kin, graded to related-ness, and perhaps those urges occasionally get misapplied to non-kin. Versions of this argument were often made in biology texts in the 1960s, to explain, for example, the evo-lution of warning cries in birds (Williams 1966, p. 206).

That explanation is not terribly satisfying, for several reasons. First, non-kin altruism seems to be much more widespread than this explanation would predict. Moreover, one would expect that the profound genetic cost of misdirected kin altruism would have led to highly evolved and widespread mechanisms to recognize one's own kin, yet it is an almost universal problem in the animal kingdom that half of all parents (males) are, by the very nature of sexual reproduction, unsure of the paternity of their offspring.

Evolutionary theorists have discovered a deeper, simpler explanation for non-kin altruism: just like the illusion of kin 'altruism', non-kin 'altruism' is not altruism at all if what is going on is the payment of a direct cost in exchange for a less direct, but nonethe-less palpable, benefit. Biologists have long known of a phenomenon, later dubbed by evolutionary theorists as 'return effect altruism', in which individual animals act in ways that appear in isolation to be altruistic, but which, when viewed in a larger, often social context, clearly confer an adaptive advantage on the allegedly altruistic actor. Bird warn-ing cries are a good example. Even a purely 'altruistic' cry—that is, one whose frequency does not depend on the proximity of kin—can convey a net adaptive advantage. Although giving such a cry can be extremely costly to the individual in the short-run (and, in fact, so costly that there is no long-run left), it also can trigger responsive cries in other nearby prey animals. Because many predators have coevolved strategies to give up the hunt if they hear too many cries, '[w]arning your [unrelated] neighbour that a predator is nearby may be the quickest way to get the predator to move on elsewhere' (Trivers 1971).

In addition to return-effect altruism, biologists have also long recognized that appar-ently altruistic behaviours are sometimes just one side of symbiotic relationships, and that when one measures the net costs and benefits of the symbiotic whole the behaviours can make perfect adaptive sense, for both participants. For example, symbiotic cleaning behaviours are fairly widespread in the ocean—more than 45 species of fishes and six species of shrimp are known to be cleaners, and innumerable species of fishes serve as hosts (Feder 1966). For both the cleaner (who spends enormous energy benefiting the host) and the cleaned (who resists the temptation to swallow the cleaner), the individual behaviours seem maladaptive when viewed in isolation. However, when considered together, and taking into account the costs of not being cleaned (that is, the damage done to the host fish by ectoparasites), the difficulty and danger of finding a cleaner, the site specificity of cleaners, the lifespans of cleaners, and the ability of hosts to find the same cleaner repeat-edly, theorists have demonstrated that cleaning behaviours can confer a net adaptive advantage on both the cleaner and the cleaned (Trivers 1971).

However, traditional symbiosis is not the only kind of 'reciprocal altruism', as theorists have labelled this sort of mutually beneficial interaction. It is a much more generalized, and indeed central, aspect of evolution itself. Robert Trivers was among the first evolu-tionary biologists to recognize that when one considers not just the survival behaviours of a single individual in isolation, but also that that individual must make guesses about the survival behaviours of his competitors and prospective mates, optimum solutions exist that involve a mix of aggressive and cooperative strategies, with the cooperative strategies often taking the form of a time-delayed exchange, or what evolutionary theorists have come to call reciprocal exchanges.

Trivers showed that animals engage in a whole host of complex reciprocal exchanges, even with (and, indeed, especially with) unrelated individuals that can accrue to their net long-term individual benefit, even if they seem to be to their net short-term individual disadvantage. If the net long-term advantage sufficiently outweighs the net short-term cost, the behaviour can become adaptive and animals can inherit a tendency to act in ways that appear 'altruistic'.

Displays of aggression also have obvious adaptive value, when viewed not in isolation but as an exchange between individuals. John Maynard Smith demonstrated that the kinds of 'graded signals', as he called them, seen in displays of aggression, make perfect evolutionary sense when one considers not just the obvious benefits of aggression but also its obvious and not-so-obvious costs—being killed or injured, or having one's mate lured away during combat by a 'sneaky male'. Perhaps more importantly, Smith demonstrated that both within and between species, when both the costs and benefits of behaviours are carefully considered, including the delayed costs and benefits in reciprocating, natural selection operates to drive individuals (and populations) to a relatively stable distribution of behavioural strategies, strategies he called 'evolutionarily stable strategies' (Maynard Smith 1982).

Of course, aggression, displays of aggression, cleaning symbioses and warning cries are just a tiny part of the behavioural toolbox. In recent years, evolutionary biologists have examined a whole host of others kinds of reciprocal behaviours, both in humans and non-humans, including foraging, communication, nepotism, sibling rivalry, parent–child conflict, habitat selection, predator–prey interaction and even learning (Dugatin 2001). Game theorists have added a mathematical rigour to the analysis of reciprocal exchanges, treating them as a set of multiple non-zero-sum games. Evolutionarily stable strategies are the Nash equilibria (Nash 1950) for the particular 'game' in question, under the constraints biologists believe were operating when a particular strategy evolved.

In intensely social species like humans, reciprocity seems to play an especially important role. After all, our evolved behavioural tendencies are the product of a long and complex interaction between our individual ancestors and the small groups in which they evolved, and living in groups requires rather sophisticated mechanisms to regulate relationships between members. The social behaviours we evolved in that environment are central to what we now view as human nature.

Any group needs rules for admission and exclusion. Thanks to the combination of our large brains, our ability to speak and our intense social natures, it seems we literally evolved an instinct for rules. In fact, our brains and our language structures are themselves most probably tools we evolved to increase the efficiency of our reciprocal social exchanges (Pinker 1994). Being in a group at all—following rules, enforcing violations, accepting punishment—is a constant series of reciprocal trade-offs between short-term individual gains/losses ('Should I steal that pile of food our hunters brought in today?') and long-term individual gains/losses ('Do I want to stay in this group and benefit from mate availability and economies of scale in food gathering and defense?') (Axelrod & Hamilton 1981). The scientific literature is now flush with studies of reciprocity, or 'cooperation' as some biologists now prefer (Burnstein *et al.* 1994; Dugatin 2001; Brown & Moore 2000; Gintis *et al.* 2003).

It now appears beyond cavil that all animals, including humans, have evolved tendencies to behave in certain predictable manners under certain conditions. Of course, the extent to which these ultimate tendencies actually express themselves, how they interact with an individual's proximate environment and, in the case of higher-order animals, their learned behaviour, continues to be open to great debate.

But how do brains turn evolutionarily stable strategies into behaviours? Before turning to that profoundly important question, I consider three general classes of human behaviours, which I propose are genetically based and which may inform much of the foundations of law.

1.6 Three core human principles

It appears that humans, and indeed all intensely social animals, have a predisposition to follow three central behavioural rules: (i) promises to reciprocate must be kept (contract); (ii) reciprocal exchanges must be voluntary (tort and criminal); and (iii) serious violations of the first two principles must be punished (enforcement).[3] These three rules form the nucleus of a kind of neo-natural law that I suspect is part of our inherited natures, and therefore is both universal and relatively invariant.

This is a profoundly different view of justice than the incomplete evolutionary views of people like Holmes and Spencer. Under this construct, we have an instinct for justice not because justice is 'a brooding omnipresence in the sky', as Holmes once derisively described efforts to externalize the law (Holmes 1917), but because we are the complex products of an evolution that made such social behaviours adaptively beneficial to our individual survival.

There is compelling game-theoretic evidence that all humans are indeed armed with versions of these three internal principles, which classical economics cannot explain but which become entirely rational if we look at our behaviours as a constellation of evolved reciprocal exchanges. For example, in the so-called 'ultimatum game', involving two players, A and B, player A is given money (or useful goods) and both players are told that A must choose a fraction to offer to B. Both players know the total amount available for division. They are also told that if B accepts the offer, the money will be divided as A has proposed, but that if B rejects, neither player gets anything. Classical economics, which assumes that A and B will act in unbounded 'self-interest', predicts that A will offer next to nothing, and that no matter how small the offer, B will accept it. Neither prediction holds true.

In industrial societies, A offers an astonishingly 'altruistic' average of *ca.* 40%, simultaneously acknowledging that this exchange should be roughly equal, that A should probably get a little more because he is the one who started out with the money,[4] and that if he offers much less B will reject and neither will get anything. In fact, offers of less than 30% are frequently rejected (Gintis 2000). These same general results occur in pre-industrial cultures (Henrich *et al.* 2001).[5]

Just as with classically 'altruistic' behaviours, this kind of behaviour is not altruistic at all. Humans have built-in regulators, evolved over a eons of intense social interaction, that tell us not to be unfair to each other, lest today's player A will become tomorrow's player B. That these preferences for a generalized kind of fairness are the adaptive product of evolutionary pressures is clear not only from their human universality, but also from the fact that other intensely social primates exhibit similar test behaviours (Brosnan & de Waal 2003).[6] That these preferences are bound up with evolved *social* behaviours is clear because when the other player is a stranger (or worse still, a computer), people tend to revert to more classically self-interested behaviours (Cook & Hegtvedt 1992). However, our hunches about a universal natural justice are still far ahead of the supporting science. The most difficult gap is in the neurology of behaviour.

The challenge is that brains, not genes, generate behaviour. Although our brains are themselves the ultimate product of evolution, neuroscientists have yet to discover the behavioural analogue to DNA—the mechanism by which our brains transmit behavioural predispositions to us, but there is encouraging and exciting evidence from the science of neuroeconomics.

1.7 The promise of neuroeconomics

As the mechanisms of the brain are being uncovered in both humans and non-humans, neuroscientists are doing two important things: (i) they are isolating and studying the actual brain structures involved in decision-making; and (ii) from these discoveries they are piecing together a new probabilistic paradigm of how brains make decisions, a paradigm that may go a long way toward explaining how adaptive behaviours are expressed in individuals and then transmitted across generations. A remarkably comprehensive and clear exposition of these developments can be found in Paul Glimcher's new book (Glimcher 2003).

As Glimcher reminds us, Rene Descartes believed that all human behaviour could be divided into two fundamentally different categories: simple behaviours, which were the deterministic motor responses of given sensory inputs; and complex behaviours (or what we would call 'cognitive' behaviours), which Descartes saw as the indeterminate product of unknown and unknowable forces, and which he simply called 'the soul' (Descartes 1649). For centuries, this Cartesian dualism has both enlightened and burdened neuroscientists examining the etiology of behaviour.

It enlightened the investigation because, by focusing on simple motor reflexes, it allowed investigators to discover quite a lot about the neural pathways between stimulus and response. However, it also profoundly burdened the investigation because it presumed that what was going on in the brain in these so-called simple motor reflexes was the same sort of deterministic and essentially linear transmissions that were observed elsewhere along the neural path. In this reflex model of simple behaviours, the brain does very little more than reflect the stimulus signal back to the appropriate response path. However, as discussed in more detail below, evidence is accumulating that when the brain 'decides' what the 'appropriate' response path should be, something is going on that is much more complicated than the reflex model predicts.

Of course, Cartesian dualism also had the effect, and indeed the intended effect, of cleaving the behavioural world into two mutually exclusive pieces: the scientifically accessible reflex piece and the mysterious, religious, scientifically inaccessible cognitive piece. Neurological research on non-cognitive behaviours proceeded apace, but research on cognitive behaviours was, at least early on, condemned to the realm of the metaphysical. Advances in neuroscience are driving a fundamental synthesis between these two realms.

Many neuroscientists believe that all behaviour can be explained by combining a sufficient number of reflexive units in a sufficiently complex way, and that the very notion of a separate and distinct kind of 'cognitive' mechanism is a false dichotomy created simply to avoid touchy issues about consciousness and free will. For example, as early as 1950, the renowned German physiologist Erik Von Holtz and a colleague wrote:

> The sooner we recognize that the [higher functions] which leave the reflex physiologist dumbfounded in fact send roots down to the simplest basal functions of the CNS, the sooner we shall see that the previously terminologically insurmountable barrier between the lower levels of neurophysiology and higher behavioural theory simply dissolves away.
>
> (Von Holtz & Middelstaedt 1950)

At the time of Von Holtz's predictions, Cartesian dualism still dominated the study of brain anatomy and function. Most 1950s textbooks divided the cortex into three functional parts: sensory, motor and what was dubbed 'association', which is a word that had its origins in Pavlov's conditioned associations, but which came to be a kind of catch-all all category corresponding to Descartes' 'complex' (Glimcher 2003, p. 233).

The association parts of the cortex remained shrouded in mystery primarily for technical reasons. Researchers could measure the activity of single sensory and motor neurons by exposing those neurons in anaesthetized subjects. But association neurons could not be explored in this manner because anaesthetized subjects are unconscious, and therefore cannot 'associate'—that is, do any of the cognitive activities presumed being done in these areas of the cortex.

This technical limitation was overcome in the late 1950s, when researchers perfected a technique of inserting tiny wires into the cortices of conscious subjects (Glimcher 2003, pp. 233–234). From that moment on, and accelerated by many other technological advances, including functional magnetic resonance imaging (fMRI), a flood of data began to be gathered about the association areas of the cortex, and the data started to suggest that the essentially Cartesian distinctions between sensory, motor and association were not at all accurate. Perhaps Von Holtz was right. Perhaps the 'cognitive' function occurring in the association part of the cortex was merely a complicated arrangement of reflexes.

But it turns out that the classical reflex model is a very poor predictor of whole categories of determinate behaviours, no matter how many simple reflex circuits we postulate, and no matter how complex the connections. For example, rhythmic behaviours—like stepping—have simply not lent themselves to any kind of modelling based on combinations of reflexive pathways (Glimcher 2003, p. 111). Moreover, electrode studies of many of these rhythmic behaviours show neural activity that is quite different, both in kind and intensity, than one would expect from a reflex model (Glimcher 2003, pp. 111–112).

As result of these difficulties, some neuroscientists are suggesting that Descartes' dualism should be closed in the other direction—by positing that there are really no reflexes, and that all behaviours are the product of a much more complicated process. In an amazing experiment in 1987, James Gnadt and Richard Andersen discovered that a portion of the parietal cortex associated with saccadic eye movements—gaze-aligning movements that rotate the eye at high speeds when an animal switches its gaze from one object to another—and which had been categorized as sensory, exhibited a suspiciously cognitive kind of pre-movement memory. When saccadic neurons in the parietal cortex of macaques trained to stare at a primary visual stimulus were activated by a secondary visual stimulus, those neurons not only remained active after the visual stimulus was removed, but remained active until the macaques moved their eye to gaze at the remembered location of the secondary stimulus. As Gnadt and Andersen put it, these saccadic neurons 'appeared to be related to the pre-movement planning of saccades in a manner which we have chosen to describe as *motor intention*' (Gnadt & Andersen 1988).

That very phrase—motor intention—sounds quite strange to ears conditioned to 400 years of Cartesian dualism, and perhaps even stranger to more modern adherents of the all-reflex approach. Neurons whose function was presumably sensory (we might even say 'autonomic') turn out to behave in a surprisingly cognitive way. What we thought was a simple sensory/motor reflex—detect a new object and move the eye to it—turns out to involve a cognitive delay—detect a new object, remember its location, and decide later whether to move the eye to the remembered location.

It seems Von Holtz's synthesis is being realized, but in the opposite direction. Even the simplest 'reflexes' may involve neural activities once thought to be associated with 'cognition'. However, where does all this leave us in our hunt for a connection between genes and behaviour?

In recent years, Paul Glimcher and other neuroscientists have suggested an answer. Because it is becoming apparent that the distinction between 'reflex' and 'cognition' is artificial, perhaps the distinction between 'determinate' and 'indeterminate' is also artificial. Perhaps the brain—both in its 'simple' and 'complex' activities—is a probability machine rather than some contraption that inexplicably switches back and forth between reflexive/determinate outcomes (burn your hand, pull it back) and cognitive/indeterminate outcomes (you decide you will walk home today rather than take the bus). Perhaps all behaviours are represented in the brain by a set of probability distributions, which are then continuously influenced by the interaction between ultimate causes (the initial probabilities that evolution built into brains) and proximate causes (the particular environmental challenges brains are called upon to solve).

In this model, the 'reflex' is just an extreme kind of probability distribution—one with a very high probability bunched near a single action, the response. When you burn your hand, it is extremely likely (but not determinate) that your brain will decide to pull the hand back. The high probability of that particular action masks its inherently indeterminate (and cognitive) character. Likewise, when you decide to walk home rather than take the bus, you are also engaging a distribution of probable behaviours, though the probabilities are more evenly distributed over a wider range, leaving you with the conscious sense that you 'decided' what to do. But in both cases, according to the probabilistic model, the particular 'decision' is an indeterminate outcome bounded only by the probability distribution of all outcomes.

Glimcher and his colleagues have performed a series of spectacular neurological experiments strongly suggesting that the brain works exactly in this probabilistic way. Using a variety of neurobiological techniques to study the neural firings in the brains of monkeys and humans as they make decisions during various kinds of games, the experimenters found that when the strength and frequency of those firings are accumulated and plotted over time, they look virtually identical to the probabilistic outcomes in decision-making by individuals over time—the so-called 'utility function' of modern economics (Glimcher 2003, pp. 322–336; Glimcher et al. 2004). This is a remarkable result, suggesting an essential unity between the way a single brain makes a single decision, and the patterns that emerge when brains make many decisions over time.

Thus, although we cannot predict whether the brain of any particular person will offer 40% in the ultimatum game, we can surmise that the population-wide average of 40% reflects the fact that the brains in that population have a probability distribution for this behaviour that peaks near 40%. The genius of the probabilistic model is that it preserves the indeterminacy (free will?) of a particular individual's behaviour, while explaining the perfectly determinate behaviour of large groups of individuals, or of a single individual over many trials. It also suggests the real possibility that some behaviours are heritable, because brains have of course been inherited.

To complete this second post-Darwinian revolution, neuroscientists will need to discover exactly how behavioural probability distributions are encoded in the brain. When and if that happens, neuroeconomics may do for the evolution of behaviour what Watson and Crick did for the evolution of physical traits.

1.8 Law as an expression of evolved probabilistic behaviours

Of course, law is a special kind of game, a sort of meta-game, where the thing in play is not a direct payoff, but the very question of what should be the rules of the game. Law may well 'evolve' in the short run in the way Holmes suggested. But if it is true that humans have evolved a set of basic social behaviours to navigate our way through the social world, and that those basic social rules form the core of a kind of natural justice, then law may well have evolved in a much deeper and profound way.

At those critical points where judges, juries or legislatures have to make decisions, those decisions may not be the valueless preferences Holmes presumed. They may not be the arbitrary behavioural cousins of the mutation, waiting for time and survival pressures to sort the useful from the useless. They may instead be preferences that reflect the interaction between the case at hand and neuroeconomically evolved, probabilistic, norms that all judges, jurors and legislators carry inside their brains. It seems likely that we cannot help but to give some distributed weight to the core principles that promises should be kept, that social exchanges should be voluntary and that serious violations of these two aspects of our imbedded social contract should be punished.

We might therefore reformulate Holmes's axioms this way, at least with regard to that portion of the body of law we believe is encompassed by our core of natural justice:

(i) If you want to know what the law is, look at it as would a 'good man'[7], someone who is not interested in the outcome of a dispute but recognizes that one day he may be subject (in either direction) to the rule derived from the dispute.
(ii) Law is nothing more than a prophecy of what rules good people are likely to agree are well settled.
(iii) 'Duty', whether in contract or tort, is a prediction of how we would agree in advance to treat one another, without knowing ahead of time whether we will be the breacher or breachee, the tortfeasor or the injured, the criminal or the victim, the defendant or the sentencing judge.
(iv) The law should not be embarrassed to label some of its most basic rules in moral and ethical terms, because that is exactly what they are.

1.9 The relationship between freedom and justice

The economist Paul Rubin has written a provocative book arguing that the freedom to leave one group and join another, and thus avoid coercion by dominants, is a deep part of our evolved natures as humans (Rubin 2002). Rubin argues that our profound sense of individuality, which has survived in tandem with our profound social natures, was a kind of ultimate veto over both dominant and collectivist excess. Exit freedom had the effect of imposing constraints on dominant individuals in the group: if a few powerful individuals got too powerful, they risked loss of members, and thus loss of some of the net advantage of living in groups. Likewise, even the majority in any group had to keep a keen eye on majoritarian excess.

Justice is what happens when our deepest social axioms—which, as I have suggested, themselves contain an embedded core of justice—are given efficient expression. The key to these social axioms is that they are the evolved product of *reciprocal* social exchanges. That is, the small groups in which we evolved contained an important element of freedom— the freedom to enter into mutually beneficial social interactions, the freedom to decline to do so, and, as Rubin points out, the freedom to leave the group and go join another. Laws enacted or developed without these complimentary forces in play will themselves tend to be unjust.

Thus, a dictator is inclined to write laws that are not just, both because the dictator is unlikely to become an enforcement object of his own laws and because he may have the power to limit his subjects' exit. Those laws will tend to reflect only the dictator's unconstrained self-interest, not the social connections out of which the dictator, and all of us, evolved.

By contrast, the deepest social connections that bind us bind us only because, in the end, we are free to disregard them. They have become powerful precisely because they must have had enough long-term utility to overcome their short-term costs, and to keep us from exercising our freedom to exit the group. They do not achieve that status if they are forced upon all group members by some a *priori* collective will. Individuals, not groups, are the functional units through which genes act, and social norms become adaptive only because they confer a net benefit to individuals. Thus, collectivist regimes are also inclined to write laws that are unjust.

Ultimately, as Rubin so powerfully argues, there is an inextricable evolutionary link between justice and democracy. The ability of any justice system to accommodate the biological tension between individual freedom and social norms depends to a great extent on its own ability to develop those norms as a free expression of social consensus. The best laws work because they efficiently confer, and express, enough long-term benefits on enough individuals that those individuals are willing to remain in the group and pay the short-term price of compliance. The genius of democracy is that it provides a continuous feedback mechanism on these social norms, constantly recalibrating them to current individual preferences.

In effect, democracy creates a market for the governed, in which conflicting preferences for individual freedom and social restraint compete freely to obtain optimal results. This is hardly a new insight, but what may be new is the evolutionary vision that suggests democratic institutions are not artificial constructs, but rather are expressions of our own evolved, and complimentary, desires for freedom and social stability. If we say that 'justice' represents our biologically embedded tendency to accommodate the tension between self and others, a tension that presupposes we have the freedom to act selfishly or selflessly, then our best institutions are those that most efficiently express that accommodation.

Rubin argues that a democratic nation with a free market economy is the highest expression of the human spirit simply because humans are built for freely entering into mutually beneficial reciprocal exchanges with other humans and because democracy is the most efficient accommodation between social constraint and individual freedom. Admittedly, Rubin's thesis, and indeed mine in this essay, both depend on many assumptions about the conditions under which humans evolved. Although palaeontologists and anthropologists are learning more and more about the ecological details of the so-called 'era of evolutionary adaptivity'—that portion of the Palaeolithic 50,000 to 100,000 years ago when the current human genome is thought to have emerged—much remains unknown.

For example, we do not know much about the ecological conditions that caused humans to stop living in small mobile groups of mostly related hunter–gatherers and start living in larger sedentary groups of mostly unrelated hunter–gatherers, although some anthropologists have speculated that this change was driven by population pressures (e.g. Tudge 1998; Carniero 2000). That transition, which preceded the transition to horticulture then agriculture, is a key to understanding the extent to which non-kin reciprocity may have shaped our genome. Regardless of when and how the sedentary transition happened, it seems highly unlikely that groups as large as 'nations' have existed long enough to have had any adaptive impact, except possibly as misinterpreted cues for social behaviour grounded on a much smaller scale.

Nevertheless, Rubin's core insights about the evolutionary relationship between economic and political freedom are tantalizing, and are precisely the kind of interdisciplinary approach that is beginning to shed light on the nature of humans and their institutions, including law.

1.10 Conclusion

Advances in neuroeconomics are suggesting the physical mechanisms by which animal behaviours are inherited. All behaviours—whether simple motor reflexes or high-order cognition—may be generated not by a collection of determinate stimulus/response pathways, but rather by the indeterminate triggering of a particular behaviour from a probabilistic distribution of possible behaviours. These insights have profound implications, not only for the paradox of free will and the interaction of the mind and body, but also for the foundations of law.

The idea that some behaviours are heritable as an array of probabilities meshes quite nicely with what evolutionary theory and game theory have been teaching us about human behaviour. We are the products of evolutionary forces that shaped us to survive as individuals, but in small intensely social groups. Our very being is about accommodating the ancient tension between self and others by passing all our decisions through a distribution of probabilities that has a built-in shape, and that peaks at three Nash equilibria: (i) do not break promises; (ii) exchange things, don't just take them; and (iii) punish serious violations of (i) and (ii).

Because these core principles are only peaks in a distribution of probable behaviours, there is no doubt that there will be great individual variation in behaviours. Indeed, the variations between individuals, and in individuals over time seem to take on the same distribution shape as the internal brain distributions. These core principles are a kind of behavioural fractal. The paradox of predictable macroeconomic patterns appearing out of unpredictable microeconomic choices is neatly solved if the machines we use to make our choices are themselves probability machines.

Of course, the majesty of the brain, and what makes it the king of adaptive tools, is that brains can learn—they can, over time, change the shape of their decision curves.

Experience, whether gained from actual encounters between a brain and the world, or through the accumulated and communicated wisdom of other brains, can alter the initial probability distributions with which our models were originally equipped. In fact, this constant feedback loop between the outside world and the brain's representation of the outside world is precisely what brains are all about.

The ultimate nurture/nature debate may thus collapse into a quantitative debate about the malleability of our initially set decision curves. Although the proximate effects of culture can hardly be overestimated when we are talking about a machine built to soak up experience, it is equally clear that the initial settings matter too.

I suspect we will discover that our deepest social instincts—of the kind I postulate in this essay—operate like our deep language structures. They form a template upon which the syntax of human interaction can unfold. There are endless variations in behaviour among individuals and among cultures (just as there are language variations), but, in the end, my guess is that we will discover that the syntax of social interaction is universal and invariant. The deepest roots of law express those universal and invariant rules of social syntax.

Holmes's insights about the relationship between individual decisions and the false majesty of the law were profound and powerful applications of what little was then known about evolution and human nature. However, his resonating logic has led us to the ironic precipice of denying our own humanity. Holmes understood only half of the engine of human evolution—that we, as individuals, are the product of a relentless struggle to survive. He did not realize that in the course of that struggle, the path upon which evolution took us was a path of intense social cooperation.

As a judge, who every day imposes drastic penalties on the free-riders we manage to detect and capture, I must confess that it is comforting to contemplate that the law is not merely a lubricant of market preferences or a collection of arbitrary predilections of the ruling class. It may well reflect our deepest commitments to each other, commitments that are at the heart of our evolved natures as social animals.

I thank Albert Alschuler, Paul Glimcher, Oliver Goodenough, Richard Posner, Paul Rubin and the anonymous peer reviewers, all of whom provided comments on earlier drafts of this essay. I also thank the late Margaret Gruter and all my friends at the Gruter Institute for Law and Behavioral Research for their contributions and inspiration.

Endnotes

1. Two of the most insightful modern heirs to Hume are probably Antonio Damasio (1994) and Robert Frank (1988).
2. I am hardly the first person to propose a biologically driven return to a natural sense of justice. See, for example, Masters & Gruter (1992). See also the groundbreaking work of Owen Jones (2001a,b) on the relationship between law and biology.
3. There is, of course, a fourth fundamental behaviour, shared by many social and non-social species alike: the recognition of property rights. The notion that things possessed by one individual cannot be taken by others may well be the most fundamental of all evolved behaviours, because survival is itself bound up with the use of things (food and shelter, for example). Indeed, the three core human principles that I posit in this essay are arguably derivative of the notion of property: it may be that living in groups, and its attendant reciprocity, is simply a strategy to deal with the problem of scarce resources. But I leave a discussion of property to my colleague Jeffrey Stake.

4. This is a version of the so-called 'endowment effect' (Kahneman 1991), and it seems to operate even where, as in the ultimatum game, the property 'owner' had no original claim to the money. Possession, it turns out, may be nine-tenths of the law because even fleeting possession evokes powerful feelings of entitlement.
5. There were some interesting differences between industrial and pre-industrial societies. A's offer tends to be lower in pre-industrial societies (26% mean) than in industrial societies (40% mean). There was also more variation in A's offer in pre-industrial societies than in industrial cultures. The lowest offers occurred in societies where the incidence of cooperation and market practices was low, and here rejection was rare. Offers were higher where exchange was more frequent. However, where local custom imposed on B a future obligation to reciprocate at a time to be determined by A, even offers greater than 50% were sometimes refused (Henrich *et al.* 2001).
6. There are, nevertheless, important differences between the 'economies' of humans and other primates. For example, it appears that although capuchins and chimpanzees have a primitive ability to monetize goods, they are unable to recognize different denominations of money (Brosnan 2004).
7. When I say 'good man' or 'good people' in these neo-Holmesian formulations, I simply mean people whose ordinary social constraints—that is, their evolved accommodations between short-term self-interest and long-term self-interest—have not been disabled.

References

Alschuler, A. W. 2000 *Law without values: the life, work and legacy of Justice Holmes*. University of Chicago Press.
Axelrod, R. & Hamilton, W. D. 1981 The evolution of cooperation. *Science* **211**, 1390–1396.
Brosnan, S. F. 2004 Primate economics, presented at the Gruter Institute for Law and Behavioral Research, Squaw Valley, CA, 22 May 2004.
Brosnan, S. F. & de Waal, F. 2003 Monkeys reject unequal pay. *Nature* **425**, 297–299.
Brown, W. M. & Moore, C. 2000 Is prospective altruist-detection an evolved solution to the adaptive problem of subtle cheating in cooperative ventures? *Evol. Hum. Behav.* **21**, 25–37.
Burnstein, E., Crandall, C. & Kitayama, S. 1994 Some Neo-Darwinian rules for altruism: weighing cues for inclusive fitness as a function of the biological importance of the decision. *J. Person. Soc. Psychol.* **67**, 773–789.
Carniero, R. L. 2000 The transition from quantity to quality: a neglected causal mechanism in accounting for social evolution. *Proc. Natl Acad. Sci. USA* **97**, 12 926–12 931.
Casebeer, W. D. 2003 Book review: evolution and the capacity for commitment. *Hum. Nat. Rev.* **3**, 12–14.
Cook, K. & Hegtvedt, K. 1992 Empirical evidence of the sense of justice. In *The sense of justice: biological foundations of law* (ed. R. Masters & M. Gruter), pp. 187–210. Newbury Park, CA: Sage Publications.
Damasio, A. R. 1994 *Descartes' error: emotion, reason, and the human brain*. New York: Putnam.
Dawkins, R. 1989 *The selfish gene*, 2nd edn. Oxford University Press.
Dawkins, R. 1999 *The extended phenotype: the long reach of the gene*. Oxford University Press.
Descartes, R. 1649 *L'homme*. Cambridge, MA: Harvard University Press. [*Treatise on man*, 1972 translation by T. S. Hall.]
Dugatin, L. A. 2001 Subjective commitment in nonhumans: what should we be looking for, and where should we be looking?. In *Evolution and the capacity for commitment* (ed. R. Neese), pp. 120–137. New York: Russell Sage.
Frank, R. H. 1988 *Passions within reason: the strategic role of the emotions*. New York: W.W. Norton.
Feder, H. M. 1966 Cleaning symbioscs in the marine environment. *Symbiosis* **1**, 327–380.
Gintis, H. 2000 *Game theory evolving*. Princeton University Press.

Gintis, H., Bowles, S., Boyd, R. & Fehr, E. 2003 Explaining altruistic behavior in humans. *Evol. Hum. Behav.* **24**, 153–172.

Glimcher, P. W. 2003 *Decisions, uncertainty, and the brain: the science of neuroeconomics*. Cambridge, MA: MIT Press.

Glimcher, P. W., Dorris, M. C., Bayer, H. M., & Lau, B. 2004 Physiologic utility theory and the neuroeconomics of choice. *Games Econ. Behav.* (In the press.)

Gnadt, J. W. & Andersen, R. A. 1988 Memory related motor planning activity in posterior parietal cortex of macaque. *Exp. Brain Res.* **70**, 216–220.

Hamilton, W. D. 1964 The genetical evolution of social behavior. *J. Theor. Biol.* **7**, 1–52.

Henrich, J., Boyd, J., Bowles, S., Camerer, C., Fehr, E., Gintis, H. & McElreath, R. 2001 In search of homo economicus: behavioral experiments in fifteen small-scale societies. *Am. Econ. Rev.* **91**, 73–78.

Holmes, O. W. Jr 1881 *The common law*. Cambridge, MA: Harvard University Press.

Holmes, O. W. Jr 1897 The path of the law. *Harv. Law Rev.* **10**, 457–478.

Holmes O.W., Jr 1917 Southern Pac. Co. v. Jensen, 244 US 205, 222.

Hume, D. 1748 *Enquiries concerning human understanding and concerning principles of morals*, 3rd edn. Oxford: Clarendon. [1975 edition, ed. L.A. Selby-Bigge.]

Jones, O. D. 2001a Time-shifted rationality and the law of law's leverage: behavioral economics meets behavioral biology. *Northwestern Univ. Law Rev.* **95**, 1141–1205.

Jones, O. D. 2001b Proprioception, non-law and bio-legal history (2001 Dunwody Distinguished Lecture in Law). *Florida Law Rev.* **53**, 831–874.

Kahneman, D. 1991 The endowment effect, loss aversion, and status quo bias. *J. Econ. Perspect.* **5**, 193–194.

McGinnis, J. O. 1996 Original constitution and our origins. *Harv. J. Law Pub. Pol.* **19**, 251–261.

Masters, R. D., Gruter, M. (eds) 1992 *The sense of justice*. Newbury Park, CA:Sage

Maynard Smith, J. 1982 *Evolution and the theory of games*. New York: Cambridge University Press.

Nash, J. F. 1950 Equilibrium points in n-person games. *Proc. Natl Acad. Sci. USA* **36**, 48–49.

Nozick, R. 1974 *Anarchy, state and utopia*. New York: Basic Books.

Pinker, S. 1994 *The language instinct*. New York: W. Morrow.

Plato *ca.* 360 B.C. *The republic*. New York: Colonial Press. [1901 edition, translated by B. Jowett.]

Posner, R. A. 1983 *The economics of justice*. Cambridge, MA: Harvard University Press.

Posner, R. A. 1992 *Essential Holmes: selections from the letters, speeches, judicial opinions and other writings of Oliver Wendell Holmes Jr.* University of Chicago Press.

Rawls, J. 1971 *A theory of justice*. Cambridge, MA: Harvard University Press.

Rubin, P. H. 2002 *Darwinian politics: the evolutionary origin of freedom*. New York: Rutgers.

Trivers, R. L. 1971 The evolution of reciprocal altruism. *Q. Rev. Biol.* **46**, 35–57.

Tudge, C. 1998 *Neanderthals, bandits, and farmers: how agriculture really started*. New Haven, CT: Yale University Press.

Von Holtz, E. & Middelstaedt, H. 1950 Das Reafferenzprinzip: Wechselwirkung zwischen Zentralnervensystem und Perepherie [The reafference principle: interaction between the central nervous system and the periphery.] *Naturwissenschaften* **37**, 464–476. In *The behavioral physiology of animals and man: the selected papers of E. Von Holtz* (ed. R. D. Martin). Miami, FL: University of Miami.

Williams, G. 1966 *Adaptation and natural selection*. Princeton University Press.

Wilson, E. O. 1975 *Sociobiology: the new synthesis*. Cambridge, MA: Harvard University Press.

Wilson, E. O. 1998 *Consilience*. New York: Knopf.

2

How neuroscience might advance the law

Erin Ann O'Hara

This essay discusses the strengths and limitations of the new, growing field of law and biology and suggests that advancements in neuroscience can help to bolster that field. It also briefly discusses some ways that neuroscience can help to improve the workings of law more generally.

Keywords: legal policy; interdisciplinary research; neuroscience

2.1 Introduction

These are exciting times for the curious and the contemplative, because the mysteries of the brain are beginning to be understood. The popular press is full of stories about studies attempting to locate the places in the brain where thoughts, perceptions, feelings and motivations are formed. For social scientists who create models of human behaviour, these findings have enormous potential theoretical value. For legal academics striving to find ways to use the law to maximize the beneficial effects of human tendencies, neuroscientific developments are potentially immensely important.

This essay proffers just a few of the myriad ways in which neuroscientific knowledge might be able to improve the law. I approach the topic as a law professor who attempts to incorporate knowledge developed in other disciplines into a behavioural model that informs decisions about legal policy. As a specialist in law and a student of neuroscience my scientific understanding is comparatively weak. In the spirit of attempting to promote interdisciplinary collaboration, however, this essay will nevertheless discuss some ways in which neuroscience carries the potential to help inform both our models of human behaviour and legal policy. In particular, this essay will discuss some ways in which neuroscience can help bolster and refine some of the implications of evolutionary theory for law. The first section of this essay will provide a brief description of the recent development, as well as some of the challenges and limitations, of the field of law and biology. The second section will discuss a few ways in which developments in neuroscience can be used to help overcome some of the challenges faced by those interested in using scientific knowledge to advance our understanding of human behaviour.

2.2 The development and challenges of law and biology

Despite the enormous potential for law and biology, the movement was a little slow to move forward. The Gruter Institute for Law and Behavioral Research, founded by Margaret Gruter, has fostered research in law and biology since 1981[1] but attention to the field by the mainstream legal academy has been limited to the past five or so years. Today there are many very talented individuals engaged in law and biology, and they have tapped into significant resources to advance our understanding of how behavioural biology informs legal policy-making.[2]

As interest in law and biology developed, the field attracted three different types of law professor. First were those law professors who were really natural scientists at heart. These professors probably should have explored careers in zoology or marine biology, as evidenced by the fact that they seem to know and care much more about the skeletal structures of mammals than they do about the Uniform Commercial Code or the Rule Against Perpetuities. For tenured law professors who missed their true calling, law and biology has become a mechanism by which they can turn avocation into vocation. While I must admit that I greatly enjoy talking with this group of individuals at conferences, these members are poorly suited to convincing the mainstream legal academy of the importance of evolutionary insights for the law. These professors tend not to be terribly interested in careful legal applications, with the result that others reading their work can too easily dismiss the movement as at best a marginally relevant interdisciplinary fad. Environmental, food and drug, and health-care policies might be important exceptions to charges of irrelevance, however, because much of the effectiveness of these policies turns on a careful understanding of current scientific knowledge. Although environmental and health-care lawyers are very much interested in biology, microbiology tends to be more directly useful to them than does evolutionary theory. Evolutionary theory can neverthe-less help these policy makers to understand and predict how human behaviours such as antibiotic and pesticide use create evolutionary pressures on both humans and non-human organisms. In any event, the 'science buffs' have had little impact on how other law professors think about human behaviour.

A second group of law professors interested in evolutionary theory include those whose normative views lack strong social scientific support. These scholars seem pre-committed to strong ideological agendas. On the right, many complain that political correctness in the social sciences prevents honest discussion of such topics as the role of women in combat, racial differences in sports and academic performance, and the inevitability of workplace sexual harassment. On the left, where the crime control model, based on notions of deterrence and retribution, is being fought, the assumptions of free will and personal responsibility that underlie current legal structures are weakened by insights from evolutionary theory. In both cases, scholars appear to be attracted to the perceived determinism of the theory.

Why does evolutionary theory attract ideological extremes? The theory itself is posit-ive, and of course, no positive theory can prove the soundness of a normative position. Moreover, nothing in the theory itself suggests that ideologically extreme positions are any more likely to follow from the theory than are more moderate positions. Instead, I believe that the extreme positions are better explained by what I will term a search cost theory of interdisciplinary work. Far too often, law professors start with a normative viewpoint that they wish to justify by reference to supporting interdisciplinary research. A writer who starts with an ideological viewpoint, or a set of priors formed from ideological beliefs, will tend to search only as far afield from legal literature as is necessary to find sufficient support for those ideological views or priors before proceeding with her legal proposals. Most mainstream normative views are already supportable with research in psychology, economics, sociology and political science. These social sciences are closer to law in terms of research methodologies, required knowledge base and terminology use than are the natural sciences, and given their backgrounds, the average law professor presumably is much more likely to have previously acquired social scientific than natural scientific knowledge. Because research in the natural sciences is more time consuming and difficult for law professors, they are much less likely to incur those costs in order to support moderate views. By contrast, those with more extreme views may find sufficient validation of those views only by bypassing the social sciences and heading for the natural sciences—here, to evolutionary theory. This biasing effect is most unfortunate for the development of the field. In fact, this ideological bias explains why 'sociobiology', the intellectual precursor to 'evolutionary theory' and 'behavioural biology' was so strongly and universally vilified by those in the social sciences. Evolutionary psychology is currently under fire for similar reasons, and behavioural biology is also beginning to be viewed suspiciously. For a survey and critical discussion of the various fields linking evolution and human behaviour, see Laland & Brown (2002).

The legal academy comfortably ignores science buffs working in the area of law and biology, regarding them as irrelevant. This second group of ideologically extreme scholars using evolutionary theory are less easily ignored but much more easily vilified. Rather than attacking the scholars and their questionable uses of evolutionary theory, however, many have simply attacked the use of evolutionary theory as dangerous. For a law review critique with references to several books that detail the abuses of biological theories, see Vogel (1997). The rest of us working in the field of law and biology bemoan the reflexive, emotional and ignorant rejection of evolutionary theory by many of our colleagues. The rejection is all the more frustrating when it is supported merely by glib comments that would have earned the rejector a grade of 'D' in high school biology. Moreover, because so much of legal literature is normatively driven, those of us who are interested in evolutionary theory for its own sake are presumed to have an ideologically extreme agenda. This assumption is often incorrect, but the resulting potential derision causes many to steer clear of law and biology.

A third and growing group of scholars has very recently brought energy to, and promise for the future of, law and biology. These academics are interested in developing the best possible models of human behaviour. For these instrumental scholars, the law is a tool used to influence what people do, but efficient and effective use of these tools requires the best possible understanding of human behaviour. A few examples include Jones (1997, 2001), Geddes & Zak (2002) and O'Hara & Yarn (2002). Behavioural biology is viewed as one of several tools that provide useful insights into human behaviour. These lawyers, as human behaviour theorists, are more likely to be deeply committed to exploring legal policy than are the science buffs, and they are less likely to be driven primarily by a normative agenda than are the ideologically extreme law and biology hobbyists. They should be neither ignored nor vilified.

Before this recent emergence of law and biology, legal scholars were busy scouring the fields of psychology and economics to build and test frameworks for human behaviour. The strengths of economic theory lie in its rigour and in its ability to generate testable predictions about human behaviour (Posner 1992, p. 17). Central to economic theory is an assumption that people act rationally in pursuit of their goals (Posner 1992, p. 3). The goals themselves are defined as elements of the person's utility function. The idea behind individual utility functions is that individuals can and do have positive preferences for many goods, services and other things. People can desire almost anything, from leisure, status and marriage to chocolate chip cookies, children and Irish setters. People are also assumed to be able to order their preferences so that at any given point a marginal increase in each of these desirables—marital quality, cookies and leisure, for example—can be rank ordered against the other desirables.

Legal academics attempting to use economic theory have generated many useful insights, but in the process, they have confronted two types of limitation. First, although individuals are allowed to prefer practically anything under economic theory, most economists are reluctant to explore the content of individual preferences (Hirshleifer 1977). Instead, they make very simple assumptions about preferences. Most commonly, they assume that people have a taste for money, and empirical work in economics typically focuses on profits or dollars as a goal of human behaviour (O'Hara & Yarn 2002). No doubt money and wealth motivate much of human behaviour, but this assumption is not always helpful in attempting to explain or predict human behaviour.

Often a desire for money sits in tension with other less quantifiable goals. For example, a growing body of legal scholarship recognizes that suit and settlement decisions often have relatively little to do with the amount of money at stake. Instead, plaintiffs often leave money on the settlement table once they receive a heartfelt apology from the defendant (O'Hara & Yarn 2002). Plaintiffs want vindication and restoration of their dignity. They may seek money too, but a single-minded assumption that they merely seek to maximize the monetary gains from suit misses important settlement dynamics that are much more likely to drive the plaintiff's decision.

At other times monetary incentives signal that something is amiss with the proposal of the 'offeror'. If, for example, the local government offers modest monetary rewards to induce people to recycle, some of the citizens will interpret the incentive as a signal that recycling levels are quite low. To the extent that people care more about complying with social norms than they do about the modest monetary payoff for recycling, then recycling levels could actually fall with the monetary incentives in place. According to Vandenbergh (2003), one implication of the norm of conformity is that people will comply with the law only if they perceive others to also comply.

In a related context, day-care centres sometimes find that parents are more rather than less likely to pick up their children late when a modest late fee is introduced. Before the imposition of the late fee, parents made greater efforts to pick up their children on time out of a sense of moral duty. With the imposition of the fine, some of the parents decided that it was worth the stated price to come a bit later (Gneezy & Rustichini 2004). Here, too, a single-minded assumption that people only care about money can lead to counterproductive policies.

Even when economists correctly identify people's goals, the assumption that people are likely to act rationally in pursuit of those goals is sometimes subject to challenge. Put differently, those who use the rational actor model are prone to ignore a variety of limitations on our abilities to gather and process information. We are prone to make mistakes owing to hindsight bias, optimism bias, endowment effects, ambiguity aversion, framing effects and other cognitive phenomena. For a description of the cognitive limitations relied on by those critical of the rationality assumption underlying economic analysis, see Mitchell (2002) and Kornhauser (2003).

The law and psychology movement is currently capitalizing on these weaknesses in the use of economic theory. The field started with several academics who were interested in learning more about mental disorders, eyewitness testimony and jury decision-making (see, generally, Satin 1995; Rachlinski 2000), but more recently law and psychology has embraced more general empirical theories of decision making. As Jeffrey Rachlinski notes:

[t]hese new, empirical theories of decision making have an interdisciplinary origin. The field consists largely of psychologists, such as Amos Tversky and Daniel Kahneman, who

refer to their work as the psychology of judgment and decision-making. It also includes many economists, however. Some economists in this field, such as Vernon Smith, embrace rational choice models, but seek to test their tenets empirically. They refer to their work as behavioral economics. Other economists, such as Richard Thaler and George Loewenstein, are skeptical of the rational choice models and use empirical research to document its flaws. These economists refer to their field by the name that many legal scholars have embraced: behavioral decision theory (BDT).

(Rachlinski 2000, p.739)

The cognitive phenomena that these scholars and experimenters have identified, including judgement biases, errors, aversions and framing effects, lack their own organizing theory (Jones 2001), however, and without a theory, we are unable to reliably predict or verify those contexts in which the cognitive phenomena are strong and when they are weak. Moreover, without a competing theory, many remain doubtful of the validity of the methodologies creating these biases (Jones 2001).

Behavioural decision theorists are beginning to focus on the operation of the human brain for a better understanding of these phenomena. Some deviations from rational choice theory stem from the fact that our capacity for attention and memory are limited (Rachlinski 2000). Other deviations originate from the fact that much of the brain's processing occurs outside of our conscious awareness, making correction of some phenomena difficult (Rachlinski 2000). And many deviations from rational choice arise from the fact that our brains are designed to respond to changes in wealth and risk rather than to their absolute levels (Rachlinski 2000). Understanding these facts about the brain is a step towards a richer understanding of these phenomena, but a greater appreciation for the contexts in which these phenomena appear requires an appreciation for the fact that our brains, like our other organs, are shaped by evolutionary pressures.

More specifically, evolutionary theory helps economists to better define the contents of the prototypical utility function (Hirshleifer 1977), and it can help those in behavioural decision theory to generate a sounder theoretical basis for some of the cognitive phenomena that are observed. As Jones (2005), a prominent law and biology scholar, explains:

All theories of human behaviour are ultimately theories about the brain. The brain is a corporeal, biological phenomenon. And modern biology makes forcefully clear that the brain's design, function, and behavioral outputs are all products of gene–environment interactions. At present, the legal system builds its models for regulating behavior using only social science components. And social sciences together typically comprise only the environmental half of the gene–environment whole.

Fortunately, this reality is beginning to change.

Moreover, evolutionary theory often feels comparatively familiar to interdisciplinary legal scholars because the methodologies of biology and economics are somewhat similar[3] in that both use game theory to generate equilibrium models of behaviour based on a type of self-interest. Put differently, the learning curve for evolutionary theory is not as steep for these scholars as would be the curve for some of the other natural sciences.

It is here, with the behavioural theorists, that law and biology is finally gaining a foothold. The advance comes with some resistance, because busy law professors still view learning about another field as problematic and view evolutionary theory with some suspicion. Some students of human behaviour are attempting to cast behavioural biology aside as unhelpful or dangerous (Rachlinski 2001; Wax 2004). Nevertheless, a growing number are appreciating the value of learning about evolutionary theory (Posner 1998, 1999; Ulen 2001; Epstein 2002, p. 1307; Luban 2004, p. 111).

The progress that law and biology is making with this third discipline-based group is aided by the fact that economists, psychologists, sociologists and political scientists are beginning to find ways to move beyond the standard social science model to incorporate behavioural biology insights directly into the social sciences (Laland & Brown 2002, p. 2; Pigliucci 2003, pp. 882–884). To the extent that a lawyer who typically uses the tools of economics or psychology sees that the academics in these fields are beginning to embrace evolutionary theory, he/she is less reluctant to draw on these tools him/herself. The insights are more quickly incorporated into legal analysis when the social sciences incorporate insights from behavioural biology into their own models. Put differently, a rich incorporation of behavioural biology into law might require that it first be heavily integrated with the social sciences. The same may be true for neuroscience.[4]

Although behavioural biology is increasingly incorporated into the social sciences, progress is hampered by three challenges that parallel the concerns about incorporating behavioural biology directly into law. The first two concerns, discussed earlier, are that evolutionary theory is irrelevant for explaining human behaviour and that, if relevant, the analysis is dangerous and politically unacceptable. A third concern raised by human behaviour theorists is that methodologically, evolutionary theory might be insufficiently rigorous. Scientific theories of human behaviour require that they be able to predict human behaviour. These predictions should enable the theory to be empirically testable and therefore falsifiable, and effective testability requires that observations of human behaviour be subject to control conditions (Rachlinski 2001). Evolutionary theory, as applied to humans, admittedly does face some challenges in these categories. Scientists are limited in the experimentation that they are allowed to perform on humans, we still have limited scientific information on the exact link between genes and behaviour, and we face extremely limited information about the timing and the content of the critically important EEA. In fact, these limitations have caused one commentator to claim that evolutionary theory is simply unscientific.

> The role that evolutionary forces have played in the development of cognitive processes, and thus in the development of law, is not readily observable. Consequently, evolutionary theories needed to explain law are not subject to empirical testing, and hence, not scientific . . . Without the ability to identify the environmental pressures that produced human cognition or the ability to compare human cognition to that of similar species, evolutionary analysis of law inevitably will lack precision and empirical support.
>
> (Rachlinski 2001, pp. 366, 370)

The charge is puzzling, for in some ways evolutionary theory has been empirically verified more exhaustively than any other. Many observed human behaviours can be ultimately explained by evolutionary theory. Moreover, the specific implications of evolutionary theory for human behaviour are themselves very often verifiable. No doubt behavioural biology can be more finely honed and therefore more useful to policymakers if theories of potentially evolved human behaviours are both informed and confirmed by empirical testing.[5] Further empirical testing is likely to proceed slowly, however, and in the interim those of us interested in evolutionary theory will have to contend with the charge that it is 'mere speculation' to assert that evolutionary pressures help to shape our tastes, personalities, cognitive thought processes, behaviour and emotions.

2.3 How can neuroscience help?

Developments in neuroscience are providing important empirical support for evolutionary claims that our brains are the product of evolutionary forces and that our brain structures influence our thoughts, feelings and actions. For those interested in evolutionary theory, neuroscientific findings are increasingly able to provide at least indirect empirical verification of the validity of the predictions of evolutionary theory. The observations not only help to test our current evolutionary theories; they also help to shape a stronger and more relevant behavioural biology. The neuroscientific focus on present manifestations of the evolution of the human brain also helps to distract attention from our paucity of knowledge about the EEA.

Moreover, in some cases, legal scholars can accept the findings of neuroscience without having to take a position in the debate about the usefulness of evolutionary theory. Stated differently, neuroscientific studies are often predicated on hypotheses generated by applying evolutionary theory to the study of the brain (LeDoux 1996; Newsome 1997; Damasio 2003). To the extent that scholars are solely interested in the behavioural phenomenon as it is observed, they are able to bypass the evolutionary psychology debate.

Neuroscientists are learning a great deal about the human brain and how it functions, and along the way we are reminded that behavioural biology has its limits as well as its powerful applications to human behaviour. In other words, we are learning how our brain seems predisposed to function, but we are also learning a great deal about its plasticity in response to environmental factors.[6] Greater knowledge about the plasticity of our cognitive processes can help to identify the limits of the implications that can be gleaned from evolutionary theory. Presumably, knowledge of the brain's plasticity coupled with knowledge about its predispositions helps us to generate a more robust theory of human behaviour than does a singular reliance on evolutionary theory.

Aside from providing contributions to the theory of human behaviour, advances in neuroscience also promise to aid the efforts of the law to better achieve just outcomes.[7] As an example, advances in neuroscience have made possible the development of 'brain printing technology' that serves as a type of high technology lie detector.[8] In essence, the technology can be used to determine which of a series of scenic images the defendant has some prior familiarity with. Several scenes can be shown to a defendant, including some aspect of the scene of the criminal activity, to get a sense of whether a defendant who claims he had absolutely nothing to do with a crime is telling the truth. The technology may evoke the same concerns about reliability and prosecutorial abuse as do more traditional forms of lie detector technologies, but at the same time it promises to aid the exculpation of innocent defendants. If it can do this successfully, then the legitimacy of the State's use of its criminal justice powers can be enhanced.

There are many other areas in which neuroscientists could focus their energies to enhance the functioning of the law, and I will use the remainder of this essay to describe a few possibilities that seem potentially promising to me. In doing so, I run the very real risk that I assume too much of the potential for neuroscientific research or too little about the current state of neuroscientific knowledge. I proceed nonetheless in the hope that at least one of the research avenues mentioned below could actually promote advancement in the law.

Agency plays an important role in the law. We often enlist others to act on our behalf, and sometimes the law imposes special fiduciary obligations on our agents to attempt to maximize the likelihood that they will fulfil their roles honourably and responsibly. Neuroscientists and neuroeconomists have learned a fair amount about our theory-of-mind mechanisms that enable us to glean and interpret the understandings, behaviour and intentions of others.[9] In interpersonal settings, we use this theory of mind mechanism to form judgements about whether another is more likely to act as 'friend' or 'foe', to forecast whether they are likely to behave coincident with our own self-interest and to make judgements about the extent to which another can be trusted. The decision about whether to trust is better understood today.

Many legal rules focus on the other end of this interpersonal dynamic, however, because they are primarily aimed at determining when we can realistically expect the agent to act in a trustworthy fashion. To try to encourage trustworthy behaviour, the law imposes on some agents' fiduciary duties of loyalty and care (Goodenough 2001). In other contexts, agents are simply prohibited from certain behaviours out of an intuition in the law that these behaviours will unduly compromise the trustworthiness of the agent's actions. For example, in some states a realtor earning a commission on the sale of real estate is barred from serving as power of attorney for the purchaser in the transaction (Walker 1922). Trustees are not permitted to commingle trust funds with personal funds.[10] Federal judges who have a pecuniary interest in one of the parties in a lawsuit are required to excuse themselves from involvement in the particular case.[11] These are all examples of situations where rule-makers question the ability of individuals to be loyal agents owing to their potentially conflicting personal interests.

In other areas of the law, however, agents need only disclose potentially conflicting situations, and the principal is left to determine how much scrutiny of the situation is warranted. A real estate attorney or divorce lawyer might for example be permitted to represent both sides of a legal matter (Galaty et al. 1974; Aronson & Weckstein 1980), and a realtor can refer clients to lenders that are financially aligned with the real estate company. Moreover, debates exist in corporate law and elsewhere about whether fiduciary duties should be contractually waivable by the parties (Blair & Stout 2001; Ribstein 2001).

The lines that are drawn and argued about in the law turn, in part, on as yet unanswered empirical assumptions about the potential trustworthiness of the agent. To what extent can, and do, we place ourselves mentally into the role of another when we are enlisted to act on their behalf? The law and legal advocates form intuitions about when that mental representation will be overridden with conflicting self-interest, but how accurate are these intuitions? People presumably vary in their trustworthiness, and our understanding of the role of the prefrontal cortex in human behaviour is improving dramatically. Much more important for legal policy purposes, however, is a need for a better understanding of the extent to which our intuitions about the limits of trustworthiness should change or vary with the behavioural context. Neuroscience might help us to better understand which sets of empirical assumptions about contextual trustworthiness are ultimately supportable.

A second place where neuroscientists can help to advance the law is in sorting deception from self-deception. *Mens rea*, or the state of mind of the defendant, is often important to our legal determinations of guilt or liability, particularly in the areas of criminal law and intentional torts. When a judge or jury is asked to make a determination about whether the defendant acted with 'knowledge', 'intent' or 'purpose', they are often forced to infer the defendant's state of mind from facts that can be gathered about his actions.

Under the Model Penal Code, for example, crimes can require one of four mental states on the part of defendant. These four categories are as follows.

(i) Crimes requiring *intention (or purpose)* to do the forbidden act (omission) or cause the forbidden result;
(ii) Crimes requiring *knowledge* of the nature of the act (omission) or of the result which will follow therefrom or of the attendant circumstances;
(iii) Those requiring *recklessness* in doing the act (omission) or causing the result (. . . the actor must in his own mind realize the risk which his conduct involves); and
(iv) Those requiring only *negligence* in so doing or causing (. . . the actor need not realize the risk in order to be negligent . . .) (LaFave 2000, pp. 229–230).

In addition, some crimes require no proof of mental state at all. These crimes are known as strict liability crimes (LaFave 2000, pp. 257–265).

When *mens rea* is disputed, the defendant claims that he did not intend to harm or that he was unaware of the consequences of his actions, and the legal decision-maker must determine whether his claim is credible. In many situations, the judge or jury must effectively determine whether the defendant is attempting to deceive them about his intentions or knowledge. This finding might in turn depend on a determination about whether the defendant, whose position is clearly unreasonable, is engaging in deceptive or self-deceptive claims. Evolutionary theorists have argued that self-deception can evolve as an effective mechanism for deceiving others (Trivers 1985, pp. 415–418; Moomol & Henzi 2000). The idea is that the telltale physiological signs of deception can be suppressed only if the actor himself is unaware of his deceptive behaviour.

Although evolutionary theorists might label self-deception as just another form of deceptive behaviour, the law often cares a great deal about the distinction between the two. For example, the crime of fraud requires not only that the defendant intended to behave the way that he did, but also that he intended to deceive and defraud his victim (LaFave 2000, p. 230). If the defendant deceived himself into believing his intentions were honourable at the point in time that he interacted with his victim, then he lacks the state of mind necessary to be guilty of fraud. More generally, under the Model Penal Code, only negligence and strict liability crimes do not require awareness on the part of the defendant about what he is doing or the likely consequences of his actions. Negligence and strict liability crimes are disfavoured in the criminal law (Parker 1993), however, so most crimes require that the defendant be consciously aware of his actions and/or their harmfulness at the time of acting. If one is, by definition, unaware of self-deception, then at least some of our concepts of legal blame do not attach to the situation. The defendant may be negligent for failing to comprehend that he was deceiving himself, but he cannot be said to have acted knowingly or intentionally.

Jurors and judges make their determinations about the defendant's state of mind based on a 'gut instinct' that may be infected by unfortunate biases or prejudices. If neuroscience could develop a more reliable way to separate deception from self-deception that could be used in the courtroom, the accuracy of these legal determinations could be greatly improved. Some evolutionary theorists posit that self-deception occurs when the conscious and subconscious hold contradictory beliefs about the self.[12] One can only hope that this, or some alternative understanding, could be more precisely identified.

Another place where the law makes blameworthiness or credibility distinctions is in those contexts where people are believed to 'snap'—that is to become suddenly unable to control their behaviour with conscious deliberations about the costs and benefits of their responses. For example, my colleague Michael Vandenbergh has begun work on the evidentiary reliability of 'excited utterance' rules given what we now know about the neuroscientific basis of the phenomenon. A second context in which the law could be better informed by neuroscience is provocation. The provocation doctrine in criminal law enables a charge of murder to be reduced to a charge of manslaughter if the defendant was provoked into killing (Perkins & Boyce 1982, pp. 84–85). In general, the provocation must be of a type that would cause the average person to lose control (Perkins & Boyce 1982, p. 87), but US courts have differed in the contexts in which the partial defence of provocation can be invoked. All courts allow the provocation defence in cases where the defendant witnesses his wife engaged in sexual relations with another man, but more difficult issues about provocation arise when the news of adultery is reported to the defendant third-hand, when the killer has been victimized by domestic violence or social taunting, and when the provocation involved a mere fist fight (Perkins & Boyce 1982, pp. 88–98). Moreover, in all states the provocation defence is unavailable if enough time passes between the provocation and the killing to enable the defendant to regain his composure (Perkins & Boyce 1982, pp. 99–101). The appropriate length of this cooling off period is left to juries and varies considerably from case to case (Perkins & Boyce 1982, p. 100). Presumably, the greater the provocation the longer the permissible cooling-off period (Perkins & Boyce 1982, p. 101). In addition, circumstances could prolong or reignite the emotional reaction (Perkins & Boyce 1982, p. 101). Although variation in the availability of, and limitations on, the use of the provocation defence are appropriate, a better understanding of the neurochemical response to varying forms of provocation might help the criminal law courts to fine tune their delivery of justice.

Finally, neuroscience can play an important role in helping the legal system to devise mechanisms for creating optimal incentives for individual and corporate behaviour. Most often injuries occur out of sheer inadvertence or ignorance of the risk of harm on the part of the injurer. The law imposes potential fines or other liabilities on these actors in an effort to draw their attention to the ways in which their behaviour can harm others. This legal response is well supported in neuroscience because it is now well understood that brains respond to changes or challenges in the environment rather than paying careful attention to all potential information available (C. Camerer, G. Loewenstein, D. Prelec, personal communication). When the law imposes a new obligation, it does so in a way calculated to gain the attention of potential injurers in the hopes of deterring future injuries. Unfortunately, if the law responds very dramatically to the problem, it risks triggering a fear response in potential defendants, and the law risks overdeterring socially useful conduct in its efforts to promote care. As Camerer *et al.* (2005) explain the phenomenon, 'much risk averse behavior is driven by immediate fear responses to risk, and fear, in turn, seems to be largely traceable to a single small area of the brain called the amygdala' (Camerer *et al.* 2005). Any nuanced neuroscientific understanding of how legal responses might catch the attention of potential injurers without causing significant reaction in the amygdala could prove enormously helpful to the development of legal development and enforcement efforts.

2.4 Conclusion

A neurologist once questioned why the lawyers at a Gruter Institute conference were so interested in learning about brain physiology. Who cares how the brain functions technically when all the lawyer really cares about is how people actually behave? The answer to his question is threefold. Some delight in learning about the science for its own sake. Others seek radical knowledge about the brain to support their radical normative views. But the third group—the one to pay attention to—hopes that a more sophisticated understanding of the brain can eventually help us to sort out the validity of competing and complementary theories of human behaviour. On a more pragmatic level, brain technologies promise to improve the legal system's delivery of justice. This essay mentions just a few of the questions that lawyers hope neuroscientists can help us resolve.

Special thanks to Owen Jones, Michael Vandenbergh, Oliver Goodenough and two anonymous referees for comments on this topic. Thanks also to the Gruter Institute for Law and the Behavioral Sciences for sparking my interest in this subject. I received research support from Vanderbilt University School of Law for this project, and, as always, I am grateful for its support.

Endnotes

1. http://www.gruterinstitute.org (visited 16 February 2004).
2. For more information on law and biology see the website for the Society for Evolutionary Analysis in Law at http://www.sealsite.org (visited 21 October 2004).
3. Charles Darwin was heavily influenced by Adam Smith's work (Gould 1995, p. 329).
4. Neuroscience too is slowly working its way into the literature of other fields. See, for example Pigliucci (2003), Casebeer & Churchland (2003), Debiec & LeDoux (2003) and Leiberman *et al.* (2003).
5. Russell Korobkin (2001) does a wonderful job of describing the intellectual synergies that can be produced by combining evolutionary theory with economic theory, experimental economics and cognitive psychology.
6. I have discussed this topic and its importance for human behavioural theorists in general, and lawyers in particular (O'Hara 2001).
7. For excellent efforts at merging the fields, see the other articles in this issue, especially Goodenough & Prehn (2004).
8. Alan Elsner, New 'brain fingerprinting' could help solve crimes, posted at http://www.rense.com/general34/newbrainfingerprinting. See also Becky McCall, Brain fingerprints under scrutiny, at http://news.bbc.co.uk/2/hi/science/nature/3495433.stm.
9. On theory of mind and its role in making cooperative decisions (see, generally, Fletcher *et al.* 1995; Happe *et al.* 1996; Frith 2001*a,b*; McCabe *et al.* 2001).
10. Restatement (Second) of Trusts § 179 (1959).
11. 28 U.S.C.A. § 455.
12. See Moomol & Henzi (2000) for a discussion of competing theories of self-deception.

References

Aronson, R. H. & Weckstein, D. T. 1980 *Professional responsibility in a nutshell.* St Paul, NY: West Publishing.

Blair, M. M. & Stout, L. A. 2001 Trust, trustworthiness, and the behavioral foundations of corporate law. *Univ. Penn. Law Rev.* **149**, 1735–1810.

Camerer, C., Loewenstein, G. & Prelec, D. 2005 Neuroeconomics: how neuroscience can inform economics. *J. Economic Lit.* (In the press.)

Casebeer, W. D. & Churchland, P. S. 2003 The neural mechanisms of moral cognition: a multi-aspect approach to moral judgment and decision-making. *Biol. Phil.* **18**, 69–194.

Damasio, A. 2003 *Looking for Spinoza: joy, sorry and the feeling brain.* Orlando, FL: Harcourt Brace.

Debiec, J. & LeDoux, J. 2003 Conclusions: from self-knowledge to a science of the self. *Ann. NY Acad. Sci.* **1001**, 305–316.

Epstein, R. A. 2002 'Let the fundamental things apply': necessary and contingent truths in legal scholarship. *Harv. Law Rev.* **115**, 1288–1313.

Fletcher, P. C., Happe, F., Frith, U., Baker, S. C., Dolan, R. J., Frackowiak, R. S. & Frith, C. D. 1995 Other minds in the brain: a functional imaging study of 'theory of mind' in story comprehension. *Cognition* **57**, 109–128.

Frith, U. 2001*a* Mind blindness and the brain in autism. *Neuron* **32**, 969–979.

Frith, U. 2001*b* What framework should we use for understanding developmental disorders? *Devl Neuropsychol.* **20**, 555–563.

Galaty, F. W., Allaway, W. J. & Kyle, R. C. 1974 *Modern real estate practice*, 13th edn. . Chicago, IL: Real Estate Education Co.

Geddes, R. & Zak, P. J. 2002 The rule of one-third. *J. Legal Stud.* **31**, 119–136.

Gneezy, U. & Rustichini, A. 2004 Incentives, punishment and behavior. In *Readings in behavioral economics* (ed. C. F. Camerer, G. F. Loewenstein & M. Rabin). (In the press.)

Goodenough, O. R. & Prehn, K. 2004 A neuroscientific approach to normative judgment in law and justice. *Phil. Trans. R. Soc. B* **359**, 1709–1726. (doi:10.1098/ rstb.2004.1552)

Goodenough, O. R. 2001 Law and the biology of commitment. In *Evolution and the capacity for commitment* (ed. R. M. Nesse), pp. 269–271. New York: Russell Sage Foundation.

Gould, S. J. 1995 *Dinosaur in a haystack: reflections in natural history.* New York: Penguin Books.

Happe, F., Ehlers, S., Fletcher, P., Frith, U., Johansson, M., Gillberg, C., Dolan, R., Frackowiak, R. & Frith, C. 1996 'Theory of mind' in the brain: evidence from a PET scan study of Asperger syndrome. *Neuroreport* **8**, 197–201.

Hirshleifer, J. 1977 Economics from a biological viewpoint. *J. Law Econ.* **20**, 1–52.

Jones, O. D. 1997 Toward an integrated model of human behavior. *J. Contemp. Legal Issues* **8**, 167–207.

Jones, O. D. 2001 Time-shifted rationality and the law of law's leverage: behavioral economics meets behavioral biology. *Northwestern Univ. Law Rev.* **95**, 1141–1205.

Jones, O.D. & Goldsmith T. H. 2005 Law and behavioural biology. *Columbia Law Rev.* **105**, 405–502.

Kornhauser, L. A. 2003 The domain of preference. *Univ. Penn. Law Rev.* **151**, 717–746.

Korobkin, R. 2001 A multi-disciplinary approach to legal scholarship: economics, behavioral economics, and evolutionary psychology. *Jurimetrics J.* **41**, 319–336.

LaFave, W. R. 2000 *Criminal law*, 3rd edn. St Paul, NY: West Publishing.

Laland, K. L. & Brown, G. R. 2002 *Sense and nonsense: evolutionary perspectives on human behavior.* New York: Oxford University Press.

LeDoux, J. 1996 *The emotional brain: the mysterious underpinnings of emotional life.* New York: Touchstone.

Leiberman, M. D., Schreiber, D. & Ochsner, K. 2003 Is political cognition like riding a bicycle? How cognitive neuroscience can inform research on political thinking. *Polit. Psychol.* **24**, 681–704.

Luban, D. 2004 A theory of crimes against humanity. *Yale J. Int. Law* **29**, 85–167.

McCabe, K., Houser, D., Ryan, L., Smith, V. & Trouard, T. 2001 A functional imaging study of cooperation in two-person reciprocal exchange. *Proc. Natl Acad. Sci. USA* **98**, 11 832–11 835.

Mitchell, G. 2002 Taking behavioralism too seriously? The unwarranted pessimism of the new behavioral analysis of law *William and Mary Law Rev.* **43**, 1907–2021.

Moomol, Z. & Henzi, S. P. 2000 The evolutionary psychology of deception and self-deception. *S. Afr. J. Psychol.* **30**, 45–51.

Newsome, W. T. 1997 Perceptual processes. In *Conversations in the cognitive neurosciences* (ed. M. S. Gazzaniga), pp. 52–68. Cambridge, MA: MIT Press.

O'Hara, E. A. 2001 Brain plasticity and Spanish moss in biolegal analysis. *Florida Law Rev.* **53**, 905–929.

O'Hara, E. A. & Yarn, D. 2002 On apology and consilience. *Washington Law Rev.* **77**, 1121–1192.

Parker, J. S. 1993 The economics of *mens rea. Virginia Law Rev.* **79**, 741–811.

Perkins, R. M. & Boyce, R. N. 1982 *Criminal law*, 3rd edn. Mineola, NY: Foundation Press.

Pigliucci, M. 2003 On the relationship between science and ethics. *Zygon* **38**, 871–894.

Posner, R. A. 1992 *Economic analysis of law*, 4th edn. Boston, MA: Little, Brown.

Posner, R. A. 1998 Rational choice, behavioral economics, and the law. *Stanford Law Rev.* **50**, 1551–1575.

Posner, R. A. 1999 *The problematics of moral and legal theory*. Cambridge, MA: Harvard University Press.

Rachlinski, J. J. 2000 The 'new' law and psychology: a reply to critics, skeptics, and cautious supporters. *Cornell Law Rev.* **85**, 739–766.

Rachlinski, J. J. 2001 Comment: is evolutionary analysis of law science or storytelling? *Jurimetrics* **41**, 365–370.

Ribstein, L. E. 2001 Law v. trust. *Boston Univ. Law Rev.* **81**, 553–590.

Satin, M. I. 1995 Law and Psychology: A movement whose time has come. *A. Surv. Am. Law* **1995**, 581–631.

Trivers, R. 1985 *Social evolution*. Menlo Park, CA: Benjamin/Cummings.

Ulen, T. S. 2001 Evolution, human behavior and law: a response to Owen Jones' Dunwody Lecture. *Florida Law Rev.* **53**, 931–946.

Vandenbergh, M. P. 2003 Beyond elegance: a testable typology of social norms in corporate environmental compliance *Stanford Environ. Law J.* **22**, 55–144.

Vogel, J. 1997 Biological theories of human behavior: admonitions of a skeptic. *Vermont Law Rev.* **22**, 425–432.

Walker, W. S. 1922 *American law of real estate agency*, 2nd edn. Cincinnati, OH: W.H. Anderson.

Wax, A. L. 2004 Evolution and the bounds of human nature. *Law Phil.* **23**, 527–591.

Glossary

EEA environment of evolutionary adaptation

Law, biology, and the brain

3

Law and the sources of morality

Robert A. Hinde

This paper argues that morality is a product of basic human psychological characteristics shaped over prehistorical and historical time by diachronic dialectical transactions between what individuals do and what they are supposed to do in the culture in which they live. Some principles are pancultural: individuals are motivated to look after their own interests, to be cooperative and kind to other group members and to look after their children. The moral precepts of every society are based on these principles, but may differ according to the vicissitudes that the society has experienced. Thus the basic principles can be seen as absolute; the precepts based on them may be specific to particular societies. Moral precepts, and the laws derived from them, are mostly such as to maintain the cohesion of the society, but some have been formulated to further the interests of those in power.

The evidence suggests that laws have been developed, by common consent or by rulers, from generally accepted moral intuitions. In general, legal systems have been formulated to deal with the more extreme infringements of moral codes. Morality prescribes how people should behave; the law is concerned primarily with how they should not. New laws, if not imposed by force, must generally be in tune with public conceptions of morality.

Keywords: law and morality; evolution of morality; development of morality; absolute principles versus culture-specific precepts; cross-cultural communication

3.1 Introduction

The relations between law and morality have been clouded by differences of opinion concerning the extent to which both law and morality are to be seen as fixed and immutable, or as labile. With respect to law, the distinction between sacred and secular, second nature in the Western world, is simply inappropriate in many societies. Even early in the second millennium BCE all imperatives of life received their value from the fact that they represented the will of the gods as conveyed by the ruler, who claimed to be accomplishing divine wishes (Bottéro 1992). And in the modern world, 'the law' is often seen as given, as what is on the statute book (e.g. Hart 1994). That leads to the view that, in considering particular cases, there should be no relation between law and morality or that, if there is, it is better for lawyers to hold to precedent and disregard it.

Nevertheless, legal theorists discuss such questions as the relative merits of principles of equality, equity, need and justice, and whether penalties are justified by principles of retribution or deterrence: morality is always there in the background (Devlin 1965; Finnis 1980; Freeman 2001). Dworkin (1973) argues that law implies principles of justice and fairness, which can be applied in judicial decisions (see Himma 2003). Furthermore, when new law becomes necessary, as when issues such as *in vitro* fertilization, genetic modification or abortion are in dispute, moral issues as purveyed by public opinion must be taken into account. Public opinion on such issues clearly has some relation to publicly accepted morality (Warnock 1998): indeed, in a democratic country, laws seen as unjust will not be respected.

In the same way, some see morality as God-given, or at least as absolute. They claim that people know what is right 'intuitively', and that science can have nothing to say on the matter. Others see morality as situation specific, differing between societies and changing with time.

While in the case of law the arguments have been well rehearsed, it is only recently that a scientific approach has been brought to bear on the nature of morality. There are ultimately only three possibilities: either our moral codes are God-given, they have been handed down by 'culture', or they have somehow been derived from human nature. I shall not consider the first possibility, except to suggest that, if moral codes have been derived from human nature, the suggestion that they are God-given is unnecessary.[1] The second possibility raises the question of where culture, including moral systems, comes from, and leads on to the third, that moral codes are ultimately derived from human nature.

This paper takes the view, based in biology, psychology and anthropology, that *morality is a product of certain basic pan-cultural characteristics of human beings, but has been shaped over prehistorical and historical time by diachronic dialectical transactions between individuals and the culture in which they live. That is, throughout human history, the behaviour, values and attitudes of individuals have continuously influenced and been influenced by the culture in which they live.* Moral principles are based in human nature, but societies and their cultures change, leading to a limited differentiation of moral codes between societies. Thus morality is neither absolute nor wholly socially constructed. (See Arenhart (1998) for a similar view reached from a somewhat different perspective.)

What does it mean to say that moral codes and values are derived from human nature? Certainly not that they are encoded in our genes, for all adult characteristics depend ultimately on both genes and environment. Nor, given the basic cross-cultural similarity between moral codes, is it likely that they are merely the 'brainchildren' of enlightened individuals. Rather, from pancultural bases moral codes have differentiated over time, largely through mutual influences between what individuals in the society do and what they are supposed to do. That interaction has depended on the vicissitudes to which the society and the individuals within it have been exposed, and has been directed mostly towards fostering smooth social relations between individuals. Thus moral codes are not rigid, but differ to some extent between societies and may change gradually over time. However, they are not infinitely flexible: the moral *precepts* in every society are related to a few pancultural *principles*. All humans have a tendency to be assertive and look after their own interests, and all have propensities to behave prosocially to kin and to other group members. The hypothesis advanced here is that moral precepts are such as to swing the balance towards prosociality so that group living is possible, though that does not mean that all so-called moral precepts facilitate group living. It is also suggested that legal systems, far from being independent of moral codes, are in large measure such as to deal with extreme infringements of moral codes.

The first section of this paper, therefore, highlights briefly the continuous interplay between biological and cultural influences in the development of morality in the individual and in the emergence and historical development of morality. It is followed by a suggestion that moral and legal systems share common roots. The final section considers the relations between law and morality: first the relevance of the current approach to situations where the legal system of one country is unacceptable to the moral code of another, and second the similarities and differences between morality and English law.

3.2 The interplay between biological and cultural influences

(a) The development of morality in the individual

The doctrine of original sin suggests that children are born evil. However, much of the behaviour that is undesirable to parents is part of natural development and/or the result of the artificial conditions of modern life. Children take delight in 'testing limits', but that is part of learning how far they can control their own environments, how far their assertiveness will take them. Equally, by 1 year of age children show behaviours that could be considered as morally good—sharing, care-taking, taking turns, sympathy, etc. (Rheingold & Hay 1980). This, of course, does not indicate a fully fledged moral capacity, and must be regarded as 'proto-moral'. Thus, young children are predisposed to develop behaviour that we consider as moral, as well as to assert themselves.

Children are also predisposed to please their parents or other adult caregivers. They like to help, to obey and imitate their parents, and they look warily at their parent if they violate a sanctioned act (Eisenberg & Fabes 1998). Biologically, this is not surprising: young primates depend on parental proximity and on obedience to parental signals for their survival. However, children are predisposed to acquire both moral (prosocial[2]) and immoral (selfishly assertive[3]) behaviour: parental treatment, depending on its nature and quality, may augment either.

The development of moral behaviour and so-called 'moral intuition' depends on numerous aspects of psychological functioning as well as on relationships with caregivers, and it is unnecessary to review its course here. The important point is that children have propensities for both prosocial and selfishly assertive behaviour, and the relative strengths that these acquire depends on their relationships with others.

In the early phase, interactions with family members are crucial: later the peer group, authority figures, cultural idols, etc., also exert their influence, but early experience is of special importance. Prosociality is most likely to be engendered by parents who are sensitive, loving, but exert reasoned control (Bowlby 1984). Parents, in turn, are influenced by their own circumstances: if the world is harsh and competitive, it is more difficult for them to be sensitive. And if the prevailing culture emphasizes assertive masculinity, they are likely to encourage this in their male children.

The internalization of moral precepts can be conceptualized in terms of the 'self-system'. Everyone acquires, primarily through observing how others behave toward them, a view of their own characteristics. Thus, one may see oneself as white Caucasian, female, a law graduate, sensitive, hard-headed, and a member of the Middle Temple with strict moral values. Data show that one tries to maintain congruency between how one perceives oneself (one's self-concept), how one sees oneself to be behaving and how one perceives others to perceive oneself (Backman 1988). Thus, if one perceives oneself as honest and to be behaving honestly, but perceives others to see oneself as deceptive, congruency must be restored. This may be achieved by trying to convince others of one's honesty, or by 'cognitive restructuring', that is by misperceiving what others say, devaluing their opinion or listening selectively to the one voice that confirms one's honesty. This provides us with a way of conceptualizing the conscience. How one sees oneself includes the nature of one's relationships with others and the rules (including moral precepts) that guide those relationships. If one sees one's behaviour as incompatible with the internalized moral rules, one experiences emotion (e.g. guilt) and may act to restore congruency. If, however, one sees oneself as behaving consistently with the moral rules one feels the pleasure of virtue.

The moral precepts that individuals acquire are best considered according to the aspect of social life with which they are concerned.

(b) Moral precepts with those perceived as kin

Certain aspects of morality can be safely ascribed to pan-cultural psychological characteristics that are the product of natural selection. (This of course does not mean that they are 'innate' and develop autonomously: they may depend on experiences common to all humans.) Most obvious here are aspects of the relationships between parents and their children and between others who see themselves as related. It is not only 'natural' for parents to love their children and children their parents, but it is considered morally right that they should do so. Prosociality between parents and their offspring is ubiquitous among mammals. Since natural selection acts to promote the survival of genes, this can reasonably be ascribed to natural selection, for the child shares half its (rare) genes with each parent. Theory predicts that prosociality with more distantly related individuals would be reduced according to the degree of relatedness (i.e. the proportion of their genes that they share): this is confirmed by data on both human and non-human species (Hamilton 1964: Betzig *et al.* 1988). Thus, varying between cultures, one has some moral obligation to act prosocially to aunts and cousins, but less than to behave prosocially to children, parents or siblings.

Interestingly, the Hebraic Commandments enjoin children to honour their parents, but not the reverse. Presumably parental love was assumed, or the Commandments were written from the parental perspective. We shall encounter other instances of moral rules prescribed with self-interest later.

The degree to which parents are expected to support their children decreases with their age. We say, 'They ought to be independent by now'. This is also in accordance with evolutionary theory. It is in the evolutionary interests of parents to look after their children only for so long as it does not overly diminish their own prospects for further reproduction. As children develop, they demand more parental resources until they demand more than the parent is prepared to give. This same biological principle also accounts for other common phenomena—for example, the difficulties that arise when a sibling is born and the care lavished on a last-born (Trivers 1974).

Certain apparent exceptions must be noted.

(i) Contraception reduces an individual's reproductive success. However, in pre-industrial societies it balances the welfare and reproductive potential of children already born against the negative effects that an immediate further conception would have on lifetime parental reproductive success. In the industrial world the use of contraception has been increased by the desire of parents for satisfactions other than those inherent in parenthood.

(ii) Infanticide has been used as a method for controlling family size, and by women who are undernourished or severely disadvantaged, who fear ostracism following the birth of an illegitimate child, or who have borne a severely congenitally abnormal child. In such cases the child would be unlikely to contribute to the parent's long-term reproductive success. In western societies step-parents, who are not biologically related to the children, are much more likely to kill or abuse children than natural parents (Daly & Wilson 1996; Jones 1997; Hrdy 1999).

(iii) Adoption. In pre-industrial societies this is usually by relatives of the parents (Silk 1980). In industrial societies its prevalence must be attributed to the desire for parenthood experienced by many adults.

Thus, many exceptions to the general rule that individuals attempt to maximize their long-term reproductive success can be understood. Such exceptions are often codified by custom. Others result from cultural desiderata other than parenthood.

(c) Relations with non-kin

Considerable insight into the dynamics of personal relationships comes from the view that relationships involve processes of exchange, individuals incurring costs (in an everyday sense) in the expectation of future rewards (e.g. Thibaut & Kelley 1959; Kelley 1979). Originally applied to marketplace transactions, exchange theories have been applied also to close personal relationships. (This does not imply that reciprocal exchange is all there is to close relationships.)

Certain consequences of this are important here. Continuity of interaction between two individuals depends on the satisfaction of both, and the rewards for a given act may lie in the future: A behaves well towards B in the expectation that B will later behave well towards him. Thus, to maintain the relationship, each participant must maximize not only his own outcomes but also those of the partner. If A does not consider B's outcomes as well as his/her own, B may opt out of the relationship and A would lose any expected return. Furthermore, initial interactions should be positive, for otherwise the other individual may refuse further interaction; trust that the partner will reciprocate, together with belief in the partner's commitment to the relationship, are essential for continuity. Therefore valuing prosociality, reciprocity, trust and commitment to the relationship follows immediately from the principle of exchange.

In the long term, the rewards exchanged must *be seen* as fair. What matters are not the resources actually exchanged, but those *perceived* as having been exchanged. Criteria of what is fair vary with the nature and age of the participants, circumstances, etc.; but always what matters is the *perception* of fairness. In some circumstances individuals do not seek to maximize their own rewards, but dislike situations in which they consider themselves to be over-benefited, feeling embarrassed or guilty (Prins *et al.* 1993). This implies that individuals are guided, perhaps unconsciously, by a contract demanding justice in personal relationships.

If reciprocity is delayed, gratitude may be accepted as an appropriate return, at least temporarily indicating that one has not incurred costs without expectation of future returns. All this occurs against a background of the moral precepts and values in one's self-system. We see individuals who express gratitude as 'polite', and value politeness.

Perception of the infringement of reciprocity requires that congruency be restored (see §2a): if met with ingratitude, one may denigrate the recipient of one's own prosocial act. Or, if one has acted unfairly oneself, one may attempt compensation, or distort one's own view of the other individual or his outcomes.

In a large group, an individual may never meet again the recipient of his prosocial action. However, the latter may express publicly his gratitude, or the prosocial act may be witnessed by others: the prosocial individual then gains a reputation for prosociality, and this will make other individuals more willing to deal with him/her in the future. Thus a reputation for generosity, or for prosociality and reciprocity, is valued (Alexander 1979; Hawkes *et al.* 2001).

Exchange theories were elaborated to explain how people behave, not how they ought to behave. But there are close parallels between exchange theories and moral codes and values. A principle of prosociality/reciprocity is preeminent in probably all societies, and a version of the Golden Rule of do-as-you-would-be-done-by is basic to all moral codes (Küng & Kuschel 1993). Some of the Ten Commandments, such as those about killing, adultery, stealing, false witness and coveting, are admonitions not to do things that one would not like to have done to oneself. Just reciprocity and prosociality are fundamental to the functioning of human groups. It is morally correct to act prosocially and to promote the welfare of others. Many recognized virtues depend on prosociality/reciprocity, for instance honesty, trustworthiness, generosity, commitment and sensitivity to others' needs.

How could one account for the ubiquity of some form of the Golden Rule across human societies and successive generations? Social groups could not be stable if individuals were predominantly selfishly assertive, but at first sight this presents a problem for evolutionary theory. Natural selection involves some individuals leaving more offspring in the next generation than others. Selfishly assertive individuals, looking after their own interests, might be expected to be more reproductively successful than prosocial ones: if so, successive generations would become progressively more assertive.

However, modelling techniques show that *cultural* selection for prosociality is possible if competition and selection both between individuals within groups and also between groups is considered. Although genetic evolution by selection between groups is at best extremely rare, the critical issue may be not that the differences between individuals should be genetic, but that they should be passed on from one individual to another by some means or other. The question then becomes, could culturally maintained similarities between individuals within a group and culturally maintained differences between groups provide a basis for group selection? Computer modelling shows that prosocial behaviour could be favoured by competition between groups under certain conditions—namely if naive individuals were to copy the behaviour most common in the group (conformism), the environments in which groups lived were heterogeneous, and groups moved from time to time. Conformism is a ubiquitous human characteristic, and the other conditions are likely to have held earlier in human history (Boyd & Richerson 1991, 1992; Sober & Wilson 1998; Wilson & Kniffen 1999). Competition between groups could have involved relative success in obtaining necessities, not necessarily actual warfare. It probably acted both at the group level, some groups being more successful than others, and at the individual level, individuals living in successful groups being more successful in spite of the costs that their prosociality incurs.

The evidence thus favours the view that prosocial behaviour and reciprocity evolved through processes of selection. The tendency to show prosocial behaviour to a related other, discussed in the previous section, implies helping another who is genetically related and therefore similarly likely to be helpful to relatives. Here, we see that prosociality to an unrelated other could be selected for if another were likely to reciprocate. In practice, each of these processes carries some of the benefits of the other. Helping a relative is helping another who is likely to help others, including the original helper. Helping an unrelated other who is likely to reciprocate means helping another who is also inclined to help others, including the original helper (Humphrey 1997).

That propensities to behave prosocially and with reciprocity are part of human nature is supported by the ubiquity of many human characteristics that support exchange. We have an acute sense of justice, are good at detecting cheating (Cosmides & Tooby 1992) and feel moral outrage when we see someone else cheating. One feels anger if unfairly treated, guilt or shame when one knows oneself to have behaved improperly (Tangney 1995). We respect honesty, fidelity, trustworthiness and commitment—virtues that are encapsulated in the concept of friendship (Frank 1988). We go to some lengths to convince others that we have these virtues. The exercise of these virtues can bring its own rewards in the shape of self-esteem and an enhanced reputation that will in turn induce others to behave positively towards oneself (Hawkes *et al.* 2001). Societies also have conventions and laws about fair-dealing that support reciprocity.

Thus, diverse aspects of human behaviour support the display of prosocial behaviour and reciprocity with in-group members. This does not mean that experience plays no part in their development in individuals. We have seen that the balance between prosociality and selfish assertiveness is influenced by experience, and there may be circumstances where unbridled selfishness pays off (De Vries 1984).

But it must not be thought that what is natural is to be seen as right, or that what is right is natural. The point is that how people actually behave, as studied by social psychologists, has many parallels with how people should behave, and that both are supported by psychological characteristics that are probably pancultural and likely to have been the product of natural selection. The principle of reciprocity is reified as a general principle and can be used to support moral precepts—'Do not hit Johnny: you would not like it if he hit you'.

The Golden Rule applied to those seen as in-group members is probably common to all cultures. However, that does not mean that all values related to it are pancultural. People in different societies have interpreted it in different ways.

(d) Status and rights

(i) Status

We have seen that, in addition to a propensity for prosociality, human infants also have a propensity to act with selfish assertiveness. Children attempt to assert their own authority. This propensity, just like that for prosociality, is affected by experience. A young man brought up in gangland in a large city is likely to take a pride in selfish assertiveness rather than prosociality.

In virtually all societies the assertiveness of individuals has led to status hierarchies. The criteria for high status differ between societies—physical strength, wealth, wisdom, beauty, gender, generosity, humility and many other qualities are valued in different societies and different contexts. The characteristic that leads to high status is either beneficial to the group (e.g. courage, generosity), or linked to envy (access to resources, women, etc.) or is a desire to possess (beauty in the opposite sex).

Status not only brings access to resources, but is also sought independently of any immediate access to resources that it may bring. High-status individuals seek to maintain the *status quo*, either because they believe it to be in the general interest or for their own purposes, whereas those low in status may seek to change it. Those in power do best if they can avoid force and use persuasion or guile to convince others that the *status quo* is in their own interests. High-status individuals may assume divine support or emphasize the moral rectitude of loyalty. And they may promote humility as a virtue, leading to reward in a later life: the Anglican catechism requires the confirmand to promise to honour the ruler and all in authority under him, and to 'order myself lowly and reverently to all my betters'.

Acceptance of low status may be facilitated by the realization that it is a good strategy: they are alright if they do not make a nuisance of themselves. Furthermore, it may become a matter of exchange, the low-status individuals profiting from the protection or benevolence of their superiors. Thus the maintenance of status differences, though resulting from assertiveness, may not be merely a matter of immediate pressure from those at the top.

(ii) Rights

Another way in which self-assertiveness is related to moral issues concerns the demand for individual autonomy and rights. Self-assertiveness is closely related to the development of selfhood and a sense of agency. Individuals strive to control their own environment and fate. Often this takes the form of seeking protection from control by those of higher status (such as parents) over actions that they consider to be outside justifiable regulation by others. Doing one's own thing, maintaining one's integrity, become matters of overriding concern. In many societies freedom of opinion, speech, movement and so on are regarded as 'inalienable'.

In practice rights are not quite 'inalienable', and differ to some extent between cultures. Limits may be set on the individuals to whom they apply: women and mentally handicapped individuals may be seen as having fewer rights than men, criminals to have no freedom of movement, enemies of the state to have no right to life. Even the so-called 'inalienable' rights are seen to have limits: freedom of expression may be seen as a universal right, but should not include the right to broadcast how to make chemical weapons. The right to autonomy is seen early in development but limits are set by cultural convention or law.

(e) Moral precepts concerned with sex and gender

The ways in which people behave and how they are supposed to behave in matters concerning the relations between the sexes are complex and diverse. Every culture has norms, some elevated to the status of moral precepts and/or secular laws, regulating sexual relations, and in none is total promiscuity allowed. For that reason, and because the socio-sexual systems of animals are equally diverse, direct comparisons with animals are extremely dubious. However, principles about the evolution of behaviour sometimes mesh surprisingly well with what we know about human behaviour.

Some societies are monogamous, some polygynous, a few polyandrous. In some a woman may profit from having intercourse with several partners because she may obtain better genes for her children, or because she thereby acquires their subsequent help in rearing her offspring (Hill & Hurtado 1996). In others biological parents do not live together, the parental role being taken by the mother's brothers (Hsu 1998). The diversity is enormous but in every culture moral codes have been elaborated to ensure that unbridled sexuality will not disrupt the social system and/or to safeguard the sexual interests of the more powerful individuals. However, invariably there is a gap between how people ought to behave and how they actually do.

Some ubiquitous characteristics of socio-sexual relations show parallels between the reproductive requirements of men and women, differences in their psychological characteristics and differences in the expectations and rules governing their sexual behaviour. Natural selection acts through reproductive success, and the reproductive requirements of the sexes differ.

In all mammals the potential lifetime reproductive success of a female is limited by the time necessary for pregnancy and (in many societies) lactation, whereas that of a male is set by the number of females fertilized. Competition between males for mates is therefore stronger than that between females, and the variance of male reproductive success is much greater than that of females. Men must compete for sexual partners and protect those they have acquired. Male aggressiveness and assertiveness, *machismo* traditions, and protective chivalry towards women are in harmony with this. Cross-cultural data indicate that adjectives such as 'aggressive', 'boastful' and others that could be called anti-social are seen as appropriate to men (Williams & Best 1982). In harmony with this, in most societies men hold the power in the social and political spheres. Not only do they compete for mates but it is also in the interests of those with power to maintain the *status quo* and order in the society to protect their wives from other men.

In addition, a woman knows that the child in her womb is her own, but a man can be cuckolded. Thus extramarital mating by a man does not lower the reproductive success of his wife unless it involves diversion of resources to another woman, but extramarital mating by a woman may result in the man expending parental care on children that are not his. In harmony with this, in probably all societies men are allowed more sexual licence than women (though male promiscuity is not necessarily seen as right). Women are expected to be chaste, modest and faithful. The difference is institutionalized with special clarity in the Muslim sphere of the *haram*, and in the association of male *machismo* with female virtue in many Catholic societies.

A child tends to be valued more by its mother than its father. The proximate reason for this may lie in feminine dispositions or in the fact that the mother has incurred more costs in rearing it. But this is also in keeping with evolutionary theory: not only may the father have been cuckolded, but also he must expend fewer resources in creating another child than must she. It is thus not surprising that, although men hold political power, in many societies women have the power in the home and control the food stores.

Again, in so far as earlier in human history, a mother needed the continuing support of a male partner, it might be expected that secure relationships would be more important to women than to men. A number of lines of evidence support this view (Gilligan 1982; Eisenberg & Fabes 1998). Adjectives such as 'affectionate', 'gentle' and 'kind' are perceived to apply more to women than to men, and empirical data show that relationships are more important to women than to men. In general, men tend to focus on justice (in keeping with their need for control in the political and social spheres), women on nurture and relationships.

Some social rules can be seen as the result of the reification of customs seen to be reproductively successful. Thus social intercourse between spouses is usually required, and some religions forbid contraception. Intercourse during menstruation may be forbidden, but that is likely to increase its frequency during the fertile period. Such practices may be in the reproductive interests of individuals, and this in turn increases the size of the community dominated by the religious specialists who uphold the moral code.

Unfortunately the origins of the cultural differences are usually lost in the mists of time (but see §4). But the parallels between biological predictions and social fact are in keeping with the view that many of the cultural expectations and stereotypes have arisen on the basis of the biological predispositions, and are the result of diachronic two way interactions between what people do and what they are supposed to do. The basic differences in predispositions between male and female neonates may be small, but they are present and are subsequently accentuated through interactions influenced by the cultural norms. Members of both sexes seek to acquire those characteristics that have brought reproductive success to their predecessors and are now seen as desirable for their gender. Members of both sexes will support norms and expectations concerning the other sex if those norms and expectations favour their own interests. From an ultimate evolutionary point of view it is in men's interests that women should be nurturing and caring, and in women's interests that the men with whom they bond should be successful in competition with other men and be good providers.

Another problem that requires integrating biological and social approaches concerns the ubiquity of incest taboos. Biologists define incest as mating between genetically closely related individuals, and both animal and human data indicate that it is biologically undesirable because of the deleterious effects of too close inbreeding on reproductive success (Grand & Bittles 1997). Anthropologists and other social scientists, impressed by the diversity of incest taboos and by the fact that the prohibitions often do not concern close genetic relatives, define incest taboos as preventing sexual relations between those whose relationship culturally debars them from having sex with each other. Most cultures do in fact discourage sexual relations between individuals closer than first cousins, in keeping with the biological view. Indeed in many cultures marriage to a member of another group may be required.

However, there are many exceptions. In some groups endogamy is encouraged, perhaps because of the difficulty of finding an unrelated spouse in a small community or because marriage to a close relative facilitates marriage arrangements, eliminates the need for dowry or bride-wealth, or ensures that possessions remain within the extended family; but outside bodies may intervene. In Europe the Christian Church discouraged close marriages, thereby weakening consanguineous ties and increasing the Church's power to obtain bequests.

There is also evidence for a psychological mechanism involving reluctance to mate with an individual who had been familiar in early life (Bevc & Silverman 2000). Thus again we see a relation between psychological propensities, the reproductive advantages that they bring, and cultural expectations and rules that may be complicated by the history and situation of the society in question.

(f) Social and religious systems

Although the parallels between psychological propensities, biological functions and moral precepts have been considered separately for several social contexts, these are not independent: the several precepts are more or less integrated in a moral system that serves primarily to maintain group cohesion. For instance, early in human evolution when groups were small, cooperative defence and hunting must have been essential for survival, and family and group loyalties must have been nearly coincident, facilitating group integrity. Sexual prohibitions are (usually) conducive to the smooth running of groups. Selfish assertiveness may be a disruptive factor, but the self-assertiveness of leaders may foster group integrity.

Many psychological mechanisms, presumably pancultural, serve in the cohesion and functioning of groups. Many cultural devices also contribute to group integrity. Social norms and moral precepts, as well as symbols such as national flags, rituals such as parades, and metaphors play a part. The metaphors (such as motherland, brothers-in-Christ) can be seen as parasitic on the consequences of kin selection. Denigration of out-group members may also result. Virtues, such as loyalty, public beneficence and courage, are presumably consequences of group living. They may acquire moral status: lack of loyalty may provoke sanctions, including ostracism, and in wartime even more severe penalties.

Group distinctiveness is also maintained by customs and moral precepts promoting differences from other groups. The dietary prohibitions of Leviticus, male circumcision and even monotheism probably contributed to maintain group distinctiveness. These are regarded as moral issues by many religious adherents. Christian missionaries sometimes promoted precepts concerned with secular matters to foster the integrity of a religious community, thereby creating an effectively separate society of converts (James 1988).

Where group integrity is of major importance to secular or religious leaders, the observance of precepts may be elevated to legal status, with heretics being burned and traitors executed. Again, basic human psychological propensities, in this case leading to the maintenance and integrity of groups, are paralleled by moral precepts, and in some extreme circumstances by the law.

3.3 Summary of the argument

On this view, therefore, there are pancultural propensities to look after one's own interests and to behave prosocially to others, especially to kin and also to in-group members. These principles are neither there in our genes, nor are they just given by an outside source. Because resources have seldom been superabundant, natural selection has ensured that individuals are endowed with a tendency to look after their own interests and those of their relatives. Because individuals have fared better as members of groups than by living singly, they also have tendencies to behave prosocially and cooperatively towards individuals perceived as members of their own group. These propensities form a basis for all moral codes.

With these as a basis, the precepts and values guiding the behaviour of individuals are a product of dialectical relations, over prehistorical and historical time, between what individuals do and what they are supposed to do according to the culture or shared understandings of the society in which they live. Morality is neither immutable nor infinitely labile, but constrained by the basic principles of selfish assertiveness and prosociality. The relative preponderance of prosocial or selfishly assertive behaviour shown by an individual will be affected by the social and physical environments that he/she and the society have experienced.

Thus, notwithstanding the view that it is fallacious to derive what ought to be from what is, this approach indicates that a scientific approach can make a major, and perhaps fundamental, contribution to understanding the bases of morality. At the group level, it leads to understanding the prehistorical, historical and current processes that lead to the range of precepts governing behaviour in a society; and at the individual level the role of the genetic constitution, and the environments encountered, on the balance between prosocial and antisocial behaviour that results. At the intra-individual level, studies of neural mechanisms may, in principle, lead to understanding how moral precepts are encapsulated in the brain, the bases of the self-system and the nature of the conscience.

Again, this is not saying that what is natural is right. The criteria of survival and reproduction by which natural selection honed the basic pancultural psychological characteristics are not the same as those we use to assess moral codes in the world today. Conventions and values change, and new discoveries demand new precepts. Selection has acted to promote lability according to current circumstances, and that can involve selfish assertiveness taking precedence over prosociality in some circumstances. In any case, the extent to which prosociality 'should' predominate over selfish assertiveness depends on the situation. Excessive unselfishness may be seen as wrong because it involves the neglect also of responsibilities, or as embarrassing because one can never repay the debts incurred.

Moral precepts are normally those that favour group integrity and integration. However, the self-assertiveness of powerful individuals may cause them to propagate precepts in their own interests, whether or not those precepts are conducive to group harmony. Since one must presume that individuals in well-integrated groups fared better than those in chaotic or disintegrating ones, prosocial or in-group cooperative precepts and behaviour must, and do, predominate over self-assertive and socially divisive ones.

3.4 The emergence of moral and legal systems

The preceding sections have assumed that certain pancultural characteristics and propensities have resulted from natural selection, and argued that they were one source of moral precepts. However, moral codes (and, as we shall see, legal systems) evolved over prehistorical and historical time. This mostly occurred long before records were available, so only indirect evidence and speculation are available. However, the issue is an important one, for it could illuminate the dynamics of moral and legal systems today. What follows, therefore, is merely a tentative scheme.

Presumably kin selection played a large part in the genesis of early human groups. Selfish assertiveness leading to competition for mates and material resources must have occurred. Nevertheless cooperative prosocial behaviour must have predominated over selfish assertiveness.

Evidence from modern hunter-gatherers, which admittedly may be misleading, suggests that early human groups tended to be egalitarian. This does not mean that status seeking was absent, but rather that individuals acted together to curb attempts at self-aggrandizement. Presumably selfish assertiveness would be seen by others as threatening their own interests.

In the absence of over-arching authority, readiness for revenge would provide the best defence against attack or exploitation. Today, revenge is central in curbing conflict in many non-literate societies (Evans-Pritchard 1940), and can be seen as a facet of the propensity for reciprocity. However, revenge, if not seen as just, can lead to escalation. Although perhaps initially a spontaneous product of selfish assertiveness, it must have been based on shared understandings about what was not acceptable behaviour. In turn, these shared understandings could have been replaced by more or less formalized rules. Perhaps this was the result of conformism: in a successful group, prosocial and cooperative behaviour must have been frequent, and conformism would lead to what most people did being transformed into what they ought to do. Formalization could have been the collective result of the experience of individuals, or the action of a charismatic leader. Collectively recognized rules could have led to punishment for non-compliance, and perhaps to rewards for those who prevented or punished anti-social behaviour. Because individuals who behave prosocially tend to receive prosociality and to be admired, prosociality would bring status and its own rewards.

Nevertheless, environmental vicissitudes must have led to differences in experience, and in the balance of prosociality and selfish assertiveness, between groups. In time, however, leaders emerged—perhaps through physical domination, or perhaps because their advice turned out to be sound. Dissent and competition for power could then have been quelled from above. It would have been in the leader's interests to maintain peace and thus the *status quo* in the society, and to promulgate rules to that end. They may also have promoted values that were in their own interests, such as the moral rectitude of humility. At an early stage leaders probably claimed divine authority for promulgating rules governing the behaviour of individuals and punishments for those who infringed them (Roth 1995).

However, leaders must be kept from exploiting their positions, and their power must be limited by appropriate institutions. Here, reciprocity may operate: for instance the leader may provide protection in return for service and respect.

Some of these processes have been documented in the development of Anglo-Saxon law. The old folk community, collectively bound to peace, came to be held together by the King. What had been *folk peace* became the *King's peace*, and offences initially seen as offences against an individual or the community were seen also as offences against the King's peace. Thus authority for retribution, originally belonging to the wronged individual or his kin or the community, became transferred to the King. Punishment involved both retribution to the wronged party (or to relatives) and an element to the King, the latter for the infringement of the folk or King's peace. Initially most offences were punished by outlawry, but later many offences were expiated by a payment, part of which went to the injured party and part to the King (Adams 1896).

However, neither moral systems nor legal systems are static. Perhaps the most important basis for change has been the dialectic between what people do and what they are supposed to do. For instance, a few decades ago divorce was regarded as disreputable in England. For a number of reasons, including the desire of women for more independence after World War II, the incidence of divorce tended to increase. As divorce became more frequent, it became more acceptable. As it became more acceptable, it became more frequent. There were also concomitant changes in the law, induced in part by the perceived consequences of conflict-filled marriages on children.

Finally, the law tends to reflect both the history and the current situation of the society. The history of the Israeli kibbutzim illustrates this. Set up mostly by individuals who had left totalitarian regimes, they presumed initially that goodwill and shared understandings would make laws unnecessary. It soon became evident that this was not enough, and laws were formulated. Each kibbutz had a General Assembly: presumably because conditions were still hard, appropriate punishment was judged not only on the rights and wrongs of the specific act, but also on the nature of the offender as assessed by his/her past contributions to the community (Saltman 1985).

Another example of the influence of the past on current morality is suggested by the differences between Western societies and some Eastern ones, such as the People's Republic of China. It has been argued that European morality is based on the importance of the individual, and stems in part from the Christian belief in individual salvation, with God sending his Son to save individual sinners. Chinese morality stems from the Confucian view of the world, which, although experiencing vicissitudes in the twentieth century, still has an underlying influence. The Earth and the Heavens were seen as constituting an ordered and harmonious system. Harmony in the relatedness of individuals was viewed as the most valuable feature of human existence. Therefore, virtue is still seen not in terms of submission to a deity, but as the building of constructive communities. Not surprisingly, the rights and duties of individuals with respect to the community are seen differently in the two systems (e.g. Huntingdon 1997).

3.5 Cross-cultural problems

Every society has experienced a different history, so inevitably moral precepts and values differ to some extent between societies. Attempts to specify moral codes must be restricted in their scope. What has become conducive to group integrity over historical time in one society may not be so in another. Furthermore, especially in modern times, circumstances are constantly changing; the dialectic between what people do and what they are supposed to do is always in flux, so that the details of moral codes may change. But prosociality must predominate: undiluted self-assertiveness inevitably leads to group disintegration.

Education should lead to greater 'understanding of' (in the sense of sympathy for) the moral precepts of other societies. Where precepts differ, a focus on human commonalities, the universal characteristics and needs of human beings, is the best starting point for the resolution of any conflict. Inevitably, people brought up in one culture, having assimilated its precepts into their self-systems, are unlikely to take easily to any other. And neither the 'missionary' course of trying to convert them by argument to one's own views, nor political pressure on the society, is likely to prove successful. Example must be the best option.

In judging the moral systems of other societies, one tends to judge them against one's own moral standards. What matters to members of another society is, in the first instance, what *they perceive* to be right. A young woman in another society might perceive it as right that she should marry the husband that her parents choose (though not all do), while we should see it as incompatible with the Golden Rule. The woman is doing what she sees as right, and probably her parents see their choice of spouse as right, though we see it differently.

There are, of course, difficult issues here: no amount of education can bring understanding of some cultural differences. Practices of burning widows, or of deserting the aged, of female genital mutilation, of killing citizens of another race, of killing to uphold family honour, are totally unacceptable to those brought up in Western society. One suspects that such practices were initially introduced by powerful individuals within the society for their own interests or what they perceived to be the interests of the group as a whole. Since they contravene the basic principle of do-as-you-would-be-done-by and deny individuals their essential rights as persons, they must be seen as unacceptable (although they may stimulate reflections on some practices in our own society, such as male genital mutilation).

But if one is tempted to make judgements, as one must be in such cases, it is important to judge separately the individual and the system. A concentration camp guard, brought up in a totalitarian state with a genocidal policy, may see it as right that he should carry out his duties. The system is, of course, despicable, but is the guard? Perhaps the key issues are the amount of choice he had and whether he could have known that his actions were wrong. Particular difficulties arise when British judges, to whom the death penalty is abhorrent, must adjudicate over the appeals of condemned individuals in another country.

Circumstances change, and sometimes values and precepts must change with them, but here a strong dose of conservatism is necessary. The moral code of a society has been honed over generations in the circumstances of that society. Values that we place on honesty, trust, compassion, responsibility and love have arisen as consequences of what we are and our need to live in a viable society with reliable interpersonal relationships. Major changes in circumstances, or new scientific developments may require innovations in the moral code, but change in our moral system must not be undertaken lightly. We must start with what has served us well so far, and remember that a code that is not acceptable to a high proportion of individuals will not be accepted.

3.6 The nature of morality in relation to the law

This final section considers how this view of the genesis of morality bears on its relations to law, with the focus primarily on English law.

First, certain questions about morality that have occupied legal theorists turn out to be non-questions. For instance:

> Are values arbitrary? Some are, some are not.
> Is morality fundamental or constructed? A bit of both.
> Is morality subjective or objective? It can be described objectively but is felt subjectively.

The preceding sections indicate that law and morality had a common source and that there have been parallels between their respective developments. Both are concerned with social order, and their development involves social processes. Many laws are formalizations of moral values—most obviously laws against killing, adultery and false witness, for example. Morality has a wider scope than the law: actions regarded as immoral are not necessarily illegal. However, in societies with some separation between the sacred and the secular, the law alone would be inadequate to maintain the cohesion of society: moral prescriptions are essential (Devlin 1958).

Early in human history, morality was probably concerned only with issues of fairly direct relevance to individual survival and reproduction. As societies became more complex its scope became wider. The same is probably true of law, which became necessary through the need for formalization and for stronger means to control severe infringements. Thus, the range of actions that can be regarded as moral/immoral is broader than those considered as legal/illegal. Occasionally, both the law and morality are concerned with behaviour that lies at the extremity of behaviour that is otherwise condoned or normal, such as marital rape.

Law has been shaped by moral values, and laws that do not have some reference to social values are seldom viable. However, a few laws and moral precepts are constructed by influential individuals, either for what they perceive as the good of the community or for their own interests. While morality prescribes how people should behave, most laws are concerned with how people ought *not* to behave.

Moral precepts are not to be seen as absolutes. They are neither ubiquitous and unchangeable, nor are they entirely culture-specific. They are based on and constrained by pancultural propensities (to behave prosocially to kin and to others perceived as in-group members and, in some cases, to further one's own interests). In a given society at a given time, they may be seen as absolutes. The law, like morality, has a certain lability, though it is seen as absolute at any one time. Scientific innovations pose new problems: changes over such issues as abortion and paid egg sharing demand legal solutions.

Some rules of conduct and some laws are concerned not so much with what is seen as right as with ensuring the smooth running of society. Thus some psychologists argue for a distinction between morals and conventions, supposing that they depend on distinct conceptual domains (Turiel 1998). Justifications for judgements about morality include promoting welfare, justice, rights, truth, loyalty, etc., whereas conventions involve merely understanding the social organization. In the same way, some laws have a clear relationship to moral principles (e.g. laws relating to murder) and others merely reify conventions (e.g. driving on the left-hand side of the road). However, the distinctions are often far from clear, and both may be seen as promoting social cohesion or the welfare of the community.

Morals are often seen as based on divine or other undefined authority, and the viability of moral precepts in a world devoid of religious believers and a religious tradition remains to be seen. Laws are now based ultimately on secular authority.

Morality is absorbed through experience into the self-systems of individuals. So-called moral intuition is not something with which humans are endowed, but is acquired in the culture in question. Law, by definition, has been imposed. Moral behaviour may be either automatic, constrained by precepts incorporated in the self-system, or intentional. Intentionality is therefore a less salient characteristic in judgements of morality than in many judgements of legal guilt.

The effectiveness of public morality is maintained by guilt processes within the individual, by social disapproval and by fear of punishment in this life or the next. Laws stipulate how (within limits) offenders should be treated.

In democracies, most law has been formulated in the interests of the society as a whole or of most individuals within it. As the example of the Israeli kibbutzim suggests, in practice the common good requires a legal system as well as moral precepts to restrict the activities of free riders. In some cases, for instance in wartime, law is imposed for the public good but against the wishes of the majority. Occasionally, as in the case of apartheid in South Africa, it is imposed against both the interests and the wishes of the majority.

So-called 'Natural Law' holds that there are objective moral principles that depend on the nature of the universe and can be discovered by reason. Although I have argued that morality is based on human nature, what is natural is not necessarily the same as what is right. Ultimately, basic principles are pancultural not because they are self-evident or accord with common practice nor because they are divinely inspired, but because individuals do better in groups.

The perceived validity of moral principles depends ultimately on their acceptance by individuals. No distinction can be made between the moral opinions of the collective and 'truth', though individuals may hold idiosyncratic moral opinions. Law, to be viable in a reasonably democratic society, must be perceived as compatible with the generally received morality (Warnock 1998). In practice, changes in the law tend to be influenced more by the morality of the élite than that of the population as a whole. Thus in the UK, the legal status of homosexual relationships was changed largely through the influence of the more educated minority.

The principle of prosocial reciprocity provides a basis for most moral precepts concerned with personal relationships or relations with the community. Reciprocity and commitment (see § 2c) also provide a basis for many laws (e.g. contract law; Goodenough 2001). It also contributes to the determination of punishments, though group coherence may demand (also) an additional penalty.

Some philosophers (e.g. Bentham) have held that no rights exist unless they are encapsulated in the law. However, in modern legal systems the law is usually based on perceived human rights, not vice versa, and rights have become a moral matter, and not mere social conventions. There is a danger in this, for individual rights must be curtailed for the good of others.

There may be moral limits to requirements to obey or not to obey the law (Devlin 1965). Similarly 'human rights' cannot be claimed by every individual, and may be limited by other aspects of the common good.

Although there is bound to be a broad resemblance between the law and morality, the coincidence is not absolute. Some acts now considered as immoral, such as slavery, have been seen as legal. Many laws prescribe behaviour that is morally neutral, such as the side of the road on which one should drive—though it must be noted that the aim of such laws is the common good. Some laws, like some moral precepts, are related to the well-being of the lawmakers or of a section of society, rather than to the common good.

Legal theory often depends on contrasting principles, such as equality, utilitarianism or justice. Most though not all moral principles are reducible to a variant of the Golden Rule (do-as-you-would-be-done-by), though that is open to different interpretations. In the historical genesis of morality, equality, utilitarianism and justice, though not unimportant, were secondary considerations, probably depending on which was most conducive to group integrity in the circumstances prevailing.

In dividing resources, neither morality nor the law provides clear guidance on the detailed principles (e.g. equality, equity, need, utilitarianism) to be followed. The first three are most likely to satisfy those immediately involved, but utilitarian distribution may favour the coherence of the group.

'The law' has usually been codified within societies and applied primarily to in-group members. However, the basic principles of selfish assertiveness and prosociality apply also to societies as entities themselves. That implies a need to frame or to re-frame laws to govern the relations between societies. Not only is it morally repulsive that vast inequalities of opportunity exist between individuals, but also between countries. The use of or threat to use nuclear weapons and other weapons of mass destruction, and even war itself, are morally unacceptable and contrary to the basic principle of prosociality: international law must not only outlaw them but also be enforceable.

The author is grateful to Lord Mustill PC, for his comments on an earlier draft.

Endnotes

1. The argument given here involves a summary of that given previously in Hinde (1999) and more especially Hinde (2002). The present paper contains only the outlines of the argument and the more essential references: greater detail is to be found in the latter book.
2. 'Prosocial' is used as a blanket term to cover diverse types of behaviour that foster the well-being of others.
3. 'Assertiveness' has positive connotations for some, negative for others. It is used here to refer to behaviours that promote one's own interests without regard for the interests of others, i.e. selfish assertiveness.

References

Adams, H. 1896 *Essays on Anglo-Saxon law*. Boston, MA: Little Brown.

Alexander, R. D. 1979 *Darwinism and human affairs*. Seattle, WA: University of Washington Press.

Arnhart, L. 1998 *Darwinian natural right: the biological ethics of human nature*. Albany, NY: State University of New York Press.

Backman, C. W. 1988 The self: a dialectical approach. *Adv. Exp. Soc. Psychol.* **21**, 229–260.

Betzig, L., Borgerhoff Mulder, M. & Turke, P. (eds) 1988 *Human reproductive behavior: a Darwinian perspective*. Cambridge University Press.

Bevc, I. & Silverman, I. 2000 Early separation and sibling incest: a test of the revised Westerman theory. *Evol. Hum. Behav.* **21**, 151–161.

Bottéro, J. 1992 *Mesopotamia: writing, reasoning and the gods*. University of Chicago Press.

Bowlby, J. 1984 *Attachment and loss*, vol. 1, 2nd edn. London: Hogarth.

Boyd, R. & Richerson, P. J. 1991 Culture and cooperation. In *Cooperation and prosocial behaviour* (ed. R. A. Hinde & J. Groebel), pp. 27–48. Cambridge University Press.

Boyd, R. & Richerson, P. J. 1992 Punishment allows evolution of cooperation (or anything else) in sizeable groups. *Ethol. Sociobiol.* **13**, 171–195.

Cosmides, L. & Tooby, J. 1992 Cognitive adaptations for social exchange. In *The adapted mind* (ed. J. H. Barkow, J. Tooby & L. Cosmides), pp. 163–228. New York: Oxford University Press.

Daly, M. & Wilson, M. 1996 Violence against stepchildren. *Curr. Dir. Psychol. Sci.* **5**, 77–81.

De Vries, M. W. 1984 Temperament and infant mortality among the Masai of East Africa. *Am. J. Psychiat.* **141**, 1189–1194.

Devlin, Lord 1958 Morals and the criminal law. Maccabaean Lecture, British Academy.

Devlin, P. 1965 *The enforcement of morals*. London: Oxford University Press.

Dworkin, R.M. 1973 The law of the slave catchers. *Times Literary Supplement*, 5 December, p. 1437.

Eisenberg, N. & Fabes, R. A. 1998 Prosocial development. In *Handbook of child psychology*, 5th edn, vol. 3 (ed. W. Damon & N. Eisenberg), pp. 701–778. New York: Wiley.

Evans-Pritchard, E. E. 1940 *The Nuer*. Oxford: Clarendon.

Finnis, J. 1980 *Natural law and natural rights*. Oxford: Clarendon.

Frank, R. H. 1988 *Patterns within reason*. New York: Norton.

Freeman, M. D. A. (ed.) 2001 *Lloyd's introduction to jurisprudence*, 7th edn. London: Sweet & Maxwell.

Gilligan, C. 1982 *In a different voice*. Cambridge, MA: Harvard University Press.

Goodenough, O. 2001 Law and the biology of commitment. In *Evolution and the capacity for commitment* (ed. R. M. Nesse), pp. 262–291. New York: Russell Sage.

Grand, J. C. & Bittles, A. H. 1997 The comparative role of consanguinity in infant and child mortality in Pakistan. *Ann. Hum. Genet.* **61**, 143–149.

Hamilton, W. D. 1964 The genetical evolution of social behaviour. *J. Theor. Biol.* **7**, 1–52.

Hart, H. L. A. 1994 *The concept of law*. Oxford: Clarendon.

Hawkes, K., O'Connell, J. F. & Blurton Jones, N. G. 2001 Hadza meat sharing. *Evol. Hum. Behav.* **22**, 113–142.

Hill, K. & Hurtado, M. 1996 *Aché life history: the ecology and demography of a foraging people.* Hawthorne, NY: Aldine de Gruyter.

Himma, K. E. 2003 Trouble in law's empire: rethinking Dworkin's third theory of law. *Oxf. J. Legal Stud.* **23**, 345–377.

Hinde, R. A. 1999 *Why gods persist.* London: Routledge.

Hinde, R. A. 2002 *Why good is good.* London: Routledge.

Hrdy, S. 1999 *Mother nature.* New York: Pantheon.

Hsu, E. 1998 Moso and Naxi: the house. In *Naxi and Moso ethnography: kin, rites, pictographs* (ed. M. Oppitz & E. Hsu), pp. 67–99. Zurich: Völkerkundemuseum.

Humphrey, N. 1997 Varieties of altruism—and the common ground between them. *Soc. Res.* **64**, 199–209.

Huntingdon, S. 1997 The West and the rest. *Prospect* **1997**, 34–39.

James, W. 1988 *The listening ebony.* Oxford: Clarendon.

Jones, O. D. 1997 Evolutionary analysis in law: an introduction and application to child abuse. *North Carolina Law Rev.* **75**, 1117–1342.

Kelley, H. H. 1979 *Personal relationships.* Hillsdale, NJ: Erlbaum.

Küng, H. & Kuschel, H.-J. 1993 *A global ethic.* London: SCM Press.

Prins, K. S., Buunk, B. P. & van Yperen, N. W. 1993 Equity, normative disapproval, and extramarital relationships. *J. Soc. Person. Relation.* **10**, 39–53.

Rheingold, H. & Hay, D. 1980 Prosocial behavior of the very young. In *Morality as a biological phenomenon* (ed. G. S. Stent), pp. 93–108. Berkeley, CA: University of California Press.

Roth, M. T. 1995 *Law collections from Mesopotamia and Asia Minor.* Atlanta, GA: Scholars' Press.

Saltman, M. 1985 'The law is an ass': an anthropological appraisal. In *Reason and morality* (ed. I. Overing), pp. 226–239. London: Tavistock.

Silk, J. B. 1980 Adoption and kinship in Oceania. *Am. Anthropol.* **82**, 799–820.

Sober, E. & Wilson, D. S. 1998 *Unto others.* Cambridge, MA: Harvard University Press.

Tangney, J. P. 1995 Recent advances in the empirical study of shame and guilt. *Am. Behav. Sci.* **38**, 1132–1145.

Thibaut, J. W. & Kelley, H. H. 1959 *The social psychology of groups.* New York: Wiley.

Trivers, R. 1974 Parent–infant conflict. *Am. Zool.* **14**, 249–264.

Turiel, E. 1998 The development of morality. *In Handbook of child development*, 5th edn, vol. 3 (ed. W. Damon & N. Eisenberg), pp. 863–932. New York: Wiley.

Warnock, M. 1998 *An intelligent person's guide to ethics.* London: Duckworth.

Williams, J. E. & Best, D. L. 1982 *Measuring sex stereotypes.* Beverley Hills, CA: Sage.

Wilson, D.S. & Kniffen, K.M. 1999 Multilevel selection and the social transmission of behavior. *Hum. Nature* **10**, 291–310.

4

Law, evolution and the brain: applications and open questions

Owen D. Jones

This paper discusses several issues at the intersection of law and brain science. It focuses principally on ways in which an improved understanding of how evolutionary processes affect brain function and human behaviour may improve law's ability to regulate behaviour. It explores sample uses of such 'evolutionary analysis in law' and also raises questions about how that analysis might be improved in the future. Among the discussed uses are: (i) clarifying cost–benefit analyses; (ii) providing theoretical foundation and potential predictive power; (iii) assessing comparative effectiveness of legal strategies; and (iv) revealing deep patterns in legal architecture. Throughout, the paper emphasizes the extent to which effective law requires: (i) building effective behavioural models; (ii) integrating life-science perspectives with social-science perspectives; (iii) considering the effects of brain biology on behaviours that law seeks to regulate; and (iv) examining the effects of evolutionary processes on brain design.

Keywords: law; evolutionary analysis in law; brain; human behaviour; behavioural biology

4.1 Introduction

The odds seem stacked against the Saharan desert ant *Cataglyphis*. It must forage alone in scorching temperatures. It must travel vast distances. It must loop and zigzag in constant pursuit of the heat-stressed prey that it must somehow locate, overcome, and then carry. Perhaps most dauntingly, with prey or without, each ant must make its way back to a small and far-distant nest entrance, out there—somewhere—in a numbingly monotonous landscape.

Yet, from the moment it starts to return, no matter where it is and no matter how peripatetic its prior wanderings, *Cataglyphis* travels a straight line back to the nest. How can this be?

To do this, each *Cataglyphis* ant needs to keep track as it travels of its changing orientation with respect to the nest, so as to know which direction to head when returning. It also needs to update its approximate distance from the nest continuously, so that when it travels in the right direction it knows when to stop and begin a local search, neither over-nor under-shooting the actual entrance.

Using an ingenious combination of observation, experiments, robotics, artificial intelligence and neurophysiology, the zoologist Rudiger Wehner has demonstrated that the *Cataglyphis* compass is updated and optically mapped against ambient light, upon emergence from the nest, with the aid of the ant's multiple polarized lenses (Wehner 2003). Even more impressively, the *Cataglyphis* distance calculator can translate the varying three-dimensional heights and inclines of wanderings into a two-dimensional map (which is necessary, for example, if the outward journey is hilly and the return route is flat). This is rather remarkable for a species ignorant of trigonometry and sporting a brain that weighs barely one ten-thousandth of a gram.

The human brain, by contrast, weighs 13 million times as much, *ca.* 1300 g. What purposes call on such power? Although the brain constitutes merely 2% of our body weight, the brain's activities consume *ca.* 20% of the calories we ingest. Given the relentlessness with which natural selection punishes waste, such an energetically costly device must provide some significant compensating benefits. What these are, how they are procured and by what processes they came to be procured are among the great questions in modern science.

The editors asked each author in this theme issue to explore various implications of modern brain science for law. Each author will probably frame these implications differently. Here is how I would frame them. Law deals in behaviour, and behaviour arises (principally) from the brain. So learning more about brain design and function should prove useful to legal thinkers, who so often are tasked with changing various aspects of human behaviour to ensure that, by and large, people behave the way society prefers.

We could preliminarily subdivide into two main contexts the usefulness of bringing law and brain science together. The first context concerns internal states: what is happening on the inside, within the brain (as it perceives, assesses and chooses, for example). The second context concerns external effects: what happens on the outside as a function of brain operation (when a person behaves in ways discernible by others).

We could further subdivide legal issues relevant to the internal states of the brain into those concerning intervention technologies and those concerning imaging technologies (Garland 2004). Intervention technologies include existing drugs, as well as drugs in development, that may enhance cognitive capabilities. For example, researchers are reportedly investigating drugs commonly used to treat depression or attention deficit hyperactivity disorders (such as selective serotonin reuptake inhibitors and noradrenaline (norepinephrine) reuptake inhibitors) for their potentially cognition-enhancing capabilities in non-depressed individuals. Efforts are apparently underway to develop drugs that boost the levels of chemicals in the brain (such as cyclic adenosine monophosphate (cAMP), cAMP response element binding protein (CREB) and glutamate) involved in amplifying memory. And transcranial magnetic stimulation, which has been shown to be capable of exciting or inhibiting various areas of the brain, may also be capable of thereby enhancing certain cognitive functions (Tancredi 2004). How, if at all, should the legal system regulate such intervention technologies?

In contrast to these intervention technologies, imaging technologies enable us to perceive non-invasively what the brain is doing when a person engages in various physical or mental tasks. These technologies include existing techniques, as well as those in development, that may eventually help us to decide (to give just three examples of many) whether a witness or defendant is competent, whether an unconscious person is brain dead or whether a person is lying (Tancredi 2004).

For example, techniques in development that use near-infrared brain scans and magnetic resonance imaging can reveal activity in the prefrontal cortex and the anterior cingulate cortex in the superior frontal gyrus, respectively. Such techniques have already started to illuminate the neural basis for social cooperation (Rilling *et al.* 2002). Will these technologies someday enable us to identify the neurophysiological predicates of 'normal' self-control or to witness the effects of brain damage on law-relevant mental processing? Some preliminary brain-imaging work is already underway that appears to show the brain-state differences between thinking about a just result to a legal conflict and applying a provided rule to resolve that conflict (Schultz *et al*. 2001). Might this someday tell us something useful about how to encourage jurors to think more or less about either justice or rules, or about how to better achieve a desired balance of the two?

A new electroencephalograph (EEG) technique can apparently detect a particular brain-wave pattern known as P-300, the presence of which, many believe, reliably indicates that the brain is recognizing a familiar stimulus (Tancredi 2004). Will these and other windows on brain function ultimately tell us anything legally useful about whether a person is lying? Will the presence of the P-300 enable us to detect lying more reliably than when traditional lie-detectors are used? Suppose the stimulus is a picture of a crime scene that a suspect denies ever visiting. Should 'brain fingerprinting' evidence that reveals an absence of a P-300 wave in the defendant's brain when he was shown a picture of the crime scene be allowed as evidence in support of his defence? Courts have only recently begun to address such questions (e.g. Terry Harrington versus State of Iowa, Supreme Court of Iowa, 659 N. W. 2d 509 (2003)).

Neuroscientific advances relating to the brain's internal states have already raised a host of legal questions concerning evidence, privacy, patents and the like (Greely 2004). What are the limits of discoverable correspondences between mental states and brain states? For some, advancing technologies raise variations on already-important questions concerning free will and responsibility (Gazzaniga & Steven 2004; Morse 2004). For others, technology offers the promise of revealing the neural bases of deciding, choosing, intending and acting.

Legal issues relevant to the external effects of brain function are somewhat different. The brain is, in many respects, a machine designed to correlate patterns of stimuli with patterns of behaviour. Behaviours relevant to law are products of perception, information-processing, emotions, deliberations, decisions and other states of the brain operating in dynamic ways that often reciprocally affect one another. Will a more detailed understanding of brain function enable us to predict a person's behaviour with the degree of confidence that different legal contexts may require? (Greely 2004). For example, would we want such an understanding to play any role in parole decisions, when the likelihood of recidivism is at issue?

The two different kinds of causes of behaviour, which biologists term 'proximate' and 'ultimate' (Mayr 1961), contribute to each of the two general contexts, discussed above, in which the legal system might attend to brain science: internal states and external effects. (Readers will recall that proximate causes involve immediate causal pathways and mechanisms; ultimate causes reflect the evolutionary pathways by which some proximate cues, rather than others, came to be correlated with some behavioural outputs, rather than others; Goldsmith & Zimmerman 2001.)

Biologists already know that proximate and ultimate causes are always present simultaneously. Every action of every organism reflects not only its unique developmental history and immediate environment but also its evolved species-typical capabilities and behavioural predispositions. To date, however, most of the law's limited attention to brain biology focuses exclusively on proximate causes. This may be because proximate causes are often easier to study. Or it may be because technological advances typically stem from studies of proximate causes and typically intervene among proximate causes.

There are probably other reasons too, but here I wish to underscore several advantages to law of knowing more about the ultimate evolutionary causes of human brain design and about the relationship between evolved behavioural predispositions and resulting behaviour.

A growing number of scholars (compiled in Jones 2004*b*) have for some time been engaged in what I have elsewhere described as 'evolutionary analysis in law' (Jones 1997*a*). Their common enterprise is to use knowledge about evolutionary processes, animal behaviour or both in ways that may further legal goals. In that enterprise, some things are known and many more are yet to be known.

In what follows, I first discuss the often under-recognized importance to law of sound behavioural models. I argue that these models—to be maximally effective—should eventually include life-science perspectives on the proximate and ultimate causes of human brain function. I then turn to raise briefly a variety of questions that need further attention as evolutionary analysis in law develops. The subsequent section offers some general thoughts about assessing and incorporating interdisciplinary perspectives, such as those from biology. The final section provides a few brief illustrations of where and how evolutionary analysis in law can be useful.

4.2 Law, biology and behavioural models

For historical reasons, the social sciences and the life sciences remain more frequently divided than their significantly overlapping interests in humans might otherwise suggest. Specifically, the study of human behaviour is too often too separated from the study of animal behaviour. Over-separation is unsound; human behaviour is a subset of animal behaviour, and therefore the studies of each must in the end reconcile with studies of the other. Over-separation is also unwise; it can obscure patterns that offer both knowledge and utility, and that can be costly.

Integrating the behavioural aspects of social sciences and life sciences into a seamless behavioural science should have particular appeal to legal policy-makers. Society often charges legal policy-makers with moving a large human population to behave more this way and less that way, consistent with democratically percolated and pre-articulated goals. And a deeper understanding of the relationship between human behaviour and the brain's design and function should prove useful to that enterprise.

There are many fields in biology that can contribute to that deeper understanding. One such field is behavioural genetics, which attempts to trace the different behaviours of different individuals to different genes among them. Another is neuroanatomy, which can reveal where and how human states originate in the brain. To these (and others) one can add evolutionary biology, which helps to illuminate how different behaviours of different individuals can flow from species-typical brains that sport highly contingent evolved algorithms (which in turn increase or decrease the probabilities of given behavioural responses in reaction to varying environmental conditions).

It may be easy for legal policy-makers to ignore or to forget that evolutionary processes influence human behaviour as well as human morphology. For one thing, legal policy-makers often ignore a great many behavioural disciplines at a time, not just biological disciplines, when they deploy insights on behaviour that typically reflect various admixtures of common sense, sociology, religion, philosophy and the like. Also, legal policy-makers typically lack significant science education, and that enables deep misunderstandings about how genes, environments and evolutionary processes interact in ways that affect resultant behaviour. And a few legal policy-makers (in common with some in the general public) may still incorrectly assume that biological explanations are inherently deterministic in a way that will often lead to justifications for bad behaviour, converting description into prescription, as if the only role for behavioural biology would be to acquit criminal defendants.

Nevertheless, there are many different ways in which human behavioural biology can offer utility in law without altering normative agendas. Carefully done, for example, evolutionary analysis in law can help to reveal the unwarranted assumptions about how and why humans behave as they do that underlie some existing legal policies. It can help us to discover useful patterns in regulable behaviour, which may lead to different regulatory strategies. And perhaps most generally, evolutionary analysis in law can help to increase law's effectiveness and efficiency.

Here is the four-step logic: (i) effective law requires an effective behavioural model; (ii) law's commonly used behavioural models are importantly incomplete; (iii) building more robust behavioural models probably requires (among other things) the integration of social-science models with life-science models; and (iv) integrating social-science models with life-science models requires familiarity with behavioural biology, including the effects of evolutionary processes on species-typical brain form and function. This logic unfolds in the following way.

First, almost anything law achieves it achieves by effecting changes in human behaviour. It effects changes, in turn, by inspiring people (or in rare cases forcing them physically) to behave differently from the way they would behave in the absence of the law's intervention. The ability to deploy legal tools to effect these changes at the least cost to society is importantly affected by the accuracy of the behavioural models on which law relies.

To put this more graphically, law is like a lever for moving behaviour, with a model of human behaviour serving as its fulcrum. That behavioural-model fulcrum consists of what we think we know about why people behave as they do. That is, the behavioural model constitutes the aggregated insights that underlie our prediction that if law moves this way, behaviour will move that way and not some other way.

Because soft fulcra are poor fulcra, we can consider the success of every legal system to depend, in part, on the solidity—that is, the accuracy and predictive power—of the behavioural model on which it both rests and relies. Flawed models will tend to yield less effective law, and legal approaches to understanding and influencing human behaviour that are based on outdated behavioural models are simply less likely to effect socially and legally desirable outcomes than are those based on more robust behavioural models. Consequently, effective law will generally require effective behavioural models.

Second, all theories of human behaviour are ultimately theories about the brain. The brain, of course, is a corporeal biological phenomenon, and modern biology makes it forcefully clear that the brain's design, function and behavioural outputs are all products of gene–environment interactions.

At present, however, the legal system tends to build its models for regulating behaviour by focusing only on the kinds of influences to which social sciences attend. Though these influences are useful to understand, they typically contribute only the environmental components of the gene–environment whole.

To put the magnitude of this oversight in sharp perspective: trying to build any human behavioural model from social sciences without life sciences is like trying to make iced tea with either water or tea leaves but not both. We know that behaviour is the result of inseparable environmental and genetic effects. Therefore, the routine omission of one of the two principal behavioural ingredients grossly oversimplifies something inherently complex, ignores interactions necessary for behaviour and renders law's general approach to behavioural models importantly inaccurate and incomplete.

Third, an objective reality underlies the influences on human behaviour. This reality cannot be captured by simplistic models that posit environmental determinism. Of course, integration of the behavioural sciences (both social and life) and behavioural influences (both proximate and ultimate) cannot guarantee perfect behavioural models. But integration, if done carefully and well, is probably a significant step towards more effective, efficient and accurate behavioural models than the ones legal thinkers commonly employ.

Integrated models, far from oversimplifying human behaviour, would reflect the most complete understanding available of the multiple and complex influences on behaviour. They would vindicate, more fully than prevailing unsupplemented social-constructivist models can alone, our species' unique history, consciousness, capabilities and richly complex behavioural processes. Consequently, building more robust behavioural models requires integrating social-science models with life-science models.

Fourth and finally, we can probably best achieve that integrated understanding of human behaviour by framing human behaviours against the backdrop of the pervasive evolutionary processes that enable and influence them. This requires a broader cross-disciplinary perspective, which at a minimum includes insights from evolutionary biology. Ideally, this would involve greater education for legal thinkers on both the immediate proximate causes of behaviours and the evolutionary causes that provide important context.

To summarize these points, then: (i) effective law requires an effective behavioural model; (ii) law's existing set of models is importantly incomplete; (iii) improving the behavioural models requires the integration of social-science and life-science models of behaviour; and (iv) such integration requires familiarity with behavioural biology. Put simply, because improving behavioural models can yield more effective legal tools and because human behaviour is influenced by the effects of evolutionary processes on the brain, greater knowledge of how evolutionary processes influence behaviour may improve law's ability to regulate it.

4.3 Several issues warranting further exploration

The editors of this theme issue encouraged the authors to raise questions about law and the brain, even when they had no answers to provide. In this section I respond to that invitation by raising a variety of topics in need of further exploration. First, I make a few general remarks, to provide context.

We already know that the gap between legal and scientific communities—in methods, assumptions, purposes and even vocabulary—is famously broad and observable in myriad contexts. For example, the gap is evident in environmental contexts, in which legal regulators attempt to balance economic interests with harms to enormously dynamic ecological systems. Also, it is evident in health contexts, in which legal regulators attempt to weigh toxicological risks against the costs of reducing those risks expressed in opaque statistics. But the law–science gap seems unusually broad in the context of human behaviour. I propose three of many possible reasons.

First, not everyone agrees that understanding more about the biology of brains and behaviours is a good thing. The historical over-division of reality into distinctly different disciplinary subcomponents (which in turn contributed to knowledge and culture gaps between disciplines) often creates turf wars over who speaks with importance on what topics. So, for example, biological perspectives on behaviour often encounter resistance from practitioners of sociology, philosophy and gender studies, as each of these disciplines has its own theories about where behaviour comes from.

Second, those who voice scepticism about biological perspectives on the brain are sometimes right. For example, they are right to raise concerns about the potential for misuse of biological information, because biology has been misused in the past. Properly understood, these are arguments more for caution than for exclusion. But caution is nonetheless often warranted. People respond differently to claims that evolutionary processes affect behaviour from the way they respond to claims that television and advertising affect behaviour.

Third, there is still widespread persistence of emotional commitment to human exceptionalism. We do not want to think that our transcendent capabilities are the products of purely terrestrial mechanisms. As my colleague Michael Saks succinctly put it in conversation: 'people don't want to be caused'.

Against this background, here are a few issues I would like to see more carefully explored in preparation for future evolutionary analysis in law. They are not unique to evolutionary analysis, but they seem particularly salient there.

(a) What standards of proof are appropriate in those contexts in which law and behavioural biology meet?

This is not as easy to answer as one might at first think. On the one hand, we generally want to base our legal approaches on well-established scientific principles. After all, why risk a change in legal policy if facts are still fuzzy? On the other hand, even brief reflection suggests that the situation is far too complicated for an approach that excludes all but well-established insights. There is an enormous literature spanning science, the history of science and philosophy of science that grapples with issues surrounding standards of proof. Although disagreements abound, it is at least presently clear that different standards of proof are customary when there are different purposes to different activities.

Basic research scientists are the most conservative, because they want to build edifices of knowledge with building blocks that are highly unlikely to be wrong. Applied scientists adopt more varying standards to meet the particular probabilities of costs and benefits in the specific contexts in which they may be working. Similarly, legal policymakers have long correlated different standards of proof with different interests at stake (Faigman 2002). Evidence sufficient for legislative action is measured differently from evidence in adjudicative contexts, for example. The latter are even further differentiated: the criminal threshold for proof 'beyond a reasonable doubt', for example, is far higher, and appropriately so, than the civil threshold of 'the preponderance of the evidence'. Law and science play very different roles, and there are very different sub-roles within each. Thus we explicitly or implicitly want there to be—and indeed need there to be—standards of proof that vary context by context.

Nevertheless, we need to know more about what this means for evolutionary analysis in law. It probably means four things at a minimum. First, it probably means that we must think harder about who within the scientific community speaks with authority when hypotheses are disputed. Second, it probably means that we should remember that risks surrounding uncertainty tend to come in pairs. That is, it is not clear that the risk in law of treating a biobehavioural hypothesis as true when it is not true is greater than the risk of treating it as untrue if in fact it is true. The magnitudes of these respective risks (false positives and false negatives) will vary by context. Third, it probably means that law should not deploy a single standard of proof for incorporating into law a biobehavioural hypothesis, since the presence of differing risks can logically support differing standards of proof. Fourth, and more specifically, it probably means that we should not *automatically* apply to the hypotheses of different disciplines whatever standard of proof is generally dominant within that discipline. To do so could, paradoxically, privilege a non-scientific perspective over a more scientific one, simply because the former is more easily supported within the discipline from which it hails.

(b) What should 'testability' mean where law and behavioural biology meet?

On the one hand, it is inherent in the notion of science that hypotheses should be testable. On the other hand, the concept of testability is often misunderstood in legal circles. Hypotheses are sometimes incorrectly deemed untestable because there are no immediately practical ways, given the existing state of technological affairs, to test the hypothesis. In fact, only some naturalistic way of testing the hypothesis is necessary to satisfy the testability criterion, even if it requires means that are beyond our current technological capacities. Something can be appropriately testable in theory, even if not *immediately* testable in fact. Also, hypotheses are sometimes incorrectly deemed untestable when the necessary tests would require clearly unethical treatment of human beings. However, this renders the tests impermissible, not impossible. Hypotheses are sometimes also incorrectly deemed untestable because it is assumed that only traditional experiments are tests. However, it is widely agreed in animal-behaviour communities that, in addition to experiments, appropriately conducted observational and comparative techniques can also test hypotheses.

Clearly, we want to test hypotheses by the best means available. But what the best means are, and what degrees of confidence different means will provide, necessarily vary. Hypotheses about proximate mechanisms are often more easily tested than hypotheses about historical pathways of evolutionary processes. How should this affect our willingness to entertain evolutionary hypotheses? And how shall we deal, in law, with the general principle that conclusions drawn from tests of hypotheses are necessarily functions of considered judgement rather than unimpeachable empirical reality? We often draw, in other contexts, conclusions about what is probably true in humans on the basis of admittedly unrealistic studies of other animals. For instance, the hypothesis that a given substance will be safe in a large population of humans with varying physical characteristics, at a particular dosage, is generally tested by tabulating adverse effects of mega-doses of that substance given to a comparatively small number of animals of a non-human species. We need to think more about what testability means in the context of law and behavioural biology.

(c) What role does the general concept of falsifiability play where law and behavioural biology meet?

Falsifiability is important. However, precisely what role falsifiability plays in science, and precisely what it means when applied in differing contexts, are not nearly as clear as they are often thought to be. On the one hand, the existence of a falsifiable hypothesis has come to be seen by many in law as an infallible discriminator between good science and non-science. (For instance, the US Supreme Court invoked the principle reverentially in Daubert versus Merrell Dow Pharmaceuticals, 509 U. S. 579 (1993).) On the other hand, the falsifiability criterion is more subtle to apply than to discuss, and it has been subjected to sufficiently strong and numerous critiques that it is rather widely regarded by scientists and philosophers of science as by no means infallible, despite its demonstrated utility. A growing literature suggests that the principle of falsifiability does not play nearly as important a role in how scientists actually conduct their research as the popular image suggests (Hempel 1966; Woodward & Goodstein 1996; Goodstein 2000; Ulen 2002).

To make matters even more complicated, the notion of falsifiability is often further misunderstood in some legal circles, because of a failure to differentiate between falsifying a hypothesis, on the one hand, and falsifying a general theoretical framework (the metatheory) from which the hypothesis is generated, on the other. That is, it is sometimes assumed in legal discussions concerning behavioural biology that if a given hypothesis about how humans might be expected to behave proves incorrect then somehow the notion is also incorrect that humans are meaningfully influenced in these behaviours by the effects of evolutionary processes on brains. That does not follow. But precisely what does follow warrants more rigorous examination.

(d) What is the proper role of parsimony in evolutionary analysis in law?

Like falsifiability, parsimony is more frequently invoked than defined. Indeed, even the literature that specifically addresses it reflects no single settled definition. In legal circles, it is sometimes incorrectly assumed that the sole criterion for parsimoniousness is the number of assumptions a theory requires, with preference to be afforded to that theory with the fewest. But this is probably importantly incomplete. Many have noted that the same claims can be formulated in so many different ways that the number of constituent assumptions is not easily determined. Moreover, even were we to employ only the definition of parsimony that counts the readily agreed number of assumptions, parsimoniousness properly favours not the theory with the fewest assumptions but rather the theory with the fewest assumptions that is consistent with all the known facts.

Further, I have on occasion observed legal scholars to comment that any theory invoking evolutionary influences on human behaviours is necessarily less parsimonious than one that assumes no such influences. After all, the reasoning goes, why complicate matters by adding in biology if culture without biobehavioural hypotheses can adequately explain a given phenomenon? This reasoning misses two important points. First, culture cannot be divorced from biology, inasmuch as all behaviour reflects the interaction between genes and environment. Second, a theory that dispenses with evolutionary history raises more complications than it dismisses. (To think that the historical context evolutionary history provides necessarily renders a given behavioural theory less parsimonious is to think that a theory of a building that starts on the ground floor is less parsimonious than a theory of a building that starts on the 50th floor, because the latter requires 49 fewer assumptions.) The important point is that parsimony, too, bears clarifying in the context of behavioural biology.

(e) What is a mechanism, and in what contexts need it be specified?

Darwin was the first to demonstrate that the effects of evolutionary processes can be meaningfully identified and understood, even if various relevant mechanisms (in his case, the particles of heredity) are not known. What will count as a mechanism for behaviours relevant to law? When should reference to a mechanism be required? And when, in any event, would knowing genetic, neuroanatomical or neurochemical mechanisms be useful in law?

   Some people reject a given evolutionary perspective on human brain functioning so long as neither the genetic nor the neuroanatomical mechanisms influencing the resultant behaviour have been identified. (I have elsewhere referred to this as 'The Argument from Missing Mechanism'; Jones 2001*d*.) On the one hand, this seems an over-conservative basis for rejecting potentially useful knowledge: we know neither the genetic nor the complete neuroanatomical pathways for sleeping behaviour or sexual desire, and yet no one seriously disputes that these are products of evolutionary, rather than purely socio-cultural, phenomena. On the other hand, it seems a mistake to forget that evolutionary processes do require actual practical mechanisms. How shall we know when mechanisms will matter to law?

(f) How shall we best understand the relationship between theories and empiricism where law and behavioural biology meet?

Some have argued that we do not need evolutionary theories, in law, because we can just observe how people behave and then formulate legal regimes accordingly. They have the advantage of common sense: who needs theory when facts will do? On the other hand, data do not collect and organize themselves into patterns from which important conclusions can be drawn. This is one of the reasons why the purely observational approach (sometimes known as inductivism, Baconian inductivism (after proponent Francis Bacon) or naive inductivism) was largely rejected as either a descriptively accurate or a normatively sufficient and appropriate approach for generating knowledge. (In part, it seemed clear that the very process of attending to some facts while ignoring others, and cross-correlating some facts with others, is necessarily a function of some pre-existing theory, however tentatively advanced.)

   To the extent that inductivism has been replaced by a less rigid and more dynamic process involving theory formulation, data collection and theory reformulation (Woodward & Goodstein 1996), what does this mean for evolutionary analysis in law? Is there any systematic way to anticipate when theory is likely to be more useful or less useful?

(g) What role should prediction play in evolutionary analysis in law?

On the one hand, we expect science to help us to predict narrow aspects of the future. For instance, science has helped us to predict with great accuracy the flight trajectory of cannon-ball after cannon-ball. On the other hand, organisms are not cannon-balls. One cannot predict with great accuracy the precise foraging pattern of even a single *Cataglyphis* ant, let alone the future behaviour of an individual human being. This cannot mean that predictions, in the life sciences, are simply unnecessary or up for grabs. Predictions in behavioural biology are inherently probabilistic. They often attend not to the behaviour of an individual but rather to the patterns most likely to emerge from the collected behaviours of a large number of individuals. That is importantly parallel to what much of law is about: trying to affect populations in probabilistic ways. So thinking that biology is unhelpful to law because it cannot predict the behaviour of a single identified individual is like thinking that meteorology is unhelpful to sailors because it cannot predict where an individual cloud will rain, or thinking that geology is unhelpful to oil companies because sometimes there is no oil where geologists think there might be. Biology and physics are sufficiently different that we expect different things from their predictions. But what else do we need to know about the process of making useful biological predictions? By what measure do we determine whether a prediction is valuable or not?

4.4 Discussion

That was but a small sampling of the questions warranting further exploration. Others include: what does biology have to tell us about how law-relevant behaviours are likely, in theory, to vary across animal populations? What does biology have to tell us about the ways in which law-relevant behaviours are likely to manifest, phenotypically, in human populations? What environmental variables are most associated with given law-relevant behaviours? What can we learn from studies of other animals about patterns in behaviours suggesting a sense of fairness, justice, property, trust, jealousy and deception? To what extent does the change from ancestral to modern environments contribute to an ability, or inability, to say something useful about evolved law-relevant features of the human brain?

Given the foregoing questions, how can we decide whether, when and how to incorporate evolutionary perspectives on the human brain, and hence on human behaviour, into law? Undoubtedly, it will require judgement on a context-by-context basis. Nonetheless, a few general remarks are in order.

It is important to distinguish the separate relationships that law and science have with reality. Speaking generally, scientists and legal policy-makers share an interest in gaining an improved understanding of reality. However, scientists and legal policy-makers are trying to achieve very different things, and this has implications for how insights from science can or should enter the legal arena. While scientists often seek an improved understanding of reality for its own sake (and ever subject to revision), legal policy-makers are instrumentalists, charged by society with juggling a number of often conflicting goals and effecting positive change in some contexts, often at some cost in other contexts.

For example, a rule that affords present justice to one category of individual may do injustice to many more in the future. A policy that increases freedom of speech may paradoxically protect harmful hostile speech. A population may want increased national security but bemoan intrusions on privacy. An elected representative may see that a majority of his constituents support a legislative outcome that will later have adverse effects that those constituents do not yet recognize and later will not want. Tax rates sufficient to ensure the safest achievable food, through governmental oversight, may be higher than citizens are willing to pay. Ensuring that drugs (for example, AIDS drugs) are safe and effective may slow their delivery to patients, some of whom may die waiting.

This is not to say that instrumentalism makes an accurate understanding of a situation irrelevant. There are in fact many ways—none of them perfect—in which legal systems encourage the discovery and incorporation of truth in legal affairs. For example, over-sight agencies, backed by government lawyers, try to ensure efficient markets by creating incentives for accurate corporate disclosures. Litigants, through discovery rules and adversarial processes, are encouraged to present and support, through evidence, truths relevant to disputes. Both elected representatives and agencies hold hearings on matters pertinent to new legislation and regulation. Freedom of the press helps expose corruption, and legal academics theorize, criticize, propose and comment.

Nevertheless, legal policy-makers must often make important choices in the absence of clear, accurate and robust understandings of a situation. Disputants may have equally supported but nonetheless materially inconsistent versions of the facts. Some relevant facts—such as a person's state of mind at the time he killed someone, allegedly in self-defence—are simply not directly knowable. And, most importantly for this discussion, circumstances may warrant legal action before scientists have achieved a high degree of certainty about a given phenomenon.

In fact, and for quite sensible reasons, we often want our legal policy-makers to act before confidence is very high or a situation is understood thoroughly. Imagine, for instance, that scientific studies suggest a possible connection between the amount of chemical x released from the smokestack of corporation y and the incidence of leukaemia in the children of local neighbourhood z, where you and your children live. How certain would you want your legislators to be of the causal relationship between the chemical and leukaemia before they intervene to prohibit—even if temporarily—the flow of chem-ical x into the air your children breathe? One hundred per cent certain? Seventy-five per cent? Even at 50% certain there are coin-flipping odds that this chemical materially increases your child's risk of developing leukaemia. For this reason, many people would prefer some regulatory action at even lower thresholds of certainty. How probable must something be before you would prefer that it be considered operationally true—for the time being—until better information comes along?

Clearly, when legal policy is at issue, we want our relative concern for certainty to vary as a function of the severity of the harms to be avoided and the benefits that might, through inaction, be foregone. The key points are these: (i) scientists and legal policy-makers undertake entirely different things; (ii) the degree of certainty to which scientists aspire is different from the degree of certainty necessary for legal action, just as we want it to be; and (iii) the degree of certainty necessary for legal action will vary as a function of the costs and benefits that a given problem and its partial solution may impose or offer, respectively.

When it comes to theories of causation that may help us achieve our goals, using the tools of law, we may often care more for utility than for reality. In this respect, evolutionary analysis in law is similar to economic analysis of law. In each case, the legal system is more concerned with the utility of the hypotheses about how humans will behave than it is with the accuracy of the factual premises on which various hypotheses about human behaviour are based.

Don't get me wrong. Accuracy is a virtue in its own right. But, just as it sometimes does not matter for legal purposes whether people consciously choose to maximize their self-interest or merely act 'as if' they were so choosing, it often will not matter whether people consciously choose behaviours that would have improved their reproductive success in ancestral or current environments, if they generally act 'as if' they were so choosing.

Consequently, when considering whether information from the biological sciences may be incorporated into legal policy-making, these conclusions emerge. First, it is perfectly appropriate, in some circumstances, to base changes in the legal system on reasonable hypotheses, as opposed to well-confirmed hypotheses. Second, it is perfectly appropriate, again in some circumstances, to base changes in the legal system on the triangulation of information from many different points, even if none of these is individually compelling.

One of several possible approaches (the discussion of which may at least illuminate several important factors to be judged) would be to ask this: is the information or approach suggested by developments in another discipline sufficiently likely to improve matters to warrant at least its temporary use in a legal context, given what is at stake? Several aspects of this approach bear further discussion.

First, this hypothetical formulation of an initial approach to interdisciplinarity in law is fundamentally sensitive to the existing state of affairs. That is, one must have some loosely quantified sense of the magnitude of existing harms, in the context under discussion. (For example, an incident of domestic physical abuse is typically far more serious than an incident of littering.)

Second, use in law is rarely a one-way ratchet. So use can be temporary and can result in periodic modifications as legal policy-makers seek improved solutions. Also, we should not neglect the potential for the legal system to be part of the hypothesis-testing enterprise. For one of the purposes to which a hypothesis can be put, in law, is to use it tentatively and selectively in an effort to test its potential utility.

Third, our approach to interdisciplinarity should be sensitive not only to the potential benefits that incorporating the perspective might bring but also to the potential harms that such incorporation may involve. A decision on whether to incorporate a biobehavioural perspective should attend to the net of the costs and benefits. Note that the question is not whether or not this perspective will single-handedly achieve some pre-articulated policy goal. The question is whether the best possible approaches incorporating this perspective stand a sufficient chance of being better than what we currently have. That is, the assessment here is comparative, not absolute, because an improvement over existing affairs may warrant use, even in the absence of a fully optimal outcome.

Finally, any useful approach probably requires some assessment of the probability that the projected benefits will come to pass. That complex assessment requires judgement as informed and sound as feasible under the circumstances, though it will be necessarily imperfect.

What all this means, in the context of human behaviour, is that the legal system should adopt an approach that is inherently sceptical, but not unduly so, scrutinizing of scientific developments, but not wholly risk averse, and calibrated by judgement of the harms avoided and the potential gains to be had. This means that, while it should encourage and expect of science all the usual rigours of science, it should not exclude proffered findings of biology any more aggressively than it excludes equally tentative proffered findings of psychology, psychiatry, sociology or economics. That is, we can, at the same time, believe on the one hand that we should aggressively seek a greater understanding of reality and believe on the other hand that we need not be certain before we act, because certainty may come either never or too late.

4.5 Examples

I have elsewhere addressed several methodological and substantive issues in evolutionary analysis in law (Jones 1997a, 1999, 2001a), and, in a recent work, Yale biologist Timothy Goldsmith and I propose more than a dozen different categories of utility, with brief examples of each (Jones & Goldsmith 2005). Below I provide a short overview of four of them: clarifying cost–benefit analyses; providing theoretical foundation and potential predictive power; assessing comparative effectiveness of legal strategies; and revealing deep patterns in legal architecture.

(a) Clarifying cost–benefit analyses

One of the advantages for law of an evolutionary approach to understanding brain design is that it can help us to clarify some of the cost–benefit analyses legal thinkers undertake when assessing various approaches to legal problems. Sometimes, an evolutionary perspective reveals that two policies, deemed independent, may trade against each other at the subsurface, such that the pursuit of either one inhibits the pursuit of the other.

For example, it is clear that the legal system is charged with attempting to reduce the sum of the costs of infanticide and the costs of reducing infanticide. It is also clear that many people would like to see the legal system reduce historically prevalent stigmatization of step-parents (and perhaps even move to bring step-parents into greater legal parity with genetic parents).

An extremely rich and broad evolutionary literature (Hausfater & Hrdy 1984; Parmigiani & vom Saal 1994; and surveyed in Jones 1997a) provides ample reason to believe that these two policies may trade against each other. Infanticide in numerous species, widely distributed across taxa, is often perpetrated by a male against an unweaned infant of a mother with whom he might (and later often does) mate. Natural selection appears to have favoured, in many species, a male predisposition towards such selective infanticide because it tends to increase the male's reproductive success. The behaviour is extremely narrowly tailored along many dimensions. For example, the risk to an unweaned infant (whose nursing causes lactational amenorrhoea, a contraceptive effect) is far greater than the risk to a slightly older infant that has ceased nursing. In humans the risk to an unweaned infant of infanticide is roughly 100-fold greater if there is an unrelated adult male in the household than if the male is the genetic father, and this risk drops off just as precipitously, post-weaning, as it does in other species.

This suggests that if the legal system were, for example, legislatively to bias the limited investigative resources of child protective services toward homes with step-parents over homes with genetic parents, when rumours of child abuse were received as to each, it might help to reduce the rate of infanticide. Of course, that benefit might come at the cost of stigmatizing the vast majority of step-parents who never abuse.

Biology cannot tell us whether to prefer preventing infanticide over preventing stigmatization. The point here, however, is that evolutionary analysis can help to sharpen the cost–benefit analysis. The cost of continuing to pursue the non-stigmatization goal may now be increased by the potential cost of a few otherwise preventable infant deaths. Alternatively, the cost of preventing those deaths may be the increased stigmatization of step-parents who never abuse. Whichever course we choose, evolutionary analysis puts the potential advantages or disadvantages in sharper relief.

(b) Providing theoretical foundation and potential predictive power

Evolutionary analysis in law may offer, at times, theoretical foundation for known human behavioural data. For example, there is, at present, no satisfying non-evolutionary foundation for a wide number of puzzling human 'irrationalities'. (Rationality, in the economic sense adopted here, refers not to procedural rationality, in the sense of conscious deliberation, but rather to substantive rationality, in the sense that the outcome of the behaviour is appropriate for achieving particular goals, given conditions and constraints, regardless of how the behaviour was actually chosen.) These puzzling irrationalities include such things as the propensity to discount future interests too steeply (over-valuing the small early gain relative to the larger later gain) or to endow an object just received with a higher value than the maximum price one would have paid to acquire it. Such seeming irrationalities matter to legal policies affecting, for example, rates of savings for retirement and the efficient distributions of property rights; these policies, like many others in law, reflect the economic assumption that people will make economically rational and efficient decisions, and if the assumption is wrong, the laws may be too. For example, people may save less for their own retirements than expected, and they may refuse to bargain away a legal right that they would have refused to purchase from someone else, making the initial distribution of rights inefficiently 'sticky'.

Existing theories purporting to explain the variety of irrationalities are largely *ad hoc*. They attribute such irrationalities to brain defects, assume they are the result of insufficient capacity or time for the complex cognitive processes necessary to reach rational decisions, or merely re-label deviations from rational choice predictions (describing endowment effects, for example, as a function of 'loss aversion'). Consequently, the theories provide no theoretical framework to explain the particular *patterns* in seeming irrationalities (such as why people would not be equally likely to exhibit gain aversion as loss aversion). They provide no underlying structure that would connect together the wide variety of highly patterned deviations from narrow economic rationality that we observe. And they provide insufficient purchase on the problem to enable prediction of as yet undiscovered patterns.

The evolutionary perspective on the human brain suggests that a great number of deviations from rational choice predictions may reflect a temporal mismatch between design features of the brain appropriate for ancestral environments and the quite different environments humans encounter in modern times. Specifically, some irrationalities may be as widely distributed as they are, in the patterns they exhibit, because they predisposed people to behave in ways that led to substantively rational outcomes in past environments. That is, they may be what I have elsewhere referred to as 'time-shifted rationalities' (TSRs) (Jones 2001*a*).

A TSR reflects the propensity of the human brain to bias perception, information processing, emotions, tastes, decision making and other states of the nervous system, as a consequence of evolutionary processes, in ways tending to increase the probability of behaviours that were adaptive, on average, in ancestral environments, even if those behaviours are maladaptive in present circumstances (Jones 2001a). Some economically irrational behaviours currently ascribed to cognitive limitations may reflect not defects, random effects or inevitable computational limitations, but rather finely tuned features of brain design that are bumping up against novel environmental features in a way that yields outcomes that are puzzlingly irrational only if measured for rationality in present environments.

Thus, for example, contemporary human patterns in discounting future interests may be out of step with novel environmental features such as (i) sharply increased median lifespans, (ii) sharply increased probabilities of minimally stable futures and (iii) the invention of currencies and financial institutions that enable long-term storage of value. In addition, patterns in over-endowing items just acquired may reflect the modern invention of abstract tradable 'rights' to receive resources in the future.

(c) Assessing comparative effectiveness of legal strategies

From economics, we know that when the cost of a good increases the demand for that good generally decreases. Similarly, from the combined insights of law and economics, we know that when the cost of a behaviour increases (through legal sanctions, for example) the incidence of that behaviour tends to decrease, and the incidence decreases along a demand curve that describes the relative sensitivity of the demand to the legal 'prices'.

Speaking quite generally, a steeper more vertical demand curve (or portion of a curve) means that it takes a greater increase in sanctions to yield a given drop in demand. A more horizontal curve (or portion of a curve) means there is a far greater drop in demand for a given increase in sanctions. So far so good. But how steep are the curves for different behaviours? What *return*—measured in decreased behaviour—will we get for a given investment in costly sanctions, for a given behaviour we seek to deter?

Slutsky's equations, economists tell us, can help us to predict the trade-offs people will make, among various alternative behaviours, given people's preferences with respect to those activities (Varian 2003). However, taking people's preferences as given is precisely what we do not want to do. We want to know enough about where those preferences come from, and what forms they are likely to take, to design maximally efficient incentives and disincentives using the tools of law.

As I have argued elsewhere (Jones 2000, 2001a,c), we can derive a general approach from the general principle of TSR. Specifically, I define 'the law of law's leverage' as follows:

> the magnitude of legal intervention necessary to reduce or to increase the incidence of any human behaviour will correlate positively or negatively, respectively, with the extent to which a predisposition contributing to that behaviour was adaptive for its bearers, on average, in past environments.
>
> (Jones 2001a, p.1190)

A more accurate (but more cumbersome) rephrasing is this: the magnitude of legal intervention necessary to reduce or to increase the incidence of any human behaviour will correlate positively or negatively, respectively, with the extent to which a behaviour-biasing information-processing predisposition underlying that behaviour (i) increased the inclusive fitness of those bearing the predisposition, on average, more than it decreased it, across all those bearing the predisposition, in the environment in which it evolved, and

(ii) increased the inclusive fitness of those bearing the predisposition more, on average, than did any alternative predisposition that happened to appear in the environment during the same period.

Consequently, it will under most circumstances be less costly to shift a behaviour in ways that tended to increase reproductive success in ancestral environments (measured, of course, in inclusive-fitness terms) than it will be to shift behaviour in ways that tended to decrease reproductive success in ancestral environments. I should not be read to suggest that evolutionary processes are not still operating on human populations. But the general point here is that the slope of the demand curve for historically adaptive behaviour that is now deemed undesirable will tend to be far steeper (reflecting less sensitivity to price) than the corresponding slope for behaviour that was comparatively less adaptive in ancestral environments. This rule is likely to hold even when the costs that an individual actually and foreseeably incurs in behaving in a historically adaptive way exceed the presently foreseeable benefits of such behaviour.

This predicts that, in criminal law, family law, torts, property and the like, behaviours involving the following things will prove more difficult to modify than the behaviour of median difficulty: mating, fairness, homicide, childrearing, status-seeking, property and territory, resource accumulation, sexuality (including infidelity and jealousy), speech, privacy, empathy, crimes of passion, moralistic aggression, risk valuation and risk taking, cooperative or altruistic behaviour, male mate-guarding and related violence and the like (Jones 2004a; Jones & Goldsmith 2005).

The law of law's leverage may offer some novel and useful insights into the different ways in which law and behaviour interact, even if it will not predict with precision either the demand curves for given behaviours or the individualized curves of a single person. By highlighting for legal thinkers the fact that the brain tends to process information in ways that tended to yield adaptive solutions to problems encountered in the environment of evolutionary adaptation, the law of law's leverage encourages the anticipation that behavioural inclinations will vary in their susceptibility to different legal tools in non-arbitrary loosely predictable ways. This may enable legal thinkers to estimate more accurately the relative costs and benefits to society of attempting to shift different human behaviours in different ways.

(d) Revealing deep patterns in legal architecture

Evolutionary analysis may also eventually provide a window into why human legal systems tend to manifest some of the features they do. My hypothesis (explored further in Jones 2001b) is that—just as beaver dams, despite their differences, all reflect the effects of evolutionary processes on beaver brains—legal systems, despite their differences, all reflect the effects of evolutionary processes on human brains. That is, it will be possible to view at least many of the largest-scale features of legal systems as reflections of human neural architecture.

Consider, for example, that we might trace the characteristics of legal regimes—with respect to a particular subject—according to four variables. *Topics* would describe the main things that people care about. *Content* would capture the normative preferences that people generally associate with that topic. *Tools* would reflect the types of legal interventions deemed useful in attempting to ensure that individuals conform to the content preferences. *Effort* would quantify the relative amount of difficulty in using that tool to ensure conformity to the content preferences. An evolutionary perspective suggests that, were we to trace the variations in these four variables for the main features of legal regimes around the world and across time, we would see a decidedly non-random macro-pattern in legal regimes. This would reflect the species-typical brain.

For example, we would expect to see great concern devoted to the acquisition of private resources. From which, perhaps, emerges a finite set of materially similar approaches to the law of property. We would expect to see concern for facilitating exchanges and gains from trade. From which, perhaps, emerge a finite set of materially similar approaches to the law of contracts. We would expect to see sharp concern for bodily safety. From which, perhaps, emerges a finite set of materially similar approaches to laws concerning crimes and torts. We would expect to see great concern devoted to the subject of mating and child-rearing. Hence family law, etc.

4.6 Conclusion

The complexity of human behaviours provides unending challenges for legal systems, which seek to regulate some of those behaviours with the tools of law. Yet, behind that complexity is an even more complex human brain, which in turn reflects the intricate interactions of genes and environments.

We know that the interaction between genes and environments is governed by evolutionary forces: natural and sexual selection, drift, gene flow and mutation. So, in theory, the more we know about the ways in which these forces ultimately affect species-typical brain design, the better we can know the subject we regulate with law and the better we may be able to guide behaviour in democratically percolated and pre-articulated directions that are socially, politically and economically desirable. It seems time, given what we know, what we do not and the tools at our disposal, that we focus more of the attention of legal thinkers on the brain itself.

Advances in neuroanatomy, neurochemistry, psychopharmacology, neuroimaging and evolutionary biology have helped us begin to fathom how the brain actually does what it does. Although this will doubtless provide no magic window on behaviour, making all causes transparent to modern science, even incremental improvements are improvements nonetheless. It seems clear that we should not exalt biology over all other sources of knowledge. At the same time, it is clear that biological perspectives on the brain, its information-processing characteristics and the behaviours to which these lead are essential components of any modern understanding of behaviour. They are consequently important for law.

I thank Michael Saks, Jane Maienschein and Richard Creath for helpful comments.

References

Faigman, D. 2002 Is science different for lawyers? Science **297**, 339–340.

Garland, B. (ed.) 2004 *Neuroscience and the law: brain, mind, and the scales of justice*. New York: Dana Press.

Gazzaniga, M. & Steven, M. S. 2004 Free will in the 21st century: a discussion of neuroscience and law. In *Neuroscience and the law: brain, mind, and the scales of justice* (ed. B. Garland), pp. 51–70. New York: Dana Press

Goldsmith, T. & Zimmerman, W. 2001 *Biology, evolution, and human nature*. New York: John Wiley & Sons, Inc.

Goodstein, D. 2000 How science works. In *Reference manual on scientific evidence*, 2nd edn, pp. 67–82. Washington, DC: Federal Judicial Center.

Greely, H. 2004 Prediction, litigation, privacy, and property: some possible legal and social implications of advances in neuroscience. In *Neuroscience and the law: brain, mind, and the scales of justice* (ed. B. Garland), pp. 114–156. New York: Dana Press.

Hausfater, G. & Hrdy, S. B. (eds) 1984 *Infanticide: comparative and evolutionary perspectives*. New York: Aldine Publishing Co.

Hempel, C. 1966 *Philosophy of natural science*. Englewood Cliffs, NJ: Prentice Hall.

Jones, O. 1997*a* Evolutionary analysis in law: an introduction and application to child abuse. *N. Carolina Law Rev.* **75**, 1117–1242.

Jones, O. 1997*b* Law and biology: toward an integrated model of human behavior. *J. Contemporary Legal Issues* **8**, 167–208.

Jones, O. 1999 Sex, culture, and the biology of rape: toward explanation and prevention. *California Law Rev.* **87**, 827–942.

Jones, O. 2000 On the nature of norms: biology, morality, and the disruption of order. *Michigan Law Rev.* **98**, 2072–2103.

Jones, O. 2001*a* Time-shifted rationality and the law of law's leverage: behavioral economics meets behavioral biology. *Northwestern Univ. Law Rev.* **95**, 1141–1206.

Jones, O. 2001*b* Proprioception, non-law, and biolegal history. *Florida Law Rev. 53*, 831–874.

Jones, O. 2001*c* The evolution of irrationality. *Jurimetrics* **41**, 289–318.

Jones, O. 2001*d* Evolutionary analysis in law: some objections considered. *Brooklyn Law Rev.* **67**, 207–232.

Jones, O. 2004*a* Evolutionary psychology and the law. In *The handbook of evolutionary psychology* (ed. D. Buss). New York: John Wiley & Sons, Inc.

Jones, O. 2004*b* Useful sources: biology, evolution, and law. See http://law.vanderbilt.edu/seal/readingsjones.htm.

Jones, O. & Goldsmith, T. 2005 Law and behavioral biology. *Columbia Law Rev.* **105**, 405–502.

Mayr, E. 1961 Cause and effect in biology. *Science* **134**, 1501–1506.

Morse, S. 2004 New neuroscience, old problems. In *Neuroscience and the law: brain, mind, and the scales of justice* (ed. B. Garland), pp. 157–198. New York: Dana Press.

Parmigiani, S. & vom Saal, S. (eds) 1994 *Infanticide and parental care*. Char, Switzerland: Harwood Academic Publishers.

Rilling, J. K., Gatman, D. A., Zen, T. R., Pagnoni, G., Berns, G. S. & Kilts, C. D. 2002 A neural basis for social cooperation. *Neuron* **35**, 395–405.

Schultz, J., Goodenough, O. R., Frackowiak, R. & Frith, C. D. 2001 Cortical regions associated with the sense of justice and with legal rules. *Neuroimage* **13**(Suppl.), S473.

Tancredi, L. 2004 Neuroscience developments and the law. In *Neuroscience and the law: brain, mind, and the scales of justice* (ed. B. Garland), pp. 71–113. New York: Dana Press.

Ulen, T. 2002 A nobel prize in legal science: theory, empirical work, and the scientific method in the study of law. *Univ. Illinois Law Rev.* 2002, 875–920.

Varian, H. R. 2003 Intermediate microeconomics, 6th edn. New York: Norton

Wehner, R. 2003 Desert ant navigation: how miniature brains solve complex tasks. *J. Comp. Physiol. A* **189**, 579–588.

Woodward, J. & Goodstein, D. 1996 Conduct, misconduct and the structure of science. *Am. Sci.* **84**, 479–490.

Glossary

TSR time-shifted rationality

5

A neuroscientific approach to normative judgment in law and justice

Oliver R. Goodenough* and Kristin Prehn

Developments in cognitive neuroscience are providing new insights into the nature of normative judgment. Traditional views in such disciplines as philosophy, religion, law, psychology and economics have differed over the role and usefulness of intuition and emotion in judging blameworthiness. Cognitive psychology and neurobiology provide new tools and methods for studying questions of normative judgment. Recently, a consensus view has emerged, which recognizes important roles for emotion and intuition and which suggests that normative judgment is a distributed process in the brain. Testing this approach through lesion and scanning studies has linked a set of brain regions to such judgment, including the ventromedial prefrontal cortex, orbitofrontal cortex, posterior cingulate cortex and posterior superior temporal sulcus. Better models of emotion and intuition will help provide further clarification of the processes involved. The study of law and justice is less well developed. We advance a model of law in the brain which suggests that law can recruit a wider variety of sources of information and paths of processing than do the intuitive moral responses that have been studied so far. We propose specific hypotheses and lines of further research that could help test this approach.

Keywords: normative judgment; moral judgment; law; emotion; intuition

5.1 Introduction

How do humans think about right and wrong? This critical question has recurred in law, philosophy, the arts and religion over the centuries. As David Hume (1739, p. 31) wrote, 'morality is a subject that interests us above all others'. More recently, this question has engaged psychology and other scientific approaches to human thought and behaviour: including the emerging science of human brain function. Interest has not abated in the twenty-first century. A recent review of neuroscientific approaches to normative judgment declared, 'the neurobiology of moral cognition is a justifiably hot topic'(Casebeer & Churchland 2003, p. 170).

Although the topic is hot, the scope of this essay is necessarily limited; it cannot hope to be a fully comprehensive treatment. Partly this is a matter of length: this is an essay, not a treatise, and so it must make simplicity of argument and selectivity of evidence a virtue. Partly it is a matter of interdisciplinary fatigue. The study of law and the brain rests on several fields: law, philosophy, economics, psychology evolutionary biology, neurology and cognitive neuroscience being, at best, a partial list. As we write this essay our expertise is stretched thin in some places, and a limited scope is perhaps a blessing. For those seeking greater detail, we have sought to provide a sufficiently broad selection of primary and secondary references to allow further pursuit.

* Author for correspondence (ogoodenough@vermontlaw.edu).

Nonetheless, we attempt to tell a complete story, one that provides not just a description of current thinking, but also sufficient historical, theoretical and methodological background to put the contemporary story in context (for additional background, see Haidt 2001; Casebeer & Churchland 2003; Greene 2003; Pigliucci 2003). We also want to foreshadow the future, exploring two of the many lines of possible research that spin out of an approach to the problems of law and justice informed by neuroscience. Finally, our goal is to tell a story that readers on both sides of the law and science divide will be able to follow. This has led to some push and pull between the authors over matters of style and assertiveness, with the scientist seeking to rein in the expansiveness of the lawyer and the lawyer seeking to set aside the caution of the scientist. A reader with a background in the disciplines related to cognitive neuroscience may wish to skip over the introductory material in § 3.

This essay is divided into five topics: (i) a review of traditional models of normative thinking, including philosophy, religion, law, psychology and economics; (ii) an introduction to the possibilities, methods, and limits of the new cognitive neuroscience; (iii) a review of recent developments in the neurobiology of normative thinking; (iv) a model of the role of law and justice in normative judgment; and (v) a sample of the kinds of investigations into concrete problems in law and justice that a neuroscientific approach makes possible.

As a final introductory matter, what do *we* mean by morals, justice and normative judgment? Definitional questions have been part of the debate as well. Some make distinctions between morals and ethics. Others distinguish conventional from moral, and both from legal. In the neuro-scientific literature, Casebeer (2003 p. 842) uses the term 'moral cognition', which he admits 'might not be a tightly defined 'natural kind' in the sense that other cognitive phenomena might be'. The arguments over these taxonomies can fill volumes (e.g. Casebeer & Churchland 2003; Haidt 2003 and the extensive surveys of moral and ethical traditions in LaFollette 2000 and Singer 1991). In the context of this essay, this long and distinguished history of argument, speculation and empirical study can only be briefly excerpted, and only a few of the most important strands identified.

For our own usage, we like the term 'normative judgment' as an inclusive description of the many flavours humans find among those things that ought to be done and those that ought not to be done, particularly in the social context of interaction with other humans. In this sense, normative judgment first involves the construction of a system (or systems) of norms, values and expectations, and, second, the evaluation of the actions of another agent, or of our own actions, made with respect to these norms, values and expectations. Our position in this essay is that the mental processes of performing this function are not unitary, but on the contrary involve some number of different approaches. We have a suspicion that these differences are at the heart of many of the historical arguments over terminology.

For this essay, we do sometimes distinguish 'moral reasoning', a relatively affect free, consciously accessible process, from other, more intuitive and emotionally based processes of normative judgment. We also sometimes follow the convention that the term 'cognitive' suggests processes on the reasoning–rational–conscious end of the spectrum as opposed to emotion-linked 'affective' processes. Others have extended 'cognitive' to encompass a wider range of mental processes, such as its use in 'cognitive neuroscience'. Please let context be your guide.

5.2 Traditional models of normative thinking: intuitionism, moral reasoning, law and the sense of justice

(a) Examples from philosophy and religion

At a gross level of description, the study of normative thinking has often divided into strands that value either intuition and emotion on the one hand, or reason on the other. One strand, called by some 'intuitionism', holds that the primary source of normative judgment comes from intuitively accessed moral sentiments (Dancy 1990). Hume (1739) provides a classic description of this approach, arguing that moral distinctions are not derived from reason, but rather from a moral sense, whose workings are not accessible to our conscious intelligence, 'morality, therefore, is more properly felt than judged of...' (Hume 1739, p. 43). Furthermore, Hume linked morality with emotional responses, or the 'passions', as he termed them. This link allowed morality to influence action in a way that pure reason never could.

Starting from these principles, Hume posited the argument often called the 'naturalistic fallacy'. Because moral sentiments are separate from facts, no logical proposition with facts alone in its predicate can contain a moral judgment in its conclusion. Only by basing an argument on a moral predicate, can a moral conclusion be obtained; facts and reason alone cannot provide a valid moral conclusion (Hume 1739; Greene 2003; Pigliucci 2003). A corollary of this was Hume's presumption that moral sentiments could not be readily reduced to facts. This left the systematic study of normative judgment somewhat high and dry: our reasoning, conscious selves cannot peer through the impenetrable fence beyond which intuition, emotion and sentiment hold sway.

In contrast to intuitionism stand moral systems which base themselves in reason. The work of Immanuel Kant is a classic example of this approach (Pigliucci 2003). Through the application of reason, Kant seeks to arrive at universal rules to govern human action: the famous 'categorical imperative' (Kant 1953; also see O'Neill 1991). A recent example in the rationalist tradition of Kantian ethics is 'A theory of justice' by John Rawls (1971). One perceived benefit of a Kantian approach is that questions of morality are open to rational, if still often introspective, study in a way that intuitionism largely defies.

Religiously grounded systems of morality add another strand to the discussion. Most religions point to divine origins or sanctions for a moral code, an approach some philosophers term the 'divine command theory' (Quinn 2000). In the Judeo-Christian Bible, God presents the 10 commandments to Moses. Muhammad receives divine guidance on moral questions which he relates to the wider world in the Koran. In the New Testament, the words of Jesus and the letters of his early followers contain many directives on the values that should form the basis of a moral life. The divine origin of values may not be susceptible to deductive proof (Quinn 2000), but it is deeply rooted in the faith of millions.

For our purposes, the next questions are the interesting ones: how do people find out and apply the content of these values? Traditional explanations for these steps sometimes cite to reason, at other times to intuition, and sometimes to both. Aquinas, for instance, argued that we perceive the general principles of 'natural law', as the divine system is sometimes called, through a kind of intuition he called 'synderesis'. We then use reason to derive secondary principles of more specific application to the needs of time and place (Gill 1995).[1]

Although the reason–intuition divide has been a particular concern of Western ethical and religious thought (Hansen 1991), the recurrence of similar distinctions in the moral traditions of non-European societies (e.g. Hourani 1985; Hansen 1991; Hallaq 1997) suggests that the distinction is not simply a localized cultural artefact.

(b) Intuition versus reason in the law

When it has bothered with introspection and internal justification, the law has both reflected these larger debates and added its own concerns. Anglo-American jurisprudence has often focused on a rules or feelings dichotomy, distinguishing between the reason-based dictates of law and an intuition-based sense of justice. This distinction has been a perennial subject for the debates and theories of the law (e.g. Austin 1832; Holmes 1881; Kelsen 1934; Hart 1961; Weinreb 1987; Gruter 1992; also see Goodenough 1997b). How one analyses problems through the application of word-based legal rules (often called 'positive law') and how one reacts to them as a matter of intuitive 'justice' (often called 'natural law') can sometimes give very different results (Goodenough 2001a). This has been demonstrated in the treatment of such issues as mandatory criminal sentencing (Smith & Cabranes 1998), the role of juries (Posner 1999; Feigenson 2000) and conflicting approaches to statutory and constitutional interpretation (Tribe 1985; Scalia 1997).

As with philosophers, legal theorists and jurists have been aware of the difficulty of penetrating into the intuitive realm of justice. Some decided that this put the topic of justice effectively beyond study:

> Justice qua absolute value is irrational. However indispensable it may be for human will and action, it is not accessible to cognition. Only positive law is given to cognition, or, more accurately, is given to cognition as a task.
>
> (Kelsen 1934, pp. 17–18)

Others, by contrast, have viewed intuitive standards as a source of legal authority. The Georgia Supreme Court used such reasoning in establishing a right of privacy in 1905:

> The right of privacy has its foundation in the instincts of nature. It is recognized intuitively, consciousness being the witness that can be called to establish its existence. Any person whose intellect is in a normal condition recognizes at once that as to each individual member of society there are matters private, and there are matters public so far as the individual is concerned. Each individual as instinctively resents any encroachment by the public upon his rights which are of a private nature as he does the withdrawal of those of his rights which are of a public nature. A right of privacy in matters purely private is therefore derived from natural law.
>
> (Pavesich v. New England Life Insurance Co. 1905, 50 S.E. 68, pp.69–70)

The intuition–reason argument was to some extent set aside in American jurisprudence with the emergence of the 'Realist School' in the middle of the twentieth century. Realism switched the focus from the source and nature of moral thinking in law to its effects as realized public policy (e.g. Llewellyn 1931), a move realism shared in psychology with behaviourism and in philosophy with utilitarianism and other forms of consequentialist ethical thought. In order to look effectively to consequences, realism requires:

> . . . the *temporary* divorce of Is and Ought for purposes of study. By this I mean that whereas value judgments must always be appealed to in order to set objectives for inquiry, yet during the inquiry itself into what Is, the observation, the description, and the establishment of

relations between the things described are to remain *as largely as possible* uncontaminated by the desires of the observer or by what he wishes might be or thinks ought (ethically) to be.

(Llewellyn 1931, p. 1236)

Jurisprudential trends as ideologically varied as law and economics and critical legal studies have used the basic assumptions of realism as a starting point (Goodenough 2001*a*).

(c) Scientific accounts of normative judgment I: moral reasoning

The past two centuries have witnessed the development of scientifically grounded understandings of human mental processes. Psychology and related disciplines have provided descriptions of increasing explanatory and predictive power (Goodwin 1999). The study of the human capacity for normative judgment has been an ongoing target in this history of enquiry. One of the most influential lines of research and theorizing has centred on a developmental model of cognitive abilities associated with Jean Piaget and Lawrence Kohlberg (e.g. Piaget 1965; Kohlberg 1969, 1981; Kohlberg & Candee 1984; Crain 2000; Haidt 2003). Building on Piaget's work, Kohlberg generated a widely cited six-stage model of the development of moral reasoning, through which, he argued, humans progress as their cognitive abilities mature and come to a more sophisticated understanding of social relations.

In his empirical studies, Kohlberg presented children and adolescents with dilemmas that contained conflicts about issues of life, interpersonal obligations, trust, law, authority and retribution. In his best known dilemma, a man named Heinz must decide whether he should break into a druggist's shop to steal a medicine that would save the life of his dying wife (Crain 2000). As Kohlberg analysed how people resolved such conflicts, he discerned a six-level progression of increasing sophistication, a progression that he linked to the development of his subject's cognitive abilities (for example, the ability for perspective-taking). One formulation describes stage 6 as follows.

> Stage 6: The universal ethical-principle orientation. Right is defined by the decision of conscience in accord with self-chosen ethical principles that appeal to logical comprehensiveness, universality, and consistency. These principles are abstract and ethical (the Golden Rule, the categorical imperative); they are not concrete moral rules like the Ten Commandments. At heart, these are universal principles of justice, of the reciprocity and equality of the human rights, and of respect for the dignity of human beings as individual persons.

(Kohlberg 1971)

This description is clearly in the Kantian tradition. It not only values and privileges conscious reasoning as the ultimate in moral cognition, but it explicitly cites the categorical imperative as an example. Kohlberg's work has had a profound influence on the scientific study of morality. With its attention set on moral reasoning, this branch of psychology has viewed emotion and intuition as disturbing factors (e.g. Sutherland 1994; see also Posner 1999), problems to be excluded from the investigation of the reasoning and judgment processes at the heart of moral thinking. As a result, much of the research on moral judgment in the latter part of the twentieth century was rooted in cognitive models, in which proper normative judgment was thought to be the result of moral reasoning.

(d) Scientific accounts of normative judgment II: a role for intuition and emotion

Of course, academia is seldom a monoculture, and there have been persistent lines of explanation in moral psychology and related disciplines that focus on emotion and intuition (LeDoux 1996; Pigliucci 2003). Emotion generally has always been a matter in study and theorizing in psychology (e.g. Darwin 1872; Plutchik 1980; Frijda 1986; Ortony *et al.* 1988; van der Meer 1989; Kemper 1990; Hatfield *et al.* 1993) and the pace has only accelerated in the past decade (e.g. LeDoux 1996; Panksepp 1998; Damasio 1999; Rolls 1999; Plutchik 2001; Davidson *et al.* 2002; Döring 2003; Haidt 2003; Solomon 2004). The contrast between rule-based decision making and intuitive, emotional judgment has been studied in a wide variety of psychological contexts (e.g. Cowan 1965; Etzioni 1988; Mellers *et al.* 1998). De Souza (1987) argued that far from being the enemy of good judgment, emotion is an essential element in rational thought.

In the context of normative judgment, Jerome Kagan (1984) and Martin Hoffman (1981) are among those psychologists who argued for the importance of emotional states in moral thinking, and even some working from the starting points of Kohlberg and Piaget acknowledge the role of affective processes as well (e.g. Damon 1988). In recent years, the interest in psychology on the role of emotion and intuition in normative judgment has flourished (Haidt 2001, 2003; Döring & Mayer 2002; Stephan & Walter 2004).

While many in law have distrusted emotion and intuition (Posner 1999), other important figures in legal psychology have argued for the importance of intuition and emotion in normative judgment (generally, Bandes 1999; Posner 2001). In 1881 Oliver Wendell Holmes Jr. wrote:

> The life of the law has not been logic: it has been experience. The felt necessities of the time, the prevalent moral and political theories, intuitions of public policy, avowed or unconscious, even the prejudices which judges share with their fellowmen, have had a good deal more to do than the syllogism in determining the rules by which men should be governed.
>
> (Holmes 1881, p. 5)

In 1996, Yale scholar Paul Gewirtz, reacting to an excessive emphasis on rational processes in judging, mused:

> All too often judges and scholars who write about law assert an inappropriately sharp distinction between the rational and the nonrational, especially between reason and emotion–invoking an overly narrow concept of reason and contrasting reason and emotion in an overly simplified manner. These discussions usually arise in the context of a traditional normative argument that judging is a realm of reason, not emotion.
>
> (Gewirtz 1996, p. 1029)

The study of juries—and their 'failures' in applying clear reasoning in their decision making—has given an empirical grounding to concerns with intuition, sympathy, emotion and heuristics in the law (e.g. Feigenson 1997, 2000; Charman *et al.* 2001). Neal Feigenson (2000) reviews a wide spectrum of this research. In coming to the broad conclusion that jurors seek to achieve what he calls 'total justice', Feigenson cites many studies indicating the role of intuitive, emotional factors in jury thinking and suggests that the goal of jurors is to integrate these with more explicitly rule-based cognition to create a satisfactory amalgam, 'which sometimes may be more justice than the law recommends' (Feigenson 2000, p.104). Others have applied a cognitive bias approach to understanding motivation in employment discrimination (Krieger 1995) and have explored the role of non-cognitive processes in criminal responsibility (Reider 1998).

Evolutionary psychology provided its own particular impetus towards a broader line of inquiry into moral reasoning. This approach looks for evolutionary explanations for human thought and behaviour (e.g. Cosmides & Tooby 1987; Laland & Brown 2002). It argues that our social responses—including our moral sense—evolved at a time when conditions were quite different than they are in contemporary society, and it predicts, at times, a mismatch between our intuitive predilections and what a more reasoned approach might provide (Jones 2001*a*). Evolutionary psychology has also argued for a high degree of continuity between human mental processes and those of other animals, particularly those of our near primate relations (e.g. Darwin 1872; de Waal 1996). Either implicit or explicit in most of these arguments is a picture of normative judgment in humans that is at odds with the Kantian empowerment of reason.

(e) Scientific accounts of normative judgment III: not a proper study

Some in psychology who followed the behaviourist approach would have avoided the debate over the nature of normative judgment altogether, arguing that science can never understand the nature of moral thinking. For the behaviourists, this grew out of a conviction that behaviour, and not the internal mental states of an actor, was the proper sphere of study (e.g. Watson 1924; Skinner 1953). It was not so much the *normative* part that put them off as it was the *judgment*. Since the 1960s (e.g. Neisser 1967), cognitive approaches and investigations of reasoning and judgment processes in experimental paradigms have largely eclipsed behaviourism in psychology.

Others, including several scholars of morality and the mind, have taken what might be called a romantic view of normative processes, questioning the susceptibility of moral cognition to systematic psychological study. Arguments from this position take many forms. Some, like Stephen Morse (2004) in his sceptical but balanced discussion, admit the theoretical possibility of describing normative judgment in material terms, but declare that the complexity of the task renders it effectively undoable. Others, including most philosophers of mind, declare the task fundamentally impossible (Morse 2004).

The more respectable version of the impossibility argument rests on the concerns about the jump from 'is' to 'ought' that are at the heart of the naturalistic fallacy, which Greene (2003) calls 'the mistake of identifying moral properties with natural properties'. But this assertion begs a question: if ought is something more than the conclusion of a particular kind of natural mental process, where does that something more come from? Even the Kantian move to duty, rationalism and universals merely shifts the exercise from one mental process to another. In all of its forms, this train of argument attributes to moral standards an independence from physical causation in the discoverable processes of the brain. And the question remains: if not physical processes, then what? At heart, the romantic approach rests on an often unacknowledged spiritualism: some non-physical standard exists 'out there' that we connect with by some kind of revelation or transcendent communication. Aquinas explored this, and it is a perfectly respectable intellectual proposition. It should, however, be acknowledged for what it is.

(f) Economics: a similar story

During the latter part of the twentieth century, moral psychology was not alone in its focus on reason as the proper mode of thought. The hugely influential discipline of neoclassical economics rested many of its explanations on rational actor models of human psychology (Kahneman 2002). Irrational, intuitive and emotion-driven thought and action were seen by some in this context as aberrations, and not part of what people *should* or, in fact, *did* do (Posner 1999, 2001; Korobkin & Ulen 2002; McKenzie 2003).

In recent years, the rationality assumption has been effectively challenged. Robert Frank was among those raising the opposition, notably in his 'Passions within reason: the strategic role of the emotions' (Frank 1988). Overly simplistic views of rationality have been questioned in a variety of new economic sub-disciplines, including behavioural economics (e.g. Kahneman 1974, 2002; Tversky & Kahneman 1974, 1981; Kahneman & Tversky 1979; Korobkin & Ulen 2002), experimental economics (e.g. Smith 1982, 1991; McCabe & Smith 2000), and neuroeconomics (e.g. McCabe *et al.* 1996, 1998, 2001; Glimcher 2003; Hoffman 2004; Zak 2004). The awarding of the Nobel Prize in economics in 2002 to Daniel Kahneman and Vernon L. Smith for their work in these fields marked the recognition by the discipline that a broader cognitive model, more firmly rooted in empirical study, was necessary for economics to progress.

5.3 Advances of cognitive neuroscience

New knowledge is allowing us to reconsider our theories of normative judgment and to apply powerful new tools to its study. Advances in our understanding of the brain, its functions, and the ways in which those functions shape the nature of human thought, together with emerging tools of neuroscientific investigation, allow us to lift the veil that has hidden the workings of the brain and mind, whether intuitive or rational, from objective study. We believe that we are in the early stages of what will be a highly productive period in the study of normative thinking.

Many of the recent advances in this process have been made possible by a collection of technological and theoretical developments often referred to as cognitive neuroscience. This somewhat flexible label (coined, the story goes, during a New York taxi ride in the late 1970s (Gazzaniga *et al.* 2002)) covers an approach that seeks to integrate into the study of human thought, our rapidly emerging knowledge about the structure and functions of the brain, and about the formal properties of agents and decision-making processes (e.g. Marr 1975; Gazzaniga *et al.* 2002; Frakowiak *et al.* 2004; see also the *Journal of Cognitive Neuroscience* and *Trends in Cognitive Sciences*, passim). Although cognitive neuroscience was well launched before the advent of such imaging technologies as PET and fMRI, the availability of non-intrusive methods that allow us to establish functional connections between mental tasks and specific anatomical structures has increased its power and accelerated its application (Savoy 2001; Frackowiak *et al.* 2004).

The great advantage of the cognitive neuroscience approach is that we now can bring together psychological models of cognitive and affective processes, experimental paradigms, various behavioural and psychophysiological measurements and functional brain imaging techniques. Therefore we are no longer dependent on observations of the behaviour or introspection and self-report alone as the basis for examining thought. Rather, we can formulate and test hypotheses about the whole chain from the 'input' of the senses through the 'processing' in the brain and on to the 'output' of action and behaviour. Some traditional psychology, at the behaviourist extreme, was left with a mysterious 'black box' as the explanation for the central part of this chain, a limitation the behaviourists sought to convert into a virtue. By untangling human brain function itself and relating it to the processes of sensation, thought and action under study, we can offer much more complete and competent descriptions and explanations of human psychology (e.g. McCrone 1999; Humphreys & Price 2001; Miller 2003; Frackowiak *et al.* 2004). By way of simple-minded analogy, one could develop a useful science of automobiles without ever opening up the hood or bonnet of a car, but it would rely on explanations such as 'the car's desire to move inspires its motive force'. With the engine exposed, a much more complete explanation is possible.

By combining the best of traditional psychology and its related disciplines with the new approaches of cognitive neuroscience, mental activities as diverse as visual perception, memory, language use, emotion, deduction and consciousness have begun to yield some of their secrets (Frackowiak *et al.* 2004). In recent years the thought processes related to social cognition in general (Blakemore *et al.* 2004) and normative judgment in particular (Haidt 2001, 2003; Casebeer 2003; Casebeer & Churchland 2003; Greene 2003; Pigliucci 2003; Moll *et al.* 2003) have also become a target for this kind of study. The boundary that Hume and Kelsen could not cross is becoming permeable. Before turning to a survey of recent developments in the neurobiology of normative judgment, however, it is useful to review aspects of the cognitive neuroscience approach that have particular application to this study.

(a) Richer cognitive models

The new neuroscience rejects the unitary models of human thought that have informed some branches of philosophy and psychology since the time of Descartes (Damasio 1994; Restak 1994); rather, it is comfortable with cognitive complexity. The principle of sorting and prioritizing multiple pathways is reflected in the nature of neuronal network processing (e.g. Smith & Ratcliff 2004) and appears to function at much 'higher' levels of activity as well. For instance, in describing the effect of emotion on decision making, Joseph LeDoux has contrasted the image of a quick, unconscious 'low road' through the amygdala with a slow, conscious 'high road' through the sensory cortex in the brain (LeDoux 1996). In a similar vein, Kahneman & Frederick (2002) argue for a 'dual process model' which has room for both intuitive and deliberative processes:

> The essence of such a model is that judgments can be produced in two ways (and in various mixtures of the two): a rapid, associative, automatic, and effortless intuitive process (sometimes called System 1), and a slower, rule-governed, deliberate and effortful process (System 2). System 2 'knows' some of the rules that intuitive reasoning is prone to violate, and sometimes intervenes to correct or replace erroneous intuitive judgments. Thus, errors of intuition occur when two conditions are satisfied: System 1 generates the error and System 2 fails to correct.
> (Kahneman 2002, references omitted; see also Evans 2003)

This application of complexity and multiplicity is not restricted to overarching models. At the level of more detailed neuroanatomy, experimentation has made progress in establishing the brain regions associated with such capacities as the different aspects of musical performance, perception and comprehension (Parsons 2003). Even the capacity to bring together and reconcile the different functional systems and processes may be carried on in particular locations. The capacity to resolve conflicts between possible responses may involve particular loci in the anterior cingulate cortex and the dorsolateral prefrontal cortex (Frith *et al.* 2004).

(b) Specialization and integration

The degree to which different mental activities rest on dedicated pieces of brain architecture has been a subject of some controversy (Savoy 2001; Posner 2003; Aron *et al.* 2004). Clearly there is a significant degree of functional localization and specialization, a principle particularly well demonstrated in the field of vision (Zeki 1990; Bartels & Zeki 2004). Although not as congruent with the subjective experience of our own minds as the old Cartesian unified model, this approach better explains the loss of particular faculties and the retention of others which can result from a stroke or other brain injury (e.g. Moore & Price 1999; Savoy 2001).

Perhaps the most assertive conception of functional separation in recent scholarship was the idea of the 'modular brain', an expression widely adopted in early 1990s (e.g. Gazzaniga 1992; Restack 1994; Frackowiak *et al.* 1997; Gigerenzer 1997), but which has more recently fallen out of use. At its most extreme, some used the metaphor that the mind resembles a Swiss Army knife, with several different, if interconnected, tools that can be brought to bear on the problems that life presents (Cosmides & Tooby 1987, 1992). Asserting this degree of specialization and segregation became controversial (Sperber 2002), and the current view takes a more balanced approach that emphasizes both specialization and integration:

> The brain appears to adhere to two fundamental principles of functional organization, functional integration and functional specialization in which the integration within and among specialised areas is mediated by effective connectivity.
>
> (Friston 2004, p. 972)

Some suggest that functional separation can take place at the level of 'primitives'. These can be thought of as quite specialized structures dedicated to a particular kind of recognition or conceptualization. The existence of primitives has been argued in contexts such as vision (e.g. Shams & von der Malsburg 2002) and motor control (e.g. Thoroughman & Shadmehr 2000; Todorov & Ghahramani 2003). Specialization can also take place a more general level, such as the clearly demonstrated involvement of the amygdala in many kinds of emotional response (Casebeer & Churchland 2003; Morris & Dolan 2004). Aron *et al.* (2004) argue for the localization of certain inhibitory responses in the right inferior frontal cortex. Many further examples could be cited.

Complicated cognitive tasks look likely to recruit a variety of regions and structures into their accomplishment. Indeed, some regions seem to specialize in functions that have quite general applicability, such as the conflict monitoring and resolving functions mentioned above. Such regions turn up over and over in a variety of imaging experiments, to the initial confusion of the researchers involved.

> In the early days of functional imaging every task seemed to activate dorsolateral prefrontal cortex (DLPFC), and every experimenter was happy to define a different role for this region.
>
> (Frith *et al.* 2004, p. 349)

In the hotly debated and controversial field of consciousness studies, some have recruited the recruitment idea as an explanation. This theory argues that what we experience as consciousness is the most extreme and general version of the recruitment strategy: a 'global workspace' that can marshal diverse resources in the brain to accomplish many tasks (Baars *et al.* 1998; Dehaene & Naccache 2001).

(c) Understanding the strategic nature of mental tasks

In pursuing the mix of modelling and empirical investigation that is at the core of cognitive neuroscience, the strategic nature of the mental task under consideration must be kept in mind. This is particularly true of mental tasks involving social relations among human actors. Traditional psychology recognized the 'actor–observer' paradox, describing the tendency for individuals to use different standards and approaches to judge their own actions as opposed to the actions of others (Duval & Wicklund 1972; Jones & Nisbett 1972; Taylor & Fiske 1975). More recently, Pizarro *et al.* (2003) have described empirical evidence for asymmetrical judgments of moral blame and praise depending on the perceived impulsiveness or considered nature of the decision. Although these kinds of double standards are widely condemned as hypocrisy, particularly when applied to benefit oneself, consideration of their strategic properties can help us to understand their occurrence.

Since the time of Adam Smith (1776), economics has correctly grasped the scale of beneficial pay-offs available to cooperative human actors. These pay-offs, and the barriers to successful cooperation posed by the opportunities of defection, are deeply imbedded in reality, and reoccur at several levels of organization in the history of living organisms (Maynard Smith & Szathmary 1995). Game theory provides a formal foundation for understanding the nature of these interactive relationships of human sociality (von Neumann & Morgenstern 1944; Binmore 1994, 1998; Fehr & Fischbacher 2004).

Games are not always symmetrical. The dynamics applicable to developing a solution for a player in one position may not be the same as those applicable to a player in a different position (McCabe *et al.* 1996, 1998, 2001). From a strategic standpoint, the answer to 'should Jane do x to John' may have a very different answer depending on whether you are Jane, John or a third party judge. It is fully possible that these different strategic dynamics could implicate different processing in the brain for what might, in its general description, be considered to be the same question. The importance of this kind of distinction is becoming better recognized in cognitive science (Camerer 2003*a,b*; Goodenough 2004).

(d) Multiple sources of information

A further complication embraced by cognitive neuroscience is the multiplicity of information sources available to the brain as it works to solve social problems. The possibilities start with our genetic information heritage. Much of this is broadly shared across humanity (Jones 2001*b*), while some may be variable and specific to individuals, one of the sources of each person's unique temperament (Larsen & Buss 2002). Nor does genetic information realize itself in a vacuum. Through the process of epigenesis, genes do their job only in conjunction with a quantity of environmental information (Hinde 2004). People also have access to a rich variety of cultural knowledge transmitted in a complementary, coevolved stream with their genetic nature (Boyd & Richerson 1982; Goodenough 2002*b*; Laland & Brown 2002; Pigliucci 2003). This cultural knowledge may itself be implicit, like the unconscious social modelling that proceeds from childhood, explicit but popular, like sayings or literature, or explicit and expert, like the law. There is also information that is personal to the individual, such as the social circumstances of her life, the day to day events that she encounters, the physical nurture or injury she has received, and her behavioural interactions with family, friends, school, etc.

The components of this mix are commonsensical; the degree to which each plays a role in a particular aspect of human thought and action can be controversial (Goodenough 1997a). What is also commonsensical is that the brain is where the combination, comparison, sorting and choice of these disparate information and memory sources is made, perhaps within a process of different systems resembling that described by Kahneman, above. Indeed, one of the functions of our relatively competent human brains is to provide and weigh alternatives. When we overlay these multiple sources of information onto the multiple pathways of thought and onto the different possible strategic positions, we realize that human normative judgment is likely to be a complicated composite, and not a unitary process. The intellectual framework of cognitive neuroscience makes the problem of understanding normative judgment and its components more complex, not less. Fortunately, with the tools of cognitive neuroscience, we can begin to work through this complexity.

(e) Methodological considerations

The methods of cognitive neuroscience involve postulating and testing functionally based hypotheses about thought. These cognitive models are developed from several sources. Traditional taxonomies of our own experience can provide a starting point. For instance, the successful investigation of the colour processing systems of the brain grew from the generally accepted, experientially based notion that colour differentiation is an important element of sight (see Zeki 1999). Similar considerations apply to normative judgment: it is a process most humans experience at a subjective level on a regular basis, and the history of intensive speculation in philosophy, religion and law has clarified the subjective descriptions. Traditional sources such as these are not without their complications, however (Churchland 1991; Keil 2003). The intuitive models of cognition that this 'folkscience' provides should be tested and refined using the proven tools of experimental psychology. Other sources for creating cognitive models include the predictions of evolutionary psychology, the descriptions of traditional psychology, and the rapidly improving understandings of cognitive neuroscience itself.

The most common method for testing these models is to seek to differentiate closely related mental tasks where the distinction between them is rooted in the hypothesis to be tested. The experimenter will seek to identify behavioural and physiological activity (or its absence) consistent with the hypothesis and inconsistent with its alternatives; if this activity is present (or absent) as predicted, the hypothesis gains support (Gazzaniga et al. 2002). The experimental tasks must be carefully designed to avoid, to the extent practicable, the presence of more than one possible source for any observed variation. Alternative possibilities are often called 'confounds', and undercut an experiment's validity. Avoiding this pitfall leads to a fundamental tension that cognitive neuroscience shares with other branches of experimental psychology. The pressure to remove confounding factors prompts researchers to strip away real-life contexts, thereby undercutting the 'ecological validity' of the targeted cognitive process. (Casebeer & Churchland 2003). Furthermore, for such cognitively complicated tasks as normative judgment, untangling the multiple processes and creating sufficiently targeted experimental tasks is inherently difficult (Casebeer & Churchland 2003).

Once the experimental tasks are set, they are given to subjects to perform, while the researchers collect a variety of data to see if there is a differentiation in physical reactions, behaviour or subjective experience that matches the hypothesized differentiation in the targeted experimental task. Investigating complex mental processes requires many different kinds of measurement. Some of these, often collectively referred to as 'behavioural data', are directly related to the performance of the task. This would include accuracy in answering and reaction time, both of which are linked to task difficulty (Wilkinson & Halligan 2004). Self reporting on subjective parameters such as task difficulty or the severity of a transgression gives its own metric of differentiation that can be compared with the behavioural measurements. Other tools of this research include such psychophysiological measures as skin conductance (linked to degrees of emotional arousal) and pupil dilation (linked to complexity of processing).

Direct physical inferences about brain function have been made for years using patients with damage to the brain resulting from injury, disease and developmental problems. These 'lesion studies' were at the centre of the early identification of some of the language areas in the brain, such as Broca's area and Wernicke's area (Finger 2000). More recently, patients with amygdala dysfunction have helped to investigate the role of that structure in emotion and emotion-linked processes (e.g. Anderson & Phelps 2001, 2002). Lesion studies have several limitations. Any ethical system of research on humans can only use naturally occurring deficits and must show sensitivity and restraint in dealing with an experimental population that is by definition mentally impaired. Furthermore, until the invention of imaging techniques that could identify deficits accurately in living subjects, the exact parameters of the injury of the subject could often only be established after death.

The invention of non-intrusive methods for spatially locating brain activity has been a significant addition to the experimental toolkit. Most prominent in recent work have been PET and fMRI. Both of these techniques give indirect measures of brain metabolism, allowing the identification of brain areas active or inhibited in mental tasks (see Friston 2004). PET uses the radioactive decay of a tracer added to the blood to provide its measurements, whereas fMRI uses the so-called BOLD signal as the basis for its measurements. In each case, the link of blood flow to functional work in the brain has been established, but subject to limitations and qualifications (e.g. Mechelli 2004). Increases in the fMRI BOLD signal lag after the onset of activity (as measured by electrical activity) by a relatively predictable 3–6 s, peaking at 5 s (Posse *et al.* 1996; Hensen 2004). Both techniques require the subject to lie immobile in a large device where it is awkward to present tasks and measure other responses. The fMRI, with its strong magnetic field and high level of noise, is particularly claustrophobic and distracting. Notwithstanding these difficulties, inventive researchers have developed clever means to present tasks and collect data with a high degree of reliability.

It is important for a non-specialist faced with imaging data to understand what it does—and does not—mean. First of all, the pretty pictures of 'brains lighting up' are actually artefacts of extensive analysis and selective presentation. In fact, at any given time of wakeful activity, many, perhaps even *all*, areas of the brain are active to some degree. The pictures show a colourful projection onto a model brain of the regions in which some statistically significant level of increase or decrease in the measurable phenomenon (blood flow) has occurred compared with a control state, often on some kind of accumulated basis over several subjects. They are *not* direct pictures in any meaningful sense.

Second, the relative activation of a particular region of the brain in the performance of a task compared with the differentiating task does not tell us that much by itself. This information is only 'spots on brains' until it is related to the target hypothesis and to the developing picture of cognitive localization and integration in the brain. A particularly nice way of linking imaging data with the targeted cognition involves establishing some kind of intensity measure for the activity in the behavioural data and demonstrating a corresponding change in intensity of response in the imaging data.

Third, the degree of spatial resolution in such images, although good and getting better, is still at a scale far coarser than the identification of particular neurons or groups of neurons (Casebeer & Churchland 2003). Finally, as with any of the experimental techniques of cognitive neuroscience, the imaging data are only as good as the underlying tasks given to the participants and the subtractions or other techniques based on these tasks allow it to be. Imaging techniques are powerful tools, but their results are not always well presented or understood.

Other techniques for measuring and localizing brain reactions include such measures of electrical activity as the EEG and MEG. These provide excellent temporal resolution of brain response (Gazzaniga *et al.* 2002).

Neurochemical studies are also an important component in the methodological mix. Although somewhat eclipsed by the recent prominence of imaging in the public and scientific imagination, neurochemistry is a necessary part of any complete functional description of brain activity (e.g. Masters & McGuire 1994; Coull & Thiele 2004). The link of serotonin and depression, although not fully understood, has been established both in science and the popular consciousness, as Robert Wright's *Slate* posting 'Is Prozac driving Wall Street' fully illustrates (Wright 2000). In considering the effect of emotion on mental processes, both the general neurochemical climate of the brain and the relative presence or absence of particular neurotransmitters are important elements (e.g. Henry 1986; Panksepp 1993).

All of these methods work best in concert with one another (Humphreys & Price 2001; Parsons 2001; Wilkinson & Halligan 2004). The profile of a fully developed field of research in cognitive neuroscience includes specific hypotheses about well-defined mental processes, a growing body of functional locations and systems linked to these hypotheses, and the support of data from behavioural experiments, lesion studies and activity measurements through imaging and other localizing techniques.

5.4 Normative judgment in the brain

Against this historical, theoretical and methodological background, we can turn to the central piece of this essay: a summary of the current 'state of play' in the neuroscientific approach to normative judgment in humans. We will first examine the model for normative judgment now animating this research, then turn to a review of lesion and imaging studies that are testing this model and its variations. Finally, we will seek to evaluate where the field is and make some predictions about where it is headed.

(a) The consensus model and its variations: emotion and intuition play important roles

The current work applying neuroscience to normative thinking has largely rejected the Kant/Kohlberg conception of normative judgment as properly seated in the realm of affect-free, rational, conscious thought. Rather, models emphasizing the role of emotion and intuition in moral judgment have been developed (Damasio 1996; Pizarro 2000; Haidt 2001, 2003; Nichols 2002; Casebeer & Churchland 2003). The social intuitionist model advanced by Haidt (2001), for instance, posits that fast, automatic and affective intuitions are the primary source of moral judgments. This article tellingly refers to an 'emotional dog and its rational tail' in its title. Haidt views moral judgments as evaluations (good versus bad) of the actions or a character of a person that are made with respect to a set of virtues held to be obligatory by a culture or subculture. In this model, conscious deliberations play only a minor causal role and are used principally to construct *post hoc* justifications for judgments that have already occurred.

(b) Concerns I: overvaluing emotion and intuition?

The emerging consensus raises its own concerns. Whereas we agree strongly with the importance of giving proper value to emotion and intuition in many forms of normative judgment, we are concerned that the pendulum may swing too far, and that cognitive processes at the reasoning end of the spectrum will undervalued. We believe that the best view of normative judgment is that it has both cognitive and affective aspects. The cognitive aspect contains factual knowledge about accepted standards of social and moral behaviour (norms and values) and rational reasoning processes. The affective aspect includes the experience and effects of emotions like guilt, sympathy, shame and anger if social or moral norms are violated. While, as Casebeer & Churchland (2003) put it, 'good moral cognition is shot-through with emotion', it is not purely emotion, either.

The totality of the evidence suggests that normative judgment consists of one or more sets of higher mental abilities, which in turn rely on a variety of disparate cognitive and affective processes, such as understanding of a situation, appraising its emotional valence, activating norms from long-term memory, maintaining a norm in working memory, comparing the norm with the present behaviour, and deciding if there is any transgression, all of which take place under the influence of emotional processes. Therefore the neural basis of normative judgments is likely to involve several brain systems and to be distributed across the large portions of the brain. That said, it is also possible that there may be dedicated elements—perhaps even primitives—for certain aspects of the process. This possibility receives some support from the work of Cosmides (1989). She presents evidence of enhanced competence in performing a logic task if the task is presented in the form of a cheater-detection story. The presence of such relatively specialized elements as components in the process would not conflict with the view of normative judgment as a complex, widely distributed system or systems.

(c) Concerns II: a better model of emotion

There is an even more fundamental difficulty with the consensus view. Notwithstanding the significant attention devoted to emotion and intuition in recent years, there is still a lack of clarity as to what they consist of in the brain (Posner 2001). It was an enthusiast for the role of emotion in normative judgment who recently admitted 'that emotion theory and research is immensely complex and that the role of the emotions in behaviour, including social judgments, is highly variable and context dependent' (Feigenson 2000, p. 447). An American judge once described the state of the law of privacy as a 'haystack in a hurricane'. Current scholarship on emotion comes close to deserving this label. Certainly the words 'heated debate' can be reasonably applied to several of its issues.

In the context of moral thought, Haidt (2003) takes a good stab at bringing some order to the field. He suggests some useful distinctions, sorting moral emotion into other-condemning emotions (contempt, anger and disgust), self-conscious emotions (shame, embarrassment and guilt), the other suffering family (sympathy and compassion) and the other praising family (gratitude, awe and elation). As satisfying as such a list can be, it still remains at heart a working hypothesis, and not yet a tested conclusion.

The authors believe that progress will be made by separating 'emotion', the sensation of arousal that we monitor in ourselves and others, from 'emotion', the functional component in mental processes. Its meaning as a sensation state strikes us as being less important to normative judgment than are the functions which the-thing-we-call-emotion-when-we-experience-it is contributing to the processing of normative tasks. In this functional sense, steady progress has been made by experimenters plugging away in a variety of contexts (e.g. Rolls 1999; Dolan 2002; Phelps 2002; Morris & Dolan 2004). These disparate results suggest that emotion acts as a great emphasizer and highlighter in the brain, an indicator of importance and urgency. Damasio, for instance, has suggested that emotion plays a key role in creating a 'somatic marker' which helps guide and prioritize decision-making processes (Damasio 1994). In the realm of memory, events that are associated with emotional states are much more likely to be transferred from working memory to long-term recollection (Morris & Dolan 2004). In the current brain, emotion drives attention towards its associated objects (Anderson & Phelps 2001). Emotion gets us up and doing. As even Hume recognized, emotion is a great translator of thought to action (Hume 1739; Rolls 1999; Schwartz 2000).

Perhaps it is not so much that emotion is a key to normative judgment as it is a key to important and effective normative judgment, normative judgment that gets our attention and gets translated into action, either with respect to our own conduct or to the reward or punishment of others (Fehr & Gächter 2002). Part of the emotion controversy revolves around how far this idea can be taken: the extent to which emotional processes influence cognition, whether fully affect-free cognitive processes exist at all, and whether we would notice them if they did, are all undecided questions (e.g. Damasio 1994, 1996, 1999; LeDoux 1996). There is evidence that emotion—or at least its frequent physical component the amygdala—is deeply and necessarily involved in social judgments (Phelps 2002).

In our view, the consensus theoretical model of moral judgment properly includes emotional involvement as an essential component. There remains, however, significant work in clarifying and testing the role or roles of this component. Furthermore, as we will argue in § 5, this component may produce consequences that the law may wish to guide and contain through the recruitment of other systems of thought.

(d) Concerns III: a better model of intuition

In our discussions so far, we have to some degree conflated intuition with emotion in discussing normative judgment. Although we are not alone in this, it is probably a mistake. It is possible for humans to make intuitive judgments about the world that have a low level of emotionality (Camerer *et al.* 2004). Consider taking an uneventful automobile drive over a familiar road or making intuitive judgments about simple grammatical errors. Put simply, intuition is a concept we use to describe mental processes that are not directly accessible to conscious monitoring or participation. Viewed this way, the property of intuition has more to do with the boundaries of self-awareness than it does with the actual competence or incompetence of the mental processes so labelled. There is no reason to suppose that intuitive processes are simple or inaccurate just because they are not directly involved in conscious thought. We certainly will not solve the problem of consciousness in this paper, but we can help de-stigmatize intuition through such a definition.

What remains interesting is the insight, going back to Hume and beyond, that certain important categories of normative judgment fall into this description. In this dimension they resemble emotional states, but they are dissimilar in other ways. The role of intuition in the study of morality may be more important for supplying a marker for some of the systems involved or cognitive mechanisms behind it than for telling us anything inherent about the properties of their processing.

(e) Lesion data

In the past decade, researchers have begun to bring real data to the study of the normative judgment in the brain. Initial attention concentrated largely on lesion data. The specific moral deficits resulting from brain trauma reported in contemporary injury studies (e.g. Anderson *et al.* 1999; Dolan 1999; see also Damasio 1997; Angrilli *et al.* 1999) and in historical patients such as the widely publicized Phineas Gage (Damasio *et al.* 1992), lend support to the proposition that at least some of the processes and structures involved in normative reasoning are dissociable from more general problem solving abilities (Casebeer & Chruchland 2003). Most of these studies point to regions in the prefrontal cortex as critical components in the formation and application of socio-moral reasoning (Casebeer & Churchland 2003). More specifically, orbitofrontal deficits have been linked to difficulties in cuing morally appropriate behaviour, and in learning moral information. Indeed, the age at which the injury occurred in this region has also been shown to have an effect on the degree and nature of the normative deficits (Anderson *et al.* 1999; Casebeer & Churchland 2003; Pigliucci 2003). Recent work on lesion patients shows orbitofrontal involvement in anticipating consequences and experiencing regret (Camille *et al.* 2004).

(f) Imaging studies: evidence for complex cognition

In the past 4 or 5 years, a flurry of fMRI studies has investigated the neural basis of normative judgment (Greene & Haidt 2002; Greene *et al.* 2001; Moll *et al.* 2001, 2002*a,b*, 2003; Heekeren *et al.* 2003, 2004). Although it is possible to raise methodological concerns about some of these studies, it is important to recall that they are pioneering efforts. The experiments take quite variable approaches. For instance, some used complex dilemmatic scenarios (Greene *et al.* 2001), others more simple ethical decision-making tasks (Moll *et al.* 2001, 2002*a,b*; Heekeren *et al.* 2003, 2004). Greene *et al.* (2001) set its dilemmas in an imaginary first person, asking what the subject would do. The others asked the subject to act as a third-party judge. The possible effects of the strategic differences between these two positions were not fully envisioned. Furthermore, the emotional content of the studies varied greatly. Some asked questions involving death and other highly emotional situations (Greene *et al.* 2001; Moll *et al.* 2002*b*), whereas others posed less fraught judgment problems (Moll *et al.* 2001; Heekeren *et al.* 2003). All of the studies requested their participants to undertake what were in effect intuitive judgments. None asked that they learn or apply any explicit set of normative rules. Finally, some of the studies showed variation in the behavioural data that supported the imaging findings; others did not.

Given these difficulties and differences, it is remarkable that these studies, taken together, point overall to a common system that may very well form the neural substrate of normative judgment: ventromedial prefrontal cortex, orbitofrontal cortex, posterior cingulate cortex and posterior superior temporal sulcus. This is not a full triumph, however. The components of this network of brain regions are each active during several tasks, e.g. control of behaviour, processing of socially relevant cues, memory and processing of emotional stimuli (Greene & Haidt 2002). Rather than identifying a 'moral centre' of the brain, what we are seeing so far is moral judgment as a cognitive-affective process building on several contributing components (Casebeer & Churchland 2003). The challenge of seeking to disentangle the different cognitive and affective processes contributing to normative judgment is certainly important, but as Greene & Haidt (2002, p. 523) suggest, '[. . .] if one attempts to 'deconfound' moral judgment with everything that is not specific to moral judgment (emotion, theory of mind, mental imagery, abstract reasoning, and so on) there will almost certainly be nothing left'.

If the identification of these regions and the conclusions flowing from it holds up in further experimentation, the challenge for understanding intuitive normative judgment shifts, at least in part, from one of localization to one of integration: can we better understand how these different brain systems act together to perform such a complicated task? Careful experimental manipulation and differentiation of the components contributing to moral judgments and of the processes through which they work together will be necessary to construct a better description of how moral judgment works in the brain. A comparison with other kinds of judgment tasks, such as evaluative judgments on simple preferences (Zysset *et al.* 2002) and grammatical judgments (Wartenburger *et al.* 2003), may also prove productive.

In addition to establishing a target system for intuitive normative judgment, many of the fMRI studies found that brain regions linked with emotional processing are also active during moral judgments (Greene *et al.* 2001; Moll *et al.* 2001, 2002*a,b*; Heekeren *et al.* 2003; for review see Greene & Haidt 2002; Moll *et al.* 2003). As in the lesion data, the orbitofrontal cortex was often implicated. This structure receives a direct projection from the amygdala (Morris & Dolan 2004), with its established roll in the emotions and social judgment generally. These findings support the model that emotion plays a role in normative judgment, or at least in the kinds of normative judgment posed to the subjects in these experiments.

(g) Conclusions on current theory and research

Current work on the application of neuroscientific methods to normative judgment has made significant progress, both at the level of modelling and theory, and at the level of functional mapping. Work so far is consistent with the idea that normative judgment consists of systems involving several subprocesses, which frequently include an emotional component. We may still be in the early days of this effort, but we are well started along the road. A clearer set of models, based on results so far and a fuller understanding of the roles of emotion and intuition, and a better use of traditional behavioural measures in conjunction with imaging, will help speed further progress.

5.5 A model for law: recruitment across the composite

So far in our story, neuroscientific examination of normative judgment has been modelled to recognize the importance of emotion and intuition. With respect to naive, personal judgments—Hume's moral sense—we agree that this focus is appropriate. We do not think, however, that it reveals the full picture of how humans can and do attack problems of judging right and wrong. The emerging picture of normative judgment suggests interrelated sets of capacities, drawing on multiple sources of information, to solve strategic dilemmas of expectation, reliability and punishment. As we have seen, cognitive neuroscience acknowledges that there are potentially several processes and several information sources that may be recruited to perform a particular mental task.

We suggest that the law is an example of just such a recruitment system, one that is located not only in the internal processes of the brain but at least in part in the external mediums of language-based culture. In this view, law is potentially the most complete and competent avenue for normative judgment, combining both of Kahneman's systems, as it were. Law makes possible the kind of complex societies that would be impossible if we could only rely on our evolved 'primary equipment', characterized by intuition and emotion, to provide the rules and responses of normative judgment. Kahneman & Frederick (2002, p. 50) remind us that intuition is not the end of the story, 'because intuition can be overridden or corrected by self-critical operations, and because intuitive answers are not always available'.

Law is neither all reason nor all emotion; it is neither all explicit rules nor intuitively accessed principles of justice; it is a composite. In some instances, such as the American standard for determining negligence, law makes an explicit appeal to intuitive processes of risk assessment and avoidance, asking the question what would a 'reasonable person' have done in a like circumstance (Restatement 2nd of Torts, § 283). In establishing the requirements for the waiver of a warranty on goods sold in normal commerce, law provides an explicit, word-based rule in the Uniform Commercial code (§ 2–316) that operates through deductive logic application.

In determining culpability and meeting out punishment, the delay inherent in procedures of criminal law can intercede to prevent the quicker action of emotion driven judgments of immediate justice. Although some emotional content is probably inevitable and necessary in reviewing criminal allegations, letting the quick, intuitive and emotional impulse to punish dissipate before judgment and action take place may lead to preferable results in a complex society. Lynching is a quick phenomenon, 'shot through' with emotion. Left to their own devices, the operation of the intuitive, emotion linked, primary punishment impulses can lead to escalating tit-for-tat retaliation cycles, whether the actors are the Hatfields and the McCoys of US feuding fame (Waller 1988) or US military jailors and Iraqi militants in Baghdad. Legal process provides different pathways for normative judgment that can lead to superior strategic solutions for all concerned. In this context, legal process acts in the role of Kahneman's second system, working with the strengths of the first system but stepping in as well to correct its failings.

We believe that law is uniquely situated to move back and forth throughout the entire composite of brain capacities, strategic positions and information sources. Sometimes the law will empower or act in concert with emotion, both to make use of the best aspects of emotion-driven judgment and to preserve law's emotional validity to its subjects (Deigh 1999). At other times law will filter certain emotions out (Nussbaum 1999). Although the law will not always be successful in constructing better solutions to the opportunities and challenges of sociality and cooperation, the well-demonstrated relationship between a reliable rule of law and high levels of economic growth (Zak & Knack 2001) suggests that legal systems are having some success in providing solutions with better outcomes than intuitive systems alone could provide.

(a) Can we test this model?

We believe that this model can be tested. After all, the law is a rich source of cognitive and behavioural data. Its taxonomies are not simply 'folk science' (Churchland 1991; Davies & Stone 1995; Keil 2003). Law is, in its own way, an investigative science, a learned and academic discipline which probes into the nature of human thought (Langdell 1887; Goodenough 2001a). The classic legal process of seeking to articulate the mental landscape on issues of right and wrong into word-based rules is a rigorous intellectual exercise, relentlessly tested back against reality in hundreds and thousands of *in vivo* experiments: actual human disputes (Goodenough 1996). Although such data are not 'scientifically' controlled in the traditional sense, generally recognized distinctions in the law represent widely held, cited and tested approaches, which have their own empirical validity as a starting point for investigation of the psychology and mechanisms depicted (Goodenough 2001b). Just as moral reasoning studies can start with the reason–intuition distinction, we suggest that the widely recognized law–justice dichotomy is sufficiently well established through legal scholarship and application to justify using it as a testable hypothesis.

(b) Empirical approaches to law and justice in the brain

Unlike naive normative judgment, law and justice have not yet sparked broad neurobiological research activity. One of us (O.R.G.) has participated in preliminary fMRI work seeking to compare the activations of subjects, using in some instances their intuitive sense of justice, and in others a legalistic rule to judge manufacturer blame in product injury scenarios. The rule in this experiment was in the form of a deductive syllogism. Initial results (Schultz et al. 2001) showed differences between the law and justice conditions and implicated orbital frontal and prefrontal regions for the justice condition: results generally consistent with the fMRI experiments on moral reasoning described above. Unpublished results using a larger sample and random effects analysis (J. Schultz, O. R. Goodenough, R. Frackowiak and C. D. Frith, unpublished data) suggest that performing the legal rule task recruits regions in the right parietal cortex, an area that has been implicated in other studies of deductive logic tasks and in the 'mental model' theory of deductive reasoning (Goel et al. 2000; Goel & Dolan 2001, 2003; Parsons & Osherson 2001; Knauff et al. 2003). Although only a start, this finding provides some initial support for the recruitment hypothesis of law.

5.6 Possible applications to problems of legal design and enforcement

So far, our discussion of the application of neuroscience to law has been at a highly theoretical level. Law as a discipline, however, is generally less interested in abstract knowledge than in the solution to very particular problems. 'What can you do for me today?' is law's motto. We believe that an understanding of the brain and the application of cognitive neuroscience has a lot to offer in addressing concrete concerns of legal doctrine and administration. In this final section, we will discuss two potential topics at the intersection of law and the brain that are of particular interest to the authors: (i) the effect of emotional arousal on jury decisions of culpability; and (ii) the ineffectiveness of intellectual property laws to inspire widespread voluntary compliance.

(a) The effect of emotionally arousing evidence on jury decision making

The rules governing the admissibility of evidence in a trial in the USA are generally aimed at filtering out evidence of low reliability or low probative value. One class of rules, however, is aimed at excluding evidence that might be both reliable and probative, but which would also be *prejudicial*. One codification of this approach is 'Rule 403' of the Federal Rules of Evidence. It provides:

> Although relevant, evidence may be excluded if its probative value is substantially outweighed by the danger of unfair prejudice, confusion of the issues, or misleading the jury, or by considerations of undue delay, waste of time, or needless presentation of cumulative evidence.

Tanford (1989, p. 831) sums up the concerns that animate Rule 403: 'if evidence threatens to frustrate [the objectives of a fair trial], by wasting time, confusing the issues, or *arousing the emotions of jurors* [emphasis added], it should be excluded'. A typical context for arguments over this rule is the desire of a prosecutor to show the most gruesome available pictures of the corpse and crime scene in a murder trial to establish the facts of the crime and the desire of the defence to keep them out.

It could be argued that this rule reflects the fundamental assumption in reason-valuing philosophy, psychology and law that emotions and cognitive processes are antagonistic and that emotions are detrimental to sound moral reasoning and moral judgment (Posner 1999, 2001). The rule could also be justified not as a denial of the importance of emotion, but rather as its validation. The underlying assumption here is that emotional loading can be so powerful that it simply becomes the dominant influence, and may lead to results unrelated to the underlying truth or falsity of the criminal accusation. Jury instructions that commonly tell jurors not to be influenced by emotion (Feigenson 1997) raise similar questions.

The role of emotion in a Rule 403 context is an empirical question, and one that has not been sufficiently tested. As Posner, no friend of emotion in judgment, puts it:

> the law has an elaborate set of doctrines for fending off dangerous intrusions of emotion into the judicial process . . . . A proper understanding and critique of these rules [of evidence] might profit greatly from a careful examination of them in the light cast by the systematic study of the role of emotions in law.

(Posner 1999, p. 327)

Feigenson, who is a friend of emotion, writes:

> Those inclined to take emotions in law seriously need whatever guidance empirical research
> can offer about how particular emotions work, what stimuli provoke them, and what effects
> they are likely to have on the various processes of legal judgment, so that they may think
> most productively about whether and how the law should respond to those emotions.
>
> (Feigenson 2001, p. 457)

Studies by Bodenhausen *et al.* (1994*a*, *b*) have shown the influence of emotions on social and quasi-legal judgements in the context of stereotyping. A recent study in which one of us (K.P.) participated (Heekeren *et al.* 2004) investigated the effect of the presence of violence on simple ethical and semantic judgments. We found that presence of violence during moral judgments (but not during semantic judgments) lead to significantly reduced response times and higher immorality ratings, i.e. an interaction of content and task.

We would like to follow up on this approach, first of all to collect expanded behavioural data on the impact of unrelated emotional loading on moral judgment and secondly to clarify how a change in amygdala activity modulates other brain regions engaged in the judgment process (ventromedial prefrontal cortex and posterior superior temporal sulcus) and in which temporal sequence. Such an investigation will require the combination of fMRI with psychophysiological tools of measurement, such as skin conductance and pupil dilation, and/or other brain imaging modalities such as EEG or MEG (cf. Dale & Halgren 2001). We believe that a better understanding of these processes will help guide courts as they interpret Rule 403.

(b) Investigating processing differences between property and intellectual property law

Intellectual property law provides a second example of a programme for possible research based in a neuroscientific approach to legal problems. Intellectual property is becoming increasingly important around the world, and considerable progress has been made in defining the explicit rule structure in both domestic and international law (e.g. Ryan 1998; Merges 2000; Mossinghoff 2000; Goodenough 2002*a*). The problem of promoting *compliance* with these improved legal structures has proved less tractable (Goodenough 2002*a*). This is true not only in such countries as Russia (e.g. Miller 2000) and China (e.g. Allison & Lin 1999; Fan 1999), but also in the USA as well, as widespread music copying through the Internet demonstrates (e.g. A&M Records Inc. versus Napster Inc. 2000, 114 F.Supp. 2d 896 (N.D. Cal.); A&M Records versus Napster Inc. 2001, 239 F.3d 1004 (9th Cir.)) (Landen 2001; Green 2002; see generally Lehman 1995).

To some extent, improved compliance can be produced by better top-down enforcement. The well-publicized campaign by the industry in 2002 to sue grandmothers and teenagers for illegally downloading music files has had some success in diminishing really blatant copying (Colletti 2003; Morrisey & James 2003). The recent adoption by the European Union of a new Intellectual Property Rights Enforcement Directive has extended the possibility of such a campaign to Europe (Lillington 2004).

But compliance rests as much in the expectations and inhibitions of the individuals in society as it does in the adoption of statutes and directives. The very technology that makes information valuable makes copying trivial and nearly undetectable, and for many, many people there is no subjective feeling that such taking is really culpable. Why do people who would feel guilt over taking a pencil happily copy programmes, songs and films without a qualm? Our admittedly anecdotal experience suggests that those cheerfully making illegal copies can often tell you, without any embarrassment, that copyright law exists. It just doesn't change their behaviour. On a very basic level, these copiers do not seem think that this kind of behaviour is *really* wrong.

Our hypothesis is that there is little or no affective component to the understanding of intellectual property in these people. To be effective, a programme to promote intellectual property compliance must not simply make people aware that such laws exist; it must also convince people that the violation of such laws is a serious injustice, invoking the emotional systems in the brain related to such a response (Goodenough 2002*a*). As Casebeer (2003, p. 846) concludes, 'emotion, reason and action are bundled together'.

In proposing this idea, we are turning our recruitment conception of the law back on itself. The ability to recruit passionless processes may be an advantage in some contexts, but it can also be a problem if carried too far. We suggest that some rules—such as our taboos on the theft of tangible objects—exist both in our articulated codes and in our emotionally and intuitively grounded sense of justice. Such rules are likely to be highly internalized in members of society and to evoke the kind of emotional response that will lead to general acceptance, personal observance and vigorous enforcement. In other cases, there may be laws that make excellent sense from an abstract 'policy' standpoint, but which have little support in the mental processes associated with the sense of justice, with predictable results. Our system of intellectual property may be such a case.

Why might there be an emotional deficit at the heart of copyright law? Two possibilities suggest themselves. Some would argue that it is just a matter of education, experience, socialization and fear of punishment. This was the position of the 1995 Working Group on Intellectual Property Rights of the Information Task Force, which suggested that ignorance and confusion were at the heart of the compliance problem and advocated popular education about the law (Lehman 1995). Another possibility is that the mental differences arise from some more fundamental, perceptual differences that implicate an emotional involvement in perceptions about the theft of tangible property but fail to do so for intellectual property. How could this come about?

One answer lies in the important strategic differences between tangible property and intellectual property. Although the solution of assigning ownership in an asset to a particular person is similar, the presenting problem that this is called on to solve is different. Current explanations for the evolvability of property focus on the utility to all players of ownership conventions to defuse rivalry over limited and consumable resources (Maynard Smith & Parker 1976; Stake 2004). Such conventions do not depend on any existing relationship between the parties, but rather an identification between the one of the parties and the resource in question.

It has frequently been noted that intellectual property is not a 'rivalrous' resource. When someone reads a book or listens to a song, that generally does not consume it and exclude someone else from doing the same thing (e.g. Wagner 2003), although there are circumstances where information use can be competitive (e.g. Aviram & Tor 2004). Rather, protecting intellectual property is more in the nature of secret keeping, or holding to a binding promise (Goodenough 2001*b*). In such a context, inhibitions on exploitation and use *do* depend on a relationship between the parties.

It is plausible, if still only a hypothesis, that these strategic differences are represented as cognitive primitives at some point in the recognition of the moral dilemma. If so, we could further imagine that the primitive for a property structure works best with a tangible object and (perhaps) land. Although property may be a good theoretical solution for allocating rights in intangible products of the intellect, it may be that the perceptual equipment of the human brain is simply not set up to recognize them as proper objects for emotionally reinforced normative judgment.

Such a model is currently only speculation. Nonetheless, it has the potential for testing by applying the methods of cognitive neuroscience. Theory arguments suggest that such a difference might exist. From the standpoint of lesion data, we are not aware of any reports of differential property-observing deficits that would support the idea of a property primitive. Nonetheless, such deficits could be masked by other cognitive capacities picking up the slack, i.e. property for the lesion patient becomes more like intellectual property in the rest of us. Given the economic and societal importance of the subject matter and the possibility that expanded knowledge can help shape more effective policy, we believe that this is a legal concern that could repay systematic exploration, using all the tools of cognitive neuroscience.

5.7 Conclusions

The study of normative judgment through the methods of cognitive neuroscience is appropriately hot. Although the discipline is only in the early stages of a complex programme of investigation, we have already seen progress arising from an improved consensus model and data collection using imaging and lesion studies. Normative judgment is well on the way to being a well developed branch of neuroscientific studies. We suggest, however, that there is still some lack of clarity in the underlying modelling of normative processes, and believe that further work, particularly on the nature of emotion and intuition, will yield even better results.

The neuroscientific inquiry into law and justice is in a much earlier phase. A neuroscientific approach, however, has suggested a model for the law involving the broad recruitment and deployment of different systems of mental capacities and sources of information. We can also identify specific areas where neuroscientific methods and data may be of interest to law and policy. There is a great deal of detailed, interdisciplinary work to do; there is also the promise of significant advances to be made.

We thank the Gruter Institute for Law and Behavioral Research, and in particular its executive directors, Monika G. Cheney and the late Dr Margaret Gruter, for their encouragement and financial support for the work reflected in this essay. We thank Professor Paul Zak for his suggestions on an earlier version of this essay. We are also deeply grateful for the learning, advice, collaboration and experimental support of the Berlin NeuroImaging Center (supported by the BMBF), particularly Professor Arno Villringer, its director; Dr Hauke Heekeren; Dr Isabell Wartenburger and of the Wellcome Department of Imaging Neuroscience at University College London; particularly Dr Johannes Schultz, Professor Chris Frith, Professor Semir Zeki, Professor Ray Dolan and Professor Richard Frackowiak. We also thank Professor Elke van de Meer (Department of Psychology, Humboldt-University, Berlin) and Professor Hans-Peter Schwintowski (Department of Law, Humboldt-University, Berlin).

Endnote

1. The relations among religious belief, cognitive processes and brain function are themselves targets of scientific study (e.g. Boyer 2003).

References

Allison, J. R. & Lin, L. 1999 The evolution of Chinese attitudes toward property rights in invention and discovery. *Univ. Pennsylvania J. Int. Econ. Law* **20**, 735–791.

Anderson, A. K. & Phelps, E. A. 2001 Lesions of the human amygdala impair enhanced perception of emotionally salient events. *Nature* **411**, 305–309.

Anderson, A. K. & Phelps, E. A. 2002 Is the human amygdala critical for the subjective experience of emotion? Evidence of intact dispositional affect in patients with amygdala lesions. *J. Cogn. Neurosci.* **14**, 709–720.

Anderson, S. W., Bechara, A., Damasio, H., Tranel, D. & Damasio, A. R. 1999 Impairment of social and moral behavior related to early damage in human prefrontal cortex. *Nature Neurosci.* **2**, 1032–1037.

Angrilli, A., Palomba, D., Cantagallo, A., Maietti, A. & Stegagno, L. 1999 Emotional impairment after right orbito-frontal lesion in a patient without cognitive deficits. *Neuroreport* **10**, 1741–1746.

Aron, A. R., Robbins, T. W. & Poldrack, R. A. 2004 Inhibition and the right inferior frontal cortex. *Trends Cogn. Sci.* **8**, 170–177.

Austin, J. 1832 *The province of jurisprudence determined*, 5th edn., 1885, reprinted 1995. Cambridge University Press.

Aviram, A. & Tor, A. 2004 Overcoming impediments to information sharing. *Alabama Law Rev.* **55**, 231–279.

Baars, B. J., Newman, J. & Taylor, J. G. 1998 Neuronal mechanisms of consciousness: a relational global workspace framework. In *Toward a science of consciousness II: the second Tucson discussions and debates* (ed. S. Hameroff, A. Kaszniak & J. Laukes), pp. 269–278. Cambridge, MA: MIT Press.

Bandes, S.A. 1999 In *The passions of law.* New York University Press.

Bartels, A. & Zeki, S. 2004 The chronoarchitecture of the human brain: functional anatomy based on natural brain dynamics and the principle of functional independence. In *Human brain function*, 2nd edn (ed. R. S. J. Frackowiak, K. J. Friston, C. D. Frith, R. H. Dolan, C. J. Price, S. Zeki, J. Ashburner & W. Penny), pp. 201–229. San Diego, CA: Academic.

Binmore, K. 1994 *Game theory and the social contract, vol. 1: playing fair*. Cambridge, MA: MIT Press.

Binmore, K. 1998 *Game theory and the social contract, vol. 2: just playing (economic learning and social evolution)*. Cambridge, MA: MIT Press.

Blakemore, S.-J., Winston, J. & Frith, U. 2004 Social cognitive neuroscience: where are we heading? *Trends Cogn. Sci.* **8**, 216–222.

Bodenhausen, G. V., Kramer, G. P. & Susser, K. 1994*a* Happiness and sterotypic thinking in social judgment. *J. Personality Social Psychol.* **66**, 621–632.

Bodenhausen, G. V., Sheppard, L. A. & Kramer, G. P. 1994*b* Negative affect and social judgment. The differential impact of anger and sadness. *European J. Social Psychol.* **24**, 45–62.

Boyd, R. & Richerson, P. J. 1982 Cultural transmission and the evolution of cooperative behavior. *Hum. Ecol.* **10**, 325–351.

Boyer, P. 2003 Religious thought and behavior as by-products of brain function. *Trends Cogn. Sci.* **7**, 119–124.

Camille, N., Coricelli, G., Sallet, J., Pradat-Diehl, P., Duhamel, J.-R. & Sirigu, A. 2004 The involvement of orbitofrontal cortex in the experience of regret. *Science* **304**, 1167–1170.

Camerer, C. F. 2003*a* Behavioral studies of strategic thinking in games. *Trends Cogn. Sci.* **7**, 225–231.

Camerer, C. F. 2003*b* Enhanced: strategizing in the brain. *Science* **300**, 1673–1675.

Camerer, C. F., Loewenstein, G. F. & Prelec, D. 2004 Neuroeconomics: how neuroscience can inform economics. *J. Econ. Lit.* (In the press.) Available online at http://papers.ssrn.com/sol3/papers.cfm?abstract_id=590965.

Casebeer, W. D. & Churchand, P. S. 2003 The neural mechanisms of moral cognition: a multiple-aspect approach to moral judgment and decision-making. *Biol. Philosophy* **18**, 169–194.

Casebeer, W. D. 2003 Moral cognition and its neural constituents *Nature Rev. Neurosci.* **4**, 841–846.

Charman, E. A., Honess, T. M. & Levi, M. 2001 Juror competence and processing style in making sense of complex trial information. In *Psychology in the courts international advances in knowledge* (ed. R. Roesch, R. R. Corrado & R. Dempster), pp. 83–96. London: Routledge.

Churchland, P. M. 1991 Folk psychology and the explanation of human behavior. In *The future of folk psychology: intentionality and cognitive science* (ed. J. Greenwood), pp. 51–70 Cambridge University Press.

Colletti, D. J. Jr 2003 Technology under siege: peer-to-peer technology is the victim of the entertainment industry's misguided attack. *George Washington Law Rev.* **71**, 255–271.

Cosmides, L. 1989 The logic of social exchange: has natural selection shaped how humans reason? Studies with the Wason selection task. *Cognition* **31**, 187–276.

Cosmides, L. & Tooby, J. 1987 From evolution to behavior: evolutionary psychology as the missing link. In *The latest on the best: essays on evolution and optimality* (ed. J. Dupre), pp. 277–336. Cambridge, MA: MIT Press.

Cosmides, L. & Tooby, J. 1992 Cognitive adaptations for social exchange. In *The adapted mind* (ed. J. Barkow, L. Cosmides & J. Tooby), pp. 163–228. New York: Oxford University Press.

Coull, J. & Thiele, C. 2004 Functional imaging of cognitive psychopharmacology. In *Human brain function*, 2nd edn (ed. R. S. J. Frackowiak, K. J. Friston, C. D. Frith, R. H. Dolan, C. J. Price, S. Zeki, J. Ashburner & W. Penny), pp. 303–327. San Diego, CA: Academic.

Cowan, T. A. 1965 *Non-rationality in decision theory*. Berkeley, CA: Space Sciences Laboratory, University of California.

Crain, W. C. 2000 *Theories of development*, 4th edn. Upper Saddle River, NJ: Prentice-Hall.

Dale, A. M. & Halgren, E. 2001 Spatiotemporal mapping of brain activity by integration of multiple imaging modalities. *Curr. Opin. Neurobiol.* **11**, 202–208.

Damasio, A. R. 1994 *Descartes' error: emotion, reason, and the human brain*. New York: G.P. Putnam's Sons.

Damasio, A. R. 1996 The somatic marker hypothesis and the possible functions of the prefrontal cortex. *Phil. Trans. R. Soc. Lond.* B **351**, 1413–1420.

Damasio, A. R. 1997 Neuropsychology: toward a neuropathology of emotion and mood. *Nature* **386**, 769–770.

Damasio, A. R. 1999 *The feeling of what happens: body and emotion in the making of consciousness*. New York: Harcourt.

Damasio, H., Grabowski, T., Frank, R., Galaburda, A. M. & Damasio, A. R. 1992 The return of Phineas Gage: clues about the brain from the skull of a famous patient. *Science* **264**, 1102–1108.

Damon, W. 1988 *The moral child*. New York: Free Press.

Dancy, J. 1990 Intuitionism. In *A companion to ethics* (ed. P. Singer), pp. 411–420. Oxford: Blackwell.

Darwin, C. 1872 *The expression of emotion in man and animals*. New York: D. Appleton and Company.

Davidson, R. J., Scherer, K. R. & Goldsmith, H. H. 2002 *Handbook of affective sciences*. Oxford University Press.

Davis, M., Stone, T. 1995 In *Folk psychology: the theory of mind debate* Oxford: Blackwell.

Dehaene, S. & Naccache, L. 2001 Towards a cognitive neuroscience of consciousness: basic evidence and a workspace framework. *Cognition* **79**, 1–37.

Deigh, J. 1999 Emotion and the authority of law: variation on themes in Bentham and Austin. In *The Passions of law* (ed. S. Bandes), pp. 285–308. New York University Press.

de Souza, R. 1987 *The rationality of emotion*. Cambridge, MA: MIT Press.

de Waal, F. B. M. 1996 *Good natured: the origins of right and wrong in humans and other animals*. Cambridge, MA: Harvard University Press.

Dolan, R. J. 1999 On the neurology of morals. *Nature Neurosci.* **2**, 297–299.

Dolan, R. J. 2002 Emotion, cognition, and behavior. *Science* **298**, 1191–1194.

Döring, S. A. 2003 Explaining action by emotion. *Phil. Q.* **53**, 214–223.

Döring, S.A. & Mayer, V. 2002 In *Die Moralität der Gefühle*. Berlin: Akademie.

Duval, S. & Wicklund, R. A. 1972 *A theory of objective self-awareness.* New York: Academic.

Evans, J. S. B. T. 2003 In two minds: dual-process accounts of reasoning. *Trends Cogn. Sci.* **7**, 454–459.

Etzioni, A. 1988 Normative-affective factors: towards a new decision-making model. *J. Econ. Psychol.* **9**, 125–150.

Fan, J. 1999 The dilemma of China's intellectual property piracy. *UCLA J. Int. Law Foreign Affairs* **4**, 207–236.

Fehr, E. & Fischbacher, U. 2004 Social norms and human cooperation. *Trends Cogn. Sci.* **8**, 185–190.

Fehr, E. & Gächter, S. 2002 Altruistic punishment in humans. *Nature* **415**, 137–140.

Feigenson, N. 1997 Sympathy and legal judgment. *Tennessee Law Rev.* **65**, 1–78.

Feigenson, N. 2000 *Legal blame: how jurors think and talk about accidents.* Washington, DC: American Psychological Association.

Feigenson, N. 2001 'Another thing needful': exploring emotions in law. (Reviewing the passions of law, Susan A. Bandes editor.). *Const. Comm.* **18**, 445–461.

Finger, S. 2000 *Minds behind the brain: a history of the pioneers and their discoveries.* Oxford University Press.

Frackowiak, R. S., Friston, K. J., Frith, C. D., Dolan, R. J. & Mazziolta, J. C. 1997 *Human brain function.* San Diego, CA: Academic.

Frackowiak, R. S., Friston, K. J., Frith, C. D., Dolan, R. J., Price, C. J., Zeki, S., Ashburner, J. & Penny, W. 2004 *Human brain function,* 2nd edn. San Diego, CA: Academic.

Frank, R. H. 1988 *Passions within reason: the strategic role of the emotions.* New York: W.W. Norton.

Fridja, N. 1986 *The emotions.* Cambridge University Press.

Friston, K. 2004 Functional integration in the brain. In *Human brain function,* 2nd edn (ed. R. S. J. Frackowiak, K. J. Friston, C. D. Frith, R. H. Dolan, C. J. Price, S. Zeki, J. Ashburner & W. Penny), pp. 971–997. San Diego, CA: Academic.

Frith, C., Gallagher, H. & Maguire, E. 2004 Mechanisms of control. In *Human brain function,* 2nd edn (ed. R. S. J. Frackowiak, K. J. Friston, C. D. Frith, R. H. Dolan, C. J. Price, S. Zeki, J. Ashburner & W. Penny), pp. 329–362. San Diego, CA: Academic.

Gazzaniga, M. S. 1992 *Nature's mind.* New York: Basic Books.

Gazzaniga, M. S., Ivry, R. B. & Mangum, G. R. 2002 *Cognitive neuroscience: the biology of the mind.* New York: W.W. Norton.

Gewirtz, P. 1996 On 'I know it when I see it'. *Yale Law J.* **105**, 1023–1047.

Gigerenzer, G. 1997 The modularity of social intelligence. In *Machiavellian intelligence II: extensions and evaluations* (ed. A. Whiten & R. W. Byrne), pp. 264–288. Cambridge University Press.

Gill, R. 1995 *A textbook of Christian ethics.* Edinburgh: T. & T. Clark.

Glimcher, P. 2003 *Decisions, uncertainty, and the brain: the science of neuroeconomics.* Cambridge, MA: MIT Press.

Goel, V. & Dolan, R. J. 2001 Functional neuroanatomy of three-term relational reasoning. *Neuropsychologia* **39**, 901–909.

Goel, V. & Dolan, R. J. 2003 Explaining modulation of reasoning by belief. *Cognition* **87**, B11–B22.

Goel, V., Buechel, C., Frith, C. D. & Dolan, R. J. 2000 Dissociation of mechanisms underlying syllogistic reasoning. *Neuroimage* **12**, 504–514.

Goodenough, O. R. 1996 *Privacy and publicity: society, doctrine and the development of law.* London: The Intellectual Property Institute.

Goodenough, O. R. 1997a Biology, behavior, and criminal law: seeking a responsible approach to an inevitable interchange. *Vermont Law Rev.* **22**, 263–294.

Goodenough, O. R. 1997b Retheorizing privacy and publicity. *Intellectual Property Q.* **1**, 37–70.

Goodenough, O. R. 2001a Mapping cortical areas associated with legal reasoning and with moral intuition. *Jurimetrics,* **41**, 429–442.

Goodenough, O. R. 2001b Law and the biology of commitment. In *Evolution and the capacity for commitment* (ed. R. M. Nesse), pp. 262–291. New York: Russell Sage Foundation.

Goodenough, O. R. 2002*a* The future of intellectual property: broadening the sense of 'ought'. *Eur. Intellectual Property Rev.* **24**, 6–8.

Goodenough, O. R. 2002*b* Information replication in culture: three modes for the transmission of culture elements through observed action. In *Imitation in animals and artifacts* (ed. K. Dautenhahn & C. L. Nehaniv), pp. 573–585. Cambridge, MA: MIT Press.

Goodenough, O. R. 2004 Responsibility and punishment: whose mind? A response. *Phil. Trans. R. Soc. B* **359**, 1805–1809. (doi:10.1098/rstb.2004.1548)

Goodwin, C. J. 1999 *A history of modern psychology*. New York: Wiley.

Green, M. 2002 Note: Napster opens Pandora's Box: examining how file-sharing services threaten enforcement of copyright on the internet. *Ohio State Law J.* **63**, 799–831.

Greene, J. 2003 From neural 'is' to moral 'ought': what are the moral implications of neuroscientific moral psychology? *Nature Rev. Neurosci.* **4**, 847–849.

Greene, J. & Haidt, J. 2002 How (and where) does moral judgment work? *Trends Cogn. Sci.* **6**, 517–523.

Greene, J., Sommerville, R. B., Nystrom, L. E., Darley, J. M. & Cohen, J. D. 2001 An fMRI investigation of emotional engagement in moral judgment. *Science* **293**, 2105–2108.

Gruter, M. 1992 An ethological perspective on law and biology. In *The sense of justice: biological foundations of law* (ed. R. D. Masters & M. Gruter), pp. 95–105. Newbury Park, CA: Sage.

Haidt, J. 2001 The emotional dog and its rational tail: a social intuitionist approach to moral judgment. *Psychol. Rev.* **108**, 814–834.

Haidt, J. 2003 The moral emotions. In *Handbook of affective sciences* (ed. R. J. Davidson, K. R. Scherer & H. H. Goldsmith), pp. 852–870. Oxford University Press.

Hallaq, W. B. 1997 *Islamic legal theories*. Cambridge University Press.

Hansen, C. 1991 Classical Chinese ethics. In *A companion to ethics* (ed. P. Singer), pp. 69–81. Oxford: Blackwell.

Hart, H. L. A. 1961 *The concept of law*. Oxford: Clarendon.

Hatfield, E., Cacioppo, J. T. & Rapson, R. L. 1993 *Emotional contagion*. Cambridge University Press.

Heekeren, H. R., Wartenburger, I., Schmidt, H., Schwintowski, H. P. & Villringer, A. 2003 An fMRI study of simple ethical decision-making. *Neuroreport* **14**, 1215–1219.

Heekeren, H. R., Wartenburger, I., Schmidt, H., Prehn, K., Schwintowski, H. P. & Villringer, A. 2004 Influence of bodily harm on neural correlates of semantic and moral decision-making. *Neuroimage.* (In the press.)

Henry, J. P. 1986 Neuroendocrine patterns of emotional response. In *Emotion: theory, research, and experience*, vol. 3 (ed. R. Plutchik & H. Kellerman), pp. 37–60. New York: Academic.

Hensen, R. 2004 Analysis of fMRI time series. In *Human brain function*, 2nd edn (ed. R. S. J. Frackowiak, K. J. Friston, C. D. Frith, R. H. Dolan, C. J. Price, S. Zeki, J. Ashburner & W. Penny), pp. 793–822. San Diego, CA: Academic.

Hinde, R. A. 2004 Law and the sources of morality. *Phil. Trans. R. Soc. B* **359**, 1685–1695. (doi:10.1098/ rstb.2004.1542)

Hoffman, M. 1983 Affective and cognitive processes in moral internalization. In *Social cognition and social behavior* (ed. E. T. Higgins, D. N. Ruble & W. W. Hartup), pp. 236–274. Cambridge University Press.

Hoffman, M. B. 2004 The neuroeconomic path of the law. *Phil. Trans. R. Soc. B* **359**, 1667–1676. (doi:10.1098/ rstb.2004.1540)

Holmes, O. W. Jr 1881 *The common law*. Boston: Little, Brown & Co.

Hourani, G. 1985 *Reason and tradition in Islamic ethics*. Cambridge University Press.

Hume, D. 1739–40 *A treatise of human nature*. Variously reprinted, and available at http://socserv2.mcmaster.ca/~econ/ugcm/3ll3/hume/treat.html.

Humphreys, G. W. & Price, C. J. 2001 Cognitive neuropsychology and functional brain imaging: implications for functional and anatomical models of cogntion. *Acta Psychologica* **107**, 119–153.

Jones, E. E. & Nisbett, R. E. 1972 The actor and the observer: divergent perceptions of the causes of behavior. In *Attribution: perceiving the causes of behavior* (ed. E. E. Jones, D. Kanouse,

H. H. Kelley, R. E. Nisbett, S. Valins & B. Weiner), pp. 79–94. Morristown, NJ: General Learning Press.

Jones, O. 2001*a* Time-shifted rationality and the law of law's leverage: behavioral economics meets behavioral biology. *NW U. Law Rev.* **95**, 1141–1206.

Jones, O. 2001*b* Evolutionary analysis in law: some objections considered. *Brooklyn Law Rev.* **67**, 207–232.

Kagan, J. 1984 *The nature of the child*. New York: Basic Books.

Kahneman, D. 1974 Cognitive limitations and public decision making. Science and absolute values. In *Proc. Third Int. Conf. on the Unity of the Sciences*, pp. 1261–1281. London: International Cultural Foundation.

Kahneman, D. 2002 *Autobiography*. Stockholm: Nobel Museum. Available at http://www.nobel.se/economics/laureates/2002/kahneman-autobio.html.

Kahneman, D. & Frederick, S. 2002 Representativeness revisited: attribute substitution in intuitive judgment. In *Heuristics & biases: the psychology of intuitive judgment* (ed. T. Gilovich, D. Griffin & D. Kahneman), pp. 49–81. Cambridge University Press.

Kahneman, D. & Tversky, A. 1979 Prospect theory: an analysis of decisions under risk. *Econometrica* **47**, 313–327.

Kant, E. 1953 *Groundwork of the metaphysic of morals* (trans. H. J. Paton). New York: Harper & Row.

Kelsen, H. 1934 *Reine Rechtslehre, Einleitung in die Rechtswissenshaftliche Problematik*. Leipzig: Franz Deuticke. Translated in *Introduction to the problems of legal theory*, 1992. Oxford: Clarendon.

Kemper, T.D. 1990 In *Research agendas in the sociology of emotions* Albany, NY: State University of New York Press.

Keil, F. C. 2003 Folkscience: coarse interpretations of a complex reality. *Trends Cogn. Sci.* **7**, 368–373.

Knauff, M., Fangmeier, T., Ruff, C. C. & Johnson-Laird, P. N. 2003 Reasoning, models, and images: behavioural measures and cortical activity. *J. Cogn. Neurosc.* **15**, 1–15.

Kohlberg, L. 1969 Stage and sequence: the cognitive-developmental approach to socialization. In *Handbook of socialization theory and research* (ed. D. A. Goslin), pp. 347–480. Chicago, IL: Rand McNally.

Kohlberg, L. 1971 The concepts of developmental psychology as the central guide to education: examples from cognitive, moral, and psychological education. In *Proc. Conf. Psychology and the Process of Schooling in the Next Decade: Alternative Conceptions* (ed. M. C. Reynolds). Reprinted at http://www.xenodochy.org/ex/lists/moraldev.html.

Kohlberg, L. 1981 *The philosophy of moral development*. New York: Harper & Row.

Kohlberg, L. & Candee, D. 1984 The relationship of moral judgment to moral action. In *Morality, moral behaviour and moral development* (ed. W. Kurtines & J. Gewirtz), pp. 52–73. New York: Wiley.

Korobkin, R. B. & Ulen, T. S. 2002 Law and behavioral science: removing the rationality assumption from law and economics. *California Law Rev.* **88**, 1051–1144.

Krieger, L. H. 1995 The content of our categories: a cognitive bias approach to discrimination and equal employment opportunity. *Stanford Law Rev.* **47**, 1161–1248.

LaFollette, H. 2000 In *The Blackwell guide to ethical theory*. Oxford: Blackwell.

Laland, K. N. & Brown, G. R. 2002 *Sense and nonsense: evolutionary perspectives on human behavior*. Oxford University Press.

Landen, J. J. 2001 Beyond Napster: an enforcement crisis in copyright law? *N. Kentucky Univ. Law Rev.* **28**, 713–720.

Langdell, C. C. 1887 Teaching law as a science. *Am. Law Rev.* **21**, 123–125.

Larsen, R. & Buss, D. M. 2002 *Personality: domains of knowledge about human nature*. Boston: McGraw-Hill.

LeDoux, J. 1996 *The emotional brain: the mysterious underpinnings of emotional life*. New York: Simon & Schuster.

Lehman, B. 1995 Intellectual property and the national information infrastructure. In *The Report of the Working Group on Intellectual Property Rights, Information Infrastructure Task Force.* Available at http://www.uspto.gov/web/offices/com/doc/ipnii/.

Lillington, K. 2004 EU copyright directive a bad case of 'Eurogarbage'. *Irish Times* 19 March 2004, 56.

Llewellyn, K. N. 1931 Some realism about realism. *Harvard L. Rev.* **44**, 1222–1264.

McCabe, K. A. & Smith, V. 2000 A two person trust game played by naive and sophisticated subjects. *Proc. Natl Acad. Sci. USA* **97**, 3777–3781.

McCabe, K. A., Rassenti, S. G. & Smith, V. L. 1996 Game theory and reciprocity in some extensive form experimental games. *Proc. Natl Acad. Sci. USA* **93**, 13421–13428.

McCabe, K. A., Rassenti, S. G. & Smith, V. L. 1998 Reciprocity, trust and payoff privacy in extensive form experimental games. *Games Econ. Behav.* **24**, 10–23.

McCabe, K. A., Houser, D., Ryan, L., Smith, V. & Trouard, T. 2001 A functional imaging study of cooperation in two-person reciprocal exchange. *Proc. Natl Acad. Sci. USA* **98**, 11832–11835.

McCrone, J. 1999 *Going inside.* London: Faber and Faber.

McKenzie, C. R. M. 2003 Rational models as theories—not standards—of behavior. *Trends Cogn. Sci.* **7**, 403–406.

Marr, D. 1975 Approaches to biological information processing. *Science* **190**, 875–876.

Masters, R.D. & McGuire, M.T. 1994 In *The neurotransmitter revolution: serotonin, social behavior, and the law.* Carbondale, IL: Sothern Illinois University Press.

Maynard Smith, J. & Parker, G. A. 1976 The logic of asymmetric contests. *Anim. Behav.* **24**, 159–175.

Maynard Smith, J. & Szathmary, E. 1995 *The major transitions in evolution.* Oxford University Press.

Mechelli, A. 2004 Detecting language activations with functional magnetic resonance imaging. In *Human brain function*, 2nd edn (ed. R. S. J. Frackowiak, K. J. Friston, C. D. Frith, R. H. Dolan, C. J. Price, S. Zeki, J. Ashburner & W. Penny), pp. 583–596. San Diego, CA: Academic.

Mellers, B. A., Schwartz, A. & Cooke, A. 1998 Judgment and decision making. *A. Rev. Psychol.* **49**, 447–477.

Merges, R. P. 2000 One hundred years of solicitude: intellectual property law, 1900–2000, in symposium of the law in the twentieth century. *California Law Rev.* **88**, 2187–2240.

Miller, D. E. 2000 Combatting copyright infringement in Russia: a comprehensive approach for western plaintiffs. *Vanderbilt J. Transnational Law* **33**, 1203–1222.

Miller, G. A. 2003 The cognitive revolution: a historical perspective. *Trends Cogn. Sci.* **7**, 141–144.

Moll, J., Eslinger, P. J. & Oliveira-Souza, R. 2001 Frontopolar and anterior temporal cortex activation in a moral judgment task: preliminary functional MRI results in normal subjects. *Arq Neuropsiquiatr.* **59**, 657–664.

Moll, J., Oliveira-Souza, R., Bramati, I. E. & Grafman, J. 2002a Functional networks in emotional moral and nonmoral social judgments. *Neuroimage* **16**, 696–703.

Moll, J., Oliveira-Souza, R., Eslinger, P. J., Bramati, I. E., Mourao-Miranda, J., Andreiuolo, P. A. & Pessoa, L. 2002b The neural correlates of moral sensitivity: a functional magnetic resonance imaging investigation of basic and moral emotions *J. Neurosci.* **22**, 2730–2736.

Moll, J., Oliveira-Souza, R. & Eslinger, P. J. 2003 Morals and the human brain: a working model. *Neuroreport* **14**, 299–305.

Moore, C. J. & Price, C. J. 1999 A functional neuroimaging study of the variables that generate category-specific object processing differences. *Brain* **122**, 943–962.

Morse, S. J. 2004 New neuroscience, old problems. In *Neuroscience and the law: brain, mind and the scales of justice* (ed. B. Garland), pp. 157–198. New York: Dana Press.

Morris, J. & Dolan, R. 2004 Functional neuroanatomy of human emotion. In *Human brain function*,2nd edn(ed.R.S.J. Frackowiak, K. J. Friston, C. D. Frith, R. H. Dolan, C. J. Price, S. Zeki, J. Ashburner & W. Penny), pp. 365–396. San Diego, CA: Academic.

Morrissey, S. & James, P. 2003 The cut-price solution to growth of music piracy. *The Times* 21 October 2003, features, 9.

Mossinghoff, G. J. 2000 National obligations under intellectual property treaties: the beginning of a true international regime. *Federal Circuit Bar J.* **9**, 591–603.

Neisser, U. 1967 *Cognitive psychology*. New York: Appleton.

Nichols, S. 2002 Norms with feeling: towards a psychological account of moral judgment. *Cognition* **84**, 221–236.

Nussbaum, M. 1999 'Secret sewers of vice': disgust, bodies, and the law. In *The passions of law* (ed. S. A. Bandes), pp. 19–62. New York University Press.

O'Neill, O. 1991 Kantian ethics. In *A companion to ethics* (ed. P. Singer), pp. 179–185. Oxford: Blackwell.

Ortony, A., Clore, G. L. & Collins, A. 1988 *The cognitive structure of the emotions.* Cambridge University Press.

Panksepp, J. 1993 Neurochemical control of moods and emotions: amino acids to neuropeptides. In *Handbook of emotions* (ed. M. Lewis & J. M. Haviland), pp. 87–107. New York: The Guilford Press.

Panksepp, J. 1998 *Affective neuroscience: the foundations of human and animal emotions.* Oxford University Press.

Parsons, L. M. 2001 Integrating cognitive psychology, neuroimaging, and neurology. *Acta Psychologica* (Special issue on cognitive neuroscience) **107**, 155–181.

Parsons, L. M. 2003 Exploring the functional neuroanatomy of music performance, perception and comprehension. *Ann. NY Acad. Sci.* **930**, 211–231.

Parsons, L. M. & Osherson, D. A. 2001 New evidence for distinct right and left brain systems for deductive and probabilistic reasoning. *Cerebral Cortex* **11**, 954–965.

Phelps, E. A. 2002 The cognitive neuroscience of emotion. In *Cognitive neuroscience: the biology of mind*, 2nd edn (ed. M. S. Gazzaniga, R. B. Ivry & G. R. Mangun), pp. 536–537. New York: Norton.

Piaget, J. 1965 *The moral judgment of the child.* New York: Free Press.

Pigliucci, M. 2003 On the relationship between science and ethics. *Zygon* **38**, 871–894.

Pizarro, D. 2000 Nothing more than feelings? The role of emotions in moral judgment. *J. Theory Social Behav.* **30**, 355–375.

Pizarro, D., Ulmann, E. & Salovey, P. 2003 Asymmetry in judgments of moral blame and praise: the role of perceived metadesires. *Psychol. Sci.* **14**, 267–272.

Plutchik, R. 1980 *Emotion: a psychoevolutionary synthesis.* New York: Harper & Row.

Plutchik, R. 2001 The nature of emotions. *Am. Sci.* **89**, 344–350.

Posner, E. A. 2001 Law and the emotions. *Georgetown Law J.* **89**, 1977–2012.

Posner, M. I. 2003 Imaging a science of mind. *Trends Cogn. Stud.* **7**, 450–453.

Posner, R. 1999 Emotion versus emotionalism in law. In *The passions of law* (ed. S. Bandes), pp. 309–329. New York University Press.

Posse, S., Muller-Gartner, H. & Dager, S. R. 1996 Functional magnetic resonance studies of brain activation. *Seminars Clin. Neuropsychiatry* **1**, 76–88.

Quinn, P. L. 2000 Divine command theory. In *The Blackwell guide to ethical theory* (ed. H. LaFollette), pp. 53–73. Oxford: Blackwell.

Rawls, J. 1971 *A theory of justice.* Cambridge, MA: Harvard University Press.

Reider, L. 1998 Toward a new test for the insanity defense: incorporating the discoveries of neuroscience into moral and legal theories. *UCLA Law Rev.* **46**, 289–342.

Restak, R. M. 1994 *The modular brain: how new discoveries in neuroscience are answering age-old questions about memory, free will, consciousness, and personal identity.* New York: Charles Scribners Sons.

Rolls, E.T. 1999 *The brain and emotion.* Oxford University Press.

Ryan, M. P. 1998 *Knowledge diplomacy: global competition and the politics of intellectual property.* Washington, DC: The Brookings Institution.

Savoy, R. L. 2001 History and future directions of human brain mapping and functional neuroimaging. *Acta Psychologica* **107**, 9–42.

Scalia, A. 1997 Common law courts in a civil law system: the role of the United States federal courts in interpreting the constitution and laws. In *A matter of interpretation* (ed. A. Gutman), pp. 3–48. Princeton University Press.

Schultz, J., Goodenough, O. R., Frackowiak, R. & Frith, C. D. 2001 Cortical regions associated with the sense of justice and with legal rules. *Neuroimage* **13** (Suppl. 1), S473.

Schwarz, N. 2000 Emotion, cognition, and decision making. *Cogn. Emotion* **14**, 433–440.

Shams, L. & von der Malsburg, C. 2002 Acquisition of visual shape primitives. *Vision Res.* **42**, 2105–2122.

Singer, P. 1991 In *A companion to ethics*. Oxford: Blackwell.

Skinner, B. F. 1953 *Science and human behavior*. New York: Macmillan.

Smith, A. 1776 *An inquiry into the nature and causes of the wealth of nations*. Variously reprinted, including Amherst, New York, Prometheus Books (1991). Available at http://www.econlib.org/library/Smith/smWN.html, from which the quotations here are drawn.

Smith, P. L. & Ratcliff, R. 2004 Psychology and neurobiology of simple decisions. *Trends Neurosci.* **27**, 161–168.

Smith, R. & Cabranes, J. A. 1998 *Fear of judging: sentencing guidelines and the federal courts*. University of Chicago Press.

Smith, V. L. 1982 Microeconomic systems as an experimental science. *Am. Econ. Rev.* **72**, 923–955.

Smith, V. L. 1991 Rational choice: the contrast between economics and psychology. *J. Political Econ.* **99**, 877–897.

Solomon, R.C. 2004 In *Thinking about feeling: contemporary philosophers on emotions*. Oxford University Press.

Sperber, D. 2002 In defense of massive modularity. In *Language, brain and cognitive development: essays in honor of Jacques Mehler* (ed. E. Dupoux), pp. 47–57. Cambridge, MA: MIT Press.

Stake, J. E. 2004 The property 'instinct'. *Phil. Trans. R. Soc. B* **359**, 1763–1774. (doi:10.1098/rstb.2004.1551)

Stephan, A. & Walter, H. 2004 In *Moralität, Rationalität und die Emotionen*. Ulm: Humboldt Universitätsverlag.

Sutherland, S. 1994 *Irrationality: the enemy within*. Harmondsworth, UK: Penguin Books.

Tanford, A. J. 1989 A political-choice approach to limiting prejudicial evidence. *Indiana Law J.* **64**, 831–872.

Taylor, S. E. & Fiske, S. T. 1975 Point of view and perceptions of causality. *J. Personality Social Psychol.* **32**, 439–445.

Thoroughman, K. A. & Shadmehr, R. 2000 Learning of action through adaptive combination of motor primatives. *Nature* **407**, 742–747.

Todorov, E. & Ghahramani, Z. 2003 Unsupervised learning of sensory-motor primitives. In *Proc. 25th Annual Int. Conf. of the IEEE Engineering in Medicine and Biology Society*, New York: IEEE.

Tribe, L. H. 1985 *Constitutional choices*. Cambridge, MA: Harvard University Press.

Tversky, A. & Kahneman, D. 1974 Judgment under uncertainty: heuristics and biases. *Science* **185**, 1124–1131.

Tversky, A. & Kahneman, D. 1981 The framing of decisions and the psychology of choice. *Science* **211**, 453–458.

van der Meer, E. 1989 Impacts of emotions on conceptual structures. In *Cognition in individual and social contexts. Proc. XXIV Int. Congress of Psychology*, vol. 3 (ed. A. F. Bennett & K. M. McConkey), pp. 349–356. Amsterdam: Elsevier.

von Neumann, J. & Morgenstern, O. 1944 *Theory of games and economic behavior*. Princeton University Press.

Wagner, R. P. 2003 Information wants to be free: intellectual property and the mythologies of control. *Columbia Law Rev.* **103**, 995–1034.

Waller, A. L. 1988 *Feud Hatfields, McCoys, and social change in Appalachia 1860–1900*. Chapel Hill, NC: University of North Carolina Press.

Wartenburger, I., Heekeren, H. R., Abutalebi, J., Cappa, S. F., Villringer, A. & Perani, D. 2003 Early setting of grammatical processing in the bilingual brain. *Neuron* **37**, 159–170.

Watson, J. 1924 *Behaviorism*. New York: Norton.

Weinreb, L. L. 1987 *Natural law and justice*. Cambridge, MA: Harvard University Press.

Wilkinson, D. & Halligan, P. 2004 Opinion: the relevance of behavioural measures for functional-imaging studies of cognition. *Nature Rev. Neurosci.* **5**, 67–73.

Wright, R. 2000 Is Prozac driving Wall Street? *Slate* 3 March 2000. Available at http://slate.msn. com/id/76624/.

Zak, P. J. 2004 Neuroeconomics. *Phil. Trans. R. Soc. B* **359**, 1737–1748. (doi:10.1098/rstb. 2004.1544)

Zak, P. J. & Knack, S. 2001 Trust and growth. *Econ. J.* **111**, 295–321.

Zeki, S. 1990 The motion pathways of the visual cortex. In *Vision: coding and efficiency* (ed. C. Blakemore), pp. 321–345. Cambridge University Press.

Zeki, S. 1999 *Inner vision: an exploration of art and the brain*. Oxford University Press.

Zysset, S., Huber, O., Ferstl, E. & von Cramon, Y. D. 2002 The anterior frontomedian cortex and evaluative judgment: an fMRI study. *Neuroimage* **15**, 983–991.

Glossary

BOLD	blood oxygen level dependent
EEG	electroencephalogram
fMRI	functional magnetic resonance imaging
MEG	magnetoencephalogram
PET	positron emission tomography

Neuroeconomics and the law

6

The brain and the law

Terrence Chorvat* and Kevin McCabe

Much has been written about how law as an institution has developed to solve many problems that human societies face. Inherent in all of these explanations are models of how humans make decisions. This article discusses what current neuroscience research tells us about the mechanisms of human decision making of particular relevance to law. This research indicates that humans are both more capable of solving many problems than standard economic models predict, but also limited in ways those models ignore. This article discusses how law is both shaped by our cognitive processes and also shapes them. The article considers some of the implications of this research for improving our understanding of how our current legal regimes operate and how the law can be structured to take advantage of our neural mechanisms to improve social welfare.

Keywords: law; neuroeconomics; neuroscience

6.1 Introduction

For centuries, the study of human behaviour has been distinct from the study of the natural world. Because of the complexity of the brain and our historic lack of understanding of its operations, social science has not focused on the brain, but instead attempted to study that which can be analysed: behaviour itself (Goodenough 2001). For example, Sigmund Freud first began his study of human behaviour with physiological mechanisms but ended this research because the basic science had not yet advanced sufficiently to directly aid him in the understanding of behaviour (Gazzaniga *et al.* 2002). Arguably, his approach to human behaviour ended up deriving more from philosophies of Hegel and Schopenauer than from neuroscientists such as Golgi and Cajal (Jones 1961; Ledoux 2002).

However, in recent decades it has become clear that neuroscience can contribute a great deal to our understanding of human behaviour. Because of recent advances in a variety of disciplines, we are now beginning to witness a merging of the hard and social sciences. Many researchers in human behaviour and biology have adopted an approach, referred to as cognitive neuroscience, that integrates psychology, biochemistry, neurology, evolutionary biology and related sciences to further our understanding of human behaviour (Gazzaniga *et al.* 2002).

Because social scientists have been studying human behaviour for well over a century, they have catalogued a wide array of behaviour and have developed many theories that attempt to explain these behaviours. This detailed observation has been invaluable in building a solid base from which to understand human behaviour. However, one problem is that the theories developed in attempting to explain behaviour are often contradictory. One can see this in the contrasting views of human decision-making used in psychology

* Author for correspondence (tchorvat@gmu.edu).

and standard economics, which famously disagree over the degree to which humans behave rationally (Brocas & Carrillo 2003). This disagreement results in part from the fact that a behaviour itself leaves us with only an artefact which we must then interpret. For any given behaviour, it may be hard to determine if subjects were somehow rationally calculating their choices to maximize either their long-run or short-run interest, or if some other process is involved. Neuroscience can help us to sort through the various possible explanations of behaviour by allowing us to better discriminate between the competing models as a result of the information it gives us about brain mechanisms used to make the decision.

It has long been hypothesized that biological mechanisms can have direct control of our behaviour in particular areas (Lieberman *et al.* 2003). Merely understanding that there may be genetic influences on behaviour does not tell us how this behaviour is created nor how the mechanism used for one problem may influence other types of behaviour. Cognitive neuroscience can help us to resolve these questions, by directly examining the neural mechanisms involved.

One of the most important areas of human behaviour is the creation and enforcement of law. Because the meaning of the term 'law' is not self-evident, we need to be clear that for purposes of this article, the term 'law' means explicit rules by which communities of humans govern themselves. Therefore, law is not custom or other implicit rules that derive from genetic predisposition or cultural mores. Under this definition, only human communities have law, because only human communities have developed communication abilities of a sufficient complexity to consciously decide and promulgate rules (Posner 1983).

Because law can change and these changes are subject to selection pressures, law itself also undergoes evolution. As with other cultural institutions, law probably has experienced a coevolution with the human genome (Bowles *et al.* 2003). There is a continuous interplay between the environment which acts on us in such a way that we create laws to address the problem we confront. These laws then interact with neural mechanisms to create behaviour. This behaviour then affects our environment, completing a circle as illustrated in figure 6.1.

This article examines the implications of the recent research in cognitive neuroscience to study of law. In particular, it examines the effects of the environment on the brain that might lead humans to create law, the effects of law on the neural mechanisms used to perceive and make decisions about the appropriate behaviour, as well as the effect of behaviour on the environment. Traditionally, economics has assumed that the effects of law on the brain operate through what are referred to as utility functions. These are functions which determine the value of any state of the world. It is assumed that humans behave so as to rationally choose the optimal behaviour given their own utility functions

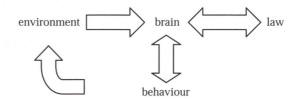

Fig. 6.1 The interaction between the environment, human brains, law and behaviour.

(Mas-Colell *et al.* 1995). Cognitive neuroscience indicates that the actual mechanisms involved are far more complicated than assumed in standard utility theory. This article will first discuss two questions that are foundational to understanding humans behaviour which has particular relevance to the study of law: how the brain maintains cognitive control and how it is able to engage in social interaction which involves trust. It then discusses some of the research that has been performed on how the brain deals with problems directly applicable to law. Finally, it discusses how this research impacts our understanding of the development and function of law.

This article will not discuss some areas of neuroscience research that are commonly addressed in legal scholarship, such as the impact of neuroscience on notions such as insanity and culpability or related notions such as ability to form intent in contact, tort and criminal law. Its focus is the development and the effect of law on the main body of society. As with any area of research, the implications of the research that has already been conducted may be significantly modified by future research. Although we have learned an astonishing amount about the neural basis of human decision making, we are also discovering new information quite literally every day. The intent of this article is to describe some of these findings and how they affect our models of human behaviour and how these affect our understanding of the law.

6.2 Relevant cognitive neuroscience

(a) Neuroscience and the basic issues that each brain must solve

We have seen in the past few decades a massive increase in our understanding of the mechanisms we use to perceive the world around us and those we use to make decisions. Of particular relevance to the study of law are the advances in the understanding of human decision making. To see the impact of neuroscience on the study of law, we will first discuss two key problems directly relevant to legal questions: how human brains maintain cognitive control and how the neural mechanisms are involved in decisions of whether to trust as well as whether to reciprocate trust.

(i) Cognitive control

Cognition is a costly resource. Because brains are finite and because there is a pay-off to increasing our understanding of the world, the constraints on the capabilities of our brains can seriously affect the manner in which functions are performed (Simon 1987). Two key questions are then how does the brain decide which problems it will address, and once this selection has been made, what neural mechanisms are used to solve the problem? The responses to these questions essentially create an economics of neural function. Not surprisingly, it appears that the answers are governed by rules similar to those that economists and operations research specialists use in their optimization calculations. In particular, many biologists argue that the brain consists of modules that solve particular kinds of problems (Wood & Grafman 2003). There are clear evolutionary advantages to this. Humans are confronted with only a finite, although very large, set of problems. Solving the specific problems presented, and having tissues structured for solving those problems would be more efficient than having general purpose tissues, which would probably be more costly, and not as well adapted (Roland & Zilles 1998).

The starting point for understanding the modern research on how specific structures of the brain are adapted for certain functions is the work of Korbinian Brodmann, who in 1909 discovered that the neurons in different areas of the brain exhibit different types of cytoarchitecture (Brodmann 1909). He hypothesized that these different types of tissue performed different functions. This hypothesis has been largely confirmed. Of course, in discussing localization of function, one must also note that generally many different areas of the brain are often invoked in any addressing any single problem. Function is therefore both localized and distributed. The particular pattern for any individual problem is to some degree unique to that problem although it may share similarities with other problems. In some ways this can be can be analogized to an alphabet. A particular sound is represented by a letter (localized), but to write a word or sentence, many letters are required (distributed function).

Because there are a nearly infinite number of stimuli in the world at any given time, to focus on any object, we must decide to ignore some stimuli and focus on others. Even after we are aware of a 'problem', we have many potential mechanisms to use to address the issues it raises. For example, we may react 'emotionally' or 'irrationally'. The research in cognitive neuroscience suggests that different methods of problem solving are located in different parts of the brain. As evidence of this, patients with damage to the ventor-medial PFC are unlikely to exhibit emotional responses to stimuli, whereas those patients with dorsolateral PFC damage appear to have problems in cognitive processing of tasks that do not seem to evoke emotional processing (e.g. the Wisconsin card sorting tasks)[1] (Gazzaniga et al. 2002). Interestingly, both types of reasoning seem to be necessary for optimal problem solving. Because of cognitive limits, it is not the case that one should always use either cognitive processing (or more colloquially 'logic') or affective processing (more colloquially 'emotion'), which has been conditioned by evolutionary pressures to punish or reward behaviour. Because of these conflicts, and the lack of inherent superiority of one mechanism over the other, there needs to be some mechanism to resolve these conflicts. A significant amount of research now focuses on how this resolution occurs. The goal of this research is to discover how we maintain cognitive control over our state of mind as well as our actions (Riling et al. 2002).

One region of the brain that is clearly involved in cognitive conflict resolution is the ACC. This area is currently thought to be involved in registering a conflict between regions. Some researchers argue that after a conflict is recognized, various areas of the PFC also become active and that the choice of regions activated depends on the cognitive requirements of the problem presented (Ponchon et al. 2002). In addition, the context in which the problem is presented may have a significant impact on the mechanism used to address the problem (Metcalfe & Mischel 1999).

Many of the mechanisms used by the brain to deal with situations of cognitive conflict are illustrated in the ultimatum game (which is discussed in § 2b(ii)). The neurological studies of how players of this game make decisions illustrate the mechanisms the brain uses to resolve the conflict between deciding whether to accept money (something generally desired), but at the same time also accepting what individuals are likely to view as an unfair bargain, or to choose to reject the money and enforce fairness. Similar mechanisms appear to be invoked whenever actions against the subject's immediate self-interest are chosen.

How decisions are made and to what extent legal rules affect the various decision mechanisms of cognitive or emotional processing are key questions for the academic study of the law. Some economists have argued that even self-destructive behaviours can best be modelled as rational choices (Becker *et al.* 1991). Whereas others, generally psychologists, argue that these behaviours are the result of lack of control and these individuals did not set out to become criminals or addicts, but these are the results of cognitive or emotional deficits. Both sides have significant evidence for their arguments. The neuroscience of decision making can help us both to understand these situations as well as understand the effects of legal rules in addressing these problems.

(ii) Trust and theory of mind

Another area of research with particular relevance to legal scholarship relates to the notions of trust and TOM. By 'trust', we mean the willingness to behave in such a way that only makes sense if you believe that others will reciprocate any benefits to you extend to them. Robert Axelrod's famous experiments discussed in his books (Axelrod 1982, 1997) describe how cooperation can evolve even in a population of completely self-interested individuals (Samuelson 2002). Even with these arguments, however, the subject of precisely how such trusting and reciprocal behaviour evolved is the subject of some debate (Gintis *et al.* 2003; Nowak *et al.* 2004).

Without some theory of how others will react, many of the predictions of game theory become indeterminate. To illustrate this, consider the centipede game. This game is essentially an multi-round version of the trust game (which is described in § 2b(iii)). The rounds in this game are structured in such a way that if you believe the other player will defect in the next round, you should defect in the current round. However, if they will cooperate in the next round, it makes sense to cooperate in this round as well. Therefore, the predicted strategy of the other player determines your optimal strategy (Camerer 2003*a*, pp. 94–95). The model of the other's persons mind is often referred to as a TOM. The notion of trust and TOM are intimately tied together because inherent in trust must be some theory of what is occurring in mind of the other player (Firth 2001).

Other mechanisms are also involved in trusting behaviour. It appears that trusting behaviour involves an ability to suppress the immediate response to simply take what is in front of them and defect in favour of longer-term goals, which may invoke reciprocity and other social mechanisms. Therefore conflict control is also important (Riling *et al.* 2002).

A relatively simple version of a TOM would be to assume that the other person will do what we would do in the same situation (Stahl & Haruvy 2003; Ramnani & Miall 2004). Recent evidence indicates that determining the actions of others activates regions of the brain that attempt to determine how others will behave by attempting to see how they themselves might behave. The primary areas involved in deriving the TOM appear to be the medial PFC, the related area of the OFC, paracingulate cortex, the temporal poles and the posterior STS (Frith & Frith 2003).

Notions of trust and trustworthiness are integral to our understanding of legal regimes. Degrees of trust, reciprocity and cooperation matter in nearly all areas of law including contracts, business organization law and tax law. The degree of trust in the society matters crucially in structuring nearly all legal rules. In many ways, our institutions in the Western world are dependent on fairly high degrees of trust and trustworthiness. Trust and trustworthiness keep many individuals from violating promises and reduce the incidence of bribery, decrease cheating on tax rules, etc., which then in turn reduce monitoring costs and allow for a more efficient society (Zak & Knack 2001). However, because trust appears to be related to both positive and negative reciprocity (McCabe & Smith 2000; Camerer 2003*b*), there is also a downside to reliance on these mechanisms. When the rules are violated, then harmed individuals often desire to impose greater penalties than are socially optimal. This may result from the evolutionary advantage of having a reputation for over-reacting to violations (Posner 1983). If modern society were to rely on the intuitive mechanisms for enforcement of agreements, for example in the form of vengeance, society would have both over- and under-deterrence of many offences.[2] Furthermore, those who are given power to make decisions about how to spend public money may use these tools for profiting themselves at the expense of society at large. To the extent this occurs, this tends to break down society and governmental structures. Therefore, the optimal set of rules will diminish the opportunities for governmental agents to take these kinds of actions, while still allowing them some freedom to exercise their presumably better knowledge concerning public policy.

This issue raises one of the key problems that law attempts to address: monitoring costs. Even if two parties agree to perform certain actions, how is it that each party attempts to ensure the other side will perform? Monitoring can be a major feature of any agreement. Law can therefore reduce transactions costs by helping to reduce monitoring costs. By studying how it is that we can actually motivate people to behave in optimal manner, we can understand how to reduce monitoring costs. One of the more interesting findings along this line is that CEOs of corporations might actually be more trustworthy than the average person (Fehr & List 2002). Perhaps the process by which they are selected will choose those who are more trustworthy. However, there also may be other explanations of the results. For example, it is not clear if CEOs are innately more trustworthy or if they simply know how to manipulate individuals more. To the extent that already existing processes select for trustworthy behaviour, law makers need to take care not to harm the processes that help to foster trust already in place.

(b) Five areas of neuroscience research of particular application to law

This section discusses five of the most important areas of current research in cognitive neuroscience that concern the understanding of law and its effects: the neurobiology of moral questions, the neural functioning of individuals in ultimatum games and trust games, the neurobiology of social rejection, and finally the research concerning how conscious decisions become automated over time. The section also discusses how this research may help to explain some of the cultural differences we observe in behavioural game-theory experiments and how this can help us to structure rules to encourage socially optimal behaviour.

(i) The resolution of moral dilemmas

Questions, such as what is moral reasoning and how we reason morally, are among the most important questions for legal scholarship. Do we base these decisions on rational reasoning based on explicit rules, or on non-conscious processing (i.e. gut feelings) or something in between? Some argue morality is based on explicit moral reasoning (such as Kantian moral theory) which is independent of any evidence, others that it derives from habits of thought and action that we developed over time (such as Aristotlean virtue ethics). Knowing the answer is important if we wish to influence these decisions by legal rules.

Some fundamental neurological experiments in this area have been conducted by a team at Princeton University (Greene *et al.* 2001). They have investigated the neural mechanisms involved in the reactions of subjects to standard hypothetical moral dilemmas. While using functional magnetic resonance imaging technology to image the brains of the subjects, they asked several questions, including how the subjects would respond if faced with the situation of a train coming down a track, and if they did nothing, the train would hit a car on the track and five people would be killed, and if they pressed a button the train would move down a sidetrack and only one person would be killed. As has been known for many years, most people report they would choose to press the button. Interestingly, the response is quite different if a similar, but slightly different, situation is presented. In this second moral dilemma, the subjects would have to push the person next to them onto the track, killing the other person. Here, most people answer they would not do that. The study shows that the parts of the brain that are actively involved in the decision to push the person are similar to those involved in fear and grief. The decision to flip the switch, which would also result in killing a human, involved far fewer emotional reactions. In particular, the areas more likely to be active in personal moral dilemmas (such as pushing the person on to the tracks) were areas of the medial frontal gyrus (in Broadman areas 9–10), the posterior cingulate gyrus and the bilateral STS. These areas are normally involved in social–emotional processing (Greene & Haidt 2002). The non-moral or impersonal dilemmas (e.g. switching the train track) tend to activate areas in the dorsolateral PFC and the parietal cortex (normally involved in calculation) and executive function (Dehaene 1996). For those subjects who did decide to push the person next to them, one might argue that 'logic' or cognitive processes prevailed over 'emotion'. Interestingly, those who did decide to push the other person took significantly longer in making this decision than those who chose not to push the other person (a difference of 5 s for those who would not push the person versus 6.75 for those who would). There was very little difference between the brain activation or decision time between impersonal moral dilemmas and non-moral dilemmas (less than one-half of a second). This would tend to indicate that the more impersonal the decision becomes, the more we can be 'rational' or rather adopt socially optimal decision-making mechanisms. This suggests that certain types of moral decision making involve a fair amount of social thinking and invoke notions of positive and negative reciprocity, and personalization. Other more recent experiments confirm that the regions of the brain involved in moral processing are also the same regions used in social cognition (Moll *et al.* 2002*a*). One recent study by Moll *et al.*(2002*b*) attempted to separate out the regions involved in moral judgements as opposed to those involved in emotional processing. They found that moral situations differentially activated the STS and the OFC. One key distinction between this experiment and the Greene experiment is that here the subjects were merely reacting to stimuli, not making decisions about how to behave.

Consistent with these experiments as well as many others, it appears that the method of reasoning changes depending on the nature of the problem presented. This may have many applications for our understanding of law and the legal system. For example, in attempting to understand how juries reach the decisions they do, we can see that individuals may make socially optimal choices more when they keep the subjects of the decision at a distance. If the decision is personalized in some way, this can, in and of itself, alter the decision. Of course, more work needs to be done to fully understand what kinds of situations result in personalization and the precise way in which reasoning processes differ between personal and impersonal situations. To the extent that these conclusions from these experiments bear up in further experiments, society may have an interest in depersonalizing problems that are presented to decision-makers. In addition, objectivity may require more than simply not being related or having a direct stake in the outcome. These and other experiments suggest even having to face someone is enough to invoke personal and social triggers (Ledyard 1995). This research may also indicate that society needs to frame interactions so that the 'personalization' will result in actions that are in accord with what is socially optimal, rather than being in conflict with it (e.g. attempt to use personalization to obtain optimal cooperation). One hopes that further research in this area will examine how individuals personalize problems when the stakes to personalization are high.

The decision of whether to take action or not involves apparently both cognitive mechanisms and trust and reciprocity and social mechanisms. Interestingly, the experiments reveal a fair degree of heterogeneity in the population of whether the social mechanism trumps the cognitive or vice versa. Not everyone chose the 'personal' decision over the socially optimal. Furthermore, these experiments suggest the application of the results of one or a group of experiments to a complicated moral situation may not necessarily be straightforward. It appears that moral reasoning is spread across many neural mechanisms (Casebeer & Churchland 2003) and which mechanism dominates for any one problem is complex issue. Any one moral problem may be approached in a very different manner than one that many seem to be similar. Therefore, an important line of future research is to attempt to understand the mechanisms by which problems are interpreted. In particular, how problems become perceived as social and how at other times problems can be interpreted as 'simply' cognitive problems is one of the key questions for understanding the impact of law on behaviour.

(ii) The ultimatum game

The ultimatum game has been one of the most important games used to differentiate actual human behaviour from those of standard non-cooperative game theory. In the standard version of this game, there are two players. The first player is given a 'stake', which can be divided in any way that the first player chooses; however, the second player can veto this distribution, in which case both players get nothing. The traditional game theoretic prediction was that the first player would keep almost all the 'stake', reasoning that the second player will take whatever they can get. Experimental research indicates that this is not generally what occurs. Often, first players offer 40–50% of the stake to the second players. An important feature of the ultimatum game research is that the behaviour of the subjects is generally highly dependent on the particular context in which these decisions are made (Henrich 2000). For example, the offers are substantially reduced if the players competed for the right to be the first player, or if they are framed as competitors (Hoffman *et al.* 1994). Various theories have been created to explain behaviour in the ultimatum game, such as inherent fairness or reciprocity (Fehr & Schmidt 1999).

In studying the neural mechanisms activated by playing the ultimatum game, one study found that 'unfair' offers resulted in activation of areas related both to cognition (e.g. the dorsolateral PFC) and emotion (e.g. the anterior insula) (Sanfey *et al.* 2003). The insula is a cortical region often active in the sensations of disgust, such as bad smells (Camerer *et al.* 2004). There was higher activity in the insula for rejected offers than for accepted offers indicating that emotion and in particular disgust or similar emotions, was part of the motivation in the rejections (Damasio *et al.* 2000; Sanfey *et al.* 2003). The ACC activation indicates that there was a cognitive conflict between accepting the money and the emotional desire to be treated fairly. The brains of the first players were not imaged in this study, because the first players, unbeknown to the second players, were computers.

We suspect that in the case when the status as 'first player' is earned the other players will expect to earn less and so there will be less disgust with lower offers (Holroyd *et al.* 2003). This result would be consistent with both the neural mechanism of cognitive control revealed in this experiment, as well as those revealed in other experiments on rewards (Breiter *et al.* 2001).

(iii) Trust games

Another group of experiments with particular relevance to understanding the creation and function of law are those involving 'trust' games. Trust games involve situations in which one player can increase the pay-off for both players, but for this increase to occur the first player must choose to allow the second player to decide how to split both the amount contributed by the first player and the surplus. That is, the first player would have to trust that the second player will reciprocate the first player's 'contribution' and return some of the added pay-off. Alternatively, the second player could choose to 'defect' (i.e. not exhibit trustworthy behaviour) and optimize their own utility (see figure 6.2). In general, over half the population exhibits both trusting and trustworthy behaviour (Berg *et al.* 1995).

One neuroeconomic study indicates several interesting features of trust games. This study was conducted on 12 right-handed subjects. This experiment had several interesting results. First, those who trusted generally activated similar regions of the brain (in particular, Brodmann areas 8 and 10), which are generally thought to be involved in

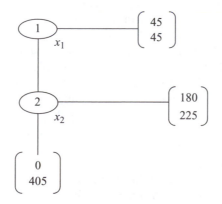

Fig. 6.2 Diagram of the decision tree for the trust game. In the trust game, the first player can either decide to move right, opting to award each player a pay-off of 45, or move down, which gives the second player the ability to decide the outcome of the game. If the second player moves right, the first player will get a pay-off of 180 and the second player will get a pay-off of 225. If the second player moves down, the first player will get a pay-off of 0, and the second player will get a pay-off of 405. In moving down, the first player is effectively trusting the second player to reward the first player by moving left, rather than defecting by moving down.

social cognition. In addition, those who chose not to cooperate generally had patterns of brain activation similar to those who were playing against a machine (McCabe *et al.* 2001). This argues that those who choose to trust are conceiving of the problem as a social problem. Conversely, this evidence indicates that those who did not cooperate perceived the problem more simply as one of maximizing their own utility.

In another study which examined the neurobiology of trust behaviour (Riling *et al.* 2002), 36 right-handed women were studied in trust games. The researchers found that those who trusted were more likely to have higher activation of the nucleus accumbens, the caudate nucleus, ventormedial frontal and orbitofrontal cortex and the rostral ACC. These areas are all commonly involved in emotional processing. They studied what mechanisms are used to overcome that natural desire to defect and take the prize in favour of exercising reciprocal altruism. This study seems to indicate that emotional responses may be important in trust as well.

(iv) The interplay between rejection and other forms of enforcement

Some evolutionary psychologists argue that social rejection might be encoded in our brain as pain because those who are motivated to maintain group relations would be more likely to survive. Therefore, finding pain and suffering in social rejection may be an optimal evolutionary response for individuals (La Ferrara 2003). In a noisy environment, individuals should be sensitive to perceptions of others about reciprocity and trustworthiness, and should be motivated to maintain positive relations even if they themselves are unaware of a violation. If these models are correct then, social exclusion can be a significant enforcement mechanism. One study that supports this view (Eisenberger *et al.* 2003) found that the ACC was more active when a participant was excluded from a virtual ball-toss game played on the computer with others. The researchers noted that physical pain also activates the ACC in similar way, and as discussed earlier, the ACC seems to be a conflict-monitoring circuit.[3] In addition, the authors found significant activity in the right ventral PFC which is thought (through efferent connections to ACC) to be involved in the regulation of pain. Thus, the activation from intentional social exclusion is similar to what one finds when actual physical pain occurs (Coghill *et al.* 1999). The researchers also compared this with the activation in situations where the subjects were excluded from the game, but were told this was because of technical difficulties. Here, they found that there was also ACC activation, but the activation in the right ventral PFC was significantly less. This could be explained if the subjects still experienced some conflict from being excluded, but it was not as acute as when they were intentionally excluded.

These findings might help to explain how culture can constrain individuals. We desire to be in the 'in-group', but not necessarily as a result of a conscious rational calculation of the benefits it will generate for us. To see how this might apply to the law, one should first note that penalties meted out by legal authorities can either conflict with or align themselves with group pressures. To the extent the latter happens, enforcement of the laws may be cheaper and more effective. Because social pressure can create actual pain, the law should attempt to align this pain with the socially desired behaviour.

(v) Automation

Another key finding in neuroscience is the ability for the brain to 'automate' processes that had previously required conscious thought, thereby conserving cognitive resources.

The idea is that if there is a behaviour that we commonly perform, we simply begin to perform the action without much thought (Heiner 1983). In fact, the brain is continually 'automating' much of our behaviour (Gazzaniga *et al.* 2002). As many have pointed out, it would be impossible to make all the calculations we need for daily life consciously. Perhaps the most familiar example of 'automation' is learning to ride a bicycle. We have to do it consciously at first, but then over time we simply do it 'without thinking' (Roth 2004). This occurs because conscious processing is apparently more costly than unconscious processing. That cognitive processing is a scarce resource has been understood for decades, whereas unconscious parallel processing seems significantly less limited (Miller 1956). This process may help to explain behaviour such as that observed in the ultimatum game when the same subjects (who are in the position of player two) are knowingly playing with a computer, and the computer has given them a 'bad' deal, they may still attempt to punish it. This indicates personification or at least the carrying over of models that one uses in everyday life to situations where personal models are not particularly helpful. To the extent that behaviour becomes automated, this may have effects on things such as compliance with law, or systematic biases which can have detrimental effects of society.

A variety of theories have been proposed to explain how this occurs. Marcus Raichle and Steven Peterson have proposed a 'scaffold to structure theory'. Under this theory, learning a task first requires conscious processing until the memory is consolidated. Once the brain activity is learned, brain activity and involvement change, or in terms of the model, the scaffolding is removed. Using positron emission tomography scans, they demonstrated that conscious processing uses a different network of brain regions than does learned unconscious processing. Another study examined the neural activity of expert chess players playing largely by intuition (Chabris & Hamilton 1992). For novices, the lightning fast play of experts is impossible, whereas for those with the proper level of experience, this type of play is automatic. The research in this area indicates that there is a high activation in the PFC during the process of learning a task, but as it is learned, the parietal, temporal and sub-cortical regions become relatively more active. If, as is often thought, 'executive function' is similar to conscious functions, these findings are indicative of lower conscious activation in the learned task. By this mechanism, the brain economizes on scarce cognitive resources.

This research has a variety of consequences for legal scholarship. For example, cultural differences in trust games and ultimatum games may be a result of automated processes that result from observing others around them and developing certain notions of trust and trustworthiness in similar situations (Henrich 2000). Law is intended to create context in which cooperative and other socially optimal behaviour is beneficial. This research indicates that such learned behaviour can in fact be altered (Ledoux 2002), yet to the extent it has become automated, it may take time and significant resources to alter behaviour in the preferred manner. In addition, one of the hopes for the law is that it will be able to influence behaviour even when it is too costly to monitor behaviour directly. To the extent we understand how behaviour and decisions are automatic, we can hopefully use this to influence choices and 'automate' trust and trustworthiness.

That culture can have a significant impact on the way in which initial decisions are made is shown by the experiments in which initial behaviour is different and more cooperative than after multiple rounds of behaviour (Palfrey & Prisbey 1997). At a minimum, we need to establish a framework in which cooperative behaviour that already exists is not unlearned. One study conducted by a group of very prominent evolutionary psychologists, game theorists and others shows that initial behaviour in economics experiments generally reflects the everyday level of cooperation within the society (Henrich *et al.* 2001).

6.3 The impact of cognitive neuroscience on the study of law

(a) The development of the law

Many authors have discussed how a basic form of society could exist without laws as we use the term (Ellickson 1994). In such situations, custom or other norms have arisen over time without an explicit central authority issuing them. It is often discussed how Homeric Greek society and Medieval Icelandic society, as exhibited in the epics written about them, seem to have existed without central authorities to promulgate rules (Miller 1996). These societies probably exemplify the environment in which human brains evolved, i.e. without explicit authority and with frequent repeat interactions. Evolutionary psychology and neuroeconomics demonstrate that our brains are well adapted to dealing with personal exchange: monitoring and reaching optimal levels of cooperation within reasonably small groups. How these norms and conventions are created is probably a result of the coevolution of culture and genetic expression (Bowles *et al.* 2003). As many authors have noted, a modern society could not really exist entirely based on reputation. We simply have too many small interactions with too many people for this to function. However, there are probably intermediate situations in which certain members or groups of society may function as go-betweens trusted by all members of society (McCabe & Smith 2000). But even in these situations reputation is the operative force. It is merely that certain members of society have been allocated the task of coordinating the trust relationships, which can economize on the number of goodwill accounts. In fact, even modern society relies to an enormous degree on reputation and repeat dealing. Most interactions, above a certain minimal threshold, that we have on a daily basis involve a fair amount of personal interaction. In a world where there is repeated interaction all the time, someone who calculates whether they will cooperate each time will be spending too many resources on making these calculations. Therefore having a default of cooperation results in saving cognitive energy.

Impersonal exchange is often a much more efficient exchange mechanism, as the Internet merchants like eBay have demonstrated. It is probably the case that, for most goods the most efficient supplier of the goods does not personally know those who value the goods the most, and so impersonal exchange can be substantially more efficient in many circumstances than personal exchange.

One way to understand the development of law is through the framework put forth by Tooby & Cosmides (1996) to explain human behaviour. This approach focuses on the interplay between the adaptive or evolutionary problem which the behaviour in question evolved to address, the cognitive programme used to solve this problem, and the particular neurophysiological mechanism used to enact this cognitive programme. One of the benefits of this approach is that it helps us to understand both the original benefits of the behaviour, as well as the limitations the solutions impose on us today.

Our brains developed at a time when the economies of scale of the existing technologies were relatively limited. In such circumstances, personal exchange is a very efficient model of trade. At some point in human evolution, technology developed in such a way that many products could be more efficiently produced for large groups than they could for small groups. Therefore, to take advantage of these technologies, humans needed to develop institutions that could foster trust in these larger groups (Arrow 1974). At first, intermediate steps, such as those previously described of having go-betweens or 'middle-men' may have been sufficient (McCabe & Smith 2000). However, mechanisms such as this can create high transaction costs if sufficiently large groups need to be involved (for example, one can think of the transaction costs of the Silk Road). Although these regimes worked for many years and in many places where the technology that existed did not require mass population for its optimal operation, as technology developed further, there became advantages to trading over larger areas. Legal regimes that allow one to seek restitution even from parties one does not know personally increases willingness to deal with those with whom one has not yet had repeated dealings. For these legal regimes not to collapse, there needs to some mechanism of enforcement which all parties trust. Many authors have discussed the development of law and the efficiency of legal regimes in these circumstances (North 1991). However, all of these legal regimes involve individuals whose reasoning mechanisms are adapted to different situations. By studying precisely how these mechanisms function, as well as how other decision-making mechanisms operate, we can better understand the limits and proper scope of law.

As discussed above, for a non-governmental state to function (as they did in Homeric Greece and medieval Iceland), there must a great deal of positive and negative reciprocity (e.g. revenge).[4] In addition, because game-theoretic concerns are important, understanding the other person's strategy is also important. This means that mechanisms such as TOM are crucial for such societies. When transactions beyond the family or local group were necessary, these would generally involve interacting with individuals who were either known to the group, or who were members of a family that had frequent interactions with the group (La Ferrera 2003). In the society that existed in many ancient cultures, people knew each other very well, or certainly knew the reputation of those connected to those with whom they are dealing. Therefore, the information about parties' behaviour was not as asymmetric as is the case with the impersonal dealing we have today. In addition, because of these and other personalizing features of these relationships, such as repeat bargaining and social sanctioning, behaving in a cooperative manner was very likely to be favoured. If the rational strategy is to cooperate, one can see how it is efficient to save cognitive calculation by simply having this as the initial first offer. This would be optimal because most decisions most of the time are made on the basis of heuristics and emotion, and such processing is cheaper.

(b) The impact of law

In small groups with repeat interactions, generally private law as we know it is not necessary. Honour and similar behavioural restraints would ensure that the parties to agreements would not generally defect, because in such situations reputation and the threat of punishment matter. Hence, early societies were probably able to solve these simple material allocation problems fairly easily once modern humans evolved. However, as discussed above, as larger social interactions became both possible and necessary, reliance on these mechanisms of personal reciprocity became suboptimal. First, where reputations are either not well known, or if the impact of defection in one case would not significantly impact reputation, trust can be diminished. Second, it is not always optimal from a social perspective that contracts are honoured, and so there needed to be some mechanism to ensure that agreements are not over-enforced as well.

Neural mechanisms that may have evolved to punish 'defectors' within a group are suboptimal for many important functions in large societies. We may prefer to use these 'personal' mechanisms for interacting with others because they involve use of fewer cognitive resources than impersonal bargaining. Personal exchange appears to be more automatic. However, impersonal exchange can often be more efficient and can allow for fewer resources spent on developing networks, etc. that are not directly productive. So for society to advance further, there would need to be some mechanism that would both allow impersonal bargaining to occur by linking it to generally applicable cognitive patterns, as well as reducing the effects of patterns of cognition applicable to personal bargaining which may impede impersonal bargaining.

One of the key functions of law is to create at least some minimal levels of trust between persons who have not previously had reason to trust each other. This can actually help to foster a greater network of trust relationships by creating networks of interactions. That is, exchanges that might not take place because of an initial lack of trust will now occur, and because of these transactions more goodwill accounts are generated, where they would not have been before. By facilitating impersonal exchange, law may be helping to foster greater and more efficient investment in personal exchange as well. One cautionary note about this description is that because law is generally generated by a subgroup, it most probably will operate to promote that subgroup's welfare. Therefore, it is not necessarily the case that law will always create the optimal level of impersonal exchange if that will come at the expense of the ruling groups welfare. However, legal regimes are only likely to be selected if they do not create enormous amounts of social strife and to the extent one group reduces the welfare of society, there will be pressure to change.

Legal enforcement of agreements is likely to create at least two positive effects. It reduces the loss to the individual from potential defection by others, which would both encourage more interactions and reduce the desire to spend resources on offensive and defensive capabilities. In addition, because those who are defected against do not share in the benefits of defection, a successful evolutionary strategy would be to punish defection by others excessively. Others will be less likely to defect against those who adopt this strategy. As a consequence, neural mechanisms have developed to exhibit punishment behaviour even when it is not efficient from a societal perspective (for example, the punishment behaviour of ultimatum games). Therefore, a key element of law may be to diminish the desire for negative reciprocity to the socially optimal level.

In many ways, one can argue that the effect of law is to operate in connection with impersonal exchange as a substitute for the trust mechanisms that operate in personal exchange. We discussed earlier how these trust mechanisms can help to ensure optimal behaviour. Law then needs to foster optimal behaviour in the absence of standard personal bargaining.

One thing that is clear from the experimental economics literature is that the institutional structure used can have a large impact on the efficiency of the outcome (Smith 1982). To be effective, an institution has to be able to convey messages to the members of the society in a form that they will be able to interpret and which will cause them to generate optimal exchange solutions. Therefore an efficient institution will be structured to account for our desires for personal exchange and the neural mechanisms of social exchange used in personal exchange.

Governmental agents will attempt to develop institutions to encourage compliance with their decisions. In so doing, it will have to implicitly or explicitly rely on the neural mechanisms discussed early to encourage compliance with public obligations. Often the government will attempt to rely on mechanisms that were developed for both negative and positive reciprocity to encourage compliance. As discussed earlier, emotional or automatic processes allow for quick reactions which can save on 'expensive' cognitive processing. If it can frame violations of its rules as defections from social norms, they are more likely to be punished and often private punishment is enough to enforce this obligation. To the extent that society is able to frame defection as cheating and invoke social sanctions, enforcement will become easier. It is likely that compliance with directives of newly formed governments that differ from traditional obligations will evoke only cognitive and rational responses, at least initially. Those societies that have attempted to supplant smaller group loyalties too quickly have often been unsuccessful, whereas those who were able to co-opt local individuals with influence and leaders of pre-existing social groups have been more successful. In so doing, they are able to align social sanctions with the new regulatory structure. Therefore, initially explicit rules may be necessary to enforce compliance, but if over time others begin to observe general compliance, they too may begin to comply regularly, and not only because of rational calculation (Carpenter 2004).

Governments that are able to develop institutions which extend the scope of trust and trust-like relationships are likely to yield efficient outcomes. The neurological evidence indicates that individuals are likely to switch from perceiving a situation as one of impersonal exchange to viewing it as one of personal exchange, with very little change to the underlying facts. This particular feature of human behaviour can both help to foster optimal social behaviour (e.g. cooperation with those we barely know) and create harmful social behaviour (e.g. the awarding of the benefits of public funds to friends of governmental agents). Interestingly, research that is being conducted in areas like neuromarketing may be able to help governments to understand the impact of various types on institutional structure.

It is likely that punishment of violations will always have to be part of the arsenal of any government authority, because of the heterogeneity of the population. In fact, the problem may be even more entrenched owing to the evolutionary game theoretic predictions that such heterogeneity is a stable equilibrium (Harsanyi 1973).[5]

6.4 Conclusion

In many ways the creation of modern society, with its reliance on impersonal exchange, is astounding, given the preference for personal bargaining that we exhibit. Many institutions have developed to make use of the mechanisms that we have for trust and reciprocity. For example, it is often said that soldiers do not fight for the army as whole as much as they fight for their immediate platoon or squad. By organizing soldiers into groups of a size where repeat interactions are common, they each will begin to behave cooperatively with other and will behave altruistically as well. This is an example of a social ordering that was explicitly created to take advantage of particular features of human behaviour. Research shows that human behaviour is a function of a complex interaction of neural mechanisms. By understanding the neural mechanism, which we use to solve problems, we can hope to create laws and other rules that will help to foster socially optimal behaviour. Such research has already given us important insights into behaviour. However, future research is likely to be able to tell us how to significantly enhance compliance with law at a minimal cost and to encourage better forms of social interaction. This research will probably completely change the way we view nearly every area of law.

T.C. thanks the Law and Economics Center and the Lawrence Cranberg Fellowship for their support. Both authors thank Oliver Goodenough and two anonymous reviewers for their comments.

Endnotes

1. The Wisconsin Card Sorting Task involves sorting cards that have objects on them that vary along three dimensions: shape, colour and number. The cards are to be sorted according to a method determined by the experimenter, but not explicitly told to the subjects. The subjects learn the rule by trial and error, or by feedback from the experimenter as to whether a particular sorting is in accord with the rule or if it violates it.
2. One might very well not wish to break a contract with a powerful person, even if such a breach might be efficient, but one might violate contracts or commit torts against a powerless person with impunity.
3. In particular, it activated the dorsal ACC.
4. One should note that when we say that reputation and other features of repeat interaction were sufficient to ensure cooperation, we are not saying that defection never occurred. Rather that the level of defection was sufficiently low so that the basic parts of the system households, clans or other groups, were able to function.
5. To some extent heterogeneity would be predicted under Harsanyi's model whenever the Nash equilibrium involves a mixed strategy.

References

Arrow, K. 1974 *The limits of organization*, p. 23. New York: W. W. Norton & Co.

Axelrod, R. 1982 *The evolution of cooperation*. New York: Basic Book.

Axelrod, R. 1997 *The complexity of cooperation*. Princeton, NJ: Princeton University Press.

Becker, G., Grossman, M. & Murphy, K. 1991 Rational addiction and the effect of price on consumption. *Am. Econ. Rev.* **81**, 237–241.

Berg, J., Dickhaut, J. & McCabe, K. 1995 Trust reciprocity and social history. *Games Econ. Behav.* **10**, 122–142.

Bowles, S., Choi, J.-K. & Hapfensitz, A. 2003 The co-evolution of individual behaviors and social institutions. *J. Theor. Biol.* **223**, 135–147.

Breiter, H., Aharon, I., Kahneman, D., Dale, A. & Shizgal, P. 2001 Functional imaging of neural responses to expectancy and experience of monetary gains and losses. *Neuron* **30**, 619–639.

Brocas, I. & Carrillo, J. (eds) 2003 *The psychology of economic decisions*, vol. **1**. *Rationality and well-being*. New York: Oxford University Press.

Brodmann, K. 1909 *Verlgleichende lokalistionslehre der grosshirnrinde*. Leipzig, Germany: J. A. Barth.

Camerer, C. 2003a *Behavioral game theory*. Princeton, NJ: Princeton University Press.

Camerer, C. 2003b Behavioural studies of strategic thinking in games. *Trends Cogn. Neurosci.* **7**, 225–231.

Camerer, C., Lowenstein, G. & Prelec, D. 2004 Neuroeconomics: how neuroscience can inform economics. Cal Tech. working paper.

Carpenter, J. 2004 When in Rome: conformity and the provision of public goods. *J. Socio-econ.* **33**, 395.

Casebeer, W. & Churchland, P. 2003 The neural mechanisms of moral cognition: a mulitple-aspect approach to moral judgment and decision-making. *Biol. Philosophy* **18**, 169–194.

Chabris, C. & Hamilton, S. E. 1992 Hemisphere specialization for skilled perceptual organization by chess masters. *Neuropsychology* **30**, 47–57.

Coghill, R., Sang, C., Maigong, J. & Iadroca, M. 1999 Pain intensity processing within the human brain: a bilateral distributed mechanism. *J. Neurophysiol.* **82**, 1934–1943.

Damasio, A., Grabowski, T. J., Bechara, A., Damasio, H., Ponto, L. L. B., Parvizi, J. & Hichwa, R. D. 2000 Sub-cortical and cortical brain activity during the feeling of self-generated emotions. *Nature Neurosci.* **3**, 1049–1056.

Dehaene, S. 1996 The organization of brain activations in number comparison. *J. Cog. Neurosci.* **8**, 47–68.

Eisenberger, N., Lieberman, M. & Williams, K. 2003 Does rejection hurt? An fMRI study of social exclusion. *Science* **302**, 290–292.

Ellickson, R. 1994 *Order without law.* Cambridge, MA: Harvard University Press.

Fehr, E. & List, J. 2002 The hidden costs and returns of incentives: trust and trustworthiness among CEOs. University of Zurich working paper, no. 134.

Fehr, E. & Schmidt, K. 1999 A theory of fairness, competition and cooperation. *Q. J. Econ.* **114**, 817–868.

Frith, U. 2001 Mind blindness and the brain in autism. *Neuron* **32**, 969–979.

Frith, U. & Frith, C. D. 2003 Development and neurophysiology of mentalizing. *Phil. Trans. R. Soc. B* **358**, 459–473. (doi:10.1098/rstb.2002.1218)

Gazzaniga, M., Ivry, R. & Magnun, G. 2002 *Cognitive neuroscience*, 2nd edn. New York: W. W. Norton.

Gintis, H., Bowles, S., Boyd, R. & Fehr, E. 2003 Explaining altruistic behavior in humans. *Evol. Hum. Behav.* **24**, 153–172.

Goodenough, O. 2001 Mapping cortical areas associated with legal reasoning and moral intuition. *Jurimetrics* **41**, 429–442.

Greene, J. & Haidt, J. 2002 How and where does moral judgment work. *Trends Cogn. Neurosci.* **6**, 517–523.

Greene, J., Sommerville, R. B., Nystrom, L., Parley, J. & Cohen, J. 2001 An fMRI investigation of emotional engagement in moral judgment. *Science* **293**, 2105–2108.

Harsanyi, J. 1973 Games with randomly distributed payoffs: a new rationale for mixed strategy equilibrium points. *Int. J. Game Theory* **2**, 1–23.

Heiner, R. 1983 The origin of predictable behavior. *Am. Econ. Rev.* **73**, 560–595.

Henrich, J. 2000 Does culture matter in economic behavior? Ultimatum game bargaining among Machiguenga of the Peruvian Amazon. *Am. Econ. Rev.* **90**, 973–979.

Henrich, J., Boyd, R., Bowles, S., Camerer, C., Fehr, E., Gintis, H. & McElreth, R. 2001 In search of *Homo economicus*: behavioral experiments in fifteen small-scale societies. *Am. Econ. Rev.* **91**, 73–79.

Hoffman, E., McCabe, K., Shacat, K. & Smith, V. 1994 Preferences, property rights and anonymity in bargaining games. *Games Econ. Behav.* **7**, 346–380.

Holroyd, C., Nieuwehuis, S., Yeung, N. & Cohen, J. 2003 Errors in reward prediction are reflected in the event-related brain potential. *Neuroreport* **14**, 2481–2484.

Jones, E. 1961 *The life and work of Sigmund Freud.* New York: Basic Books.

La Ferrara, E. 2003 Kin groups and reciprocity: a model of credit transactions in Ghana. *Am. Econ. Rev.* **93**, 1730–1751.

Lieberman, D., Tooby, J. & Cosmides, L. 2003 Does morality have a biological basis? An empirical test of the factors governing moral sentiments relating to incest. *Proc. R. Soc. B* **270**, 819–826. (doi:10.1098/rspb.2002.2299)

Ledoux, J. 2002 *The synaptic self*. New York: Viking Books.

Ledyard, J. 1995 Public goods. In *The handbook of experimental economics* (ed. J. Kagel & A. Roth), 111–194. Princeton, NJ: Princeton University Press.

McCabe, K. & Smith, V. 2000 Goodwill accounting and the process of exchange. In *Bounded rationality: the adaptive tool-box* (ed. G. Gigerenzer & R. Selten). Cambridge, MA: MIT Press.

McCabe, K., Houser, D., Ryan, L., Smith, V. & Trouard, T. 2001 A functional imaging study of cooperation in two-person reciprocal exchange. *Proc. Natl Acad. Sci. USA* **98**, 11 832–11 835.

Mas-Colell, A., Whinston, M. & Green, J. 1995 *Microeconomic theory*. New York: Oxford University Press.

Metcalfe, J. & Mischel, W. 1999 A hot-cool analysis of the delay of gratification: the dynamics of willpower. *Psychol. Rev.* **106**, 3–19.

Miller, G. 1956 The magical number seven, plus or minus two: some limits on our capacity for processing information. *Psychol. Rev.* **101**, 343–352.

Miller, W. I. 1996 *Blood taking and peace making: feud, law and society in Saga Iceland*. University of Chicago Press.

Moll, J., de Oliveira-Souza, R., Eslinger, P. J., Bramati, I. E., Mourão-Miranda, J., Andreiuolo, P. A. & Pessoa, L. 2002*a* The neural correlates of moral sensitivity: a functional magnetic resonance imaging investigation of basic and moral emotions *J. Neurosci.* **22**, 2730–2736.

Moll, J., de Oliveira-Souza, R., Bramati, I. E. & Grafman, J. 2002*b* Functional networks in emotional moral and non-moral social judgments. *Neuroimage* **16**, 696–703.

North, D. 1991 Institutions. *J. Econ. Persp.* **5**, 97–112.

Nowak, M. A., Sasaki, A., Taylor, C. & Fudenberg, D. 2004 Emergence of cooperation and evolutionary stability in finite populations. *Nature* **428**, 646–650.

Palfrey, T. & Prisbey, J. 1997 Anomalous behavior in linear public goods experiments: how much and why? *Am. Econ. Rev.* **87**, 829–846.

Ponchon, J. B., Levy, R., Rossati, P., Leherily, S., Poline, J. B., Pillon, B., Le Bihan, D. & Du Bois, B. 2002 The neural system that bridges reward cognition in humans: an fMRI study. *Proc. Natl Acad. Sci. USA* **99**, 5669–5674.

Posner, R. 1983 *The economics of justice*. Cambridge, MA: Harvard University Press.

Ramnani, N. & Miall, R. C. 2004 A system in the human brain for predicting actions of others. *Nature Neurosci.* **7**, 85–90.

Riling, J., Gutman, D., Zeh, T., Pagnoni, G., Berns, G. & Kilts, C. 2002 A neural basis for social cooperation. *Neuron* **35**, 395–405.

Roland, P. & Zilles, K. 1998 Towards an understanding of integration of brain function: structural divisions and functional fields in the human cerebral cortex. *Brain Res. Rev.* **26**, 37.

Roth, G. 2004 The quest to find consciousness. *Sci. Am. Mind* **4**, 36–38.

Samuelson, L. 2002 Evolution and game theory. *J. Econ. Persp.* **16**, 47–66.

Sanfey, A., Rilling, J., Aronson, J., Nystrom, L. & Cohen, J. 2003 The neural basis of economic decision-making in the ultimatum game. *Science* **300**, 1755–1758.

Simon, H. 1987 Bounded rationality. In *The new Palgrave: a dictionary of economics* (ed. J. Eatwell, M. Milgate & P. Newman), pp. 266–286. London: Macmillan.

Smith, V. 1982 Microeconomics as experimental science. *Am. Econ. Rev.* **72**, 923–955.

Stahl, D. & Haruvy, E. 2003 Level-*n* bounded rationality in two-player two-stage games. University of Texas, Department of Economics working paper, 25 November.

Tooby, J. & Cosmides, L. 1996 The psychological foundations of culture. In *The adapted mind: evolutionary psychology and the generation of culture* (ed. Barkow, L. Cosmides & J. Tooby), pp. 19–136. New York: Oxford University Press.

Wood, J. & Grafman, J. 2003 Human prefrontal cortex: processing and representational perspectives. *Nature Neurosci.* **4**, 139–147.

Zak, P. & Knack, S. 2001 Trust and growth. *Econ. J.* **111**, 295.

Glossary

ACC   anterior cingulate cortex
CEO   chief executive officer
OFC   orbital frontal cortex
PFC   prefrontal cortex
STS   superior temporal sulcus
TOM   theory of mind

7

Neuroeconomics

Paul J. Zak

This paper introduces an emerging transdisciplinary field known as neuroeconomics. Neuroeconomics uses neuroscientific measurement techniques to investigate how decisions are made. First, I present a basic overview of neuroanatomy and explain how brain activity is measured. I then survey findings from the neuroeconomics literature on acquiring rewards and avoiding losses, learning, choice under risk and ambiguity, delay of gratification, the role of emotions in decision-making, strategic decisions and social decisions. I conclude by identifying new directions that neuroeconomics is taking, including applications to public policy and law.

Keywords: reward; brain; trust; emotions; strategy; neuroimaging

7.1 Introduction

Neuroeconomics is an emerging transdisciplinary field that uses neuroscientific measurement techniques to identify the neural substrates associated with economic decisions. 'Economics' here should be interpreted in the broadest possible sense as any (human or non-human) decision process that is made by evaluating alternatives. A classic non-human example is 'optimal foraging' where, for example, an ungulate must decide when to expend energy to move from the patch of grass it is currently eating to a different location with an uncertain quantity and quality of grass. A human example would be whether to accept a job as a stock analyst at Goldman Sachs for $100 000 per year but with few future pay increases or advancement versus a job as a stockbroker for a small company starting at $40 000 per year but with the potential for much greater income if successful (and the risk of being fired if not). Both of these examples can be expressed mathematically as constrained optimization problems that generate empirically testable predictions. A prediction in the human example is that a person who is more risk averse (in a precisely defined and agreed upon mathematical sense) is more likely to take the 'safe' $100 000 per year job, whereas someone who is less risk averse will gravitate towards the job as a stockbroker.

Economics is typically defined as the science characterizing the optimal allocation of scarce resources. Note: economics is *not* about money (surprisingly, economics has produced very few deep insights about money!) even though money is a convenient way to determine how much someone cares about something. Fundamentally, economics models individuals valuing rewards and choosing among alternatives. I prefer this definition of economics as it maps economic decisions straightforwardly into the neural substrates that produce these decisions. Specifically, each decision involves (i) obtaining information from the environment regarding possible actions, (ii) valuing those actions, and (iii) choosing between them. Each of these three tasks is, in principle, measurable. Further, this hierarchy of how decisions are made can further be broken down into sub-tasks, including determining one's objective(s), filtering incoming information, accessing memories of related events, using heuristics and identifying constraints on cognitive processing (e.g. energy or time constraints). These, too, are measurable.

Neuroeconomics is a natural extension of bioeconomics (Hirshleifer 1985; Gheslin & Landa 1999; Hirshleifer & Zak 2004). The bioeconomics research programme uses evolutionary biology to build models that predict human behaviour (e.g. Zak 2002; Zak & Park 2002). A second progenitor of neuroeconomics is behavioural economics, a field that uses findings from cognitive psychology to better model human decision-making (Camerer 2004). Whereas bioeconomics has focused primarily on ultimate causes of behaviour and behavioural economics has focused on how our evolved psychologies affect decisions, the neuroeconomics research programme seeks to discover proximate causes of choice behaviour. It is proximate causes that probably provide the most leverage when seeking to affect behaviour through policy. For example, introducing laws that seek to influence individual behaviour can be done more effectively and precisely when the proximate mechanisms producing the behaviour are known.

Because of the focus on decisions, neuroeconomics is not limited to studying humans (and should not be). I date the first paper in neuroeconomics as the 1999 *Nature* article by Michael Platt and Paul Glimcher (discussed later), which used an economic approach to understand how rhesus monkeys choose between two cued rewards. Indeed, neuroeconomics is improving research methods and providing new insights on both sides of the shop, i.e. in 'neuro' and in 'econ'. The first plenary meeting of neuroeconomists, organized by Greg Berns of Emory University, was held in autumn 2003. Out of the 30 researchers attending, roughly one-third had a Ph.D. in neuroscience, one-third had a Ph.D. in economics, and one-third had an M.D. This indicates the broad potential of neuroeconomics across disciplines, including clinical applications.

The economics of choice can be broken down into two primary branches, and research in neuroeconomics has a similar split. The first is solitary choice. Solitary choices are made with little or no input from others and are non-strategic. The job candidate in my example above already has the job offers and must consider which to choose—this is an individual optimization problem. Such problems are represented mathematically by individuals maximizing a 'utility function' subject to a set of constraints (e.g. an income–expenditure constraint, a time constraint, etc.). A utility function, say $U(c)$, is a mapping from consumption of 'stuff', c, into a measure of subjective happiness, U. 'Stuff' can be anything from commodities to sunsets to leisure time. Using a utility function as a person's ultimate objective is consistent with maximizing genetic fitness (Robson 2001; Zak & Denzau 2001).

Predictions from a solitary choice model are made by finding an *equilibrium*, where the preferred choice produces maximal utility subject to the constraints the person faces and the rules governing the environment of choice. The presumption that human beings have a utility function came from descriptions of the behaviour of gamblers by Daniel Bernoulli in the eighteenth century and is the most foundational notion in economics. Solitary constrained utility maximization predicts behaviour in impersonal exchange (e.g. in markets), generally quite well. This model of decision-making works less well when the decision-maker has incomplete or ambiguous information, or is influenced by others' behaviours (herding) or intangibles other than measurable 'stuff' enter into the utility function. Modifications to the classical utility maximization model for these situations have been proposed, but extensive tests of competing models have not produced an accepted new general theory (Kahneman 2004).

The second branch in the study of choice is strategic choice. Continuing with the example of the job seeker, before obtaining the job offer, he or she probably behaved strategically because the rivalry to get a job offer was with other people. Strategies might include buying a new suit to appear professional and successful, wearing a brightly coloured tie or scarf to be memorable, designing a clever resume to generate attention, finding out who the other interviewees are so as to disparage their skills or education to the interviewer, etc. Decisions with socially strategic elements can be described mathematically using game theory. A game-theoretic model of behaviour requires a description of the people in the game, the information each has or can obtain, the actions available to each player, and the pay-off expected from each strategy. A Nash equilibrium of a game identifies an optimal strategy conditional on everyone else in the game also behaving optimally. Game theory models decisions more complex than isolated utility maximization, and its predictive record is more mixed (Camerer 2004).

In summary, economics is the science of decision-making, decisions that both involve others and those that do not. For this reason, economic models can be applied to a wide range of species and behaviours. Neuroscience, on the other hand, has an exquisite arsenal of measurement modalities, but historically has focused on characterizing a quite limited set of behaviours. Therefore, there is a natural affinity between neuroscience and economics as one has produced and tested many behavioural models without asking what produces the behaviour, whereas the other is able to open the black box that generates behaviours but is searching for interesting behaviours to study.

The expected benefits of neuroeconomics on each side of the shop are high. For economics, neuroeconomic research will lead to the building of models that predict economic and social behaviours better and that are grounded in neurobiology. This will allow economists to answer fundamental questions they are unable to address now such as: why do two individuals faced with the same information and incentives make different choices? Why does the same individual sometimes make choices that are inconsistent? How much is choice behaviour affected by childhood development, if at all? Currently, most answers to economic questions focus on average choices, rather than individual or temporal variation in choices, and model building has a 'what-if' quality where new models are often built without any motivating data. In the application of economic models to policy, most laws seek to circumscribe extreme behaviours, not average behaviours, so an understanding of the interpersonal and intertemporal variation in choices is fundamental to effective public policy.

On the neuroscience side, neuroeconomics provides a host of well-studied and (often) interesting decision tasks that are begging to have their neural 'underpinnings' identified. For example, social cognitive neuroscience is an exciting and important new field (Adolphs 2003), and game-theoretic models of social interactions are an obvious source of tasks to study. Economic models supply the structure of the social interaction as well as (usually) field-tested behavioural predictions, saving researchers from having to reinvent the wheel. Such game-theoretic models are often fairly complex, and neuroeconomics is moving neuroscientists to study tasks that approach those that humans actually do in their daily lives. Finally, because economic models have objective behavioural measures, usually involving monetary transfers, neuroeconomic experiments engage subjects' attention better and have added control compared with tasks that are simply passive (e.g. viewing photographs) or in which the subjects are asked to 'imagine' themselves doing something. Most neuroeconomists also follow the ethic in experimental economics that prohibits the deception of subjects. With a guarantee of no deception, subjects make choices without trying to 'game' the experimenters by figuring out what they are 'really' looking for.

7.2 Basic brain facts and terminology

There are roughly 100 billion neurons in the human brain, with each neuron directly connected to between 1000 and 10 000 other neurons. Brain tissue can be separated into grey matter (neurons) and white matter (axons and dendrites, the connections between neurons). Grey matter makes up 40% of the brain, but consumes 94% of the brain's oxygen owing to the firing of action potentials (electrical pulses) that allow one neuron to communicate with other neurons. The cortex (from the Latin for bark) is the outer surface of the brain that is used for information processing and higher mental functions. Because the human brain is folded (to pack more cortical tissue into the skull), a brain region may be identified as being on a gyrus (hill, plural gyri) or in a sulcus (valley, plural sulci).

The brain is grossly divided into four sections: the frontal, temporal, parietal and occipital lobes (see figure 7.1). Each lobe performs several functions, containing smaller structures that do specific tasks, often in concert with other brain regions through connections called projections. The brain sits on top of the brain stem, which leads to the spinal column. A cauliflower-shaped structure, the cerebellum, sits below the occipital lobe and adjacent to the brainstem. A common way to identify cortical regions in the brain is by using 'Brodmann's Areas', which are numbered from 1 to 47. These are

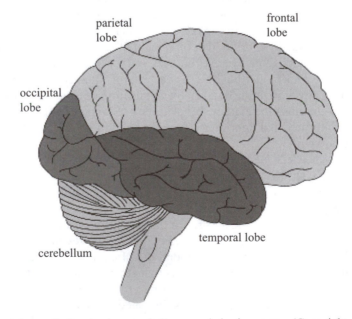

Fig. 7.1 The lobes of the brain, cerebellum and brain stem. (Copyright Mark Dubin; printed here with permission. First published online: See http://spot.colorado.edu/~dubin/talks/brodmann/brodmann.html.)

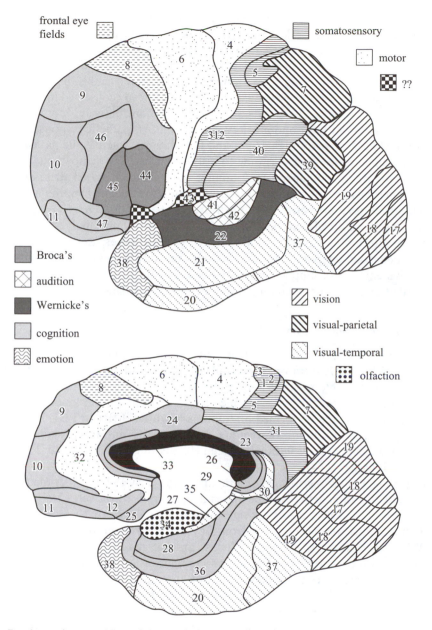

Fig. 7.2 Brodmann's areas. (Copyright Mark Dubin; printed here with permission. First published online: See http:// spot.colorado.edu/~dubin/talks/brodmann/brodmann.html.)

abbreviated BAx, where x is the integer corresponding to that region. German physician and anatomist Korbinian Brodmann (1868–1918) identified brain regions based on similar cellular and laminar structures (see figure 7.2).

Because the brain is three-dimensional, identifying locations requires specialized terminology. Terms for locations of brain regions include: dorsal (top, from the Latin for back); ventral (bottom facing the central axis, from the Latin for belly) or basal; rostral (front, from the Latin for beak) or anterior; caudal (back, from the Latin for tail) or posterior; superior (towards the top); inferior (towards the bottom); medial/mesial (middle); lateral (away from mid-line); and orbital (above the eyes, from the Latin orbita meaning eye sockets). Generally, brain regions that are ventral and inferior tend to be phylogenetically older than dorsal and rostral regions, with older regions mostly conserved in lower animals.

Much of the nervous system is outside of volitional control (is autonomic). There are two opposing sides to the autonomic nervous system. Sympathetic responses are associated with the four Fs (fright, flight, fight and fornication), whereas the parasympathetic nervous system activates when it is time to rest and digest. The sympathetic is arousing, and the parasympathetic relaxes; maintaining the balance between these sides of the autonomic nervous system is essential to health and growth. The hypothalamus, a basal midbrain structure, exerts primary control over the autonomic nervous system. Most emotional responses are also automatic and rapid. Primary emotional responses emanate from the brain's limbic structures. The limbic system (limbus, Latin for edge) is grey matter in the medial temporal lobe, and includes the amygdala (associated with positive and negative emotions), hippocampus (associated with long-term memory), cingulate cortex (attention and error detection) and olfactory cortex (smell).

(a) Measurement of brain activity

Neuroscientists use a variety of measurement modalities to gauge neural activity, including PET, fMRI, EEG/ERP, intra-or extracellular recording of electrical activity of single neurons, bioassays of blood, urine and cerebral spinal fluid, responses to drug infusions, as well as studies of patients with specific central nervous system lesions. Most of the neuroeconomics research performed on humans has used fMRI or PET, both of which provide high spatial resolution of regional brain activity during particular tasks with moderate to low temporal resolution (between 100 ms and 2 s for fMRI, and 30 s or more for PET; see Buckner 2003).

PET imaging was first performed on humans in the early 1970s. Experimental subjects are injected with a radioactive isotope that emits positrons (positively charged electrons). Subjects then lie in a ring of crystal detectors and a camera that captures radioactive decay (when a positron meets an electron they annihilate each other and emit gamma rays). When neurons fire they deplete glucose and oxygen and require increased blood flow to resupply these substances. Blood flows to neurons roughly proportionally to their firing rates. PET measures the accumulation of the radioactive tracer in brain regions; regions metabolizing glucose faster receive more blood flow and emit more gamma rays. A computer algorithm constructs the measurements of regional cerebral blood flow in three dimensions as an indirect measure of neural activity. The use of radioisotopes with short half-lives places a 1 h time limit on PET experiments and restricts subjects to two studies per year.

fMRI was first used on humans in 1992, and produces 3D renderings of regional neural activity. The data obtained by fMRI are BOLD signals that indirectly measure regional neural and synaptic activity by examining the amount of oxygenated to deoxygenated blood (the haemo-dynamic response). Neural firing increases the demand for oxygenated blood (oxyhaemoglobin). Because deoxyhaemoglobin is paramagnetic, it produces a measurably larger signal relative to oxyhaemoglobin when perturbed by a short radio-frequency pulse. These differences are small and can be measured only in a very powerful magnet (currently MRI scanners used for humans have magnets from 1 to 8 T; a 1 T magnet is 20 000 times stronger than the magnetic field on the Earth's surface). Higher field-strength magnets increase resolution (up to 1 mm^3) but also increase the noise associated with signal detection. This makes the analysis more difficult because external confounds must be eliminated. Magnetic fields are not associated with any adverse health effects (Kangarlu *et al.* 1999), though very powerful magnets (4 T or more) can induce temporary dizziness and a metallic taste in the mouth. fMRI experiments are limited in time only by the subject's ability not to fidget or fall asleep, and can be repeated on the same subject indefinitely.

Both fMRI and PET use a 'subtraction' method to statistically identify regional neural activation during a task. This is done by measuring brain activity during the task of interest and then removing activation measured in a control task. The control task is often 'baseline' neural activity (e.g. staring at a fixation point), though better studies use control tasks that are closer to the task of interest. For example, if the task is to choose between two alternatives involving monetary rewards, a good control task would be giving the subject a monetary reward absent choice. The subtraction then removes the activation in the brain from simply receiving (or anticipating) reward and identifies brain regions active in making the choice. Choosing a good control task is a major feature of these experiments, and readers of this literature should be sceptical of the results if the experimental design is poor. Both PET and fMRI correlate tasks with regional brain activity; demonstrating causation requires others methods discussed below.

Montague *et al.* (2002) at Baylor College of Medicine's Human Neuroimaging Laboratory have provided an important advance to study regional brain activity during social interactions that they call 'Hyperscanning.' Hyper-scanning allows two or more subjects in MRI scanners in different locations to interact simultaneously through the Internet with behavioural and even visual and auditory feedback between subjects while measuring brain activity. This literally allows researchers to see one person's brain affect another person's brain. So far, Montague and collaborators have hyperscanned eight subjects simultaneously. Their proprietary software synchronizes stimulus presentation and BOLD signal acquisition across subjects and locations. Hyperscanning opens up fMRI from single-to multiple-subject studies and will see increasing use in the coming years to answer questions in social cognitive neuroscience and the neuroeconomics of social decisions.

EEGs/ERPs use between 16 and 256 scalp electrodes to measure the electrical activity of large groups (more than one million) of neurons. EEGs are used clinically to help diagnose neurological disorders, especially epilepsy, by examining the synchronicity, frequency and amplitude of EEG tracings called 'waves' while a patient sits or lies down. ERPs differ from EEGs in that experimental subjects are given specific tasks to do that may provoke regional brain activation. The characteristics of ERP waves identify regional excitatory or inhibitory neural activity. ERPs provide higher temporal resolution than fMRI or PET (*ca.* 10 ms) but lower spatial resolution. The other advantages of ERP over fMRI or PET are its relatively low cost, less demanding statistical analyses (two dimensional versus three dimensional), and greater freedom of movement for subjects. The disadvantages of ERPs include low spatial specificity, subject performance fatigue that occurs because many trials are required per subject to reduce background noise and artefact, and potential problems with inter-subject comparisons because consistent electrode placement depends on a careful identification of bony landmarks that vary across subjects. Some laboratories have now combined ERP and fMRI to obtain high temporal resolution together with high spatial resolution.

Measuring the firing rates of single neurons in the brain requires that a microelectrode be attached to, or inserted into, the neuron cell body. Neuron cell bodies vary in size from 4 to 100 μm (a micrometre is one thousandth of a millimetre), and obtaining internal or external recordings from a neuron often damage or destroy it. Single neuron firing measurements offer the highest level of spatial specificity, but are seldom performed on humans. Some surgical patients have electrode grids place on the convexity of the brain or deeper inside the brain ('depth electrodes') that measure the activity of a few neurons, and these patients have occasionally been used in research. Animals are more commonly used when recording the firing of single neurons.

Bioassays provide an indirect measure of neural activity, and have the advantage of being able to identify cascades of activity that produce behaviour, as well as facilitating the investigation of individual-specific confounds. Obtaining biological material, such as blood, is invasive and the act of obtaining the sample may affect what is being measured (e.g. hormones or neurotransmitters). Combining bioassays with other measurement techniques allows researchers to triangulate neural activity within a single experiment.

Using pharmaceuticals in experiments is an important method to induce behaviour, i.e. to move from correlation to causation, and its use in neuroeconomics is just beginning. Similarly, comparing the behaviour of patients with focal brain lesions with healthy controls is also an important step in establishing the necessity of a brain region for a particular behaviour. Several laboratories, including my own, are studying brain-damaged patients but have not yet published their findings. Temporary brain lesions or neural hyperactivation can be induced by focusing a magnet field on the convexity of the brain using TMS. I am not aware of any neuroeconomics experiments using TMS, but it is an important (though not completely risk-free) technique that can be used to ascertain causation.

7.3 Major findings in neuroeconomics

The research topics studied by neuroeconomists fall into two major categories: (i) identifying the neural processes involved in decisions in which standard economic models predict behaviour well; and (ii) studies of 'anomalies' where the standard models fail. For the latter, often several alternative models have been proposed with different behavioural assumptions that predict decisions equally well and therefore the 'true' sources of behaviour are unknown (Camerer 2004). Research in category (i) is often headed by a neuroscientist or an M.D., where much of the research in (ii) is led by economists. Many research teams now include both economists and neuroscientists/M.D.s and consequently the breakdown of research into these two categories is beginning to blur. Because of the rapid growth of the neuroeconomics literature, the review here will be incomplete by the time this issue goes to press, but I maintain an updated neuroeconomics reading list at my laboratory Web site, http://www.pauljzak.com.

(a) Reward acquisition

All animals need to obtain resources to survive, and the neural structures needed for reward acquisition are primitive and well conserved across species. Choice execution is preceded by the evaluation of the reward associated with each choice, but the evaluative substrate was unknown. Platt & Glimcher (1999) trained rhesus monkeys in a colour-cued eye saccade task. The correct left or right saccade was rewarded with a squirt of juice. These researchers suspected that area LIP was being used to evaluate rewards as projections from the visual cortex converge in area LIP before being relayed to the motor cortex for execution. Platt and Glimcher measured the firing rate of 40 neurons in area LIP in three monkeys as they varied the juice reward for the correct saccade either in absolute amount, or probabilistically (i.e. for the latter, each correct saccade was rewarded with juice with a given probability). They found that 62.5% of area LIP neuron activation was correlated with expected gain. These findings for area LIP were recently replicated and extended by Newsome's laboratory (Sugrue *et al.* 2004).

Glimcher *et al.* (2005) go further, to argue that the utility function that economists presumed existed to explain behavioural data is a physiological reality in area LIP. That is, area LIP neurons do not behave 'similar to' a utility function, but 'are' a physiological utility function in monkey brains (i.e. area LIP neurons perform the calculations needed to determine utility). However, this does not preclude the existence of other brain regions that are utility functions (see below). Glimcher *et al.* (2005) support this claim by showing that area LIP firing rates can be used to predict the behaviour of monkeys in several reward acquisition tasks. Work with humans using fMRI is currently underway in Glimcher's laboratory to determine if the human homologue of area LIP is also a physiological utility function (Nelson *et al.* 2004).

Reward acquisition requires a motivating mechanism to obtain the reward as well as the ability to predict reward size to gauge the effort needed to pursue the reward. Schultz *et al.* (1997) review single-neuron firing studies of juice rewards in non-human primates and identify dopaminergic neurons in the ventral tegmental area and substantia nigra as processing rewarding stimuli, activating during novel stimuli, and most importantly, firing proportional to the error of the actual to the expected reward. They introduce the temporal difference mathematical model to show how dopamine neuron activity can be used to predict an animal's behaviour as it learns about rewards.

Dopaminergic neurons are particularly dense in the nucleus accumbens in the ventral medial region, and this region has strong projections to the medial forebrain, which is active in many decision-making tasks. Although cocaine, methamphetamines, humour, and even viewing faces of attractive women by heterosexual men produce acute activation in the nucleus accumbens (Aharon *et al.* 2001; Mobbs *et al.* 2003), recent experiments have shown that dopamine release is not the same as pleasure (Garris *et al.* 1999). Indeed, activation in the nucleus accumbens and ACC (BA23/24/31/31/32) is associated with attentional demands. Breiter *et al.* (2001) used event-related fMRI to examine regional activation to the expectation and realization of monetary gains and losses for 12 human subjects. Monetary awards were made without any subject choice in this experiment. They showed that expected and actual rewards were associated with significant haemo-dynamic responses in the SLEA and orbital gyrus. In addition, activation in the nucleus accumbens, SLEA and hypothalamus tracked the highest monetary values. Gains produced predominant activation in the right hemisphere (particularly the nucleus accumbens and hypothalamus), whereas losses produce greater left hemisphere activity (especially the left amygdala). These findings appear to indicate that gains produced neural rewards, whereas losses provoked emotional responses associated with fear or regret.

Knutson *et al.* (2001) further dissociate the anticipation of reward with its realization by having nine subjects respond with a button push to a coloured cue in an fMRI study. A rapid button push for a yellow cue produced a $1 reward, a rapid response to a blue cue was not rewarded, and a red cue required no response. After each trial, subjects were told how much they earned on that trial and in total. Knutson and colleagues acquired fMRI signals, before and after subjects received feedback on reward or no reward. Anticipation of reward produced activity in the dopamine-receptor-rich ventral striatum (consisting of the substructures caudate nucleus and putamen), whereas notification that a reward was earned (approximating reward consumption) produced primary activation the MPFC.

In a follow-up study with a larger reward ($5), Knutson *et al.* (2003) show that the MPFC (BA 10/32), posterior cingulate cortex (BA 26/30) and parietal cortex (BA 7) activate during the notification of a monetary reward. Interestingly, when rewards were anticipated but *not* obtained, the MPFC showed decreased activation relative to baseline (no outcome). The MPFC has the densest dopaminergic innervation of any cortical region and Knutson and colleagues argue that this region serves as a utility function, whereas the nucleus accumbens guides reward anticipation and learning. An excellent review of this literature is Knutson & Peterson (2005) where the authors make the point that subjective states associated with utility must have an emotional basis—utility must be felt to be valuable—and the MPFC and the OFS circuit appear to map 'wanting' into 'having'.

Montague & Berns (2002) also review the reward and prediction literature. They propose a predictor-valuation model for reward that uses the OFS circuit. Similar to Glimcher's claim for area LIP and Knutson's promotion of MPFC, Montague and Berns provide an array of evidence that OFS values rewards (and punishments). They also provide evidence that reward/punishment evaluation in OFC is separate from the error prediction feature of mid-brain dopamine neurons that innervate it.

Dickhaut *et al.* (2003) had nine subjects choose between pairs of lotteries in a PET study. Some of the lotteries produced gains whereas others produced losses (subjects received an initial endowment of $190). Behaviourally, they find risk aversion over gains but not losses, with average response times for loss lotteries 500 ms slower than choices over gains. When compared with a risky reference lottery, gains minus losses produced OFC activation. By contrast, when the reference lottery was a certain payment, gains minus losses produced primary activation in the cerebellum and parietal cortex. Losses minus gains activated dorsal parietal and frontal cortices whether the reference lottery was risky or certain. This report demonstrates how varying the stimulus and/or measurement modality can produce quite different regional activation maps than other similar studies have found. Interpretive caution is called for.

All reward evaluation requires 'emotion' in that ventromedial areas associated with dopamine activate to motivate subjects to acquire resources, and dopamine-innervated cortical regions appear to value resources. It is possible that OFS, MPFC and area LIP *all* value rewards (i.e. are physiological utility functions), with an undiscovered brain region (perhaps prefrontal) determining final valuation when these regions provide conflicting assessments. The asymmetry between gains and losses is also an issue requir-ing further study by, for example, replicating some of the experiments discussed in this section. Finally, additional research is needed to elucidate the temporal dependence of subcortical and cortical circuits identified in reward evaluation and consumption.

(b) Certainty, ambiguity and gratification delay

Neuroscience research has shown that emotions are an important physiological guidance system for choice. For example, Damasio (1994) reported the inability of patients with selective damage to the OFC to execute choices. Kahn *et al.* (2002) showed that amygdala activation was predictive of an anticipated loss. Emotional activation during decisions may be more likely to occur with incomplete information, risk, or choice in a social context. For tasks in which the best decision is difficult to determine through cogitation, emotional markers provide additional information that can guide choice.

The suppression of limbic responses may be part of what makes human choice different from choice by animals. This was investigated in a fascinating field study by Lo & Repin (2002). These researchers proposed that professional foreign exchange traders would have emotional responses to market volatility while trading. With permission from a Boston brokerage firm, they 'wired up' 10 traders for 1 h each to obtain data on six physiological measures while the traders managed currency contracts of one million US dollars and larger. Lo and Repin simultaneously measured activity in the currency markets. All traders exhibited heightened cardiovascular and electrodermal states during periods of market volatility. More generally, rapid market movements provoked traders' sympathetic nervous systems; this can be interpreted as emotional responses. Interestingly, longer job tenure was associated with reduced sympathetic responses for a given amount of market volatility. This suggests that either experienced traders learned over time to suppress their emotions, or that more emotionally reactive traders left to take other less personally stressful jobs. Lo and Repin were not allowed to obtain data on traders' performance in markets, so we do not know if emotional responses diminished (or improved) the ability to make money. These researchers are currently examining this issue by bringing professional money managers into the laboratory and requiring them to trade to earn monetary returns in simulated markets.

Smith *et al.* (2002) examined the same data as Dickhaut *et al.* (2003) but investigated the role of ambiguity. An ambiguous lottery is one in which the likelihood of one or more of the pay-offs occurring is not fully specified. For example, the subject is asked to choose between lotteries A and B, where A guarantees a payment of $10, and B pays $20 if a red ball is pulled from an urn, and $0 if a blue ball is pulled; the urn contains 90 balls, and at least 50 are red. (Try this yourself: do you prefer lottery A or B? Most people are ambiguity-averse and choose A.) Smith and colleagues report strong activation in the OFC and intraparietal sulcus for gains subtracted from losses without ambiguity. Subtracting risky losses from gains after removing ambiguous lottery choices produced activation in the cerebellum and dorsomedial cortex. This suggests that losses activated cortical regions associated with calculation, while gains activated the older ventromedial system. Ambiguity alone produces small amounts of ventromedial and limbic activation.

Unpublished research by Rustichini *et al.* (2004) used a similar paradigm with 12 subjects choosing between 96 pairs of certain, risky, ambiguous and partly ambiguous lotteries in a PET study. Subjects showed strong ambiguity aversion, but ambiguous and partly ambiguous choices did *not* generate activation in brain regions associated with emotions (e.g. OFC or amygdala). Rather, ambiguous choices were associated with rostrofrontal activation, with substantial deactivation in ventromedial regions. Similar to work from Glimcher's laboratory, Rustichini *et al.* (2004) find strong parietal activation when subjects chose the certain lottery (but they did not explore a parametric relationship between activation and reward amount). There is no consistency between the findings of Rustichini *et al.* (2004) and Smith *et al.* (2002) about the neural substrates associated with ambiguity during choice. I consider this issue important and unresolved.

A major behavioural difference separating humans from other animals is our ability to postpone current gratification for a later (larger) reward. Behaviourally, humans exhibit a strong desire for current reward and rapidly devalue future rewards (Laibson *et al.* 1998). Recent work by McClure *et al.* (2004) used fMRI to examine how the brain decides between current versus delayed rewards. In this study, all rewards were monetary, with current rewards paid immediately after scanning, and delayed rewards paid between two and six weeks later. Delayed rewards always exceeded current rewards. McClure and collaborators found that immediate reward primarily activated the ventral striatum, medial OFC and medial prefrontal cortex. Delayed rewards differentially activated the lateral prefrontal cortex and inferior parietal cortex. These areas were particularly active when the difference between immediate and postponed rewards was small. The authors conclude that choosing between immediate and delayed gratification constitutes a battle between limbic structures that activate for current reward and newer cortical regions that evaluate trade-offs.

(c) Learning and strategy

Both the dopaminergic system and emotional responses are important in learning what is valuable or dangerous as animals navigate the world. These systems, and others, update memories of past experiences using the present experience so the animal has a basis for making informed future decisions. In a very careful study, Barraclough *et al.* (2004) investigated reinforcement learning and reward encoding in two rhesus monkeys trained to play a variant of 'matching pennies' against a computer using three different strategies. Matching pennies is a very simple game in which optimal behaviour is a 'mixed strategy' or randomization over choices. The canonical game has two opponents choosing to show either a head or a tail on a penny, and putting the coins down simultaneously on a table. If both pennies show the same face (i.e. either both heads or both tails), player A wins the pennies; otherwise player B wins. The monkeys did this task using eye saccades and juice rewards.

Barraclough and colleagues found that for all the algorithms they used, monkeys learn very quickly to behave optimally by randomizing their choices. A reinforcement learning statistical model fitted the monkeys' choices quite well showing that the history of play by the computer affected the monkeys' current choices. These researchers also recorded the firing of 132 separate neurons in the DLPFC during monkey choices. The firing rate of 37% of DLPFC neurons measured was affected by the previous reward, while the firing rate of 39% of these neurons was influenced by the previous choice. This indicates that the DLPFC may be part of the neurophysiology of reward acquisition, especially when this involves memory-dependent strategic decisions. In humans, the DLPFC, which activates during working memory tasks, may be another physiological utility function. That is, the current value of a reward may be affected by the memories of obtaining similar rewards. If this result is confirmed by other studies (especially in humans), it suggests an important modification to the classical economic model of utility.

Learning involves, of course, more than one brain area and more than one neuro-transmitter. For example, the neurotransmitter glutamate and N-methyl-D-aspartate receptors are critical for the neural basis of learning in which connections between neurons are strengthened, called LTP (see Riedel *et al.* 2003). Reinforcement learning also appears to require neural activation in the amygdala and OFC (see the excellent review and a proposed mathematical model in Dayan & Balleine (2002)). Future neuroeconomic research on learning should explore the roles of glutamate and LTP.

(d) Cooperation

Intraspecies cooperation with non-kin is an issue that has attracted substantial attention but is still not well-understood (Boyd *et al.* 2003; Brosnan & de Waal 2003). Particularly stark is costly cooperation in one-shot interactions with the opportunity to defect without punishment. Even in this setting, humans are highly cooperative (Smith 1998; Fehr & Rockenbach 2003). The ability to cooperate has, potentially, positive and negative neural reinforcers. The positive is the (internal and external) reward obtained by being cooperative. The negative may be the neural correlates associated with the loss of a larger reward and the neural activity resulting from social condemnation by one's trading partner after being uncooperative (for a mathematical model of prosocial emotions see Bowles & Gintis (2003)).

Neuroeconomists have sought to identify the neural substrates associated with cooperative behaviour. An early and important contribution by McCabe *et al.* (2001) reported fMRI data for subjects interacting in real-time by computer with another person outside the scanner. McCabe *et al.* (2001) hypothesized that cooperative behaviour would require that subjects use a brain region associated with 'theory of mind' in which a person is able to anticipate what another will do by imagining himself/herself in the same situation. Most humans, except those under 5 years old and most autistics, have a fully operational theory of mind, and it has been localized to include a region in the medial OFC (BA10) as well as several other regions (Frith & Frith 2003). McCabe *et al.* (2001) provided an incentive for cooperative behaviour by using a binary choice version of the 'trust game' (Berg *et al.* 1995) where subjects can earn more money if they cooperate, but cannot communicate except by transferring money to each other through their choices. Subjects denoted DM1 and DM2 made sequential choices for the dollar amounts shown in figure 7.3, alternating the roles of DM1 and DM2. In figure 7.3, DM1 either ends the interaction by providing pay-offs of $0.45 for DM1 and DM2 (moving left), or transfers control to DM2 (moving right). When DM1 yields control of the game to DM2, he or she signals trust in DM2. DM2 then can be trustworthy, earning $1.80 for DM1 and $2.25 for DM2 (left), or can be non-trustworthy causing DM1 to earn $0, and DM2 to earn $4.05 (right). Note that the 'pie' increases from $0.90 to $4.05 (450%) when DM1 chooses to transfer control to DM2.

In a conjunction analysis of cooperative moves by DM1s and DM2s, McCabe *et al.* (2001) find that BA10 is indeed more active (i) than when subjects were not cooperative, and (ii) relative to a control task where subjects were informed that they were interacting with a computer that moved left or right with known probabilities. The authors argue that BA10 is part of the neural architecture that allows gratification delay in order to obtain larger rewards through cooperation. A possible confound in this study is that to generate sufficient fMRI signal, DM1–DM2 pairs made 80 choices in the same dyad so subjects were able to build reputations for cooperation during the experiment. It is also worth mentioning three important aspects of this study. First, there was no deception: the

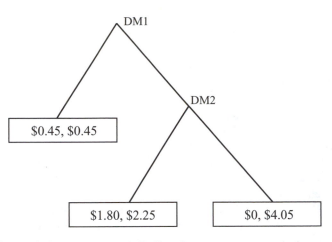

Fig. 7.3 The binary-choice trust game. Dollar figures are, respectively, pay-offs for DM1 and DM2 at each node.

DM in the MRI scanner actually interacted in real time with another human being (a reasonably difficult technical hurdle). Second, the control task was identical to the treatment task but simply removed the intentionality associated with decisions. This allowed these researchers to cleanly extract the neural components of intention. Third, the neuroanatomical hypothesis for activation in BA10 allowed the acquisition of fMRI data optimized for high signal: noise in the region of interest providing higher-quality data.

The binary trust game is an iterated PD, where DM1 and DM2 choose to either cooperate or defect. A PD is a strategic interaction in which both parties gain by behaving cooperatively, but are unable to coordinate cooperation; the dominant strategy (choice) is for both DMs to choose to be non-cooperative ('defect'), injuring both DMs by producing low or negative pay-offs. Rilling *et al.* (2002) examined cooperation versus defection when 36 female subjects played 20 or more rounds of the trust game against a human or computer opponent programmed to react in several ways to the other's choices (e.g. tit-for-tat). Removing the pure monetary effect using a condition where the subject knows she is playing against a computer (for the same dollar amount), the social aspect of cooperation produced activation in the anteroventral striatum, right ACC and OFC.

The conclusion from this study is that cooperation is rewarding (striatum), requires attention and the mediation of the conflicting concerns of making more money but behaving in socially less acceptable ways (ACC), and has an emotional component (OFC). Defection by DM1 with cooperation by DM2 was associated with deactivation of the striatum, with a similar deactivation when choosing the cooperative node with a computer partner. The region with the strongest activation during cooperation is the somatosensory association cortex (BA7), consistent with Antonio Damasio's somatic marker theory (Damasio 1994) linking emotions 'experienced' in the body with decisions. (The somatosensory association cortex in the posterior parietal lobe activates during memory, attention and emotional responses to objects.) Rilling *et al.* (2002) partly replicate the finding of McCabe *et al.* (2001) of BA10 activation, but only when subjects cooperated while playing a computer that also moved to the cooperative node, but not in the human–human treatment.

Sanfey *et al.* (2003) used fMRI to analyse another economic task involving cooperation, with their major results associated with the consequences of not cooperating. Sanfey and colleagues had subjects make decisions in the ultimatum game, a sequential decision task to determine the split of a sum of money between two people. For example, DM1 is given $10 and told to offer an integer split to DM2, without seeing or communicating with him or her. DM2 can then accept the split and the amounts are paid, or can reject the split and both DMs earn nothing. Behaviourally, when DM1s offer less than 30% of the money, DM2s nearly always reject offers. From a purely economic point of view, a rejection of any money is 'irrational' because some money is expected to be preferred to none, but humans are social beings and there is clearly a social aspect to this game. DM2s also report feeling angry when a DM1 offers a stingy split.

Sanfey *et al.* (2003) modified the ultimatum game to generate only the following DM1–DM2 offers: {$5, $5}, {$7, $3}, {$8, $2} and {$9, $1}. Only DM2s were scanned. A computer played the role of DM1, but Sanfey *et al.* (2003) deceived subjects into believing that they were playing with another human to simplify the protocol (all subjects reported that they believed this). On some trials, the researchers told DM2s that they were playing against a computer as a control task. Unfair offers differentially activated the anterior insula, DLPFC and ACC. Activation in all three regions was greater for unfair offers from humans than from a computer. Their major finding is that insula activation increased with the unfairness of the offer from a human. Insular cortex activation has previously been associated with disgust, pain, hunger and thirst. Sanfey and colleagues concluded that low offers in the ultimatum game are rejected because of a sense of disgust, while DLPFC activation may be signalling the importance of acquiring money.

Interpersonal trust is the most powerful predictor at the country level of whether nations will experience rising living standards or will remain trapped in poverty (Zak & Knack 2001). Zak *et al.* (2004) examine whether there is a physiological correlate associated with the receipt of a signal of trust that motivates individuals to be trustworthy (that is, to reciprocate trust). Drawing on research with rodents on social recognition and attachment, Zak and colleagues proposed that the neuroactive hormone OT would process signals of trust and induce trustworthy behaviour. They used a variant of the trust game in which all DMs received a $10 show-up payment and were randomly assigned to dyads. DM1s were prompted to send an integer amount, including zero, of their $10 show-up money to the DM2 in their dyad. The amount sent was removed from DM1's account, and was tripled in DM2's account. DM2s were then told the tripled amount that they were sent and the total in their accounts. Next, DM2s were prompted to send some amount back to the DM1 in their dyad, including zero. All interactions were mediated by computer, and subjects were fully informed of the structure of the interaction and the consequences of their choices. Participants where also told that they would only make a single decision.

In this experiment, DMs made decisions serially, and immediately after each decision went to an anteroom and had 28 ml of blood drawn from an antecubital vein. All experiments began at 13.00, a trough in diurnal hormone variation. Zak and colleagues showed that DM2s receiving trust signals had OT levels almost twice that of DM2s in a control task in which DM2s received random (unintentional) monetary transfers of the same average amount as in the treatment task. In addition, higher OT levels in DM2s were strongly associated with trustworthy behaviour. None of nine other hormones measured, except for progesterone, responded to the trust signal nor were associated with DM2 behaviour. Women in the study who were ovulating (progesterone level more than

3 ng/ml) were less trustworthy than other subjects. Progesterone is known to inhibit OT uptake. This finding indicates that OT is the primary hormone responding to signals of trust (i.e. the behavioural effect is caused by OT and not another hormone). There were no overall gender differences. Their analysis shows that OT is released in response to a signal of trust (the experimental state), rather than being a primary trait of subjects (i.e. DM1s with high OT levels did not behave any differently than other DM1s as these subjects did not receive a trust signal). Zak's team concludes that OT, which activates the parasympathetic system and facilitates dopamine release, is a positive physiological motivator of cooperation.

7.4 The future: convergent evidence

One of the important lessons neuroscience can teach economics is the necessity of convergent evidence before a finding is accepted as 'proved'. This typically means using different measurement modalities, subject groups (especially atypical groups), and moving from correlation to causation. An example of this research using economic decision tasks but absent neurophysiological measurement is the study of autistics by Hill & Sally (2003). They compared the behaviour of healthy children and adults with age-matched patients diagnosed with autistic spectrum disorder as they made choices in the PD, ultimatum and dictator games. (In the dictator game, DM1 is given a monetary endowment and chooses to give some amount of it to an unknown DM2; DM2 does not make a choice. Healthy adult DM1s typically offer 10% or less to DM2s in this game which is designed to measure altruistic behaviour.) They report that autistics were no less likely to cooperate, but did not learn to be strategic in repeat play as did healthy subjects. Some of this failure to learn strategy appeared to derive from a lack of a theory of mind by autistics, yet even healthy young children (*ca.* 6 years old) learned this. The authors suggest that part of the difference in behaviour is occurring because autistics have not developed social 'fairness' rules that most healthy individuals have internalized through repeated social interactions. The veracity of this claim would be clarified with measurements of neural activity.

A second example of the need for convergence comes from Knutson's laboratory (Bjork *et al.* 2004) who replicated the paradigm of Knutson *et al.* (2003) using 12 adolescents (ages 12–17 years) and 12 young adults (ages 22–28 years) as subjects. Rewards for the correctly cued colour choice were $0.20, $1 or $5, and choices were designed so that subjects were correct 70% of the time. Gain acquisition in both age groups similarly activated the MPFC. Interestingly, while anticipation of gains activated the ventral striatum in both groups, adolescents had a significantly lower average BOLD signal than young adults for the same sized reward. These data indicate that one reason adolescents may engage in risky behaviours is to compensate for hypoactive reward activity in their brains. It also suggests that to fully understand anticipation and consumption of rewards, one cannot only study young healthy adults.

The above review of the neuroeconomics literature is, by necessity, truncated and subject to my own biases. Other discussions of the neuroeconomics literature and methodology can be found in Camerer (2004), Camerer *et al.* (2004), the 2002 special issue of *Neuron* (Cohen & Blum 2002), a special issue of *Games and economic behavior* (2005) and the book by Glimcher (2003).

7.5 Neuroeconomics and the law

One of most important areas that neuroeconomics can contribute to is the law. Laws (or more generally institutions as defined by Douglass North (1990)) specify the 'rules of the game'; yet not everyone follows these rules. Neuroeconomics experiments that vary the 'laws' and allow subjects to make choices under several legal regimes could be an important step towards better public policy. Such experiments could provide a deep understanding into the usefulness of laws that are either 'carrots' or 'sticks'. For example, when an action results in a harsh punishment (e.g. experimentally, a decrement of money), why do some subjects still choose to do this? What drives such behaviour? How much of it can be traced to nature and nurture? Do known criminals have different neural activity than non-criminals? The number of interesting questions is manifold. The late Margaret Gruter, of the Gruter Institute for Law and Behavioral Research, called this field 'neurojurisprudence'. The economic part is important experimentally because it allows the imposition of accept-able and valued rewards and punishments for behaviours in an experimental setting.

A specific legal example is property crime. Property crime (larceny) is little impacted by most punishments, an increased likelihood of detection, or the provision of presumed alternative leisure activities such as nighttime basketball (Zak 2000). More effective laws might be designed if the neural activation associated with obtaining property illegally, but risking punishment, were characterized. This is straightforward to do in a neuroeconomic experiment using, for example, the 'power-to-take' game (Bosman & van Winden 2002). Neural activity can be measured as rewards and punishments are varied to determine why most punishments fail to deter larceny, and to search for those that are likely to work. The neural activity of larcenists could be compared in this experiment with non-criminals to understand recidivism. In addition, humans appear to have a strong sense of ownership of physical property. Behaviourally, people value an item more when they possess it than when they do not (Camerer 2004). This suggests that people might pay more to protect property than the expected loss associated with its expropriation. There may be neural clues to this behaviour that might suggest why individuals may not want to trade off a given amount of theft for less police protection and lower taxes. This is one example of neuroeconomic–neurojurisprudence complementarity, but many more surely exist. Note that there are a host of important technical and ethical issues that this example opens up, including using averaged brain data to determine policy, using brain-scanning data to identify criminals, appropriate statistical thresholds to determine if something has been demonstrated, etc. The reader is referred to the discussion of these topics by Goodenough & Prehn (2004) and Greene & Cohen (2004) in this issue.

Another transdisciplinary field that also impacts questions of law is neuroethics (Greene & Haidt 2002; Moreno 2003). The notion that some behaviours are almost universally considered wrong is among the first issues that neuroethicists have studied. Greene et al. (2001) showed, using fMRI, that personal moral dilemmas (e.g. whether it is morally acceptable to personally kill one person to save five others from certain death) activated cortical areas associated with social cognition, including the medial OFC (BA9/10), posterior cingulate (BA39) and angular gyrus (BA39). Interestingly, regions associated with working memory (BA46, BA7/40) exhibited reduced neural activity during personal moral dilemmas. A legal implication of this research is that laws designed to prohibit personal moral violations must activate brain regions associated with understanding others to be effective.

In fMRI research similar to that of Greene *et al.* (2001) (though with substantially different control tasks), Moll *et al.* (2002) found that moral judgements are associated with significant BOLD signals in the medial OFC, as well as in the temporal pole (BA38) and superior temporal sulcus (BA21/22). This provides support for the role of emotions in moral judgments. Both the Greene and Moll studies could be extended using neuroeconomic methods (e.g. using monetary rewards and punishments) so that subjects' choices have weight and their attention is consistently focused on the task. Further, by varying the 'costs' of immoral behaviour, the robustness of moral disgust could be probed.

7.6 Conclusion

The nineteenth century economist Thorstein Veblen wrote in 1898 that 'Economics, properly understood, is simply a branch of biology'. Human beings are a biological species doing what every other species seeks to do: survive and reproduce (albeit with a larger brain than most other species). These activities require that choices be made to acquire resources, i.e. to process environmental signals, value alternatives and chose among them. Resource acquisition may also require that we interact with other humans, sometimes strategically. Neuroeconomics provides a unified framework to measure neurophysiological activity during the process of choice, and in doing so opens a window into human nature.

References

Adolphs, R. 2003 Cognitive neuroscience of human social behaviour *Nature Rev. Neurosci.* **4**, 165–178.

Aharon, I., Etcoff, N., Ariely, D., Chabris, C. F., O'Connor, E. & Breiter, H. C. 2001 Beautiful faces have variable reward value: fMRI and behavioral evidence. *Neuron* **32**, 537–551.

Barraclough, D. J., Conroy, M. L. & Lee, D. 2004 Prefrontal cortex and decision making in a mixed-strategy game. *Nature Neurosci* **7**, 404–410.

Berg, J., Dickhaut, J. & McCabe, K. 1995 Trust, reciprocity, and social history. *Games Econ. Behav.* **10**, 122–142.

Bjork, J. M., Knutson, B., Fong, G. W., Caggiano, D. M., Bennett, S. M. & Hommer, D. W. 2004 Incentive-elicited brain activation in adolescents: similarities and differences from young adults. *J. Neurosci* **24**, 1793–1802.

Bosman, R. & van Winden, F. 2002 Emotional hazard in a power-to-take game experiment. *Econ. J.* **112**, 147–169.

Bowles, S. & Gintis, H. 2003 Prosocial emotions. Santa Fe Institute working paper no. 02-07-028.

Boyd, R., Gintis, H., Bowles, S. & Richerson, P. J. 2003 The evolution of altruistic punishment. *Proc. Natl Acad. Sci. USA* **100**, 3531–3535.

Breiter, H. C., Aharon, I., Kahneman, D., Anders, D. & Shizgal, P. 2001 Functional imaging of neural responses to expectancy and experience of monetary gains and losses. *Neuron* **30**, 619–639.

Brosnan, S. F. & de Waal, F. B. M. 2003 Monkeys reject unequal pay. *Nature* **425**, 297–299.

Buckner, R. L. 2003 The hemodynamic inverse problem: making inferences about neural activity from MRI signals. *Proc. Natl Acad. Sci. USA* **100**, 2177–2179.

Camerer, C. F. 2004 Behavioral Game Theory: Experiments in Strategic Interaction. Princeton: Princeton University Press.

Camerer, C. F., Loewenstein, G. & Prelec, D. 2005 Neuroeconomics: how neuroscience can inform economics. *J. Economic Lit.* **43**, 9–64.

Cohen, J. D. & Blum, K. I. 2002 Reward and decision. *Neuron* **36**, 193–198.

Damasio, A. R. 1994 *Descartes' error: emotion, reason, and the human brain.* New York: Avon Books.

Dayan, P. & Balleine, B. W. 2002 Reward, motivation, and reinforcement learning. *Neuron* **36**, 285–298.

Dickhaut, J., McCabe, K., Nagode, J. C., Rustichini, A., Smith, K. & Pardo, J. V. 2003 The impact of the certainty context on the process of choice. *Proc. Natl Acad. Sci. USA* **100**, 3536–3541.

Fehr, E. & Rockenbach, B. 2003 Detrimental effects of sanctions on human altruism. *Nature* **422**, 137–140.

Frith, U. & Frith, C. D. 2003 Development and neurophysiology of mentalizing. *Phil. Trans. R. Soc. B* **358**, 459–473. (doi:10.1098/rstb.2002.1218)

Gheslin, M. & Landa, J. T. 1999 The emerging discipline of bioeconomics: aims and scope of the journal of bioeconomics *J. Bioecon.* **1**, 5–12.

Garris, P. A., Kilpatrick, M., Bunin, M. A., Michael, D., Walker, O. D. & Wightman, R. M. 1999 Dissociation of dopamine release in the nucleus accumbens from intracranial self-stimulation. *Nature* **398**, 67–69.

Glimcher, P. W. 2003 *Decisions, uncertainty, and the brain: the science of neuroeconomics.* Cambridge, MA: MIT Press.

Glimcher, P. W., Dorris, M. C., Bayer, H. M. & Lau, B. 2005 Physiologic utility theory and the neuroeconomics of choice. *Games Econ. Behav.* **2**, 213–256.

Goodenough, O. R. & Prehn, K. 2004 A neuroscientific approach to normative judgment in law and justice. *Phil. Trans. R. Soc. B* **359**, 1709–1726. (doi:10.1098/rstb. 2004.1552)

Greene, J. & Haidt, J. 2002 How (and where) does moral judgment work? *Trends Cogn. Sci.* **6**, 517–523.

Greene, J. & Cohen, J. 2004 For the law, neuroscience changes nothing and everything. *Phil. Trans. R. Soc. B* **359**, 1775–1785. (doi:10.1098/rstb.2004.1546)

Greene, J. D., Sommerville, R. B., Nystrom, L. E., Darley, J. M. & Cohen, J. D. 2001 An fMRI investigation of emotional engagement in moral judgment. *Science* **293**, 2105–2108. (doi: 10.1126/science.1062872)

Hill, E. & Sally, D. 2003 Dilemmas and bargains: autism, theory-of-mind, cooperation and fairness. Working paper, University College London.

Hirshleifer, J. 1985 The expanding domain of economics. *Am. Econ. Rev.* **75**, 53–68.

Hirshleifer, J. & Zak, P. J. 2004 The bioeconomics of social behavior: introduction. *J. Bioecon.* **6**, 1–2.

Kahn, I., Yeshurun, Y., Rotshtein, P., Fried, I., Ben-Bashat, D. & Hendler, T. 2002 The role of the amygdala in signaling prospective outcome of choice. *Neuron* **33**, 983–994.

Kahneman, D. 2004 Maps of bounded rationality: psychology for behavioral economics. *Am. Econ. Rev.* **93**, 1449–1475.

Kangarlu, A., Burgess, R. E., Zhu, H., Nakayama, T., Hamlin, R. L., Abduljalil, A. M. & Robitaille, P. M. 1999 Cognitive, cardiac, and physiological safety studies in ultra high field magnetic resonance imaging. *Magn. Reson. Imag.* **17**, 1407–1416.

Knutson, B. & Peterson, D. 2005 Neurally reconstructing expected utility. *Games Econ. Behav.* **2**, 305–315.

Knutson, B., Fong, G. W., Adams, C. M., Varner, J. & Hommer, D. 2001 Dissociation of reward anticipation and outcome with event-related fMRI. *NeuroReport* **12**, 3683–3687.

Knutson, B., Fong, G. W., Bennett, S. M., Adams, C. S. & Hommer, D. 2003 A region of mesial prefrontal cortex tracks monetarily rewarding outcomes: characterization with rapid event-related fMRI. *NeuroImage* **18**, 263–272.

Laibson, D., Repetto, A. & Tobacman, J. 1998 Self-control and savings for retirement. *Brook. Papers Econ. Act.* **1**, 91–196.

Lo, A. W. & Repin, D. 2002 The psychophysiology of real-time financial risk processing. *J. Cogn. Neurosci.* **14**, 323–339.

McCabe, K., Houser, D., Ryan, L., Smith, V. & Trouard, T. 2001 A functional imaging study of cooperation in two-person reciprocal exchange. *Proc. Natl Acad. Sci. USA* **98**, 11 832–11 835.

McClure, S. M., Laibson, D. I., Loewenstein, G. & Cohen, J. D. 2004 Separate neural systems value immediate and delayed monetary rewards. *Science* **306**, 2105–2108. (doi:10.1126/science.1100907)

Mobbs, D., Greicius, M. D., Abdel-Azim, E., Menon, V. & Reiss, A. L. 2003 Humor modulates the mesolimbic reward centers. *Neuron* **40**, 1041–1048.

Moll, J., de Oliveira-Souza, R., Bramati, I. E. & Grafman, J. 2002 Functional networks in emotional moral and non-moral judgments. *NeuroImage* **16**, 696–703.

Montague, R. P. & Berns, G. S. 2002 Neural economics and the biological substrates of valuation. *Neuron* **36**, 265–284.

Montague, P. R., Berns, G. S., Cohen, J. D., McClure, S. M., Pagnoni, G., Dhamala, M., Wiest, M. C., Karpov, I., King, R. D., Apple, N. & Fisher, R. E. 2002 Hyperscanning: simultaneous fMRI during linked social interactions. *Neuro-Image* **16**, 1159–1164.

Moreno, J. D. 2003 Neuroethics: an agenda for neuroscience and society. *Nature Rev. Neurosci.* **4**, 149–153.

Nelson, A. J., Heeger, D. J., McCabe, K., Houser, D., Zak, P. & Glimcher, P. W. 2004 Expected utility provides a model for choice behavior and brain activation in humans. Abstract No. 20.12. Society for Neuroscience.

North, D. 1990 *Institutions, institutional change and economic performance*. Cambridge University Press.

Platt, M. L. & Glimcher, P. W. 1999 Neural correlates of decision variables in parietal cortex. *Nature* **400**, 233–238.

Riedel, G., Platt, B. & Micheau, J. 2003 Glutamate receptor function in learning and memory. *Behav. Brain Res.* **140**, 1–47.

Rilling, J. K., Gutman, D. A., Zeh, T. R., Pagnoni, G., Berns, G. S. & Kilts, C. D. 2002 A neural basis for social cooperation. *Neuron* **35**, 395–405.

Robson, A. J. 2001 Why would nature give individuals utility functions? *J. Polit. Econ.* **109**, 900–914.

Rustichini, A., Dickhaut, J., Ghirardato, P., Smith, P. & Glimcher, P.W. 2004 Expected utility provides a model for choice behavior and brain activation in humans. Abstract No. 20. 12. Society for Neuroscience.

Sanfey, A. G., Rilling, J. K., Aronson, J. A., Nystrom, L. E. & Cohen, J. D. 2003 The neural basis of economic decision-making in the ultimatum game. *Science* **300**, 1755–1758. (doi: 10.1126/science.1082976)

Schultz, W., Dayan, P. & Montague, P. R. 1997 A neural substrate of prediction and reward. *Science* **275**, 1593–1599. (doi: 10.1126/science.275.5306.1593)

Smith, K., Dickhaut, J., McCabe, K. & Pardo, J. 2002 Neuronal substrates for choice under ambiguity, risk, certainty, gains, and losses. *Mngmt Sci.* **48**, 711–718.

Smith, V. 1998 The two faces of Adam Smith. *South. Econ. J.* **65**, 1–29.

Sugrue, L. P., Corrado, G. S. & Newsome, W. T. 2004 Matching behavior and the representation of value in the parietal cortex. *Science* **304**, 1782–1787. (doi: 10.1126/science.1094765)

Zak, P. J. 2000 Larceny. *Econ. Govern.* **1**, 157–179.

Zak, P. J. 2002 Genetics, family structure, and economic growth *J. Evol. Econ.* **12**, 343–365.

Zak, P. J. & Knack, S. 2001 Trust and growth. *Econ. J.* **111**, 295–321.

Zak, P. J. & Denzau, A. 2001 Economics is an evolutionary science. In *Evolutionary approaches in the behavioral sciences: toward a better understanding of human nature* (ed. A. Somit &S. Peterson), pp. 31–65. New York: JAI Press.

Zak, P. J. & Park, K.-W. 2002 Population genetics and economic growth. *J. Bioecon.* **4**, 1–37.

Zak, P. J., Kurzban, R. & Matzner, W. 2004 The neurobiology of trust. *Ann. NY Acad. Sci.* **1032**, 224–27.

Glossary

ACC   anterior cingulate cortex
BOLD   blood oxygen-level dependent
DLPFC   dorsolateral prefrontal cortex

DM1   decision maker 1
DM2   decision maker 2
EEG   electroencephalogram
ERP   evoked response potential
fMRI   functional magnetic resonance imaging
LIP   lateral intraparietal
LTP   long-term potentiation
MPFC   mesial prefrontal cortex
OFC   orbitofrontal cortex
OFS   orbitofrontal–striatal
OT   oxytocin
PD   Prisoner's Dilemma
PET   positron emission tomography
SLEA   sublenticular extended amygdala
TMS   transcranial magnetic stimulation

Decision making and evidence

8

A cognitive neuroscience framework for understanding causal reasoning and the law

Jonathan A. Fugelsang* and Kevin N. Dunbar

Over the past couple of decades, there have been great developments in the fields of psychology and cognitive neuroscience that have allowed the advancement of our understanding of how people make judgements about causality in several domains. We provide a review of some of the contemporary psychological models of causal thinking that are directly relevant to legal reasoning. In addition, we cover some exciting new research using advanced neuroimaging techniques that have helped to uncover the underlying neural signatures of complex causal reasoning. Through the use of functional imaging, we provide a first-hand look at how the brain responds to evidence that is either *consistent* or *inconsistent* with one's beliefs and expectations. Based on the data covered in this review, we propose some ideas for how the effectiveness of causal reasoning, especially as it pertains to legal decision-making, may be facilitated.

Keywords: causation; causality; legal; decision-making; functional magnetic resonance imaging; neuropsychology

8.1 Introduction

The human mind has evolved many cognitive tools including abstraction, counterfactual thought, deduction and induction, for a vast variety of circumstances that are applied differently depending on the task at hand. Central to these domain general processes is causal thinking. An individual's ability to determine if a precipitating event was the cause of an outcome is essential for making sense of the complex world in which we live. Indeed, many of the learning and evaluative processes in which individuals engage pertain to the development and testing of causal models portraying the relationship between variables of interest (Dunbar 1995; Fugelsang *et al.* 2004). Such causal reasoning processes are evident in tasks ranging from simple everyday reasoning, such as why one's computer crashes, to complex scientific discovery, such as the formulation of the 'Universal Law of Gravitation' in the *Principia* by The Royal Society's former president Isaac Newton (Newton 1999).

This ability to infer causality is not only crucial for human reasoning in general, but also more specifically to the application of law. The legal system often asks lawyers, jurors and judges to determine if an individual's actions were responsible for a specific outcome. In so doing, the legal system requires that individuals reason about the evidence presented to them in an *unbiased* manner, formulating a judgement of causality if and only if the evidence presented to them overwhelmingly depict the acts of the defendant as causally responsible for the outcome under question.

* Author for correspondence (jafugels@uwaterloo.ca).

In the present essay, we address two main questions that are directly relevant to such legal reasoning: (i) what sources of information do people use to evaluate causality, and (ii) to what degree do people evaluate evidence about causality in an *unbiased* manner? To answer these questions we will discuss both behavioural and fMRI experiments conducted in our laboratory and others.

8.2 Legal decision-making and causal reasoning

Whereas much decision-making research in the legal domain has focused on the content-oriented (i.e. substance of the trial itself) aspects of legal decision-making (e.g. Matlon 1986), research on the extra-legal aspects of legal decision-making (i.e. decision-making strategies of individuals) has primarily been conducted by cognitive and social psychologists (see Pennington & Hastie (1990) for a comprehensive review). Perhaps not surprisingly, much of this work has focused on criminal jury decision-making processes, especially as they pertain to judgements involving more serious crimes often involving capital punishment (e.g. Constanzo & Constanzo 1994; Wiener *et al.* 1995). The ability of jurors to make decisions in a non-arbitrary and *unbiased* manner in these situations is of obvious importance. Courts ask jurors to set aside personal beliefs and biases to make judgements in favour of, or against, a defendant based solely on the facts of the case presented to them. This *unbiased* application of the law is crucial, not only for obvious judicial reasons, but also to maintain consistency among rulings within and across jurisdictions. As alluded to in § 1, one's ability to make such judgements is directly related to one's ability to effectively attribute causality when presented with evidence. This evidence can come from a variety of sources and often involves the construction of causal chains of events, whereby the link between the actions of the defendant and the outcome under question may be separated by several intermediate variables, each with a specific probability of occurring (Einhorn & Hogarth 1986). Indeed, this is not an easy task.

Researchers in both cognitive and social psychology have developed several models that capture different aspects of this causal reasoning process. The predominant view of causality in the psychological literature over the past two decades has dealt with the extent to which people induce causality based on observed statistical covariation-based evidence (e.g. Jenkins & Ward 1965; Rescorla 1968; Kelley 1973; Allan & Jenkins 1980; Einhorn & Hogarth 1986; Cheng & Novick 1990, 1992; Cheng 1997; White 2002). These models of causality stem from the Humean philosophy of radical empiricism (Hume 1978), which is based on the assumption that events that covary are more likely to be judged as causally related than events that do not covary. Such models typically propose computational algorithms by which reasoners are thought to derive an estimate of causality from such observable correlated events, and delineate conditions under which the covariation between variables of interest can be used to infer causality.

There are several different models of causal reasoning, each proposing different accounts of how people induce causality based on observed statistical covariation. Most derive estimates of the degree of covariation based on computing statistical contrasts between the presence and absence of events and outcomes. Perhaps the most popular contemporary model of causality that is based on this covariation principle in the recent psychological literature is the Power PC theory (Cheng 1997; Novick & Cheng 2004). According to this model, an individual considers both the probability of the effect occurring in the presence of the cause [$P(e/c)$] and the probability of the effect occurring in the absence of the cause [$P(e/\sim c)$]. Specifically, Cheng and her colleagues propose that the perceived causal relationship between variables of interest is a function of both the cause's covariation with the given effect [quantified as $P(e/c) - P(e/\sim c)$] and the inverse of the base rate [$1 - P(e/-c)$] of that effect. That is, reasoners are suggested to view an individual or an event as a cause of a specific outcome to the extent that the individual or event raises the likelihood of the outcome above some baseline of the outcome occurring when the individual or event is absent. Specifically, the extent to which smoking may be judged as causally responsible for the incidence of lung cancer in a group of patients would depend, not only on the degree to which smoking and lung cancer co-occur together, but also the degree to which lung cancer occurs in the absence of smoking. Proponents of this and other similar covariation-based models (e.g. Cheng & Novick 1990, 1992; White 2002) claim that people are sensitive to the covariation between the cause and effect, and then use this information to derive a measure of the causal link or liability of the causal candidates in question.

An alternative account for how people may judge an individual or an event as liable for an outcome concerns the extent to which that individual or outcome is judged to be a rare or an abnormal event in the given situation. Hilton & Slugoski (1986) have proposed such a model, the Abnormal Conditions Focus model. They propose the causal inference progresses in two stages. The first stage is proposed to involve a judgement about the degree to which a candidate is perceived to be *necessary* for the occurrence of the effect. For example, both oxygen and flame are necessary, but not sufficient variables required for paper to burn; in the absence of either event, paper would not burn. Consequently, both causes would be selected during the first stage of reasoning. The second stage of reasoning involves selecting the abnormal variable from the set of *necessary* causes identified by the first stage of reasoning. That is, a cause is selected that departs from that which is normal for the given circumstances. Hilton and Slugoski provide a helpful example that clarifies these two components. They note that the speed of a train, the weight of the railway cars, and a faulty rail are all necessary components for a train to derail. However, the faulty rail is the one component that is likely to be selected as causally relevant, because it is the single feature from the set that is abnormal for the everyday operation of trains.

Whereas the former models stress the role of observed covariation-based evidence, other cognitive models have examined the degree to which people judge causality based on their beliefs and expectations about what events have the *capacity* or *power* to produce specific outcomes. These models stem from the philosophical tradition of Immanuel Kant (1965) who proposed that causality is an inherent law of nature, not merely an emergent property of statistical regularity. Harre & Madden (1975; see also Hart & Honore 1959; White 1989, 1995; Ahn *et al.* 1995) have elaborated on this philosophical tradition by positing that certain objects are perceived to possess stable properties whose power to produce a specific outcome is based on the 'chemical, physical, or genetic natures of the entities involved' (p. 5). For example, individuals may judge smoking to be causally related to the development of lung cancer owing to their beliefs about the carcinogenic properties of inhaling tobacco, independently of the degree to which they may be thought to correlate in the actual environment.

Harre and Madden further elucidate the relationship between causal agents and enabling conditions. That is, a specific causal outcome is thought to occur only under the appropriate enabling conditions. For example, an individual may possess the disposition to commit a violent crime; however, this disposition may only result in a violent act if the individual is intoxicated. In this example, *intoxication* would act as the enabling or releasing condition that allows the disposition of the individual (that is, to be aggressive) to be released. Based on these defining features of causality, causal roles are defined conceptually, rather than based solely on observing correlations between variables in the environment. The assessment of causal hypotheses, therefore, is thought to be mainly a matter of seeking some object believed to possess the power to produce the effect in question and then determining if the appropriate releasing conditions are present to enable the power of the object to exert the effect (see Dunbar 2002) for an example of this phenomenon in scientists reasoning 'live' in their laboratories). In many cases, this search for an object that possesses the power to produce a specific outcome may supersede the search for evidence about the covariation between variables of interest (e.g. White 1989; Ahn *et al.* 1995).

8.3 Integrating evidence with one's beliefs and expectations

Recently, our laboratory and others have been conducting several behavioural experiments examining the degree to which an individual's beliefs and expectations (derived from information about the inherent properties of objects) influence how they make causal decisions about covariation-based evidence. Several studies have found that individuals appear to have great difficulty evaluating evidence that is inconsistent with their beliefs. For example, research in a variety of disciplines including cognitive psychology (e.g. Bruner *et al.* 1956; Wason 1968; Mynatt *et al.* 1977; Koriat *et al.* 1980; Klayman & Ha 1987; Evans 1989), judicial reasoning (e.g. Hendry & Shaffer 1989; Pennington & Hastie 1993; Simon 2004; Simon *et al.* 2004) and medical reasoning (e.g. Elstein & Bordage 1979) have all demonstrated examples of biases in evidence-based decision-making. The typical finding is that people are more likely to attend to, seek out and evaluate evidence that is consistent with their beliefs, and ignore or downplay evidence that is inconsistent with their beliefs. In a series of experiments conducted in our laboratory, we have examined how reasoners appear to use their prior knowledge and expectations to *constrain* how they evaluate covariation-based evidence.

In one series of studies we (Fugelsang *et al.* 2004) created a causal thinking situation where participants were asked to test the effectiveness of novel drugs designed to produce a particular outcome. The plausibility of the causal theories was manipulated by presenting participants with a brief introductory statement, which depicted a causal theory that contained either a plausible mechanism of action or an implausible mechanism of action. This manipulation was intended to induce a specific belief about how the potential cause may produce an expected outcome. Evidence was then provided to participants in a trial-by-trial format where they viewed multiple trials of evidence for each type of drug. Under some conditions the candidate cause covaried strongly with an expected outcome; under other conditions the candidate cause covaried weakly with an expected outcome. Here, for example, evidence of a strong covariation would be *consistent* with their beliefs and expectations based on a plausible theory and *inconsistent* with their beliefs and expectations based on an implausible theory.

The basic finding is that people weight the covariation-based evidence stronger when it follows from a theory that contains a plausible mechanism of action than when the evidence follows from a theory that contains an implausible mechanism of action (see Fugelsang & Thompson 2000, 2003; Fugelsang & Dunbar 2005). We have argued that this could be seen as a useful heuristic given the potentially infinite number of covarying causes for every given effect occurring in the natural environment. Using one's beliefs and expectations to *filter* out evidence for implausible theories serves to make the task of building causal theories from evidence achievable. Of course, this heuristic does have a drawback in that potentially valid evidence may be discounted if it is inconsistent with a theory that an individual has strong beliefs in.

8.4 Brain-based correlates of complex causal reasoning

An exciting recent approach to the study of human reasoning and decision-making has accompanied the advent of advanced functional brain imaging techniques such as positron emission topography, event-related potentials and fMRI. Using these new techniques, we are able to get a first-hand look at how the brain responds during complex reasoning. Recent work by several cognitive neuroscientists has examined the neurological underpinnings of a variety of complex reasoning and decision-making processes including problem solving (Goel & Grafman 1995; Colvin *et al.* 2001; Fincham *et al.* 2002), analogical reasoning (Wharton *et al.* 2000; Kroger *et al.* 2002; A. Green, J. Fugelsang, N. Shamosh and K. Dunbar, unpublished data), inductive reasoning (Goel & Dolan 2000; Seger *et al.* 2000) and deductive reasoning (Osherson *et al.* 1998; Parsons & Osherson 2001; Goel & Dolan 2003). The major research approach has been to have participants take part in a task that taps a specific reasoning process of interest (e.g. deductive reasoning) and contrast that with a control task that contains much of the same visual and cognitive stimulation but devoid of the specific reasoning process of interest. By contrasting the task-related brain activations of the specific reasoning task with the control task, researchers are able to measure the unique brain activity associated with the specific reasoning process of interest.

We (Fugelsang & Dunbar 2005) have taken a slightly different approach in our research programme on the neural underpinning of complex causal reasoning. Rather than using fMRI to uncover specialized neural circuitry for causal thinking, we have been examining how reasoning with statistical covariation-based evidence that is either consistent or inconsistent with participants' beliefs recruits brain networks that have been implicated in several more domain general cognitive processes. Specifically, we have been using fMRI to uncover the mechanisms by which statistical evidence is integrated with one's beliefs and expectations about that evidence in the brain.

The main question that motivated this research programme was the extent to which people might be more inclined to attend to and assimilate evidence that is consistent with their beliefs, while treating evidence that is inconsistent with their beliefs as error. If that was the case, there are several key brain networks that might be the neural signature of these processes. For example, research in behavioural and cognitive neuroscience has indicated that there are several different brain networks that are invoked during learning (e.g. McDermott *et al.* 1999; Poldrack *et al.* 2002) and in error detection and conflict monitoring (e.g. Botvinick *et al.* 2001; Holroyd & Cole 2002; Kerns *et al.* 2004; Yeung *et al.* 2004) that may be invoked for these different conditions. Based on our prior behavioural research, we predicted that different networks related to learning and conflict monitoring may show increased activity when participants are receiving evidence that is consistent, or inconsistent, respectively, with their beliefs and expectations.

Using a similar paradigm to that of our behavioural experiments, we measured the task-related blood oxygen-level-dependent response as participants observed evidence on the effectiveness of drugs designed to relieve depressive symptoms. The plausibility of the theory of action of the drug and whether the data were consistent or inconsistent with the theory were varied. We found that when people were reasoning with evidence that was *consistent* with their beliefs, a distinct network of brain regions widely associated with learning and memory were significantly activated, including the caudate and the parahippocampal gyrus. By contrast, when the evidence was *inconsistent* with people's beliefs, a different pattern of activation occurred that is widely associated with error detection and conflict resolution, including the anterior cingulate cortex, posterior cingulate and the precuneus. A graphical depiction of this brain-based model of these findings is depicted in figure 8.1 where symbols in light grey depict the observed brain network activated when beliefs and evidence are *consistent*, and symbols in dark grey depict the observed brain network activated when beliefs and evidence are *inconsistent*. These findings provide a neural instantiation for the behavioural interactions between beliefs and evidence that we covered in § 3. Specifically, people's beliefs and expectations may act as a *biological filter* during evidence evaluation by selectively recruiting learning mechanisms for evidence that is consistent with their beliefs and error detection mechanisms for evidence that is inconsistent with their beliefs.

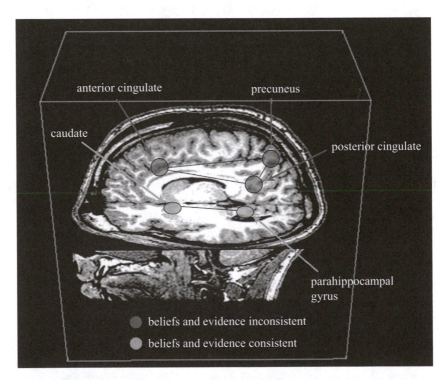

Fig. 8.1 A graphical depiction of a brain-based model displaying the two dissociated networks involved with belief and evidence integration in causal reasoning. Light grey symbols depict the observed brain-based network preferentially recruited when people's beliefs and the observed evidence are *consistent*, and dark grey symbols depict the observed brain-based network preferentially recruited when beliefs and evidence are *inconsistent*.

8.5 Further implications for legal decision-making

In this essay, we have covered a variety of experimental studies that demonstrate how people's evaluation of evidence is highly influenced by their beliefs about the objects and events under consideration. That is, people typically *do not* evaluate evidence in an atheoretical manner; rather they use their beliefs and expectations to guide their assessment of the evidence given to them (e.g. Evans *et al.* 1983; Fugelsang *et al.* 2004). This inter-play between one's beliefs and evidence has a distinct neural signature, in that evidence that is consistent with one's beliefs is more likely to recruit neural tissue involved in learning and memory, whereas evidence that is inconsistent with one's beliefs is more likely to invoke neural tissue associated with error detection and conflict monitoring.

These findings have important implications for legal reasoning. Specifically, the human brain appears to be specifically sensitive to the degree to which evidence, in the form of statistical information, is consistent with the expectations of the individual. Is this something that the brain does automatically, or do people have conscious cognitive control over this process? Indeed, the answer to this question may have large implications for how one can hope to minimize the influence of such biases when they hinder legal decision-making. The finding that these brain-based dissociations occur when evidence is first being evaluated suggests that people may be unable to set aside their beliefs and expectation when making judgements about causality. These data are corroborated by some recent findings by Fugelsang & Thompson (2003). They provided data that showed that individuals were unable to gauge the degree to which their beliefs and expectations influenced their evaluation of statistical evidence. Taken together, these findings suggest that individuals may not be entirely aware of the extent to which their expectations influence their decisions when judging evidence.

Judges and lawyers are very aware that people can be biased in their reasoning. Our results indicate that there may be brain-based underpinnings for these biases. Knowing that one's beliefs can hinder reasoning, and that this may occur at an automatic or uncon-scious level, what additional strides can be taken to minimize the influence of one's beliefs when they may hinder legal reasoning? Several researchers have found that instructions developed to augment the relevance of normative information can reduce the impact that one's beliefs have on their reasoning (Evans 2002; Evans *et al.* 1994). Specifically, Evans and colleagues have found that instructions that emphasize the role of logical form of a problem can result in a decrease in the influence of the content of the scenarios. In addi-tion, Dunbar (1993) found that altering the goal of a reasoner could be very effective in switching a reasoner's strategy from one of confirmation seeking to disconfirmation seeking.

An important avenue for future research would be to examine the role of making individuals cognizant of the potential biasing effects of their beliefs before they engage in legal reasoning. Laying out potential alternative hypotheses before the presentation of evidence may minimize the influence of specific beliefs on the part of the individual asked to weigh the evidence. In addition, the biasing effects of beliefs on evidential evaluation and subsequent judgements are surely influenced by several factors related to the acquisi-tion and maintenance of those beliefs. For example, beliefs may vary in terms of several variables, such as personal relevance, age of initial acquisition and original source of acquisition, that may be orthogonal to the strength of those beliefs. In addition, the extent to which such extra-legal factors (e.g. belief biases in decision-making) influence different content-oriented factors of the judicial process (e.g. judges' instructions, examination of witnesses and the use of exhibits) is still relatively unknown. Further cross-talk between cognitive neuroscientists and legal academics and professionals will do much to inform these future research endeavours.

The authors thank the Honorable Judge Morris Hoffman, Professor Kenneth Kreiling and Professor Oliver Goodenough for providing discussions on various aspects of the research contained in our essay. Research reported in this essay has been funded by grants from Dartmouth College, and the Natural Sciences and Engineering Research Council of Canada.

References

Ahn, W., Kalish, C. W., Medin, D. L. & Gelman, S. A. 1995
The role of covariation versus mechanism information in causal attribution. *Cognition* **54**, 299–352.

Allan, L. G. & Jenkins, H. M. 1980 The judgements of contingency and the nature of response alternatives. *Can. J. Psychol.* **34**, 1–11.

Botvinick, M., Braver, T., Barch, D., Carter, C. & Cohen, J. 2001 Conflict monitoring and cognitive control. *Psychol. Rev.* **108**, 625–652.

Bruner, J. S., Goodnow, J. J. & Austin, G. A. 1956 *A study of thinking*. New York: NY Science Editions.

Cheng, P. W. 1997 From covariation to causation: a causal power theory. *Psychol. Rev.* **104**, 367–405.

Cheng, P. W. & Novick, L. R. 1990 A probabilistic contrast model of causal induction. *J. Pers. Soc. Psychol.* **58**, 545–567.

Cheng, P. W. & Novick, L. R. 1992 Covariation in natural causal induction. *Psychol. Rev.* **99**, 365–382.

Colvin, M. K., Dunbar, K. & Grafman, J. 2001 The effects of frontal lobe lesions on goal achievement in the water jug task. *J. Cogn. Neurosci.* **13**, 1129–1147.

Constanzo, S. & Constanzo, M. 1994 Life or death decisions: an analysis of capital jury decision-making under the special issues sentencing framework. *Law Hum. Behav.* **18**, 151–170.

Dunbar, K. 1993 Concept discovery in a scientific domain. *Cogn. Sci.* **17**, 397–434.

Dunbar, K. 1995 How scientists really reason: scientific reasoning in real-world laboratories. In *Mechanisms of insight* (ed. R. J. Sternberg & J. Davidson), pp. 365–395. Cambridge, MA: MIT Press.

Dunbar, K. 2002 Science as category: implications of *in vivo* science for theories of cognitive development, scientific discovery, and the nature of science. In *Cognitive models of science* (ed. P. Caruthers, S. Stich & M. Siegel), pp. 154–170. New York: Cambridge University Press.

Einhorn, H. J. & Hogarth, R. M. 1986 Judging probable cause. *Psychol. Bull.* **99**, 3–19.

Elstein, A. S. & Bordage, G. 1979 Psychology of clinical reasoning. In *Health psychology: a handbook* (ed. G. Stone, F. Cohen & N. Adler), pp. 333–367. San Francisco, CA: Jossey-Bass.

Evans, J. St B. T. 1989 *Bias in human reasoning: causes and consequences*. Hove: Psychological Press.

Evans, J. St B. T. 2002 Logic and human reasoning: an assessment of the deduction paradigm. *Psychol. Bull.* **128**, 978–996.

Evans, J. St B. T., Barston, J. L. & Pollard, P. 1983 On the conflict between logic and belief in syllogistic reasoning. *Mem. Cogn.* **11**, 295–306.

Evans, J. St B. T., Newstead, S. E., Allen, J. L. & Pollard, P. 1994 Debiasing by instruction: the case of belief bias. *Eur. J.Cogn. Psychol.* 6, 263–285.

Fincham, J. M., Carter, C. S., van Veen, V., Stenger, V. A. & Anderson, J. R. 2002 Neural mechanisms of planning: a computational analysis using event-related fMRI. *Proc. Natl. Acad. Sci. USA* **99**, 3346–3351.

Fugelsang, J. A. & Dunbar, K. (2005(1)) Brain-based mechanisms underlying complex causal thinking. *Neuropsychologia*. **483**, 1204–1213.

Fugelsang, J. & Thompson, V. 2000 Strategy selection in causal reasoning: when beliefs and covariation collide. *Can. J. Exp. Psychol.* **54**, 13–32.

Fugelsang, J. A. & Thompson, V. A. 2003 A dual-process model of belief and evidence interactions in causal reasoning. *Mem. Cogn.* **31**, 800–815.

Fugelsang, J. A., Stein, C., Green, A. & Dunbar, K. 2004 Theory and data interactions of the scientific mind: evidence from the molecular and the cognitive laboratory. *Can. J. Exp. Psychol.* **58**, 132–141.

Goel, V. & Dolan, R. J. 2000 Anatomical segregation of component processes in an inductive inference task. *J. Cogn. Neurosci.* **12**, 110–119.

Goel, V. & Dolan, R. L. 2003 Explaining modulation of reasoning by belief. *Cognition* **87**, 11–22.

Goel, V. & Grafman, J. 1995 Are the frontal lobes implicated in 'planning' functions? Interpreting data from the Tower of Hanoi. *Neuropsychologia* **33**, 623–642.

Harre, R. & Madden, E. H. 1975 *Causal powers: a theory of natural necessity*. Oxford: Basil Blackwell.

Hart, H. & Honore, A. 1959 *Causation in law*. Oxford: Clarendon.

Hendry, S. H. & Shaffer, D. R. 1989 On testifying in one's own behalf: interactive effects of evidential strength and defendant's testimonial demeanor on jurors' decisions. *J. Appl. Psychol.* **74**, 539–545.

Hilton, D. & Slugoski, B. 1986 Knowledge-based causal attribution: the abnormal conditions focus model. *Psychol. Rev.* **93**, 75–88.

Holroyd, C. B. & Cole, M. G. H. 2002 The neural basis of human error processing: reinforcement learning, dopamine, and error-related negativity. *Psychol. Rev.* **109**, 679–709.

Hume, D. 1978 *A treatise of human nature*. Oxford University Press. [Original work published 1739.]

Jenkins, H. & Ward, W. 1965 Judgments of contingency between response and outcomes. *Psychol. Monogr.* **7**, 1–17.

Kant, I. 1965 *Critique of pure reason*. London: Macmillan & Co. [Original work published 1781.]

Kelley, H. 1973 The process of causal attribution. *Am. Psychol.* **28**, 107–128.

Kerns, J. G., Cohen, J. D., MacDonald, A. W., Cho, R. Y., Stenger, A. & Carter, C. S. 2004 Anterior cingulate conflict monitoring and adjustment in control. *Science* **303**, 1023–1026.

Klayman, J. & Ha, Y. 1987 Confirmation, disconfirmation, and information in hypothesis testing. *Psychol. Rev.* **94**, 211–228.

Koriat, A., Lichtenstein, S. & Fischhoff, B. 1980 Reasons for confidence. *J. Exp. Psychol. Learn.* **6**, 107–118.

Kroger, J. K., Sabb, F. W., Fales, C. L., Bookheimer, S. Y., Cohen, M. S. & Holyoak, K. J. 2002 Recruitment of anterior dorsolateral prefrontal cortex in human reasoning: a parametric study of relational complexity. *Cerebr. Cortex* **12**, 477–485.

McDermott, K. B., Ojemann, J. G., Petersen, S. E., Ollinger, J. M., Snyder, A. Z., Akbudak, E., Conturo, T. E. & Raichle, M. E. 1999 Direct comparison of episodic encoding and retrieval of words: an event-related fMRI study. *Memory* **7**, 661–678.

Matlon, R. J. 1986 Factors affecting jury decision-making. *Soc. Action Law* **12**, No 41–42.

Mynatt, B. T., Doherty, M. E. & Tweney, R. D. 1977 Confirmation bias in a simulated research environment: an experimental study of scientific inference. *Q. J. Exp. Psychol.* **29**, 85–95.

Newton, I. 1999 *The principia: mathematical principles of natural philosophy*. Berkley, CA: University of California Press. [Original work published 1678.]

Novick, L. & Cheng, P. 2004 Assessing interactive causal inference. *Psychol. Rev.* **111**, 455–485.

Osherson, D., Perani, D., Cappa, S., Schnur, T., Grassi, F. & Fazio, F. 1998 Distinct brain loci in deductive versus probabilistic reasoning. *Neuropsychologia* **36**, 369–376.

Parsons, L. M. & Osherson, D. 2001 New evidence for distinct right and left brain systems for deductive versus probabilistic reasoning. *Cerebr. Cortex* **11**, 954–965.

Pennington, N. & Hastie, R. 1990 Practical implications of psychological research on juror and juror decision-making. *Pers. Soc. Psychol. Bull.* **16**, 90–105.

Pennington, N. & Hastie, R. 1993 The story model of juror decision-making. In *Inside the juror: the psychology of jury decision-making* (ed. R. Hastie), pp. 192–221. New York: Cambridge University Press.

Poldrack, R. A., Clark, J., Pare-Blagoev, E. J., Shohamy, D., Creso Moyano, J., Myers, C. & Gluck, M. A. 2002 Interactive memory systems in the human brain. *Nature* **414**, 546–550.

Rescorla, R. A. 1968 Probability of shock in the presence and absence of CS in fear conditioning. *J. Comp. Physiol. Psychol.* **66**, 1–5.

Seger, C., Poldrack, R., Prabhakaran, V., Zhao, M., Glover, G. & Gabrieli, J. 2000 Hemispheric asymmetries and individual differences in visual concept learning as measured by functional MRI. *Neuropsychologia* **38**, 1316–1324.

Simon, D. 2004 A third view of the black box: coherence based reasoning in law. *Univ. Chicago Law Rev.* **71**, 511–586.

Simon, D., Snow, C. & Read, S. 2004 The redux of cognitive consistency theories: evidence judgements by constraint satisfaction. *J. Pers. Soc. Psychol.* **86**, 814–837.

Wason, P. C. 1968 Reasoning about a rule. *Q. J. Exp. Psychol.* **20**, 273–281.

Wharton, C. M., Grafman, J., Flitman, S. S., Hansen, E. K., Brauner, J., Marks, A. & Honda, M. 2000 Toward neuroanatomical models of analogy: a positron emission tomography study of analogical mapping. *Cogn. Psychol.* **40**, 173–197.

White, P. A. 1989 A theory of causal processing. *Br. J. Psychol.* **80**, 431–454.

White, P. A. 1995 Use of prior beliefs in the assignment of causal roles: causal powers versus covariation-based accounts. *Mem. Cogn.* **23**, 243–254.

White, P. A. 2002 Perceiving a strong causal relation in a weak contingency: further investigation of the evidential evaluation model of causal judgement. *Q. J. Exp. Psychol. A* **55**, 97–114.

Wiener, R. L., Pritchard, C. C. & Weston, M. 1995 Comprehensibility of approved jury instructions in capital murder cases. *J. Appl. Psychol.* **80**, 455–467.

Yeung, N., Botvinick, M. M. & Cohen, J. D. 2004 The neural basis of error-detection: conflict monitoring and the error-related negativity. *Psychol. Rev.* **111**, 931–959.

Glossary

fMRI   functional magnetic resonance imaging

Truthfulness

9

A cognitive neurobiological account of deception: evidence from functional neuroimaging

Sean A. Spence*, Mike D. Hunter, Tom F. D. Farrow, Russell D. Green, David H. Leung, Catherine J. Hughes and Venkatasubramanian Ganesan

An organism may use misinformation, knowingly (through deception) or unknowingly (as in the case of camouflage), to gain advantage in a competitive environment. From an evolutionary perspective, greater tactical deception occurs among primates closer to humans, with larger neocortices. In humans, the onset of deceptive behaviours in childhood exhibits a developmental trajectory, which may be regarded as 'normal' in the majority and deficient among a minority with certain neurodevelopmental disorders (e.g. autism). In the human adult, deception and lying exhibit features consistent with their use of 'higher' or 'executive' brain systems. Accurate detection of deception in humans may be of particular importance in forensic practice, while an understanding of its cognitive neurobiology may have implications for models of 'theory of mind' and social cognition, and societal notions of responsibility, guilt and mitigation. In recent years, functional neuroimaging techniques (especially functional magnetic resonance imaging) have been used to study deception. Though few in number, and using very different experimental protocols, studies published in the peer-reviewed literature exhibit certain consistencies. Attempted deception is associated with activation of executive brain regions (particularly prefrontal and anterior cingulate cortices), while truthful responding has not been shown to be associated with any areas of increased activation (relative to deception). Hence, truthful responding may comprise a relative 'baseline' in human cognition and communication. The subject who lies may necessarily engage 'higher' brain centres, consistent with a purpose or intention (to deceive). While the principle of executive control during deception remains plausible, its precise anatomy awaits elucidation.

Keywords: lying; deception; executive function; prefrontal cortex; functional magnetic resonance imaging

9.1 Introduction

[L]ie . . . a false statement made with the intention of deceiving . . . .

(Chambers 1991)

[D]eception . . . a successful or unsuccessful deliberate attempt, without forewarning, to create in another a belief which the communicator considers to be untrue.

(Vrij 2001)

That deception has long been of salience to human beings is apparent in the religious texts of many civilizations. From the writings of Ptahhotep five millennia ago (Chinweizu 2001), through the Hebrew Old Testament, to later works, humans have been encouraged to be truthful: 'Thou shalt not bear false witness against thy neighbour' (Exodus 20: 16,

* Author for correspondence (s.a.spence@sheffield.ac.uk).

King James version). The presence of such injunctions suggests that humans do indeed bear false witness, not least when they are required to comment upon others. Hence, any consideration of the relationship between the 'law' and the 'brain' must take account of what humans do when they seek to deceive. Our view is that when humans lie they are probably using some of the 'highest' centres of their brains, a proposition that has implications for notions of moral responsibility.

Furthermore, the deception practised in the courtroom or the cell can be seen within a wider context. There are emerging literatures in evolutionary studies (Dunbar 2000; Byrne 2003), normal human child development (Ford 1995) and developmental psychopathology (Sodian & Frith 1992; Hughes & Russell 1993) suggesting that deception is an ability that develops naturally during childhood, and which is 'normal'. Such behaviours follow a characteristic developmental trajectory (Ford 1995; O'Connell 1998) and are impaired among humans with specific neurodevelopmental disorders (e.g. autism; Sodian & Frith 1992). Hence, there would appear to be an interesting tension between what is supposedly socially undesirable but normal (i.e. telling lies), and that which is said to be commendable but pathological (i.e. total truthfulness). Normal human social interaction may depend upon limited disclosure. Indeed, several authors have pointed out that strictly truthful communication at all times might be rather hard to live with (e.g. Ford 1995; Vrij 2001) and truth itself may be used to malicious ends while some forms of lie can be altruistic (Ford 1995). Across cultures there are more words for deception and lying than for telling the truth, an apparent discrepancy that may reflect the social sensitivity of indicating that another person is dishonest (Ford 1995).

9.2 The use of deception

> [O]ne must know how to colour one's actions and to be a great liar and deceiver. Men are so simple, and so much creatures of circumstance, that the deceiver will always find someone ready to be deceived.
>
> (Machiavelli 1999, p. 57)

Tactical deception is defined as a behaviour that forms part of the normal repertoire of an animal but which is deployed in such a way that it appears to mislead a conspecific, to the advantage of the index organism (Byrne 2003). Drawing on the available evolutionary evidence, Byrne (2003) speculated that tactical deception probably emerged within the primate lineage some 12 Myr ago, thereby inferring sufficient cognitive capacity among primate species at that time.

Studies of contemporary non-human primates suggest that some form of purposeful deception occurs in those closest to man (in terms of their evolutionary lineage), and that, at the level of species, neocortical volume is related to the frequency of such observed deception (Byrne 2003). 'Simply knowing the ratio of the brain taken up by the neo-cortex, divided by the volume of the rest of the brain, enables us to predict 60% of the variance in the amount of deception that is observed in the species concerned' (Byrne 2003, p. 51).

Why might deception arise within primate colonies? Adenzato & Ardito (1999) suggest that deception facilitates individual autonomy within the constraints of group living. To be able to do what he/she wishes, especially in the face of hierarchical restraint, an organism must be able to mislead others. Adenzato and Ardito suggest that deceiving organisms rely upon two cognitive psychological mechanisms: 'theory of mind', by which they mean the ability of the organism to infer what others are thinking, and 'deontic reasoning', by which they mean an appreciation of social rules and the consequences of their transgression. Hence, it only makes sense to speak of 'deception' among primates if the animal concerned gives some indication that it understands how the current situation appears to the conspecific it is deceiving, and if there is some advantage to that deception (e.g. avoidance of punishment or access to reward).

Given the normal appearance of lying and deception during childhood (Ford 1995; O'Connell 1998), several authors have speculated upon the (teleonomic) purpose served by such behaviours in human life. These accounts have little to say about the mechanism by which deception emerged during evolution. However, at the level of the individual human child, one speculation has been that deceit delineates a boundary between the 'self' and the 'other', specifically between the child and her mother (Ford et al. 1988). Learning at the age of 3 or 4 years that he/she can know something that his/her mother does not know (which itself implies a developing theory of mind) establishes for the child the limit of his/her mother's knowledge, and allows the child some degree of control. Indeed, this experience of control (over information) might drive the 'pathological lying' seen later in life, among dysfunctional adolescents and adults (Ford et al. 1988). Following this argument, the ability to lie is dependent upon the liar's recognition that his/her thoughts are not known to others; and that different individuals' understandings of the world may diverge. Hence, deliberate deception is dependent upon the acquisition of a capacity for theory of mind, a capacity that has been the subject of functional neuroimaging studies (Fletcher et al. 1995; Gallagher & Frith 2003).

It is worth noting that lying may be prosocial in certain contexts. It may ease social interaction, by way of compliments and information management. By contrast, precisely truthful communication at all times would be difficult and perhaps rather brutal. Hence, it is unsurprising that 'normal' subjects admit to telling lies on most days (Vrij 2001). Social psychological studies, often of college students, suggest that lies facilitate impression management, especially early on in a romantic relationship (Vrij 2001). Hence, given that theory of mind is a prerequisite for deception, and that deception eases social communication, it is unsurprising that disorders of social interaction (such as autism) are associated with an inability to deceive, and social communication that may appear insensitive (Sodian & Frith 1992; Hughes & Russell 1993; Happe 1994).

Of course, deception is a vital skill in the context of conflict, especially between social groups, countries or intelligence agencies (e.g. Latimer 2001). When practised under these circumstances it might even be perceived as a moral 'good' (depending on one's affiliation). However, when an individual subject is branded a liar, any advantage formerly gained may be lost. Although fluent liars might make entertaining companions (at times), being known as a liar is unlikely to be ultimately advantageous (Vrij 2001).

9.3 Principles of executive control

Control of voluntary behaviour in everyday human life is crucial but likely to be constrained by cognitive, neurobiological resources (Baddeley 1966; Passingham 1996; Spence et al. 2002). Control (or executive) functions are not necessarily 'conscious', although their contents may access awareness (Badgaiyan 2000; Jack & Shallice 2001).

Executive functions include problem solving, planning, the initiation and inhibition of behaviours, and the manipulation of useful data in conscious working memory (e.g. the telephone number about to be dialled, the ramifications of the lie about to be told). These functions engage specific regions of the PFC (see figures 9.1 and 9.2), though they also involve distributed brain systems. There seems to be a principle to the cognitive architecture of executive control. 'Higher' centres such as the PFC are essential to adaptive behaviour in novel or difficult circumstances, while lower, slave systems, implicating posterior and sub-cortical systems, may be sufficient to perform routine or automated tasks (e.g. riding a bike while thinking of something else; figure 9.2; Shallice 1988, 2002; Passingham 1996).

A recurring theme in the psychology of deception is the difficulty of deceiving in 'high stake' situations: information previously divulged must be recalled, emotions and behaviours 'controlled', information managed (Vrij 2001). The latter resemble executive tasks. Hence, much of the liar's behaviour may be seen, from a cognitive neurobiological perspective, as falling on a continuum with other situations in which behavioural control is exerted, albeit using limited resources (hence, subjects will exhibit decrements in performance while attempting to perform dual or multiple tasks concurrently; Passingham 1996). A liar might therefore 'slip up' if distracted, mistakenly uttering the truth.

Liars may also 'give away' deception by their motor behaviours. While telling complex lies they may make fewer hand and arm movements ('illustrators'; Ekman & Friesen 1972; Vrij 2001). The slowing of behaviour exhibited by liars has been termed the 'motivational impairment effect' (Vrij 2001).

9.4 Lying as a cognitive process

Deceiving another human subject is likely to involve multiple cognitive processes, including theory of mind concerning the victim's thoughts (their ongoing beliefs) and the analysis

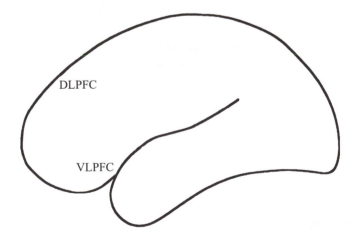

Fig. 9.1 Cartoon illustrating two regions of PFC implicated in behavioural control. The brain is viewed from the left side. DLPFC has been particularly implicated in the generation of behaviours (especially novel or 'internally generated' behaviours; Frith *et al.* (1991); Spence *et al.* (1998)); VLPFC has been implicated in response inhibition and reversal (Starkstein & Robinson 1997). VLPFC is markedly activated in our experimental lying protocols (see figures 9.3 and 9.4).

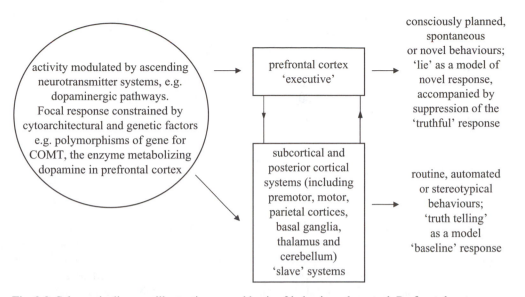

consciously planned, spontaneous or novel behaviours; 'lie' as a model of novel response, accompanied by suppression of the 'truthful' response

prefrontal cortex 'executive'

activity modulated by ascending neurotransmitter systems, e.g. dopaminergic pathways. Focal response constrained by cytoarchitectural and genetic factors e.g. polymorphisms of gene for COMT, the enzyme metabolizing dopamine in prefrontal cortex

subcortical and posterior cortical systems (including premotor, motor, parietal cortices, basal ganglia, thalamus and cerebellum) 'slave' systems

routine, automated or stereotypical behaviours; 'truth telling' as a model 'baseline' response

Fig. 9.2 Schematic diagram illustrating neural basis of behavioural control. Prefrontal systems are implicated in control of complex and novel behaviour patterns, modulating 'lower' brain systems (such as basal ganglia and premotor cortices). However, constraints are imposed by genetic and neurodevelopmental factors (left) and activity is modulated by neurotransmitter function. These constraints impose limits on the envelope of possible responses emitted by the organism (Spence *et al.* 2002).

of responses made by both the liar and the victim in the context of their interaction. In the light of the above, we may posit that in the normal situation the liar is called upon to do at least two things simultaneously. He must construct a new item of information (the lie) while also withholding a factual item (the truth), assuming that he knows and understands what constitutes the 'correct' information. Within such a theoretical framework it is apparent that the truthful response comprises a form of baseline, or pre-potent response. We would predict that such a response would be made by an honest subject answering the same question or by the liar were he to become distracted or fatigued (indeed, from this perspective it is understandable why inebriation or sedation might 'release' the truth via disinhibition: *in vino veritas*). We might, therefore, propose that responding with a lie demands some form of additional cognitive processing, that it will engage executive, prefrontal systems (more so than telling the truth). Hence, we have a hypothesis that may be tested using functional neuroimaging (Spence *et al.* 2001).

That the orbitofrontal cortex may be involved in successful deception, or at least in withholding information, has been implied by Ford (1995). Drawing on the example of the 'pseudopsychopathic personality' syndrome observed after orbitofrontal lesions, Ford points out that though these patients may exhibit certain features of psychopathy (such as impulsiveness and aggression), they tend not to lie. Instead they exhibit a callous disregard for social convention and an 'honesty' that may be extremely insensitive to decorum and the feelings of others. They may be inappropriately truthful (i.e. 'tactless'). Hence, it is possible that the presence of an intact orbitofrontal cortex facilitates the telling of lies (perhaps as a consequence of response inhibition; in this case the inhibition of truthful responses). Lesions of this brain region in non-human primates produce deficits on conditional response tasks (including certain forms of the 'go, no-go' task) that may elicit perseveration (contextually inappropriate response repetition; Iversen & Mishkin 1970; Butters *et al.* 1973). In humans, lesions may also be associated with perseveration and a failure to inhibit pre-potent responses (Starkstein & Robinson 1997). Hence, from a cognitive neurobiological perspective, the pseudopsychopath of Ford (1995) utters pre-potent truths, tactlessly, because they are 'released' by orbitofrontal lesions.

9.5 Imaging deception

(a) Spence (2001)

We proposed that the inhibition of relatively pre-potent responses ('truths') would be associated with greater activation of *ventral* prefrontal regions (systems known to be implicated in response inhibition; see §4 and figure 9.1). We also proposed that the concomitant generation of 'lie' responses (in contrast to 'truths') would be associated with greater *dorsolateral* prefrontal cortical activity (this area being implicated in the generation of novel responses; Frith *et al.* 1991; Spence *et al.* 1998).

We used a simple computerized protocol in which subjects answered questions with a 'yes' or a 'no', pressing specified single computer keys. All the questions concerned activities that subjects might have performed on the day that they were studied. We had previously acquired information from each of them, concerning their activities, when they were first interviewed. However, there was an added feature of the method applied in that subjects performed these tests in the presence of an investigator who was a 'stooge', who would be required to judge afterwards whether the subjects' responses were truths or lies. The computer screen presenting questions to the subjects also carried a green or red prompt (the sequence counter-balanced across subjects). Without the stooge knowing the 'colour rule', subjects responded with truthful responses in the presence of one colour and lie responses in the presence of the other. All questions were presented twice, once each under each colour condition, so that finally we were able to compare response times and brain activity during 'truth' and 'lie' responses. We have published studies from three cohorts of subjects 'outside the scanner' (30–48 subjects in each; Spence *et al.* 2001, 2003; Farrow *et al.* 2003) and one sample of 10 subjects 'inside the scanner' (Spence *et al.* 2001), each cohort performing two variants of our experimental protocol. The brain imaging technique applied was fMRI.

Our analyses revealed that whether subjects were studied inside or outside the scanner there was a statistically significant effect of lying upon response time (it being *ca.* 200 ms longer during 'lying' compared with responding truthfully). In the scanned sample, lie responses were associated with increased activation in bilateral ventrolateral pre-frontal and anterior cingulate cortices (together with medial premotor and left inferior parietal cortices; figure 9.3). These data support the hypothesis that prefrontal systems exhibit greater activation when subjects are called upon to generate experimental 'lies' and they demonstrate (at the level of groups of subjects) that longer processing time is required to answer with a lie. However, our predictions of *which* prefrontal regions would be most activated during deception were only partly confirmed. The presence of consistent activation in ventrolateral PFCs and the minimal activation of DLPFC suggested to us that that the

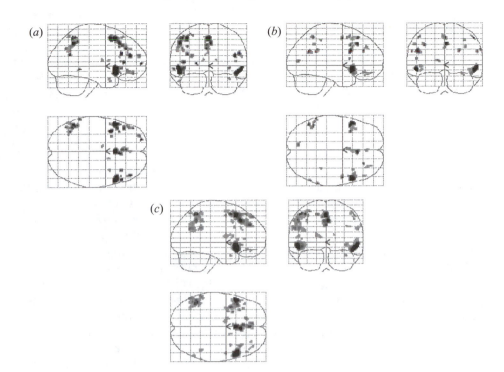

Fig. 9.3 Brain regions showing significantly greater neuronal response during lying (cf. truth telling) when answers are given manually, and questions are presented visually (*a*), or via headphones (*b*). A conjunction analysis, combining both datasets, reveals the same pattern of activation (*c*). These figures show statistical parametric maps thresholded for display purposes at $p < 0.001$ (uncorrected). In each group, the upper left figure is a sagittal view (from the right side), the upper right figure is a coronal view (from behind) and the lower left is a transverse view (from above the brain). Regions maximally activated include bilateral VLPFCs cortices and medial PFC (anterior cingulate cortex); there is also activation of left parietal cortex. (Adapted from Spence *et al*. (2001).)

inhibition of the pre-potent (truthful) response, inherent in our task, contributed most to the pattern of activity seen. While 'lying' comprised only a reversal of the pre-potent response (e.g. 'yes' for 'no') rather than an elaboration of a 'new lie', it may have been insufficiently demanding for there to be marked activation of dorsolateral prefrontal regions (see the Ganis *et al*. (2003) study).

Notwithstanding these and other limitations (described in § 5e), our finding of increased response time during lying is congruent with a recent report of a convicted murderer, filmed while lying and telling the truth (Vrij & Mann 2001). Although recounting similar material on both occasions, this subject exhibited slower speech with longer pauses and more speech disturbance when lying. He also exhibited fewer 'illustrators' (bodily movements). Previous meta-analyses of behavioural lying studies have also pointed to speech disturbance, increased response latency and a decrease in other motor behaviours in the context of attempted deception (Ekman & Friesen 1972; Vrij & Mann 2001). Although responses on our (computerized) tasks were non-verbal, the behavioural and functional anatomical profile revealed (above) may indicate a common process underlying these findings and others; namely, an inhibitory mechanism that is used by those attempting to withhold the truth (a process associated with increased response latency).

It is noteworthy that the difference between lying and truth times for all groups in our studies was *ca.* 200 ms (Spence *et al.* 2001, 2003; Farrow *et al.* 2003). This is consistent with behavioural data acquired by other authors, studying the 'guilty knowledge' test (Farwell & Donchin 1991; Seymour *et al.* 2000; see §5b).

(b) Langleben (2002)

Other groups have also used fMRI and found the PFC to be implicated in deception. Langleben and colleagues used the guilty knowledge paradigm, to test the hypothesis that subjects would activate executive, inhibitory brain regions while withholding a truthful response. Subjects were studied in a MR scanner while they made motor responses to a sequence of playing cards presented visually. The subjects each held one card, which was known to them and which they believed was unknown to the investigators (its identity comprised their 'guilty knowledge'). Subjects used a button box to respond manually 'yes' or 'no' regarding the identity of the card they held. They also answered control questions, some requiring truthful responses, and other 'non-target' questions to confirm their attention to the protocol. Denying possession of a target playing card (the 'lie') was associated with greater activation in the anterior cingulate cortex (brain coordinates 4,26,42, in a region very similar to that identified in Spence *et al.* (2001): 3,28,43; Talairach & Tournoux 1988) and left parietal cortex (in a region medial to that identified in Spence *et al.* (2001)). There were no brain regions that exhibited greater activation during truthful responding relative to the lie condition. Response times were not reported.

(c) Lee (2002)

On the basis of behavioural experiments examining the ways in which healthy subjects would set about feigning memory impairment, Lee and colleagues suggested that a real 'feigner' would take account of their response performance as they went along, so that they would not perform 'too badly' all the time (in case this provoked suspicion). To remain credible, such a malingerer would wish to perform no worse than chance when answering questions relating to their feigned deficit (e.g. their autobiographical memory). In a MR scanner subjects performed two forced-choice tasks, one relating to identifying three-digit numbers they had seen previously, the other to items of autobiographical information, for example, where they had been born (Lee *et al.* 2002). Subjects made manual responses to indicate their answers. When compared with truthful responding (on both tasks) malingering was associated with increased activation in bilateral dorsolateral pre-frontal, inferior parietal, middle temporal and posterior cingulate cortices, together with bilateral caudate nuclei. The authors did not report any areas where truthful responding elicited greater activation. Response times were not reported.

(d) Ganis (2003)

In this study the authors made a novel distinction, not emphasized in earlier studies, between lies that form part of a well-rehearsed and coherent scenario and those that are spontaneous and need not fit into such a larger narrative framework. Subjects were studied while they gave motor (button press) and vocal responses, comprising both forms of 'lie'. Their findings were that both types of lie were associated with greater activation in bilateral anterior prefrontal cortices and bilateral hippocampal gyri, while there were no reported areas of greater activation during truthful responding. On a sub-group of subjects for whom behavioural response measures were available, the authors did not find a significant difference in response times during lying and truthful responding. However, it is interesting to note that their raw data do suggest a difference of *ca.* 200 ms (whereas the mean response time for memorized-scenario lies was 838 ms, and that for spontaneous, isolated lies was 859 ms, the mean response time for truthful responses was 613 ms; Ganis *et al.* 2003). This study may have been underpowered to detect significant differences between deceptive and truthful response time.

These authors also reported some other similarities to the foregoing work. Anterior cingulate gyrus exhibited greater activation during spontaneous lies, at a focus (4,6,39) 20 mm posterior to that seen in the studies by Spence *et al.* (2001) and Langleben *et al.* (2002; See §5b). Also, they found an area of activation associated with the telling of spontaneous, isolated lies in the right Brodmann Area 47 'in a spherical (region of interest) centred at the coordinates reported in Spence *et al.* (2001)' (p. 835).

With respect to the proposed distinction between rehearsed and spontaneous lies, Ganis and colleagues report greater right frontal activation in the former and greater anterior cingulate cortex and visual cortex activity in the latter.

(e) Future directions

The scanning studies to date, including our own, have been subject to behavioural and task-related limitations: a certain artificiality, the frequent use of a non-vocal signal to transmit the deception, and the 'low stake' nature of the 'lying' involved. Some of these limitations have involved compromises imposed by the scanning technology itself. Future experimentation should seek to use other paradigms for testing the neurological components of deception, in part by expanding the kinds of tasks used.

In a current, unpublished fMRI study, we have begun to explore this kind of variation, using 'silent periods' in the scanner to allow auditory stimuli and vocal responses to be used. By studying vocal lies and by adding a 'defy/comply' condition, we posited that the following cognitive subtraction would reveal those brain regions specifically activated by lying, rather than by memory of the index event or the mere reversal of a pre-potent response:

$$\text{brain activations specific to lying} = (\text{lie-truth}) - (\text{defy-comply}).$$

This approach appears promising. Preliminary data analysis using this subtraction suggests that lying was specifically associated with activation of the following regions: right ventrolateral and orbitofrontal cortices (BA 47 and 11, respectively), right medial (BA 6) frontal gyrus, right inferior parietal lobule (BA 40) and left premotor cortex (BA 6) (table 9.1). At a less conservative statistical threshold ($p < 0.001$, uncorrected for multiple comparisons) activity in orbitofrontal regions was seen to be bilateral (figure 9.4), similar in location though not identical to that of our previous study (figure 9.2; Spence *et al.* 2001).

Table 9.1 Areas activated during lie condition in vocal lying study (relative to truthful responding and following subtraction of 'defy/comply' activations). ($p < 0.05$, corrected for multiple comparisons.)

Brain area		Talairach coordinates			
	BA	X	Y	Z	t
Right orbitofrontal PFC	11	38	40	−15	4.50
Right VLPFC	47	34	31	−2	4.22
Right premotor cortex	6	4	1	57	4.32
Right inferior parietal lobule	40	50	−60	44	4.97
Left premotor cortex	6	−10	22	66	4.40

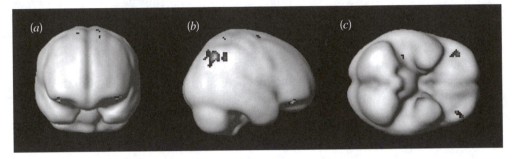

Fig. 9.4 Brain regions showing significantly greater neuronal response during lying (cf. truth telling) when lies are spoken. These figures show statistical parametric maps thresholded for display purposes at $p < 0.001$ (uncorrected, extent threshold 30 voxels). Group data are presented on a smoothed brain, viewed from the front (*a*), right lateral (*b*) and inferior (*c*) perspectives. During lying there is greater activation in bilateral ventrolateral orbitofrontal regions (left and right) and the right inferior parietal lobule (seen in (*b*)).

9.6 Comment

From a cognitive perspective the telling of lies resembles an executive process. On behavioural measures there is an increase in response time, relative to truthful responding (Spence *et al.* 2001, 2003; Farrow *et al.* 2003; see Ganis *et al.* 2003). When fMRI has been used to study experimental deception, a consistent finding has been that of increased activity in executive brain regions, specifically areas of PFC and anterior cingulate gyrus (Spence *et al.* 2001; Langleben *et al.* 2002; Lee *et al.* 2002; Ganis *et al.* 2003). So far, to our knowledge, no published fMRI study has revealed increased activation in any brain region during truthful responding (relative to deception, though the possibility of a Type 2 error cannot be unequivocally excluded).

The findings of our current study of vocal lying are consistent with key aspects of the foregoing studies. In common with our own previous study, lying is associated with increased activation in VLPFC (BA 47). In common with the work of Lee *et al.* (2002) it is also associated with increased activation in the right inferior parietal lobule (BA 40). Although greater activation of BA 47 may reflect the suppression of pre-potent, truthful responses (Spence *et al.* 2001), greater activation of BA 40 may reflect an element of online computation (where it is expedient not to lie 'too often'; Lee *et al.* 2002). Also, as in each of the preceding neuroimaging studies (Spence *et al.* 2001; Langleben *et al.* 2002; Lee *et al.* 2002; Ganis *et al.* 2003), our current study reveals no areas of the brain where truthful responding elicited increases in activation (relative to lying). Taken together, our findings are consistent with the hypothesis that lying comprises an executive process and that truthful responding constitutes a relative baseline in human cognition.

One of the weaknesses of our first study was that the activations associated with deception enacted through motor responses were confounded by the requirement for response reversal (e.g. answering 'yes' for 'no'). In the later study we attempt to control for this possible confound. Our defy/comply protocol allows us to study response suppression in another context and reveals that even after subtracting away those activations associated with response reversal in 'defiance', lying elicits greater activation in ventral prefrontal regions. The regions implicated by results to date, in our later study, again suggest that a central component of lying is the suppression of truthful (pre-potent) responses. Once again, it was the *ventral* prefrontal regions that were most activated (cf. DLPFC, figure 9.1).

9.7 The brain and the law

> The first visual record of police interrogation we have comes from a XII Dynasty tomb in Egypt, two thousand years before Christ. The image shows a man being held by three others while the fourth one beats him with a bamboo stick and the fifth, who appears to be the one in charge, supervises the procedure.
>
> (Simic 2004, p. 24)

> And if my thought-dreams could be seen, they'd probably put my head in a guillotine.
> (Bob Dylan, *It's All Right Ma, I'm Only Bleeding*)

As psychiatrists and neuroscientists, our interest in the cognitive neurobiology of deception has been motivated by a desire to understand the cognitive architecture of complex, purposeful human behaviours. We are commonly confronted with the possibility of deception in the clinical arena and its meaning may be susceptible to multiple interpretations. From a biological perspective, our findings and those of others suggest that deception engages the higher centres of the human brain and places certain demands upon the cognitive capacities of the individual who is lying. It would be naive to imagine that such a body of work might not impact upon that other 'real world' of forensic practice, at least at a theoretical level (at the moment). The question of whether or not societies should resort to lie detection is one deserving of broad societal debate and is not in itself a scientific question. However, the development of means of lie detection that are (physically) harmless to the individual concerned might be regarded as a moral good, if contrasted with the more traditional means of information extraction alluded to by Simic (2004).

Nevertheless, the right to silence and the value of non-coerced confessions as desirable elements of human behaviour are also deserving of respectful consideration and continue to attract thoughtful review (e.g. Brooks 2000). We do not have the space to do sufficient justice to these issues in the current paper so we offer the following as cautions to the premature application of brain imaging technology to the problem of lie detection. The problems we foresee include the following.

(i) *Ecological validity*: the experiments that we have reviewed have generally involved compliant subjects telling trivial lies. They have not involved the high-stake situations that might be expected to pertain in the forensic arena.

(ii) *Experimental design*: it is clear that all experimenters to date (ourselves included) have devised simple experiments of simulated deception, which facilitate analyses using simple contrasts (i.e. lie versus truth) with the theoretical assumptions inherent in such designs. Making a categorical distinction between truth and lie suggests a certain clarity but may not cohere in the 'real world', where information may be imprecise, motives mixed and elements of truthfulness contained within the lie that the subject tells. Additionally, no study reported to date has demonstrated a distinct physiological signature to 'truth', merely that 'lies' activate the brain more, particularly in executive regions.

(iii) *Statistical power*: the studies we have reviewed concern the averaged brain activities of groups of subjects and we are aware of no study to date that has provided convincing evidence of a physiology of deception at the level of the single subject. Hence, there may well be a range of individual differences and it would be premature to extrapolate from the sorts of data we have considered to the individual suspect in the courtroom or the cell.

(iv) *Can lying be 'pathological'?*: while deception is by definition a deliberate act, we are aware of conditions in which it may be conceptualized as 'pathological' (e.g. Abed 1995; Tyrer *et al.* 2001). Future theoretical work might focus upon the question of whether such a deliberate act can be pathological in nature, or whether it is instead the motivations, the reasons, driving the act that are the locus of implied pathology. It might well be that those who lie habitually are not 'abnormal liars' (i.e., they are not 'lying abnormally'), merely people who use a normal strategy to excess.

M.D.H. is supported by the Wellcome Trust, C.J.H. and V.G. are supported by a Medical Research Council (UK) Career Establishment grant awarded to S.A.S., and R.D.G. was supported by an investigator grant awarded to S.A.S. by Cephalon UK.

References

Abed, R. T. 1995 Voluntary false confessions in a Munchausen patient: a new variant of the syndrome? *Irish J. Psychol. Med.* **12**, 24–26.

Adenzato, M. & Ardito, R. B. 1999 The role of theory of mind and deontic reasoning in the evolution of deception. In *Proc. 21st Conf. Cogn. Sci. Soc.* (ed. M. Hahn & S. C. Stoness), pp. 7–12. Mahwah, NJ: Lawrence Erlbaum Associates.

Baddeley, A. D. 1966 The capacity for generating information by randomization. *Q. J. Exp. Psychol.* **18**, 119–129.

Badgaiyan, R. D. 2000 Executive control, willed actions, and nonconscious processing. *Hum. Brain Map.* **9**, 38–41.

Brooks, P. 2000 *Troubling confessions: speaking guilt in law and literature.* Chicago University Press.

Butters, N., Butter, C., Rosen, J. & Stein, D. 1973 Behavioural effects of sequential and one-stage ablations of orbital prefrontal cortex in the monkey. *Exp. Neurol.* **39**, 204–214.

Byrne, R. W. 2003 Tracing the evolutionary path of cognition. In *The social brain: evolution and pathology* (ed. M. Brune, H. Ribbert & W. Schiefenhovel), pp. 43–60. Chichester: Wiley.

Chambers 1991 *Chambers concise dictionary.* Edinburgh: Chambers Harrap.

Chinweizu 2001 From Ptahhotep to postcolonialism. *Times Literary Supplement*, 17 August, p. 6.

Dunbar, R. 2000 On the origin of the human mind. In *Evolution and the human mind: modularity language and meta-cognition* (ed. P. Carruthers & A. Chamberlain), pp. 238–253. Cambridge University Press.

Ekman, P. & Friesen, W. V. 1972 Hand movements. *J. Commun.* **22**, 353–374.

Farrow, T. F. D., Reilly, R., Rahman, T. A., Herford, A. E., Woodruff, P. W. R. & Spence, S. A. 2003 Sex and personality traits influence the difference between time taken to tell the truth or lie. *Percept. Motor Skills* **97**, 451–460.

Farwell, L. A. & Donchin, E. 1991 The truth will out: interrogative polygraphy ('lie detection') with event-related brain potentials. *Psychophysiology* **28**, 531–547.

Fletcher, P. C., Happe, F., Frith, U., Baker, S. C., Dolan, R. J., Frackowiak, R. S. J. & Frith, C. D. 1995 Other minds in the brain: a functional imaging study of 'theory of mind' in story comprehension. *Cognition* **57**, 109–128.

Ford, C. V. 1995 *Lies! Lies! Lies! The psychology of deceit*. Washington, DC: American Psychiatric Press.

Ford, C. V., King, B. H. & Hollender, M. H. 1988 Lies and liars: psychiatric aspects of prevarication. *Am. J. Psychiat.* **145**, 554–562.

Frith, C. D., Friston, K., Liddle, P. F. & Frackowiak, R. S. J. 1991 Willed action and the prefrontal cortex in man: a study with PET. *Proc. R. Soc. Lond.* B **244**, 241–246.

Gallagher, H. L. & Frith, C. D. 2003 Functional imaging of 'theory of mind'. *Trends Cogn. Sci.* **7**, 77–83.

Ganis, G., Kosslyn, S. M., Stose, S., Thompson, W. L. & Yurgelun-Todd, D. A. 2003 Neural correlates of different types of deception: an fMRI investigation. *Cerebr. Cortex* **13**, 830–836.

Happe, F. 1994 *Autism: an introduction to psychological theory*. Hove: Psychology Press.

Hughes, C. H. & Russell, J. 1993 Autistic children's difficulty with mental disengagement from an object: its implications for theories of autism. *Devl Psychol.* **29**, 498–510.

Iversen, S. D. & Mishkin, M. 1970 Perseverative interference in monkeys following selective lesions of the inferior pre-frontal covexity. *Exp. Brain Res.* **11**, 376–386.

Jack, A. I. & Shallice, T. 2001 Introspective physicalism as an approach to the science of consciousness. *Cognition* **79**, 161–196.

Langleben, D. D., Schroeder, L., Maldjian, J. A., Gur, R. C., McDonald, S., Ragland, J. D., O'Brien, C. P. & Childress, A. R. 2002 Brain activity during simulated deception: an event-related functional magnetic resonance study. *Neuro-Image* **15**, 727–732.

Latimer, J. 2001 *Deception in war*. London: John Murray.

Lee, T. M. C., Liu, H.-L., Tan, L.-H., Chan, C. C. H., Mahankali, S., Feng, C.-M., Hou, J., Fox, P. T. & Gao, J.-H. 2002 Lie detection by functional magnetic resonance imaging *Hum. Brain Map.* **15**, 157–164.

Machiavelli, N. 1999 *The prince*. London: Penguin.

O'Connell, S. 1998 *Mindreading: an investigation into how we learn to love and lie*. London: Arrow Books.

Passingham, R. E. 1996 Attention to action. *Phil. Trans. R. Soc.* B **351**, 1473–1479.

Seymour, T. L., Seifert, C. M., Shafto, M. G. & Mosmann, A. L. 2000 Using response time measures to assess 'guilty knowledge' *J. Appl. Psychol.* **85**, 30–37.

Shallice, T. 1988 *From neuropsychology to mental structure*. Cambridge University Press.

Shallice, T. 2002 Fractionation of the supervisory system. In *Principles of frontal lobe function* (ed. D. T. Stuss & R. T. Knight), pp. 261–277. Oxford University Press.

Simic, C. 2004 Adam's umbrella. *The New York Review*, 24 June, pp. 24–27.

Sodian, B. & Frith, U. 1992 Deception and sabotage in autistic, retarded and normal children. *J. Child Psychol. Psychiat.* **33**, 591–605.

Spence, S. A., Hirsch, S. R., Brooks, D. J. & Grasby, P. M. 1998 Prefrontal cortex activity in people with schizophrenia and control subjects: evidence from positron emission tomography for remission of 'hypofrontality' with remission from acute schizophrenia. *Br. J. Psychiat.* **172**, 316–323.

Spence, S. A., Farrow, T. F. D., Herford, A. E., Wilkinson, I. D., Zheng, Y. & Woodruff, P. W. 2001 Behavioural and functional anatomical correlates of deception in humans. *NeuroReport* **12**, 2849–2853.

Spence, S. A., Hunter, M. D. & Harpin, G. 2002 Neuroscience and the will. *Curr. Opin. Psychiat.* **15**, 519–526.

Spence, S., Farrow, T., Leung, D., Shah, S., Reilly, B., Rahman, A. & Herford, A. 2003 Lying as an executive function. In *Malingering and illness deception* (ed. P. W. Halligan, C. Bass & D. A. Oakley), pp. 255–266. Oxford University Press.

Starkstein, S. E. & Robinson, R. G. 1997 Mechanism of disinhibition after brain lesions. *J. Nerv. Mental Dis.* **185**, 108–114.

Talairach, J. & Tournoux, P. 1988 *Co-planar stereotaxic atlas of the human brain.* New York: Thieme.

Tyrer, P., Babidge, N., Emmanuel, J., Yarger, N. & Ranger, M. 2001 Instrumental psychosis: the Good Soldier Svejk syndrome *J. R. Soc. Med.* **94**, 22–25.

Vrij, A. 2001 *Detecting lies and deceit: the psychology of lying and the implications for professional practice.* Chichester: Wiley.

Vrij, A. & Mann, S. 2001 Telling and detecting lies in a high-stake situation: the case of a convicted murderer. *Appl. Cogn. Psychol.* **15**, 187–203.

Glossary

BA   Brodmann area
DLPFC   dorsolateral prefrontal cortex
fMRI   functional magnetic resonance imaging
MR   magnetic resonance
PFC   prefrontal cortex
VLPFC   ventrolateral prefrontal cortex

Property in biology and the brain

10

The property 'instinct'

Jeffrey Evans Stake

Evolutionary theory and empirical studies suggest that many animals, including humans, have a genetic predisposition to acquire and retain property. This is hardly surprising because survival is closely bound up with the acquisition of things: food, shelter, tools and territory. But the root of these general urges may also run to quite specific and detailed rules about property acquisition, retention and disposition. The great variation in property-related behaviours across species may mask some important commonalities grounded in adaptive utility. Experiments and observations in the field and laboratory suggest that the legal rules of temporal priority and possession are grounded in what were evolutionarily stable strategies in the ancestral environment. Moreover, the preferences that humans exhibit in disposing of their property on their deaths, both by dispositions made in wills and by the laws of intestacy, tend to advance reproductive success as a result of inclusive fitness pay-offs.

Keywords: extended phenotype; possession; intestate succession; endowment effect; inclusive fitness; paternity uncertainty

10.1 Introduction

People untrained in the law often think of 'property' as a relationship between a thing and a person. It is common for law professors to attempt to correct this lay notion by describing property as a relationship between people with respect to a thing. In denying the importance of the relationship between the person and his things, however, this professional view obscures the possibility that the institution of property rests in part on deep-seated connections to and attitudes toward things.

In the law, 'property' means rights in things. A woman has property when other persons share a respect for her relationship to some thing and are willing to enforce her rights. Embedded in the idea of property is the presumption that there are identifiable patterns in the resolutions of disputes over resources. In other words, there are criteria that determine how competing claims to assets will be resolved. It is possible that these factors, the determinants of property, are solely the product of laws and other conventions constructed by formal human organizations. Property, in such a view, rises and falls with human institutions. Bentham wrote (1914, pp. 145–147) 'there is no such thing as natural property: it is entirely the creature of the law. . . . Property and law were born together, and would die together. Before the laws property did not exist; take away the laws, and property will be no more'.

This article proposes an alternative possibility: basic components of property preceded formal institutions; fundamental principles of property are encoded in the human brain. There are obvious reasons to believe that a system for allocating rights in things could, at least in part, be hardwired into animal brains. A scarcity of resources creates competition for them, and some forms of competition result in harm to the competitors. Rivals can reduce the costs of competition by adopting strategies for determining the outcome of fights without physical damage. For example, many of nature's agonistic encounters between conspecifics are won by the larger contestant (Moretz 2003). If the larger rival is certain to win, competitors can save themselves the costs of battle by allowing the size asymmetry to settle the dispute before they actually engage in battle. Such strategies can be evolutionarily stable (Maynard Smith 1972; Maynard Smith & Parker 1976; Gibbard 1982). When an ESS is adopted by most members of a population, it cannot be invaded by the spread of any rare alternative strategy (Krebs & Davies 1997). Thus, a body is more likely to survive if its brain is equipped with rules of property incorporating ESSs for reducing the costs of allocating resources among competitors. Property is part of human biology.

This claim that legal rules are partly hardwired might evoke the counter-argument that the sheer heterogeneity of those rules belies any significant genetic component. But that argument ignores the complex and continuous feedback loop between nature and nurture. ESSs can and do fine tune themselves in many different ways over time and across populations. They can also take on cultural super-structures, extending the human phenotype (Dawkins 1982) beyond our bodies. Just as humans share a universal grammar (Pinker 1994) despite wide differences in languages, humans may share a core property 'instinct' despite differences in property law. We may have an adaptation, an evolved mental mechanism, for dealing with several of the issues that arise repeatedly with regard to resources. Like our languages, our various legal systems may be extensions of our human phenotype. Our laws, including our property laws, are part of the niches we have constructed for ourselves.

Our property instinct or mental adaptation might be nothing more than a natural inclination to learn the rules that other humans use to resolve the coordination problem inherent in resource disputes, much as we learn new words as toddlers to resolve the coordination problem inherent in communication. But it is also possible that the property instinct is more. An ability to recognize and, in appropriate contexts, adhere to specific conventions may be part of our behavioural repertoire.

For example, we may have an innate sense of alienability, a natural feeling that one person may transfer things to another. If such a tendency is heritable and adaptive, it is not difficult to imagine a more efficient and more adaptive version: in addition to transfer-ring the thing itself, it should be possible to transfer the rights to the thing. For such alienation to be proper according to our adaptation, the transfer must be voluntary. Here, the property instinct connects with an instinct for equity in reciprocal exchanges (Brosnan & de Waal 2003) and thus can be seen as one part of a sense of fairness or justice.

Another component of our property instinct is an inclination for what to do with property. Instincts may tell us not only how to transfer property, but also to whom. These donative tendencies and the laws of inheritance that reflect them are discussed below.

A property instinct could combine a general inclination to acquire rules with some spe-cific pre-wired options. For learning language, the human brain may be programmed to gather grammatical usage examples from the childhood environment (verbs preceding or following their objects and adjectives preceding or following their complements, etc.) and generalize from those examples to a conclusion that the language is 'head-first' or 'head-last' (Pinker 1994). Similarly, for learning property, the human brain might be endowed with an inclination to gather examples of resource allocation, and generalize from those examples to one of a range of available property rules. For example, humans might be programmed with three rules for initially allocating rights in a thing: to the first person to touch the thing, or to the older contestant, or to the dominant member of the group, all of which have the potential to seem 'natural'. Which of these three rules to apply would be determined by the culture in which the human grows up.

Whether evolutionary pressures acted precisely to create specific property rules or whether they created a probability distribution between sets of rules is not the focus here. It seems clear that there are certain rules of property that are recognized across a number of different species and have demonstrable adaptive value. These rules reflect what we could call a 'deep property structure' akin to the deep language structure. Recognizing this deep property structure may aid in understanding the rules of property and applying them to new situations.

10.2 First in time, first in right

Being first in time to capture or create a thing often creates some right to that thing. Historically, first discovery gave nations rights in foreign lands. The common law of property in England and the US has, as one of its cornerstones, the notion that the first person to possess a thing owns it. Could first-in-time be an ESS?

A first-in-time convention differs in an obvious way from the larger-wins convention mentioned above. The latter can be called a 'correlated' strategy because its winner is correlated to the winner in an actual physical fight (Maynard Smith & Parker 1976). Being first to possess, however, does not correlate as positively with winning the fight over a resource. Indeed, being first can be a disadvantage. A cheetah exhausted from the chase and with its kill in its mouth fights from a weaker position than a late-coming competitor that did not participate in the hunt.

First-in-time has both correlated and uncorrelated aspects: the first in time might be the fastest or smartest or otherwise possess a correlative adaptive advantage. But it is uncorrelated in that the first in time might also just be lucky. However, even if luck matters more, uncorrelated strategies can be evolutionarily stable (Maynard Smith & Parker 1976). Avoiding a physical fight by deference to the first in time is just as effective in preserving genes as avoiding a fight by deference to the larger body. An uncorrelated strategy can be evolutionarily stable even when there is a correlated strategy also available (Hammerstein 1981). Whether correlated or not, a first-in-time-wins convention built into competitors could reduce their losses from fighting over resources.

Therefore, it is theoretically possible for animals to be genetically programmed to be assertive in defending a resource they discover first and deferential when they come late (Maynard Smith & Parker 1976; Sugden 1986; Yee 2003). There is also empirical evidence that nature embedded a rule of temporal priority in our brains before culture codified it in our laws. First in time is the natural rule of sunspot ownership for speckled wood butterflies (Davies 1978; Epstein 1980), and it may be for swallowtail butterflies as well (Maynard Smith & Parker 1976). Unless we are to believe that butterflies communicate this strategy as a matter of culture, members of a species may share a genetic predisposition to be aggressive when first in time and to give up easily when the opposing conspecific was first.

It is important to stress that a first-in-time property convention, if there is one innate to humans, need not be a rigid routine that we follow in all contexts. Rather, like nearly all of our preferences, it takes the form of an inclination that sometimes predominates and at other times does not. Perhaps it plays a role only when the outcome of a fight does not matter very much (Grafen 1987). Nevertheless, just as our genes give us a taste for eating sweets and fats, our genes may incline us towards fighting harder for an item depending on whether we were first.

10.3 A natural meaning of possession

We may share with butterflies an evolved strategy that favours those who are first. But first at what? The legal answer is often 'possession'. In the words of Justice Holmes, 'possession is the beginning of ownership' (Missouri v. Holland 1920 252 US 416–435, p. 434). Possession is the root of title (Epstein 1979; Megarry & Wade 1984; Rose 1985). But that does not really answer the question. If possession is the key, what does it take to establish possession? Property law breaks possession into two elements: physical control and intent to assert control.

The intent element seems natural in that it is closely related to, if not the same thing as, willingness to fight, which in turn relates to the outcome of a physical contest over the resource. Willingness to fight may overcome inferior fighting ability. Smaller crickets defeated larger ones 30% of the time, possibly because they were more willing to fight (Hofmann & Schildberger 2001). If it matters to nature, it should not surprise us that intention matters to the law.

The other legal element of possession concerns the physical connection between the thing and its possessor. In a pair of nineteenth-century cases, Young v. Hichens (1844 12 Q. B. 518–520) and Pierson v. Post (1805 3 Caines 175–182, 2 Am. Dec. 264 (N.Y. 1886)), English and American courts confronted this question of defining the physical connection required to establish possession or occupancy. The judges hearing the cases decided that title in a wild animal belonged not to the person that first had a reasonable prospect of taking control but rather to the person that first had actual control. In Young v. Hichens, the plaintiff had nearly encircled some fish with a net when the defendant intruded. In his suit against the interloper, the plaintiff's claim rested on an assertion of possession. But the court was unwilling to find the requisite possession. Lord Denman stated (Young v. Hichens, p. 611), 'what-ever the interpretation may be put upon such terms as "custody" and "possession", the question will be whether any custody or possession has been obtained here. I think it is impossible to say that it had, until the party had actual power over the fish'.

Although property teachers often treat this important legal line as arbitrary, evolutionary theory suggests deeper roots. A strategy can work for the benefit of both parties only when both parties respond to the same environmental trigger. Both need to know when to be assertive, when to be deferential. Humans with a miscalibrated cognitive module for recognizing possession by others would have found themselves trying to obtain what was fiercely defended, whereas those who did not recognize their own possession would have failed to keep track of things that could have been easily secured. The result is that most of us descended from beings who could correctly determine who was first according to the convention.

Evolutionary theory not only suggests that humans have a common sense of possession, it suggests two points about the content of that shared sense. First, the strategy must provide a single winner in a good number of situations; it can work only if it is based on some asymmetry. But different criteria harbour differing degrees of asymmetry. When the criterion serving as the basis for the convention has too little asymmetry, fights will occur. If fights occur often, the contestants employing that strategy will not survive as often as those employing an alternative, less symmetrical and thus more determinate strategy. The forces of selection probably defined our sense of possession to be highly asymmetrical, such that it would be exclusive in many cases.

Second, the criterion that determines possession must be observable (Maynard Smith & Parker 1976). Duels between resident damselflies are usually won by the fatter contestant but cannot be settled quickly on that basis because their reserves of fat are stored inside their skeletons, out of view (Marden & Rollins 1994; Mesterton-Gibbons & Adams 1998). Crickets whose antennae have been shortened fight longer perhaps because they are less able to determine their opponent's willingness to fight (Hofmann & Schildberger 2001). For possession to work well as the hinge on which behaviour can pivot, possession has to depend on facts that can be perceived readily and reliably by the parties. Although it would help if both parties could observe whether the other is in possession, that is not strictly required. If the criterion is exclusive, it is enough that each party can tell whether he has satisfied the criterion. Conversely, the strategy of first-possession will have a hard time surviving as a strategy if a party cannot tell whether he himself has satisfied the criterion.

The results in Young v. Hichens and Pierson v. Post are completely understandable on both these points. A first-in-time strategy based on an actual grabbing of the object satisfies the requirement of high asymmetry. It will be unusual for two claimants to have hold of an object at the same time. By contrast, it would be much more common for competitors to have a 'reasonable expectation' (Young v. Hichens) or a 'reasonable prospect' (Pierson v. Post) of securing the thing at the same time and thus be in simultaneous possession. Actual grabbing is also, of course, considerably more observable than the fleeting notion of a reasonable prospect of capture, the alternative rejected by the courts.

There is evidence supporting this claim that law's physical-control rule is of biological origin. Touching may be a key ingredient in animal possession. The male speckled wood butterflies in Davies's experiments fought 10 times as long when both had touched down on vegetation as when only one had done so. Being in close proximity or having a reasonable prospect of actual contact was apparently not enough for the butterfly to form the attachment needed to fight a protracted battle. It might not be a mere coincidence that physical touching is important to the law.

Not only is touching important to possession, but animals have a means of recognizing touching by themselves, obviously, and by others. A certain group of neurons fire when a monkey grasps a piece of food in a certain way (Rizzolatti et al. 1996). Moreover, when a monkey sees either another monkey or the human experimenter grasping the food, 'mirror neurons' fire in the subject monkey. Although there are 'mirror neurons' for many actions, the fact that there are neurons activated by grasping and by observing the act of grasping suggests that there are neurons associated with recognizing possession by ourselves and others.

Thus, we may be programmed to recognize when we have a certain proximate relationship to a physical object and, by mirroring, to recognize when others have a similar relationship to an object. Our brains may then determine 'ownership' by combining that relational data with information about previous relationships, such as information about who was first in time and what voluntary transfers have occurred. Certain combinations of information—'it is in my grasp' plus 'there is no previous owner'—may throw switches in our brains making us more willing to be assertive in excluding others from the thing. Such a neurological structure could provide part of the basis for a very natural law of property.

Maynard Smith (1982) referred to this strategy—defend aggressively when one is an owner and defer to the opponent when one is an intruder—as the 'bourgeois' strategy. Owners usually defeat intruders in a number of species, from baboons (Kummer *et al.* 1974) to damselflies (Waage 1988), and similar behaviour has been observed in desert ants that mark their territories with pheromones and assert ownership when in territories marked by their colonies (Wenseleers *et al.* 2002), and in both sexes of Ozark zigzag salamanders (Mathis *et al.* 2000). In two species of colonial spider the larger conspecific wins, but if the contestants are of similar size, the resident usually defeats the intruder (Hodge & Uetz 1995).

This is not to say that all animals must follow the bourgeois strategy. One species of Mexican spider, for example, appears to follow an anti-bourgeois strategy, with the owners fleeing upon the arrival of intruders (Burgess 1976). Whether a population will evolve to bourgeois or anti-bourgeois may depend on resource-holding potential (Mesterton-Gibbons & Adams 1998). Indeed, no strategy will be an ESS in situations where it would make permanent reproductive losers of one group (Grafen 1987).

Landowners seem to follow the bourgeois strategy when they defend their lands with their lives rather than surrender them to invaders. Pape (2003) found that suicide attacks are carried out most often by persons who are trying to displace occupying invaders. 'In general, suicide terrorist campaigns seek to achieve specific territorial goals, most often the withdrawal of the target state's military forces from what the terrorists see as national homeland' (Pape 2003, p. 344).

Given the frequency of territorial behaviour in humans and other animals, it is reasonable to assume that there is some meaning of possession that is naturally shared among conspecifics. Even in the absence of law—*especially* in the absence of law—there are beneficial network externalities that arise from a common sense of ownership. When the nexus between a person and a thing becomes strong enough, he feels like the owner and others recognize him as the owner. The bourgeois strategy might have purely uncorrelated origins, or it might be based in part on an asymmetry in values. But whatever the origin, if a bourgeois strategy is part of our evolved psychological makeup, the necessary shared sense of when to be assertive and when to be deferential constitutes an innate sense of possession, and that common sense could be embodied in the common law's definition of possession. Because possession is, in turn, a block in the foundation of our law of property (Epstein 1979; Megarry & Wade 1984; Holmes, Missouri v. Holland 1920 252 US 416–435, p. 434), much of our property law could be built upon distinctions embedded in the structure of our brains.

10.4 Legal recognition of the waxing and waning of attachments

The rules that anchor the initial allocation of title in possession become easier to understand when we recognize that forming attachments may solve evolutionary problems. Clearly the ownership convention is more complicated for humans than for butterflies. Ownership, once established, can be transferred and does not evaporate as quickly.

Humans keep track of earlier occupancies. However, even in societies recognizing potentially perpetual rights, ownership does not always last forever. Ownership in captured wild animals ends when they regain their natural liberty (In re Oriental Republic Uruguay 1993 821 F. Supp. 950–956 (D. Del.); Mullett v. Bradley 1898 53 N.Y.S. 781–783 (App. Div.)). 'In all these creatures, reclaimed from the wildness of their nature, the property is not absolute, but defeasible: a property, that may be destroyed if they resume their antient wildness and are found at large' (Blackstone 1766, p. 393). Rights in personal property, in the US at least, end upon abandonment (Eads v. Brazelton 1861 22 Ark. 499, 79 Am. Dec. 88–102; Erickson v. Sinykin 1947 223 Minn. 232, 26 N.W. 2d 172–178; Blackstone 1766, p. 9; Pollock & Wright 1888) and easements may terminate by abandonment (Crossley and Sons Ltd. v. Lightowler 1867 2 Ch. App. 478–486; R. v. Chorley 1848 12 Q. B. 518–520; Iowa State Highway Commission v. Dubuque Sand & Gravel Co. 1977 258 N.W. 2d 153–154 (Iowa); Megarry & Wade 1984).

One of the most common involuntary terminations of rights occurs by virtue of the doctrine of adverse possession. This doctrine wrests legal title from the person that is the current title holder according to the records and reallocates that title to the current possessor, without the consent of the record title holder. The law of adverse possession raises a profoundly difficult issue: how can the law divest a rightful owner of his property and transfer it to a mere squatter? The normative nature of the issue explains the prominence of adverse possession in the law-school curriculum. Over the years, legal scholars have constructed many rationales for the doctrine, none of which is very compelling today, however appropriate they might once have been (Stake 2001). Can evolutionary science provide any insight into the persistence of this odd exception to our ordinary rules of perpetual ownership? Yes.

(a) Studies of birds

Experiments performed with birds indicate that the attachment to territory and the trauma of losing possession of territory increases with the length of possession. Krebs (1982) removed pairs of resident great tits from their territories, kept them in captivity, and then released them after a replacement pair had settled in the vacated territories. The replacement birds that had been in possession for 3 h contested for ownership seven times longer than they did if they had just arrived, and they contested nearly twice again as long when they had been in possession for 10 h instead of 3 h. Beletsky & Orians (1989) found that replacement red-winged blackbirds that held territories for 6–7 days could usually defeat the original owners. Tobias (1997) removed European robins from their territories and then released them at varying periods after replacements had settled into those territories. The replacement robins defeated removed robins after the replacements had been in possession for 10 days in winter, and defeated removed robins for the bulk of the territory after only a single day in spring.

The authors of the experiments interpret their results as supporting the 'value-asymmetry hypothesis'. Over time, the value to the original bird declines, but declines slowly. The value to the replacement bird increases, and increases faster than the value to the original bird declines. Eventually, the value to the replacement exceeds the value to the original and the replacement will fight long and hard enough to fend off the original. If persistence and success in fighting for control of territory correlate with the pain of dispossession, that pain increases with the length of possession.

English law of territory ownership follows nature's lead. The adverse possession doctrine conforms to the principle reflected in the bird studies, that after the passage of time the value of the territory to the new claimant is greater than the value to the old claimant. To establish title by this passage of time, the squatter has to show that for the statutory period he had possession, that such possession was adverse to the owner, that it was continuous, that it was exclusive, and that the owner was out of possession (Megarry & Wade 1984; Smith 1996). The requirement of possession assures that the squatter had physical control and the intent to maintain it. If his possession was continuous, it was unbroken by his own abandonment or by the possession of others. Thus the doctrine asks whether the adverse possessor used the land as a true owner would, whether he showed the defensive, possessive attitudes one would expect of a true owner, and whether he formed the kind of attachment that leads to increased efforts in defence of territory. The requirements assure that the squatter did indeed form the strong ties that could be cut only with great pain. Conversely, the doctrinal inquiry also establishes that the record owner was not in possession and, therefore, does not feel like the typical owner of land and, hence, would not defend it to the same degree. As between the two claimants, the law allocates the loss to the non-possessor because the loss will hurt him less.

(b) Studies of humans

The doctrine of adverse possession also fits with what we are learning about the brain from experimental psychology and economics. People often demand more to give up some thing than they would be willing to pay for the exact same thing. Thaler (1980) called this pattern of underweighting of opportunity costs the 'endowment effect'. This anomaly is a manifestation of an asymmetry of value that Kahneman & Tversky (1984) dubbed 'loss aversion'. According to the theory of loss aversion, losses from one's endowment have more subjective impact than financially equivalent gains, and losses from endowment are more painful than losses of mere prospects (Kahneman *et al.* 1990, 1991; Korobkin 2003). This difference in impact is greater than would be expected from considering declining marginal utility alone.

In two experiments reported by Kahneman *et al.* (1990), the experimenters randomly divided subjects into three groups: buyers, choosers and sellers. The sellers were given coffee mugs, the choosers were given options to acquire coffee mugs and the buyers were given nothing. Sellers indicated the least they would take for their mugs, buyers indicated the most they would pay for mugs, and choosers indicated the price at which they would rather have cash than mugs. The experimenters found that subjects endowed with mugs placed a higher value on them than the choosers or the buyers. These experiments also support the conclusion that there is an endowment effect for cash, although the effect was smaller than for the intrinsically valuable coffee mugs (Stake 1995).

The studies of bird territoriality and human endowment effects lead to the conclusion that duration of actual possession and expectation of ownership make a difference to a person's attachment to a thing. The property doctrine of adverse possession conforms to this adaptation of the brain, implicitly recognizing that the claimant in recent, lengthy, exclusive possession has formed a greater bond with the land and will fight harder for it. Property law resolves such disputes as they would be resolved in physical fights, without the need for combat.

10.5 Group protection of individual interests

The resemblance of non-human animal behaviours to human property institutions discussed so far should not be taken as sufficient to conclude that animals have what we call property. The human institution of property incorporates at least four elements. First, the owner must form some special relationship to the thing, such as being more willing to expend resources defending it. Second, conspecifics must in some way honour or respect the owner's relationship. Third, the owner must recognize that respect by others. Fourth, conspecifics as individuals or as members of the group must be willing to intervene on behalf of that owner, protecting the property from threats by challengers, whether they be conspecifics or others. On the third and fourth points, more research is needed.

Heinrich (1999) presents compelling evidence that ravens can gang together to protect their assets. He introduced a wild raven into a group of four ravens that had lived together nearly all of their lives. The four did not allow the wild raven to feed on the food pile in the aviary. With that access to food barred, the newcomer watched where the others cached emergency supplies from the food pile and tried to feed upon those caches. Although there was plenty of food to feed all five, the others killed the wild raven for her efforts to feed from their caches.

More noteworthy are three other raven stories that Heinrich (1999) presents anecdotally. According to Heinrich, Kevin McGowan climbs trees to band ravens. Not only do ravens attack him when he comes into their territory, but neighbouring ravens join in the attack to defend the territory of the residents. In separate incidents, Lorenzo Russo and Chris Walsh each reported being attacked by resident pairs. When the attacks were unsuccessful, the pairs flew off, only to return shortly with three or five helpers, respectively, who joined in attacking the human interloper. This behaviour might be explained as instances of the helper ravens acting in anticipatory defence of their own territories, or the helpers may have been relatives acting in the interests of inclusive fitness. It could be the case, however, that the behaviour was not just nepotism or immediate self interest, but that it was an instance of reciprocal behaviour, neighbour ravens joining forces in group protection of a member's property. There is a lot more research to be done, but these stories hint that even the human institution of the group acting to protect the things of an individual may have ancient biological antecedents.

10.6 What humans do with their property, and the laws of intestacy

If humans have a property instinct, it ought to include not only respect for the possessions of others, protection of one's own possessions and helping in the defence of others', but also inclinations regarding what to do with those things that have been acquired. Obviously, people use assets to keep themselves alive, the evolutionary utility of which needs no discussion. It is worth noting, however, that the law recognizes this utility by allowing individuals great freedom in consuming assets as they please. Law would undermine its own authority if it were to try to tell people how to use or not to use their things.

Very often, however, people do not consume their assets, but give them to others instead. If people have a property instinct, how do these gifts fit into that instinct? Evolutionary theory should allow us to predict donative behaviours as well as acquisitive and retentive behaviours. To whom do people give their property? In what ways does the law reflect those inclinations to make gifts? In other words, what is the phenotypical behaviour and in what way is the law an extension of that phenotype? Evolutionary analysis can parsimoniously explain several specific donative preferences and, in doing so, explain some of the basic contours in the laws that apply when someone dies without a will, the laws of intestate succession.

(a) Benefactors' blood relatives

Because a parent is just a gene's way of making another gene, selection should favour those genes that make good parents, parents who produce viable offspring and help those offspring to reproduce. There are a number of ways parents invest in their offspring (Trivers 1972). For example, female Belding's ground squirrels put themselves at risk by sounding alarms to warn other squirrels of predators. Sherman (1981) has found, however, that they are not indiscriminate in this risky warning behaviour. They make the alarm warnings more often when they have mothers, daughters or sisters nearby than when the surrounding squirrels are related less closely or not at all.

Another important means of increasing offspring survival and reproduction is the transfer of property, both tangible and intangible. Because property can be converted to food and shelter, parents, grandparents and more distant ancestors can enhance the chances that their offspring will survive by giving them property.

Actual giving conforms to the theory. Smith *et al.* (1987) found that 1000 randomly selected wills left 92.3% of the wealth to spouses and kin and only 7.7% to non-relatives. Gifts completed during the life of the donor follow a similar pattern. Anderson *et al.* (1999) studied parental investment by men. Their data indicate that children of the current mate of the donor were three times as likely to receive some money for college if they were the genetic children of the donor than if they were step-children of the donor. Children of a previous mate of the donor were four times as likely to receive some money for college if they were the genetic children of the donor than if they were step-children of the donor.

English and American laws of intestate succession follow this evolutionarily predictable pattern. The laws of descent and distribution allocate a large portion of a decedent's estate to surviving blood relatives. Indeed, if a decedent (deceased person) leaves no surviving spouse or relatives, the decedent's property escheats to the crown or state rather than going to in-laws, friends or other worthy recipients. We could explain the laws of intestacy on the theory that they were designed merely to mimic the testaments of persons who left wills. In this view, the law is simply being efficient. However, this efficiency explanation underestimates the degree to which it is important for laws of intestate succession to reflect what feels natural, or fair, or just, to those empowered to determine the rules. If the rules favouring relatives do not seem fair at some basic level, they might not last long or garner much respect.

(i) Genetic proximity

The chances that a gene or allele is passed to a child are 50%, because half of each person's genes come from each parent. The chances that a gene will reach a grandchild are only one out of four, the odds diminishing by a factor of two with each succeeding generation. A selfish gene (Dawkins 1976) should be less interested in helping more distant family members. For this reason, we would expect decedents' gifts to be concentrated in closer relatives. This prediction is confirmed by both common experience and research by Smith *et al.* (1987), who found that decedents gave 46% of their wealth to relatives one-half related, 8% to relatives one-quarter related, and less than 1% to relatives one-eighth related. Evolution has selected in the human brain an inclination to give property to others, but that inclination is biased heavily towards persons who share a close genetic relationship.

Laws of intestate succession follow this preference by providing that closer relatives take before more distant relatives. Both the English statute (Megarry & Wade 1984) and section 2–103 of the Uniform Probate Code (Langbein & Waggoner 2003), which has been adopted in many of the United States, provide that siblings, cousins and more distant relatives of the decedent take nothing if children of the decedent survive. Evolutionary theory explains the priority of closer relatives found in the laws of intestacy.

(ii) Age of recipient

Evolutionary theory also suggests that gifts to persons beyond reproductive years will create little benefit for the donor's genes and, therefore, donors are less likely to give to elderly persons than to similarly related persons of child-bearing age. Adaptive giving would be expected to be biased towards donees who are most likely to have additional children. For example, a decedent is equally related to her children, siblings and parents, but in most cases she can do her genes more good by giving her property to her children rather than her parents because her children are more likely to reproduce. Moreover, a decedent's assets passed to parents or siblings are likely to end up in the hands of nephews and nieces, who are not as closely related to the decedent as her own children.

Once again, research by Smith *et al.* (1987) confirms the prediction of evolutionary theory with regard to the behaviour of testators (persons who died with wills). The decedents in the study gave 38% to their children compared with only 8% to their siblings and nothing to their parents. Of course, there are other explanations: older relatives might also tend to be less needy because they have had more time to accrue resources. Turning from testate to intestate succession, when the law distributes assets on behalf of a decedent who has not executed a will, it tracks the general preference for younger persons, allocating the estate to the living children or their issue, if there are any, rather than to the decedent's parents or siblings (Megarry & Wade 1984; Uniform Probate Code section 2–103 (Langbein & Waggoner 2003)).

The optimal evolutionary strategy gets more complicated when there are no children and the choice of beneficiaries is between parents and siblings. When a childless person is old enough to have children, his parents are unlikely to produce many more children and it makes sense to send his assets to his siblings rather than his parents, the younger generation being generally more likely to convert resources into additional copies of the donor's genes. At about the same time that people gain the physical capacity to have children, they gain the legal capacity to execute a will, and as just noted those wills tend to allocate assets to fecund siblings over ageing parents.

However, when a person is too young to have children, it is likely that some of her siblings are also too young to have children and that her parents are still young enough to produce additional children. In such situations, it makes biological sense for her to send her assets to her parents, who may still be able to have children and in any case will be likely to spend some of the assets supporting their other children, the decedent's siblings. Indeed, if the siblings are minors, the parents will probably spend the assets more wisely and effectively on behalf of the siblings than the siblings would do themselves. Furthermore, the parents are better able to tell who in the family would benefit most from the assets and are likely to allocate the assets efficiently, allocating them to one child or spreading them around as needs be. Allocating the decedent's assets to all her siblings might spread the assets too thinly, for example. If the decedent does not have children, her genetic interests are the same as her parent's interests, and focussed giving by her parents might advance the family genes more than an automatic allocation of equal portions to all siblings would.

Most Anglo-American laws of descent and distribution conform to this biological priority by giving to parents before turning to siblings of the decedent. If the parents are dead, however, the assets will pass to the siblings. Thus the law makes a rough cut, favouring children when there are some, and then going next to parents if there are no children, which makes sense when the decedents are too young to write a will.

(iii) Paternity uncertainty and maternity certainty

An efficient gene, one designed to make the most of its resources, would build a brain that avoids wasting resources on persons who are less likely to carry that gene. Half of all parents, the male half, cannot be completely confident that their children are indeed the product of their gametes. To the extent that a man is uncertain a child is his, we should expect him to be less inclined to allocate property to that child. Conversely, we should expect to see greater giving when certainty of parenthood is higher. Once again, the pattern of actual giving tracks the evolutionary theory. Buss (1999) reports that Anderson et al. (1999) found that children of the few men who expressed uncertainty in their paternity were much less likely than the children of confident fathers to receive money for college from those fathers.

Older versions of the Uniform Probate Code expressly recognized the uncertainty surrounding paternity and the preference of men for not giving to the children of other men. Before 1990, section 2–109 provided that 'a person born out of wedlock is ... a child of the father, if ... the paternity is established by an adjudication before the death of the father or is established thereafter by clear and convincing proof...' (Langbein & Waggoner 2003). The same section also recognized that men were more likely than women to deny support to their children by its provision that mothers could inherit from their illegitimate children but fathers could do so only if they had not refused to support them. These provisions were changed to be sex-neutral in the 1990 reforms.

Despite hospital errors, human mothers, like other mammalian mothers, are nearly certain of their maternity. Given their greater confidence, evolutionary theory predicts that if all else is equal mothers will give more property to offspring than will fathers. Furthermore, evolutionary theory predicts that grandparents of either gender will give more to children of daughters than to children of sons. There are two links from a grandparent to a grandchild. Father–child links are less certain than mother–child links. Therefore, a brain built by rational, selfish genes would devote the most property to grandchildren connected by two maternal links, less to grandchildren connected by one maternal link and one paternal link, and the least to grandchildren connected by two paternal links.

This prediction was confirmed by DeKay (1995). The subjects reported getting the most in gifts from their maternal grandmother and the least from their paternal grandfather. This result is probably not a result of the general tendency of women to give more than men because, on average, the mother's father gave more property than the father's mother. Gaulin *et al.* (1997) similarly found a matrilineal bias in the investment by aunts and uncles. Both aunts and uncles showed more concern for their sisters' children than for their brothers' children. One way for genes to favour the children of sisters is to generate a stronger tie to sisters. Thus it is not surprising that Salmon & Daly (1996) found that both male and female college students were more likely to name a sister than a brother as the sibling to whom they felt closest. The warmth for sisters' offspring reflects back upon the sisters themselves.

Of course these findings reveal a lot about our attitudes towards other people. But they also reveal something about property. If the donative urge is millennia old, the sense of control over assets must stem from an even earlier date for it is hard to have a sense of how to allocate assets without first having a sense of what things are one's assets. It is a risky move for a parent to give his child property to which someone else feels attached.

(iv) Wealth of the beneficiary

In addition to age and genetic relatedness, there are other criteria that a well-adapted brain might use to determine how to allocate property within its control. Donor behaviour ought to depend on the behaviour expected of donees. Donees can use resources for a number of purposes: to survive, to attract mates and to provide for offspring. In pre-modern societies, wealth is indeed associated with reproductive success (Borgerhoff Mulder 1998); the relationship is less clear in developing and developed societies (Judge & Hrdy 1992; Low 2000). However, although any donee can make use of additional resources, they are not all equally likely to convert parental gifts of property into offspring.

Evolutionary pressure could have shaped brains to send property where it will be most efficiently deployed. One factor that affects the ability of the donee to benefit from a gift is the level of resources already available to that donee. That is, when instructing its body to shift resources to others, an efficient brain would take into account the resource level of the various potential donees.

(v) Interaction of wealth and sex of recipient

Another factor in the ability of the donees to make use of gifts in some situations might be their sex. Males and females do not have the same capacity for creating children (Low 2000). To take human examples, no woman on record has had even one-tenth as many children as Morocco's Emperor Moulay Ismail The Bloodthirsty, who claimed to have fathered more than 700 sons, and received credit for 888 children in The Guinness Book of World Records (Pinker 1997). As Pinker (1997, p. 478) puts it, '[u]nder polygyny, men vie for extraordinary Darwinian stakes—many wives versus none—and the competition is literally cutthroat'. By necessity, the high reproductive success of some males ties up the reproductive capacities of multiple females, leaving other males with no opportunities to reproduce. The result is that the variation in number of offspring is greater for males than for females. In their study of 1500 Californians who died leaving wills, Judge & Hrdy (1992) found a variance of 3.45 offspring for women, as compared with 4.34 for men.

Any sex difference in the variance in reproduction creates the potential for a difference in the reproductive pay-off from resources. For example, Judge & Hrdy (1992) found that men whose estates were above the median value left more surviving children than did men whose estates were smaller. The same was not true, however, of women; those who left more wealth did not also leave more surviving children.

Trivers & Willard (1973) deduced that there could be an interactive effect between sex and resource level. The Trivers–Willard hypothesis says that the condition of animals will influence whether they invest more resources in male or female offspring. The pay-off to additional resources is nonlinear and differs by sex. Parents who cannot endow a son with enough resources to get him a mate should invest their resources in their female children if they are to maximize their reproductive success (Hartung 1982). Parents who can put sons in a position to have more than one mate should direct more resources towards sons, or in some circumstances even concentrate them in a single son. There is evidence supporting this conjecture in the behaviour of mice (Rivers & Crawford 1974), spider monkeys (McFarland Symington 1987) and red deer (Clutton-Brock et al. 1986). Evolution could have tailored the human brain to discriminate between sons and daughters in allocating the property within its control and to determine that allocation differently depending on a number of factors, including the available resources.

The Trivers–Willard hypothesis dovetails with the ancient law of primogeniture (Boone 1986). Under primogeniture, a decedent's land passed to just one son, thereby maximizing that son's chances of becoming an alpha male and, hence, his reproductive opportunities. If the decedent had no son, his assets passed equally to his daughters, as might be adaptive according to Trivers & Willard.

One problem with this explanation of the law of descent is that it does not explain why modern lawmakers have forsaken primogeniture in favour of equal distribution among children. The older and newer rules might be reconciled by focusing on the fact that primogeniture fits the needs of wealthier decedents, whereas egalitarian, modern law fits the needs of poorer decedents. If through the ages the law has come to incorporate more of the values and sentiments of people of modest means, this might help explain why the law has shifted from the rules of primogeniture to the modern rules of more equal distribution. More likely, modern norms of equality have simply overridden the sentiments favouring a single male heir.

Studies of individually directed giving are mixed on this issue of whether humans behave as predicted by Trivers & Willard. In support of the hypothesis, Smith et al. (1987) found that while the proportion of estates given to females did not vary much according to wealth, the proportion given to males shifted from about half that of females for poor families to twice that of females for wealthy families. Other support for Trivers–Willard has been found in fifteenth and sixteenth century Portuguese families (Boone 1986), the Yomut of Turkmenistan (Irons 2000), and the Mukogodo of Kenya (Cronk 2000). However, while Judge & Hrdy (1992) did find that parents showed more favouritism among sons than among daughters, their study of California wills failed to find the other predicted interactive effect, that of greater giving to sons when there is greater wealth to give. Freese & Powell (1999) also failed to find the predicted interaction when they studied parental investment in adolescents. Borgerhoff Mulder (1998) found that survival rates in the Kipsigis of Kenya do not support Trivers–Willard, but parental investment in education does track the Trivers–Willard pattern, and increasingly so in recent years.

The Trivers–Willard hypothesis might lead to an explanation of recently heralded findings regarding likelihood of divorce (Morgan *et al*. 1988; Dahl & Moretti 2004). Dahl & Moretti examined 60 years of US Census Bureau data and found that families with one girl were 1–7% more likely to divorce than families with one boy, with the effect increasing to 7% for larger families, but decreasing to zero over recent decades. Similarly, Morgan *et al*. (1988) had earlier found that sons reduce the risk of marital disruption by 9% more than daughters. There are a number of conceivable explanations for these findings, including the possibilities that men want sons and keep marrying until they get one or that men become more involved in the family when they have a son. However, Trivers–Willard offers an explanation that is not rooted in a preference for sons or traditional gender roles. Because divorce is costly, it decreases family assets. Investing effort to keep a marriage together increases family assets available to the children, and thus could be seen as an investment in the children. Couples make a greater investment when they have a male child than when they have females. This difference in investment makes biological sense if inherited wealth is more important to a son's reproductive success than to a daughter's, which Trivers–Willard argues would be the case when the parents are rich in resources. What remains to be determined is whether the divorce rate is a function of the interaction of wealth and sex of the child.

The Trivers–Willard theory might explain the divorce data in another, somewhat backwards and as yet incompletely explained, way. Because mothers can invest less in male offspring by bearing fewer of them, the theory suggests that mothers poor in resources might produce relatively more female offspring, whereas mothers rich in resources might produce more males, although the physiological mechanism for this is unclear (McFarland Symington 1987). This prediction was borne out in an experimental field study in which female opossums given supplemental provisions produced more male offspring than did controls (Austad & Sunquist 1986), and it has been observed that female red deer (Clutton-Brock *et al*. 1986) and spider monkeys (McFarland Symington 1987) produce a higher ratio of males if they are high in rank. For human examples, consider that wives of American Presidents have borne 86 male and 58 female children (Betzig & Weber 1995), and white American mothers, who are statistically richer, have relatively more male children than black American mothers (National Center for Health Statistics 1999). Some women can anticipate divorce, certainly if they are contemplating initiating proceedings but maybe also if they sense such an inclination on the part of their husbands. Married women sensing an unmarried future are also sensing a lower level of support, and for that reason would be predicted by the Trivers–Willard theory to have more female children. In addition, such women, who have the sense that they might be unmarried at a later date, might indeed be more likely to be unmarried at a later date. Viewed after the divorce, it looks like the daughters helped cause the divorce, but instead the impending divorce perhaps helped cause the daughters.

Further research could examine the Trivers–Willard proposition in the context of both lifetime and testamentary human altruism. A study of lifetime giving might, for example, investigate whether wealthier parents in industrialized societies offer their male children disproportionately better opportunities for college educations. Inequality in such a domain would be less obvious to the donors and, hence, be less likely to be purposively overcome by persons ordinarily attentive to the social norm of equality. It also could be the case that the adaptation itself is sensitive to the perceived connection between reproductive success and wealth. In other words, if people do not see wealthier men having substantially higher numbers of children, they do not perceive a winner-take-all race and they might not feel any urge to give more to their sons. Another possibility is that modern egalitarian social norms have overcome a Trivers–Willard discriminatory adaptation, even if humans are born with one.

(b) Attracting mates

The instinct to care for one's children has no application until there are children to care for. An even more basic instinct, then, is to perform the steps needed to create offspring. One of those steps is attracting a mate, and being generous might advance that cause. A woman who sees a man being generous has some reason to believe that the man will be generous to her, helping her to survive. He might also be generous to his children (Buss 1999), helping them to survive, and helping them to attract mates (if they are generous in turn), all of which redounds to the genetic benefit of their mother. Thus, to a female brain evolved to respond to the potential benefits of charity, the generous male looks like a better prospect than the skinflint. Because generosity attracts persons who expect to be beneficiaries, generosity towards mates and potential mates brings sexual opportunities. Therefore, such giving should be expected and is consistent with the theory that people are selfish reproducers. Anderson et al. (1999) offer some evidence that men use their charity to impress potential partners. They found that a child was nearly three times as likely to receive money for college from its father or stepfather if he was living with the mother at the time the child entered college.

Gifts that become effective at the death of the donor can do little to improve the dead person's sexual opportunities. Nevertheless, Fellows et al. (1978) found that the desire to give to mates continues to the end of life. It could be that giving to spouses at death is just a vestige of the habit of giving during life. But another way to look at testamentary gifts to spouses is that, because a will is made during life, the charitable value of the will is actually enjoyed during life. Thus, testamentary giving may still be an act of courtship.

There is another biological explanation for testamentary gifts to spouses. Decedents can reasonably expect their surviving spouses to pass a portion of the gifts on to their children. Judge (1995) found that men often expressed confidence that their wives would provide for, or pass property along to, their common children. Among those estates studied by Judge & Hrdy (1992), when men died they left nearly 70% of their assets to their spouses. That men ordinarily expected a portion of these assets to reach their children is indicated by the fact that in one-quarter of the cases in which they took the unusual step of leaving less than half of their assets to their surviving spouse, they did so to leave the large bulk of their estate to children from previous marriages. When women died, they left less of their assets to their surviving spouses than did men, perhaps in part because their husbands might remarry and devote some of those resources to children of that new marriage. Indeed, when couples marry at an older age, having already produced children with previous mates, they often make premarital agreements designed to direct assets to their own children rather than to their spouses or their spouses' children.

In their basic approach, modern English and American laws of intestacy track the preference for generosity towards mates by allocating a substantial portion of the decedent's estate to the surviving spouse (Megarry & Wade 1984; Uniform Probate Code section 2–103 (Langbein & Waggoner 2003)). Some variants track the evolutionary model a bit more closely by paying attention to whether the surviving children were children of both the decedent and the surviving spouse or just one of them. Section 2–102 of the Uniform Probate Code (Langbein & Waggoner 2003) provides that more assets go to the surviving children and fewer go to the surviving spouse when the decedent leaves children whose other parent is not the surviving spouse. When the survivor was not the parent of all of the decedent's children, the decedent cannot count on as much generosity from the survivor to the decedent's children by other parents. To achieve the same balance of giving between children and spouse when the surviving spouse is less likely to give to the decedent's children, the decedent has to give more to them directly rather than relying on the survivor to be a conduit. Similarly, when the decedent was the parent of only some of the survivor's children, the decedent might not wish to support those other children as fully as the decedent's own children and so must give assets directly to the decedent's children rather than to the spouse as a proxy because the spouse will not distinguish between the children as the decedent would have wished.

There have long been limitations on the minimum that a decedent could leave to his or her surviving spouse. According to Geddes & Zak (2002) many legal systems have assured the wife one-third of the husband's estate upon the husband's death. They argue that the 'rule of one-third' increases the mother's investment in their children. If she were not guaranteed such a share, the wife would expend too little effort on mothering their children and too much effort acquiring resources for herself. If she were assured more than one-third, she would invest more in the children, but that would leave less for the men, which would not be favoured in a patriarchal legal system.

The various arguments here should not be read to contend that the law was written expressly to achieve biological goals. Some laws of intestate succession have been drafted to mimic what people would do on their own (Fellows *et al.* 1978; Beckstrom 1985), to achieve decedents' desires without need for any action by the decedents. Other normative goals include justice. But no matter which, our biology is involved. The laws of intestacy extend the human phenotype.

10.7 Conclusion

Property is more than a social invention; it is set of feelings built into our brains to solve survival problems confronting our ancestors. There are many dimensions to the property instinct, ranging from what constitutes property to what to do with property. Doubtless, these dimensions of the property instinct will be developed further, corrected and clarified, and other dimensions will be discovered as the science of behaviour progresses. Exploration and improved understanding of the property instinct should help us to place the various property laws on a more scientific footing than is possible today.

The author thanks Val Nolan Jr, Owen Jones, Jeremy Freese, Nicholas Georgakopoulos, Mitu Gulati, Erik Lillquist, Karen Parker, Sarah Brosnan, David Snyder, Robert Stake, the anonymous reviewers and especially Oliver Goodenough for their considerable help on this chapter. I could not have completed the project without research support from Indiana University School of Law–Bloomington.

References

Anderson, K. G., Kaplan, H. & Lancaster, J. 1999 Paternal care by genetic fathers and stepfathers. I. Reports from Albuquerque men. *Evol. Hum. Behav.* **20**, 405–431. (doi:10.1016/S1090-5138(99)00023-9).

Austad, S. N. & Sunquist, M. E. 1986 Sex-ratio manipulation in the common opossum. *Nature* **324**, 58–60.

Beckstrom, J. H. 1985 *Sociobiology and the law: the biology of altruism in the courtroom of the future*. Urbana, IL: University of Illinois Press.

Beletsky, L. D. & Orians, G. H. 1989 Territoriality among male red-winged blackbirds. III. Testing hypotheses of territorial dominance. *Behav. Ecol. Sociobiol.* **24**, 333–339.

Bentham, J. 1914 Of property. In *The theory of legislation*, vol. 1. *Principles of the civil code*. Part I (ed. É. Dumont), pp. 145–147. Oxford University Press.

Betzig, L. & Weber, S. 1995 Presidents preferred sons. *Politics Life Sci.* **14**, 61–64.

Blackstone, W. 1766 *Commentaries on the laws of England*, vol. **2**. Oxford: Clarendon (1979 facsimile of the 1st edn, University of Chicago Press).

Boone, J. 1986 Parental investment and elite family structure in preindustrial states: a case study of late medieval–early modern Portuguese genealogies. *Am. Anthropol.* **88**, 859–878.

Borgerhoff Mulder, M. 1998 Brothers and sisters: how sibling interactions affect optimal parental allocations. *Hum. Nature* **9**, 119–161.

Brosnan, S. F. & de Waal, F. B. M. 2003 Monkeys reject unequal pay. *Nature* **425**, 297–299. (doi:10.1038/nature01963)

Burgess, J. W. 1976 Social spiders. *Sci. Am.* **234**(3), 100–106.

Buss, D. 1999 *Evolutionary psychology: the new science of the mind*. Needham Heights, MA: Allyn & Bacon.

Clutton-Brock, T. H., Albon, S. D. & Guinness, F. E. 1986 Great expectations: dominance, breeding success and off-spring sex ratios in red deer. *Anim. Behav.* **34**, 460–471.

Cronk, L. 2000 Female biased parental investment and growth performance among the Mukogodo. In *Adaptation and human behavior: an anthropological perspective* (ed. L. Cronk, N. Chagnon & W. Irons), pp. 203–221. New York: Aldine de Gruyter.

Dahl, G. B. & Moretti, E. 2004 The demand for sons: evidence from divorce, fertility, and shotgun marriage. Draft at http://papers.nber.org/papers/W10281 last viewed on 12 October 2004.

Davies, N. B. 1978 Territorial defence in the speckled wood butterfly (*Pararge aegeria*): the resident always wins. *Anim. Behav.* **26**, 138–147.

Dawkins, R. 1976 *The selfish gene*. Oxford University Press.

Dawkins, R. 1982 *The extended phenotype: the long reach of the gene*. Oxford University Press.

DeKay, W. T. 1995 Grandparental investment and the uncertainty of kinship. Paper presented to Seventh Annual Meeting of the Human Behavior and Evolution Society, 28 June to 2 July, Santa Barbara, CA. In Buss (1999), p. 239.

Epstein, R. A. 1979 Possession as the root of title. *Georgia Law Rev.* **13**, 1221–1243.

Epstein, R. A. 1980 A taste for privacy? Evolution and the emergence of a naturalistic ethic. *J. Legal Stud.* **9**, 665–681.

Fellows, M. L., Simon, R. J. & Rau, W. 1978 Public attitudes about property distribution at death and intestate succession laws in the United States. *Am. Bar Found. Res. J.* **1978**, 319–391.

Freese, J. & Powell, B. 1999 Sociobiology, status, and parental investment in sons and daughters: testing the Trivers–Willard hypothesis. *Am. J. Sociol.* **106**, 1704–1743. (doi:10.1086/321304)

Gaulin, S. J. C., McBurney, D. H. & Brakeman-Wartell, S. L. 1997 Matrilateral biases in the investment of aunts and uncles: a consequence and measure of paternity uncertainty. *Hum. Nature* **8**, 139–151.

Geddes, R. & Zak, P. J. 2002 The rule of one-third. *J. Legal Stud.* **31**, 119–137. (doi:10.1086/339289)

Gibbard, A. F. 1982 Human evolution and the sense of justice. In *Midwest studies in philosophy, vol. VII: social and political philosophy* (ed. P. A. French, T. E. Uehling Jr & H. K. Wettstein), pp. 31–46. Minneapolis, MN: University of Minnesota Press.

Grafen, A. 1987 The logic of divisively asymmetric contests: respect for ownership and the desperado effect. *Anim. Behav.* **35**, 462–467.

Hammerstein, P. 1981 The role of asymmetries in animal contests. *Anim. Behav.* **29**, 193–205.

Hartung, J. 1982 Polygyny and inheritance of wealth. *Curr. Anthropol.* **23**, 1–12. (doi:10.1086/202775)

Heinrich, B. 1999 *Mind of the raven: investigations and adventures with wolf-birds*. New York: HarperCollins.

Hodge, M. A. & Uetz, G. W. 1995 A comparison of agonistic behavior of colonial web-building spiders from desert and tropical habitats. *Anim. Behav.* **50**, 963–972. (doi:10.1016/0003-3472(95) 80097-2)

Hofmann, H. A. & Schildberger, K. 2001 Assessment of strength and willingness to fight during aggressive encounters in crickets. *Anim. Behav.* **62**, 337–348. (doi:10.1006/anbe.2001.1746)

Irons, W. 2000 Why do the Yomut raise more sons than daughters? In *Adaptation and human behavior: an anthropological perspective* (ed. L. Cronk, N. Chagnon & W. Irons), pp. 223–236. New York: Aldine de Gruyter.

Judge, D. 1995 American legacies and the variable life histories of women and men. *Hum. Nature* **6**, 291–323.

Judge, D. S. & Hrdy, S. B. 1992 Allocation of accumulated resources among close kin: inheritance in Sacramento, California, 1890–1984. *Ethol. Sociobiol.* **13**, 495–522. (doi:10.1016/0162-3095 (92)90014-U)

Kahneman, D. & Tversky, A. 1984 Choices, values and frames. *Am. Psychol.* **39**, 341–350.

Kahneman, D., Knetsch, J. L. & Thaler, R. H. 1990 Experimental tests of the endowment effect and the Coase theorem. *J. Pol. Econ.* **98**, 1325–1348. (doi:10.1086/261737)

Kahneman, D., Knetsch, J. L. & Thaler, R. H. 1991 The endowment effect, loss aversion, and status quo bias: anomalies. *J. Econ. Perspect.* **5**, 193–206.

Korobkin, R. 2003 The endowment effect and legal analysis. *Northwestern Univ. Law Rev.* **97**, 1227–1293.

Krebs, J. R. 1982 Territorial defence in the great tit (*Parus major*): do residents always win? *Behav. Ecol. Sociobiol.* **11**, 185–194.

Krebs, J. R. & Davies, N. B. 1997 *Behavioural ecology, an evolutionary approach*, 4th edn. Oxford: Blackwell Science.

Kummer, H., Gotz, W. & Angst, W. 1974 Triadic differentiation: an inhibitory process protecting pair bonds in baboons. *Behavior* **49**, 62–87.

Langbein, J. H. & Waggoner, L. W. 2003 *Uniform trust and estate statutes*. New York: Foundation Press.

Low, B. S. 2000 Sex, wealth, and fertility: old rules, new environments. In *Adaptation and human behavior: an anthropological perspective* (ed. L. Cronk, N. Chagnon & W. Irons), pp. 323–344. New York: Aldine de Gruyter.

McFarland Symington, M. 1987 Sex ratio and maternal rank in wild spider monkeys: when daughters disperse. *Behav. Ecol. Sociobiol.* **20**, 421–425.

Marden, J. H. & Rollins, R. A. 1994 Assessment of energy reserves by damselflies engaged in aerial contests for mating territories. *Anim. Behav.* **48**, 1023–1030. (doi:10.1006/anbe.1994.1335)

Mathis, A., Schmidt, D. W. & Medley, K. A. 2000 The influence of residency status on agonistic behavior of male and female Ozark zigzag salamanders *Plethodon angusticlavus*. *Am. Midland Nat.* **143**, 245–249.

Maynard Smith, J. 1972 *On evolution*. Edinburgh University Press.

Maynard Smith, J. 1982 *Evolution and the theory of games*. Cambridge University Press.

Maynard Smith, J. & Parker, G. A. 1976 The logic of asymmetric contests. *Anim. Behav.* **24**, 159–175.

Megarry, R. & Wade, H. R. W. 1984 *The law of real property*, 5th edn. London: Stevens & Sons Limited.

Mesterton-Gibbons, M. & Adams, E. S. 1998 Animal contests as evolutionary games. *Am. Sci.* **86**, 334–341. (doi:10.1511/1998.4.334)

Moretz, J. 2003 Aggression and RHP in the Northern swordtail fish, *Xiphophorus cortezi*: the relationship between size and contest dynamics in male–male competition. *Ethology* **109**, 995–1008. (doi:10.1046/j.0179-1613.2003.00938.x)

Morgan, S. P., Lye, D. N. & Condran, G. A. 1988 Sons, daughters, and the risk of marital disruption. *Am. J. Sociol.* **94**, 110–129. (doi:10.1086/228953)

National Center for Health Statistics 1999 *Vital statistics of the United States 1993*, vol. **1**. *Natality*. Hyattsville, MD: DHHS.

Pape, R. A. 2003 The strategic logic of suicide terrorism. *Am. Political Sci. Rev.* **97**, 343–361. (doi:10.1017/S000305540300073X)

Pinker, S. 1994 *The language instinct*. New York: William Morrow.

Pinker, S. 1997 *How the mind works*. NewYork: W. W. Norton.

Pollock, F. & Wright, R. S. 1888 *Possession in the common law*, part III. Oxford: Clarendon Press.

Rivers, J. P. W. & Crawford, M. A. 1974 Maternal nutrition and the sex ratio at birth. *Nature* **252**, 297–298.

Rose, C. M. 1985 Possession as the origin of property. *Univ. Chicago Law Rev.* **52**, 73–88.

Rizzolatti, G., Fadiga, L., Gallese, V. & Fogassi, L. 1996 Premotor cortex and the recognition of motor actions. *Cogn. Brain Res.* **3**, 131–141. (doi:10.1016/0926-6410(95)00038-0)

Salmon, C. A. & Daly, M. 1996 On the importance of kin relations to Canadian women and men. *Ethol. Sociobiol.* **17**, 289–297. (doi:10.1016/S0162-3095(96)00046-5)

Sherman, P. W. 1981 Kinship, demography and Belding's ground squirrel nepotism. *Behav. Ecol. Sociobiol.* **8**, 251–259.

Smith, M. S., Kish, B. J. & Crawford, C. B. 1987 Inheritance of wealth as human kin investment. *Ethol. Sociobiol.* **8**, 171–182. (doi:10.1016/0162-3095(87)90042-2)

Smith, R. J. 1996 *Property law*, 2nd edn. London: Longman.

Stake, J. E. 1995 Loss aversion and involuntary transfers of title. In *Law and economics: new and critical perspectives, vol. 4 of critic of institutions series* (ed. R. P. Malloy & C. K. Braun), pp. 331–360. New York: Peter Lang.

Stake, J. E. 2001 The uneasy case for adverse possession. *Georgetown Law J.* **89**, 2419–2474.

Sugden, R. 1986 *The economics of rights, co-operation, and welfare*. Oxford: Blackwell.

Thaler, R. 1980 Toward a positive theory of consumer choice. *J. Econ. Behav. Org.* **1**, 39–60. (doi:10.1016/01672681(80)90051–7)

Tobias, J. 1997 Asymmetric territorial contests in the European robin: the role of settlement costs. *Anim. Behav.* **54**, 9–21. (doi:10.1006/anbe.1996.0383)

Trivers, R. L. 1972 Parental investment and sexual selection. In *Sexual selection and the descent of man, 1871–1971* (ed. B. Campbell), pp. 136–179. Chicago, IL: Aldine.

Trivers, R. L. & Willard, D. E. 1973 Natural selection of parental ability to vary the sex ratio of offspring. *Science* **179**, 90–92.

Waage, J. K. 1988 Confusion over residency and the escalation of damselfly territorial disputes. *Anim. Behav.* **36**, 586–595.

Wenseleers, T., Billen, J. & Hefetz, A. 2002 Territorial marking in the desert ant *Cataglyphis niger*: does it pay to play bourgeois? *J. Insect Behav.* **15**, 85–93. (doi:10.1023/ A:1014484229639)

Yee, K. K. 2003 Ownership and trade from evolutionary games. *Int. Rev. Law Econ.* **23**, 183–197. (doi:10.1016/S0144-8188(03)00026-7)

Glossary

ESS: evolutionarily stable strategy

Criminal responsibility and punishment

11

For the law, neuroscience changes nothing and everything

Joshua Greene * *and Jonathan Cohen*

The rapidly growing field of cognitive neuroscience holds the promise of explaining the operations of the mind in terms of the physical operations of the brain. Some suggest that our emerging understanding of the physical causes of human (mis)behaviour will have a transformative effect on the law. Others argue that new neuroscience will provide only new details and that existing legal doctrine can accommodate whatever new information neuroscience will provide. We argue that neuroscience will probably have a transformative effect on the law, despite the fact that existing legal doctrine can, in principle, accommodate whatever neuroscience will tell us. New neuroscience will change the law, not by undermining its current assumptions, but by transforming people's moral intuitions about free will and responsibility. This change in moral outlook will result not from the discovery of crucial new facts or clever new arguments, but from a new appreciation of old arguments, bolstered by vivid new illustrations provided by cognitive neuroscience. We foresee, and recommend, a shift away from punishment aimed at retribution in favour of a more progressive, consequentialist approach to the criminal law.

Keywords: law; brain; morality; free will; punishment; retributivism

11.1 Introduction

The law takes a long-standing interest in the mind. In most criminal cases, a successful conviction requires the prosecution to establish not only that the defendant engaged in proscribed behaviour, but also that the misdeed in question was the product of *mens rea*, a 'guilty mind'. Narrowly interpreted, *mens rea* refers to the intention to commit a criminal act, but the term has a looser interpretation by which it refers to all mental states consistent with moral and/or legal blame. (A killing motivated by insane delusional beliefs may meet the requirements for *mens rea* in the first sense, but not the second.) (Goldstein *et al.* 2003) Thus, for centuries, many legal issues have turned on the question: 'what was he thinking?'.

To answer this question, the law has often turned to science. Today, the newest kid on this particular scientific block is cognitive neuroscience, the study of the mind through the brain, which has gained prominence in part as a result of the advent of functional neuroimaging as a widely used tool for psychological research. Given the law's aforementioned concern for mental states, along with its preference for 'hard' evidence, it is no surprise that interest in the potential legal implications of cognitive neuroscience abounds. But does our emerging understanding of the mind as brain really have any deep implications for the law? This book is a testament to the thought that it might. Some have argued, however, that new neuroscience contributes nothing more than new details and that

* Author for correspondence (jdgreene@princeton.edu).

existing legal principles can handle anything that neuroscience will throw our way in the foreseeable future (Morse 2004).

In our view, both of these positions are, in their respective ways, correct. Existing legal principles make virtually no assumptions about the neural bases of criminal behaviour, and as a result they can comfortably assimilate new neuroscience without much in the way of conceptual upheaval: new details, new sources of evidence, but nothing for which the law is fundamentally unprepared. We maintain, however, that our operative legal principles exist because they more or less adequately capture an intuitive sense of justice. In our view, neuroscience will challenge and ultimately reshape our intuitive sense(s) of justice. New neuroscience will affect the way we view the law, not by furnishing us with new ideas or arguments about the nature of human action, but by breathing new life into old ones. Cognitive neuroscience, by identifying the specific mechanisms responsible for behaviour, will vividly illustrate what until now could only be appreciated through esoteric theorizing: that there is something fishy about our ordinary conceptions of human action and responsibility, and that, as a result, the legal principles we have devised to reflect these conceptions may be flawed.

Our argument runs as follows: first, we draw a familiar distinction between the consequentialist justification for state punishment, according to which punishment is merely an instrument for promoting future social welfare, and the retributivist justification for punishment, according to which the principal aim of punishment is to give people what they deserve based on their past actions. We observe that the common-sense approach to moral and legal responsibility has consequentialist elements, but is largely retributivist. Unlike the consequentialist justification for punishment, the retributivist justification relies, either explicitly or implicitly, on a demanding—and some say overly demanding—conception of free will. We therefore consider the standard responses to the philosophical problem of free will (Watson 1982). 'Libertarians' (no relation to the political philosophy) and 'hard determinists' agree on 'incompatibilism', the thesis that free will and determinism are incompatible, but they disagree about whether determinism is true, or near enough true to preclude free will. Libertarians believe that we have free will because determinism is false, and hard determinists believe that we lack free will because determinism is (approximately) true. 'Compatibilists', in contrast to libertarians and hard determinists, argue that free will and determinism are perfectly compatible.

We argue that current legal doctrine, although officially compatibilist, is ultimately grounded in intuitions that are incompatibilist and, more specifically, libertarian. In other words, the law *says* that it presupposes nothing more than a metaphysically modest notion of free will that is perfectly compatible with determinism. However, we argue that the law's intuitive support is ultimately grounded in a metaphysically overambitious, libertarian notion of free will that is threatened by determinism and, more pointedly, by forthcoming cognitive neuroscience. At present, the gap between what the law officially cares about and what people really care about is only revealed occasionally when vivid scientific information about the causes of criminal behaviour leads people to doubt certain individuals' capacity for moral and legal responsibility, despite the fact that this information is irrelevant according to the law's stated principles. We argue that new neuroscience will continue to highlight and widen this gap. That is, new neuroscience will undermine people's common sense, libertarian conception of free will and the retributivist thinking that depends on it, both of which have heretofore been shielded by the inaccessibility of sophisticated thinking about the mind and its neural basis.

The net effect of this influx of scientific information will be a rejection of free will as it is ordinarily conceived, with important ramifications for the law. As noted above, our criminal justice system is largely retributivist. We argue that retributivism, despite its unstable marriage to compatibilist philosophy in the letter of the law, ultimately depends on an intuitive, libertarian notion of free will that is undermined by science. Therefore, with the rejection of common-sense conceptions of free will comes the rejection of retributivism and an ensuing shift towards a consequentialist approach to punishment, i.e. one aimed at promoting future welfare rather than meting out just deserts. Because consequentialist approaches to punishment remain viable in the absence of common-sense free will, we need not give up on moral and legal responsibility. We argue further that the philosophical problem of free will arises out of a conflict between two cognitive subsystems that speak different 'languages': the 'folk psychology' system and the 'folk physics' system. Because we are inherently of two minds when it comes to the problem of free will, this problem will never find an intuitively satisfying solution. We can, however, recognize that free will, as conceptualized by the folk psychology system, is an illusion and structure our society accordingly by rejecting retributivist legal principles that derive their intuitive force from this illusion.

11.2 Two theories of punishment: consequentialism and retributivisim

There are two standard justifications for legal punishment (Lacey 1988). According to the forward-looking, consequentialist theory, which emerges from the classical utilitarian tradition (Bentham 1982), punishment is justified by its future beneficial effects. Chief among them are the prevention of future crime through the deterrent effect of the law and the containment of dangerous individuals. Few would deny that the deterrence of future crime and the protection of the public are legitimate justifications for punishment. The controversy surrounding consequentialist theories concerns their serviceability as *complete* normative theories of punishment. Most theorists find them inadequate in this regard (e.g. Hart 1968), and many argue that consequentialism fundamentally mis-characterizes the primary justification for punishment, which, these critics argue, is retribution (Kant 2002). As a result, they claim, consequentialist theories justify intuitively unfair forms of punishment, if not in practice then in principle. One problem is that of Draconian penalties. It is possible, for example, that imposing the death penalty for parking violations would maximize aggregate welfare by reducing parking violations to near zero. But, retributivists claim, whether or not this is a good idea does not depend on the balance of costs and benefits. It is simply wrong to kill someone for double parking. A related problem is that of punishing the innocent. It is possible that, under certain circumstances, falsely convicting an innocent person would have a salutary deterrent effect, enough to justify that person's suffering, etc. Critics also note that, so far as deterrence is concerned, it is the *threat* of punishment that is justified and not the punishment itself. Thus, consequentialism might justify letting murderers and rapists off the hook so long as their punishment could be convincingly faked.

The standard consequentialist response to these charges is that such concerns have no place in the real world. They say, for example, that the idea of imposing the death penalty for parking violations to make society an overall happier place is absurd. People everywhere would live in mortal fear of bureaucratic errors, and so on. Likewise, a legal system that deliberately convicted innocent people and/or secretly refrained from punishing guilty ones would require a kind of systematic deception that would lead inevitably to corruption and that could never survive in a free society. At this point critics retort that consequentialist theories, at best, get the right answers for the wrong reasons. It is wrong to punish innocent people, etc. because it is fundamentally unfair, not because it leads to bad consequences in practice. Such critics are certainly correct to point out that consequentialist theories fail to capture something central to common-sense intuitions about legitimate punishment.

The backward-looking, retributivist account does a better job of capturing these intuitions. Its fundamental principle is simple: in the absence of mitigating circumstances, people who engage in criminal behaviour *deserve* to be punished, and that is why we punish them. Some would explicate this theory in terms of criminals' forfeiting rights, others in terms of the rights of the victimized, whereas others would appeal to the violation of a hypothetical social contract, and so on. Retributivist theories come in many flavours, but these distinctions need not concern us here. What is important for our purposes is that retributivism captures the intuitive idea that we legitimately punish to give people what they deserve based on their past actions—in proportion to their 'internal wickedness', to use Kant's (2002) phrase—and not, primarily, to promote social welfare in the future.

The retributivist perspective is widespread, both in the explicit views of legal theorists and implicitly in common sense. There are two primary motivations for questioning retributivist theory. The first, which will not concern us here, comes from a prior commitment to a broader consequentialist moral theory. The second comes from scepticism regarding the notion of desert, grounded in a broader scepticism about the possibility of free will in a deterministic or mechanistic world.

11.3 Free will and retributivism

The problem of free will is old and has many formulations (Watson 1982). Here is one, drawing on a more detailed and exacting formulation by Peter Van Inwagen (1982): determinism is true if the world is such that its current state is completely determined by (i) the laws of physics and (ii) past states of the world. Intuitively, the idea is that a deterministic universe starts however it starts and then ticks along like clockwork from there. Given a set of prior conditions in the universe and a set of physical laws that completely govern the way the universe evolves, there is only one way that things can actually proceed.

Free will, it is often said, requires the ability do otherwise (an assumption that has been questioned; Frankfurt 1966). One cannot say, for example, that I have freely chosen soup over salad if forces beyond my control are sufficient to necessitate my choosing soup. But, the determinist argues, this is precisely what forces beyond your control do—always. You have no say whatsoever in the state of the universe before your birth; nor do you have any say about the laws of physics. However, if determinism is true, these two things together are sufficient to determine your choice of soup over salad. Thus, some say, if determinism is true, your sense of yourself and others as having free will is an illusion.

There are three standard responses to the problem of free will. The first, known as 'hard determinism', accepts the incompatibility of free will and determinism ('incompatibilism'), and asserts determinism, thus rejecting free will. The second response is libertarianism (again, no relation to the political philosophy), which accepts incompatibilism, but denies that determinism is true. This may seem like a promising approach. After all, has not modern physics shown us that the universe is *in*deterministic (Hughs 1992)? The problem here is that the sort of indeterminism afforded by modern physics is not the sort the libertarian needs or desires. If it turns out that your ordering soup is completely determined by the laws of physics, the state of the universe 10,000 years ago, *and* the outcomes of myriad subatomic coin flips, your appetizer is no more freely chosen than before. Indeed, it is *randomly* chosen, which is no help to the libertarian. What about some other kind of indeterminism? What if, somewhere deep in the brain, there are mysterious events that operate independently of the ordinary laws of physics and that are somehow tied to the will of the brain's owner? In light of the available evidence, this is highly unlikely. Say what you will about the 'hard problem' of consciousness (Shear 1999), there is not a shred of scientific evidence to support the existence of *causally effective* processes in the mind or brain that violate the laws of physics. In our opinion, any scientifically respectable discussion of free will requires the rejection of what Strawson (1962) famously called the 'panicky metaphysics' of libertarianism.[1]

Finally, we come to the dominant view among philosophers and legal theorists: compatibilism. Compatibilists concede that some notions of free will may require indefensible, panicky metaphysics, but maintain that the kinds of free will 'worth wanting', to use Dennett's (1984) phrase, are perfectly compatible with determinism. Compatibilist theories vary, but all compatibilists agree that free will is a perfectly natural, scientifically respectable phenomenon and part of the ordinary human condition. They also agree that free will can be undermined by various kinds of psychological deficit, e.g. mental illness or 'infancy'. Thus, according to this view, a freely willed action is one that is made using the right sort of psychology—rational, free of delusion, etc.

Compatibilists make some compelling arguments. After all, is it not obvious that we have free will? Could science plausibly deny the obvious fact that I am free to raise my hand *at will*? For many people, such simple observations make the reality of free will non-negotiable. But at the same time, many such people concede that determinism, or something like it, is a live possibility. And if free will is obviously real, but determinism is debatable, then the reality of free will must not hinge on the rejection of determinism. That is, free will and determinism must be compatible. Many compatibilists sceptically ask what would it mean to give up on free will. Were we to give it up, wouldn't we have to immediately reinvent it? Does not every decision involve an implicit commitment to the idea of free will? And how else would we distinguish between ordinary rational adults and other individuals, such as young children and the mentally ill, whose will—or whatever you want to call it—is clearly compromised? Free will, compatibilists argue, is here to stay, and the challenge for science is to figure out how exactly it works and not to peddle silly arguments that deny the undeniable (Dennett 2003).

The forward-looking–consequentialist approach to punishment works with all three responses to the problem of free will, including hard determinism. This is because consequentialists are not concerned with whether anyone is really innocent or guilty in some ultimate sense that might depend on people's having free will, but only with the likely effects of punishment. (Of course, one might wonder what it means for a hard determinist to justify any sort of choice. We will return to this issue in 11.8.) The retributivist approach, by contrast, is plausibly regarded as requiring free will and the rejection of hard determinism. Retributivists want to know whether the defendant truly *deserves* to be punished. Assuming one can deserve to be punished only for actions that are freely willed, hard determinism implies that no one really deserves to be punished. Thus, hard determinism combined with retributivism requires the elimination of all punishment, which does not seem reasonable. This leaves retributivists with two options: compatibilism and libertarianism. Libertarianism, for reasons given above, and despite its intuitive appeal, is scientifically suspect. At the very least, the law should not depend on it. It seems, then, that retributivism requires compatibilism. Accordingly, the standard legal account of punishment is compatibilist.

11.4 Neuroscience changes nothing

The title of a recent paper by Stephen Morse (2004), 'New neuroscience, old problems', aptly summarizes many a seasoned legal thinker's response to the suggestion that brain research will revolutionize the law. The law has been dealing with issues of criminal responsibility for a long time, Morse argues, that there is nothing on the neuroscientific horizon that it cannot handle.

The reason that the law is immune to such threats is that it makes no assumptions that neuroscience, or any science, is likely to challenge. The law assumes that people have a general capacity for rational choice. That is, people have beliefs and desires and are capable of producing behaviour that serves their desires in light of their beliefs. The law acknowledges that our capacity for rational choice is far from perfect (Kahneman & Tversky 2000), requiring only that the people it deems legally responsible have a *general* capacity for rational behaviour.

Thus, questions about who is or is not responsible in the eyes of the law have and will continue to turn on questions about rationality. This approach was first codified in the *M'Naghten* standard according to which a defence on the ground of insanity requires proof that the defendant laboured under 'a defect of reason, from disease of the mind' (Goldstein 1967). Not all standards developed and applied since *M'Naghten* explicitly mention the need to demonstrate the defendant's diminished rationality (e.g. the *Durham* standard; Goldstein 1967), but it is generally agreed that a legal excuse requires a demonstration that the defendant 'lacked a general capacity for rationality' (Goldstein *et al.* 2003). Thus, the argument goes, new science can help us figure out who was or was not rational at the scene of the crime, much as it has in the past, but new science will not justify any fundamental change in the law's approach to responsibility unless it shows that people in general fail to meet the law's very minimal requirements for rationality. Science shows no sign of doing this, and thus the basic precepts of legal responsibility stand firm. As for neuroscience more specifically, this discipline seems especially unlikely to undermine our faith in general minimal rationality. If any sciences have an outside chance of demonstrating that our behaviour is thoroughly irrational or arational it is the ones that study behaviour directly rather than its proximate physical causes in the brain. The law, this argument continues, does not care if people have 'free will' in any deep metaphysical sense that might be threatened by determinism. It only cares that people in general are minimally rational. So long as this appears to be the case, it can go on regarding people as free (compatibilism) and holding ordinary people responsible for their misdeeds while making exceptions for those who fail to meet the requirements of general rationality.

In light of this, one might wonder what all the fuss is about. If the law assumes nothing more than general minimal rationality, and neuroscience does nothing to undermine this assumption, then why would anyone even *think* that neuroscience poses some sort of threat to legal doctrines of criminal responsibility? It sounds like this is just a simple mistake, and that is precisely what Morse contends. He calls this mistake 'the fundamental psycholegal error' which is 'to believe that causation, especially abnormal causation, is *per se* an excusing condition' (Morse 2004, p. 180). In other words, if you think that neuroscientific information about the causes of human action, or some particular human's action, can, by itself, make for a legitimate legal excuse, you just do not understand the law. Every action is caused by brain events, and describing those events and affirming their causal efficacy is of no legal interest in and of itself. Morse continues, '[The psycholegal error] leads people to try to create a new excuse every time an allegedly valid new "syndrome" is discovered that is thought to play a role in behaviour. But syndromes and other causes do not have excusing force unless they sufficiently diminish rationality in the context in question' (Morse 2004, p. 180).

In our opinion, Morse and like-minded theorists are absolutely correct about the relationship between current legal doctrine and any forthcoming neuroscientific results. For the law, as written, neuroscience changes nothing. The law provides a coherent framework for the assessment of criminal responsibility that is not threatened by anything neuroscience is likely to throw at it. But, we maintain, the law nevertheless stands on shakier ground than the foregoing would suggest. The legitimacy of the law itself depends on its adequately reflecting the moral intuitions and commitments of society. If neuroscience can change those intuitions, then neuroscience can change the law.

As it happens, this is a possibility that Morse explicitly acknowledges. However, he believes that such developments would require radical new ideas that we can scarcely imagine at this time, e.g. a new solution to the mind–body problem. We disagree. The seeds of discontent are already sown in common-sense legal thought. In our opinion, the 'fundamental psycholegal error' is not so much an error as a reflection of the gap between what the law officially cares about and what people really care about. In modern criminal law, there has been a long, tense marriage of convenience between compatibilist legal principles and libertarian moral intuitions. New neuroscience, we argue, will probably render this marriage unworkable.

11.5 What really matters for responsibility? materialist theory, dualist intuitions and the 'boys from brazil' problem

According to the law, the central question in a case of putative diminished responsibility is whether the accused was sufficiently rational at the time of the misdeed in question. We believe, however, that this is not what most people really care about, and that for them diminished rationality is just a presumed correlate of something deeper. It seems that what many people really want to know is: was it really *him*? This question usually comes in the form of a disjunction, depending on how the excuse is constructed: was it *him*, or was it his *upbringing* ? Was it *him*, or was it his *genes*? Was it *him*, or was it his *circumstances*? Was it *him*, or was it his *brain*? But what most people do not understand, despite the fact that naturalistic philosophers and scientists have been saying it for centuries, is that there is no 'him' independent of these other things. (Or, to be a bit more accommodating to the supernaturally inclined, there is no 'him' independent of these things that shows any sign of affecting anything in the physical world, including his behaviour.)

Most people's view of the mind is implicitly *dualist* and *libertarian* and not *materialist* and *compatibilist*. Dualism, for our purposes, is the view that mind and brain are separate, interacting, entities.[2] Dualism fits naturally with libertarianism because a mind distinct from the body is precisely the sort of non-physical source of free will that libertarianism requires. Materialism, by contrast, is the view that all events, including the operations of the mind, are ultimately operations of matter that obeys the laws of physics. It is hard to imagine a belief in free will that is materialist but not compatibilist, given that ordinary matter does not seem capable of supplying the non-physical processes that libertarianism requires.

Many people, particularly those who are religious, are explicitly dualist libertarians (again, not in the political sense). However, in our estimation, even people who do or would readily endorse a thoroughly material account of human action and its causes have dualist, libertarian intuitions. This goes not only for educated people in general, but for experts in mental health and criminal behaviour. Consider, for example, the following remarks from Jonathan Pincus, an expert on criminal behaviour and the brain.

> When a composer conceives a symphony, the only way he or she can present it to the public is through an orchestra . . . If the performance is poor, the fault could lie with the composer's conception, or the orchestra, or both . . . Will is expressed by the brain. Violence can be the result of volition only, but if a brain is damaged, brain failure must be at least partly to blame.
>
> (Pincus 2001, p. 128)

To our untutored intuitions, this is a perfectly sensible analogy, but it is ultimately grounded in a kind of dualism that is scientifically untenable. It is not as if there is *you*, the composer, and then *your brain*, the orchestra. You *are* your brain, and your brain is the composer and the orchestra all rolled together. There is no little man, no 'homunculus', in the brain that is the real you behind the mass of neuronal instrumentation. Scientifically minded philosophers have been saying this *ad nauseum* (Dennett 1991), and we will not belabour the point. Moreover, we suspect that if you were to ask Dr Pincus whether he thinks there is a little conductor directing his brain's activity from within or beyond he would adamantly deny that this is the case. At the same time, though, he is comfortable comparing a brain-damaged criminal to a healthy conductor saddled with an unhealthy orchestra. This sort of doublethink is not uncommon. As we will argue in 11.7, when it comes to moral responsibility in a physical world, we are all of two minds.

A recent article by Laurence Steinberg and Elizabeth Scott (Steinberg & Scott 2003), experts respectively on adolescent developmental psychology and juvenile law, illustrates the same point. They argue that adolescents do not meet the law's general requirements for rationality and that therefore they should be considered less than fully responsible for their actions and, more specifically, unsuitable candidates for the death penalty. Their main argument is sound, but they cannot resist embellishing it with a bit of superfluous neuroscience.

Most of the developmental research on cognitive and psychosocial functioning in adolescence measures behaviors, self-perceptions, or attitudes, but mounting evidence suggests that at least some of the differences between adults and adolescents have neuropsychological and neurobiological underpinnings.

(Steinberg & Scott 2003, p. 5)

Some of the differences? Unless some form of dualism is correct, *every* mental difference and *every* difference in behavioural tendency is a function of some kind of difference in the brain. But here it is implicitly suggested that things like 'behaviours, self-perceptions, or attitudes' may be grounded in something other than the brain. In summing up their case, Steinberg and Scott look towards the future.

Especially needed are studies that link developmental changes in decision making to changes in brain structure and function... In our view, however, there is sufficient indirect suggestive evidence of age differences in capacities that are relevant to criminal blameworthiness to support the position that youths who commit crimes should be punished more leniently then their adult counterparts.

(Steinberg & Scott 2003, p. 9)

This gets the order of evidence backwards. If what the law ultimately cares about is whether adolescents can behave rationally, then it is evidence concerning adolescent behaviour that is *directly* relevant. Studying the adolescent brain is a highly *indirect* way of figuring out whether adolescents in general are rational. Indeed, the only way we neuroscientists can tell if a brain structure is important for rational judgement is to see if its activity or damage is correlated with (ir)rational *behaviour*.[3]

If everyone agrees that what the law ultimately cares about is the capacity for rational behaviour, then why are Steinberg and Scott so optimistic about neuroscientific evidence that is only indirectly relevant? The reason, we suggest, is that they are appealing not to a legal argument, but to a moral intuition. So far as the law is concerned, information about the physical processes that give rise to bad behaviour is irrelevant. But to people who implicitly believe that real decision-making takes place in the mind, not in the brain, demonstrating that there is a brain basis for adolescents' misdeeds allows us to blame adolescents' brains instead of the adolescents themselves.

The fact that people are tempted to attach great moral or legal significance to neuro-scientific information that, according to the letter of the law, should not matter, suggests that what the law cares about and what people care about do not necessarily coincide. To make this point in a more general way, we offer the following thought experiment, which we call '*The Boys from Brazil* problem'. It is an extension of an argument that has made the rounds in philosophical discussions of free will and responsibility (Rosen 2002).

In the film *The Boys from Brazil*, members of the Nazi old guard have regrouped in South America after the war. Their plan is to bring their beloved *führer* back to life by raising children genetically identical to Hitler (courtesy of some salvaged DNA) in environments that mimic that of Hitler's upbringing. For example, Hitler's father died while young Adolph was still a boy, and so each Hitler clone's surrogate father is killed at just the right time, and so on, and so forth.

This is obviously a fantasy, but the idea that one could, in principle, produce a person with a particular personality and behavioural profile through tight genetic and environmental control is plausible. Let us suppose, then, that a group of scientists has managed to create an individual—call him 'Mr Puppet'—who, by design, engages in some kind of criminal behaviour: say, a murder during a drug deal gone bad. The defence calls to the stand the project's lead scientist: 'Please tell us about your relationship to Mr Puppet...'

> It is very simple, really. I designed him. I carefully selected every gene in his body and carefully scripted every significant event in his life so that he would become precisely what he is today. I selected his mother knowing that she would let him cry for hours and hours before picking him up. I carefully selected each of his relatives, teachers, friends, enemies, etc. and told them exactly what to say to him and how to treat him. Things generally went as planned, but not always. For example, the angry letters written to his dead father were not supposed to appear until he was fourteen, but by the end of his thirteenth year he had already written four of them. In retrospect I think this was because of a handful of substitutions I made to his eighth chromosome. At any rate, my plans for him succeeded, as they have for 95% of the people I've designed. I assure you that the accused deserves none of the credit.

What to do with Mr Puppet? Insofar as we believe this testimony, we are inclined to think that Mr Puppet cannot be held fully responsible for his crimes, if he can be held responsible for them at all. He is, perhaps, a man to be feared, and we would not want to return him to the streets. But given the fact that forces beyond his control played a dominant role in causing him to commit these crimes, it is hard to think of him as anything more than a pawn.

But what does the law say about Mr Puppet? The law asks whether or not he was rational at the time of his mis-deeds, and as far as we know he was. For all we know, he is psychologically indistinguishable from the prototypical guilty criminal, and therefore fully responsible in the eyes of the law. But, intuitively, this is not fair.

Thus, it seems that the law's exclusive interest in rationality misses something intuitively important. In our opinion, rationality is just a presumed correlate of what most people really care about. What people really want to know is if the accused, as opposed to something else, is responsible for the crime, where that 'something else' could be the accused's brain, genes or environment. The question of someone's ultimate responsibility seems to turn, intuitively, on a question of internal versus external determination. Mr Puppet ought not be held responsible for his actions because forces beyond his control played a dominant role in the production of his behaviour. Of course, the scientists did not have complete control—after all, they had a 5% failure rate—but that does not seem to be enough to restore Mr Puppet's free will, at least not entirely. Yes, he is as rational as other criminals, and, yes, it was his desires and beliefs that produced his actions. But those beliefs and desires were rigged by external forces, and that is why, intuitively, he deserves our pity more than our moral condemnation.[4]

The story of Mr. Puppet raises an important question: what is the difference between Mr Puppet and anyone else accused of a crime? After all, we have little reason to doubt that (i) the state of the universe 10,000 years ago, (ii) the laws of physics, and (iii) the outcomes of random quantum mechanical events are together sufficient to determine everything that happens nowadays, including our own actions. These things are all clearly beyond our control. So what is the real difference between us and Mr Puppet? One obvious difference is that Mr Puppet is the victim of a diabolical plot whereas most people, we presume, are not. But does this matter? The thought that Mr Puppet is not fully responsible depends on the idea that his actions were externally determined. Forces beyond his control constrained his personality to the point that it was 'no surprise' that he would behave badly. But the fact that these forces are connected to the desires and intentions of evil scientists is really irrelevant, is it not? What matters is only that these forces are beyond Mr Puppet's control, that they're not really *his*. The fact that someone could deliberately harness these forces to reliably design criminals is an indication of the strength of these forces, but the fact that these forces are being guided by other minds rather than simply operating on their own seems irrelevant, so far as Mr Puppet's freedom and responsibility are concerned.

Thus, it seems that, in a very real sense, we are all puppets. The combined effects of genes and environment determine all of our actions. Mr Puppet is exceptional only in that the intentions of other humans lie behind his genes and environment. But, so long as his genes and environment are intrinsically comparable to those of ordinary people, this does not really matter. We are no more free than he is.

What all of this illustrates is that the 'fundamental psycholegal error' is grounded in a powerful moral intuition that the law and allied compatibilist philosophies try to sweep under the rug. The foregoing suggests that people regard actions only as fully free when those actions are seen as robust against determination by external forces. But if determinism (or determinism plus quantum mechanics) is true, then no actions are truly free because forces beyond our control are always sufficient to determine behaviour. Thus, intuitive free will is libertarian, not compatibilist. That is, it requires the rejection of determinism and an implicit commitment to some kind of magical mental causation.[5]

Naturalistic philosophers and scientists have known for a long time that magical mental causation is a non-starter. But this realization is the result of philosophical reflection about the nature of the universe and its governance by physical law. Philosophical reflection, however, is not the only way to see the problems with libertarian accounts of free will. Indeed, we argue that neuroscience can help people appreciate the mechanical nature of human action in a way that bypasses complicated arguments.

11.6 Neuroscience and the transparent bottleneck

We have argued that, contrary to legal and philosophical orthodoxy, determinism really does threaten free will and responsibility as we intuitively understand them. It is just that most of us, including most philosophers and legal theorists, have yet to appreciate it. This controversial opinion amounts to an empirical prediction that may or may not hold: as more and more scientific facts come in, providing increasingly vivid illustrations of what the human mind is really like, more and more people will develop moral intuitions that are at odds with our current social practices (see Robert Wright (1994) for similar thoughts).

Neuroscience has a special role to play in this process for the following reason. As long as the mind remains a black box, there will always be a donkey on which to pin dualist and libertarian intuitions. For a long time, philosophical arguments have persuaded some people that human action has purely mechanical causes, but not everyone cares for philosophical arguments. Arguments are nice, but physical demonstrations are far more compelling. What neuroscience does, and will continue to do at an accelerated pace, is elucidate the 'when', 'where' and 'how' of the mechanical processes that cause behaviour. It is one thing to deny that human decision-making is purely mechanical when your opponent offers only a general, philosophical argument. It is quite another to hold your ground when your opponent can make detailed predictions about how these mechanical processes work, complete with images of the brain structures involved and equations that describe their function.[6]

Thus, neuroscience holds the promise of turning the black box of the mind into a *transparent bottleneck*. There are many causes that impinge on behaviour, but all of them—from the genes you inherited, to the pain in your lower back, to the advice your grandmother gave you when you were six—must exert their influence through the brain. Thus, your brain serves as a bottleneck for all the forces spread throughout the universe of your past that affect who you are and what you do. Moreover, this bottleneck contains the events that are, intuitively, most critical for moral and legal responsibility, and we may soon be able to observe them closely.

At some time in the future we may have extremely high-resolution scanners that can simultaneously track the neural activity and connectivity of every neuron in a human brain, along with computers and software that can analyse and organize these data. Imagine, for example, watching a film of your brain choosing between soup and salad. The analysis software highlights the neurons pushing for soup in red and the neurons pushing for salad in blue. You zoom in and slow down the film, allowing yourself to trace the cause-and-effect relationships between individual neurons—the mind's clockwork revealed in arbitrary detail. You find the tipping-point moment at which the blue neurons in your prefrontal cortex out-fire the red neurons, seizing control of your pre-motor cortex and causing you to say, 'I will have the salad, please'.

At some further point this sort of brainware may be very widespread, with a high-resolution brain scanner in every classroom. People may grow up completely used to the idea that every decision is a thoroughly mechanical process, the outcome of which is completely determined by the results of prior mechanical processes. What will such people think as they sit in their jury boxes? Suppose a man has killed his wife in a jealous rage. Will jurors of the future wonder whether the defendant acted in that moment *of his own free will*? Will they wonder if it was *really him* who killed his wife rather than his *uncontrollable anger*? Will they ask whether he *could have done otherwise*? Whether he really *deserves* to be punished, or if he is just a victim of unfortunate circumstances? We submit that these questions, which seem so important today, will lose their grip in an age when the mechanical nature of human decision-making is fully appreciated. The law will continue to punish misdeeds, as it must for practical reasons, but the idea of distinguishing the truly, deeply guilty from those who are merely victims of neuronal circumstances will, we submit, seem pointless.

At least in our more reflective moments. Our intuitive sense of free will runs quite deep, and it is possible that we will never be able to fully talk ourselves out of it. Next we consider the psychological origins of the problem of free will.

11.7 Folk psychology and folk physics collide: a cognitive account of the problem of attributive free will

Could the problem of free will just melt away? This question begs another: why do we have the problem of free will in the first place? Why does the idea of a deterministic universe seem to contradict something important in our conception of human action? A promising answer to this question is offered by Daniel Wegner in *The illusion of conscious will* (Wegner 2002). In short, Wegner argues, we feel as if we are uncaused causers, and therefore granted a degree of independence from the deterministic flow of the universe, because we are unaware of the deterministic processes that operate in our own heads.

Our actions appear to be caused by our mental states, but not by physical states of our brains, and so we imagine that we are metaphysically special, that we are non-physical causes of physical events. This belief in our specialness is likely to meet the same fate as other similarly narcissistic beliefs that we have cherished in our past: that the Earth lies at the centre of the universe, that humans are unrelated to other species, that all of our behaviour is consciously determined, etc. Each of these beliefs has been replaced by a scientific and humbling understanding of our place in the physical universe, and there is no reason to believe that the case will be any different for our sense of free will. (For similar thoughts, see Wright (1994) on Darwin's clandestine views about free will and responsibility.)

We believe that Wegner's account of the problem of free will is essentially correct, although we disagree strongly with his conclusions concerning its (lack of) practical moral implications (see below). In this section we pick up on and extend one strand in Wegner's argument (Wegner 2002, pp. 15–28). Wegner's primary aim is to explain, in psychological terms, why we attribute free will to ourselves, why we feel free from the inside. Our aim in this section is to explain, in psychological terms, why we insist on attributing free will to *others*—and why scientifically minded philosophers, despite persistent efforts, have managed to talk almost no one out of this practice. The findings we review serve as examples of how psychological and neuroscientific data are beginning to characterize the mechanisms that underlie our sense of free will, how these mechanisms can lead us to assume free will is operating when it is not, and how a scientific understanding of these mechanisms can serve to dismantle our commitment to the idea of free will.

Looking out at the world, it appears to contain two fundamentally different kinds of entity. On the one hand, there are ordinary objects that appear to obey the ordinary laws of physics: things like rocks and puddles of water and blocks of wood. These things do not get up and move around on their own. They are, in a word, inanimate. On the other hand, there are things that seem to operate by some kind of magic. Humans and other animals, so long as they are alive, can move about at will, in apparent defiance of the physical laws that govern ordinary matter. Because things like rocks and puddles, on the one hand, and mice and humans, on the other, behave in such radically different ways, it makes sense, from an evolutionary perspective, that creatures would evolve separate cognitive systems for processing information about each of these classes of objects (Pinker 1997). There is a good deal of evidence to suggest that this is precisely how our minds work.

A line of research beginning with Fritz Heider illustrates this point. Heider and Simmel (Heider & Simmel 1944) created a film involving three simple geometric shapes that move about in various ways. For example, a big triangle chases a little circle around the screen, bumping into it. The little circle repeatedly moves away, and a little triangle repeatedly moves in between the circle and the big triangle. When normal people watch this movie they cannot help but view it in social terms (Heberlein & Adolphs 2004). They see the big triangle as *trying* to harm the little circle, and the little triangle as trying to *protect* the little circle; and they see the little circle as *afraid* and the big triangle as *frustrated*. Some people even spontaneously report that the big triangle is a *bully*. In other words, simple patterns of movement trigger in people's minds a cascade of complex social inferences. People not only see these shapes as 'alive'. They see beliefs, desires, intentions, emotions, personality traits and even moral blameworthiness. It appears that this kind of inference is automatic (Scholl & Tremoulet 2000). Of course, you, the observer, know that it is only a film, and a very simple one at that, but you nevertheless cannot help but see these events in social, even *moral*, terms.

That is, unless you have damage to your amygdala, a subcortical brain structure that is important for social cognition (Adolphs 1999). Andrea Heberlein tested a patient with rare bilateral amygdala damage using Heider's film and found that this patient, unlike normal people, described what she saw in completely asocial terms, despite that fact that her visual and verbal abilities are not compromised by her brain damage. Somehow, this patient is blind to the 'human' drama that normal people cannot help but see in these events (Heberlein & Adolphs 2004).

The sort of thinking that is engaged when normal people view the Heider–Simmel film is sometimes known as 'folk psychology' (Fodor 1987), 'the intentional stance' (Dennett 1987) or 'theory of mind', (Premack & Woodruff 1978). There is a fair amount of evidence (including the work described above) suggesting that humans have a set of cognitive subsystems that are specialized for processing information about intentional agents (Saxe *et al.* 2004). At the same time, there is evidence to suggest that humans and other animals also have subsystems specialized for 'folk physics', an intuitive sense of how ordinary matter behaves. One compelling piece of evidence for the claim that normal humans have subsystems specialized for folk physics comes from studies of people with autism spectrum disorder. These individuals are particularly bad at solving problems that require 'folk psychology', but they do very well with problems related to how physical objects (e.g. the parts of machine) behave, i.e. 'folk physics' (Baron Cohen 2000). Another piece of evidence for a 'folk physics' system comes from discrepancies between people's physical intuitions and the way the world actually works. People say, for example, that a ball shot out of a curved tube resting on a flat surface will continue to follow a curved path outside the tube when in fact it will follow a straight path (McCloskey *et al.* 1980). The fact that people's physical intuitions are slightly, but systematically, out of step with reality suggests that the mind brings a fair amount of implicit theory to the perception of physical objects.

Thus, it is at least plausible that we possess distinguishable cognitive systems for making sense of the behaviour of objects in the world. These systems seem to have two fundamentally different 'ontologies'. The folk physics system deals with chunks of matter that move around without purposes of their own according to the laws of intuitive physics, whereas the folk psychology system deals with unseen features of minds: beliefs, desires, intentions, etc. But what, to our minds, is a mind? We suggest that a crucial feature, if not the defining feature, of a mind (intuitively understood) is that it is an uncaused causer (Scholl & Tremoulet 2000). Minds animate material bodies, allowing them to move without any apparent physical cause and in pursuit of goals. Moreover, we reserve certain social attitudes for things that have minds. For example, we do not resent the rain for ruining our picnic, but we would resent a person who hosed our picnic (Strawson 1962), and we resent picnic-hosers considerably more when we perceive that their actions are intentional. Thus, it seems that folk psychology is the gateway to moral evaluation. To see something as morally blameworthy or praiseworthy (even if it is just a moving square), one has to first see it as 'someone', that is, as having a mind.

With all of this in the background, one can see how the problem of attributive free will arises. To see something as a responsible moral agent, one must first see it as having a mind. But, intuitively, a mind is, among other things, an uncaused causer. Consequently, when something is seen as a mere physical entity operating in accordance with deterministic physical laws, it ceases to be seen, intuitively, as a mind. Consequently, it is seen as an object unworthy of moral praise or blame. (Note that we are not claiming that people automatically attribute moral agency to anything that appears to be an uncaused causer. Rather, our claim is that seeing something as an uncaused causer is a *necessary but not sufficient* condition for seeing something as a moral agent.)

After thousands of years of our thinking of one another as uncaused causers, science comes along and tells us that there is no such thing—that all causes, with the possible exception of the Big Bang, are caused causes (determinism). This creates a problem. When we look at people as physical systems, we cannot see them as any more blameworthy or praiseworthy than bricks. But when we perceive people using our intuitive, folk psychology we cannot avoid attributing moral blame and praise.

So, philosophers who would honour both our scientific knowledge and our social instincts try to reconcile these two competing outlooks, but the result is never completely satisfying, and the debate wears on. Philosophers who cannot let go of the idea of uncaused causes defend libertarianism, and thus opt for scientifically dubious, 'panicky metaphysics'. Hard determinists, by contrast, embrace the conclusions of modern science, and concede what others will not: that many of our dearly held social practices are based on an illusion. The remaining majority, the compatibilists, try to talk themselves into a compromise. But the compromise is fragile. When the physical details of human action are made vivid, folk psychology loses its grip, just as folk physics loses its grip when the morally significant details are emphasized. The problem of free will and determinism will never find an intuitively satisfying solution because it arises out of a conflict between two distinct cognitive subsystems that speak different cognitive 'languages' and that may ultimately be incapable of negotiation.

11.8 Free will, responsibility and consequentialism

Even if there is no intuitively satisfying solution to the problem of free will, it does not follow that there is no correct view of the matter. Ours is as follows: when it comes to the issue of free will itself, hard determinism is mostly correct. Free will, as we ordinarily understand it, is an illusion. However, it does not follow from the fact that free will is an illusion that there is no legitimate place for responsibility. Recall from 11.2 that there are two general justifications for holding people legally responsible for their actions. The retributive justification, by which the goal of punishment is to give people what they really deserve, does depend on this dubious notion of free will. However, the consequentialist approach does not require a belief in free will at all. As consequentialists, we can hold people responsible for crimes simply because doing so has, on balance, beneficial effects through deterrence, containment, etc. It is sometimes said that if we do not believe in free will then we cannot legitimately punish anyone and that society must dissolve into anarchy. In a less hysterical vein, Daniel Wegner argues that free will, while illusory, is a necessary fiction for the maintenance of our social structure (Wegner 2002, ch. 9). We disagree. There are perfectly good, forward-looking justifications for punishing criminals that do not depend on metaphysical fictions. (Wegner's observations may apply best to the personal sphere: see below.)

The vindication of responsibility in the absence of free will means that there is more than a grain of truth in compatibilism. The consequentialist approach to responsibility generates a derivative notion of free will that we can embrace (Smart 1961). In the name of producing better consequences, we will want to make several distinctions among various actions and agents. To begin, we will want to distinguish the various classes of people who cannot be deterred by the law from those who can. That is, we will recognize many of the 'diminished capacity' excuses that the law currently recognizes such as infancy and insanity. We will also recognize familiar justifications such those associated with crimes committed under duress (e.g. threat of death). If we like, then, we can say that the actions of rational people operating free from duress, etc. are free actions, and that such people are exercising their free will.

At this point, compatibilists such as Daniel Dennett may claim victory: 'what more could one want from free will?'. In a word: retributivism. We have argued that common-sense retributivism really does depend on a notion of free will that is scientifically suspect. Intuitively, we want to punish those people who truly deserve it, but whenever the causes of someone's bad behaviour are made sufficiently vivid, we no longer see that person as truly deserving of punishment. This insight is expressed by the old French proverb: 'to know all is to forgive all'. It is also expressed in the teachings of religious figures, such as Jesus and Buddha, who preach a message of universal compassion. Neuroscience can make this message more compelling by vividly illustrating the mechanical nature of human action.

Our penal system is highly counter-productive from a consequentialist perspective, especially in the USA, and yet it remains in place because retributivist principles have a powerful moral and political appeal (Lacey 1988; Tonry 2004). It is possible, however, that neuroscience will change these moral intuitions by undermining the intuitive, libertarian conceptions of free will on which retributivism depends.

As advocates of consequentialist legal reform, it behooves us to briefly respond to the three standard criticisms levied against consequentialist theories of punishment. First, it is claimed that consequentialism would justify extreme over-punishing. As noted above, it is possible in principle that the goal of deterrence would justify punishing parking violations with the death penalty or framing innocent people to make examples of them. Here, the standard response is adequate. The idea that such practices could, in the real world, make society happier on balance is absurd. Second, it is claimed that consequentialism justifies extreme under-punishment. In response to some versions of this objection, our response is the same as above. Deceptive practices such as a policy of faking punishment cannot survive in a free society, and a free society is required for the pursuit of most consequentialist ends. In other cases consequentialism may advocate more lenient punishments for people who, intuitively, deserve worse. Here, we maintain that a deeper understanding of human action and human nature will lead people—more of them, at any rate—to abandon these retributivist intuitions. Our response is much the same to the third and most general criticism of consequentialist punishment, which is that even when consequentialism gets the punishment policy right, it does so for the wrong reasons. These supposedly right reasons are reasons that we reject, however intuitive and natural they may feel. They are, we maintain, grounded in a metaphysical view of human action that is scientifically dubious and therefore an unfit basis for public policy in a pluralistic society.

Finally, as defenders of hard determinism and a consequentialist approach to responsibility, we should briefly address some standard concerns about the rejection of free will and conceptions of responsibility that depend on it. First, does not the fact that you can raise your hand 'at will' prove that free will is real? Not in the sense that matters. As Daniel Wegner (2002) has argued, our first-person sense of ourselves as having free will may be a systematic illusion. And from a third-person perspective, we simply do not assume that anyone who exhibits voluntary control over his body is free in the relevant sense, as in the case of Mr Puppet.

A more serious challenge is the claim that our commitments to free will and retributivism are simply inescapable for all practical purposes. Regarding free will, one might wonder whether one can so much as make a decision without implicitly assuming that one is free to choose among one's apparent options. Regarding responsibility and punishment, one might wonder if it is humanly possible to deny our retributive impulses (Strawson 1962; Pettit 2002). This challenge is bolstered by recent work in the behavioural sciences suggesting that an intuitive sense of fairness runs deep in our primate lineage (Brosnan & De Waal 2003) and that an adaptive tendency towards retributive punishment may have been a crucial development in the biological and cultural evolution of human sociality (Fehr & Gachter 2002; Boyd *et al.* 2003; Bowles & Gintis 2004). Recent neuroscientific findings have added further support to this view, suggesting that the impulse to exact punishment may be driven by phylogentically old mechanisms in the brain (Sanfey *et al.* 2003). These mechanisms may be an efficient and perhaps essential, device for maintaining social stability. If retributivism runs that deep and is that useful, one might wonder whether we have any serious hope of, or reason for, getting rid of it. Have we any real choice but to see one another as free agents who deserve to be rewarded and punished for our past behaviours?

We offer the following analogy: modern physics tells us that space is curved. Nevertheless, it may be impossible for us to see the world as anything other than flatly Euclidean in our day-to-day lives. And there are, no doubt, deep evolutionary explana-tions for our Euclidean tendencies. Does it then follow that we are forever bound by our innate Euclidean psychology? The answer depends on the domain of life in question. In navigating the aisles of the grocery store, an intuitive, Euclidean representation of space is not only adequate, but probably inevitable. However, when we are, for example, planning the launch of a spacecraft, we can and should make use of relativistic physical principles that are less intuitive but more accurate. In other words, a Euclidean perspect-ive is not necessary for *all* practical purposes, and the same may be true for our implicit commitment to free will and retributivism. For most day-to-day purposes it may be pointless or impossible to view ourselves or others in this detached sort of way. But—and this is the crucial point—it may not be pointless or impossible to adopt this perspective when one is deciding what the criminal law should be or whether a given defendant should be put to death for his crimes. These may be special situations, analogous to those routinely encountered by 'rocket scientists', in which the counter-intuitive truth that we legitimately ignore most of the time can and should be acknowledged.

Finally, there is the worry that to reject free will is to render all of life pointless: why would you bother with anything if it has all long since been determined? The answer is that you will bother because you are a human, and that is what humans do. Even if you decide, as part of a little intellectual exercise, that you are going to sit around and do nothing because you have concluded that you have no free will, you are eventually going to get up and make yourself a sandwich. And if you do not, you have got bigger problems than philosophy can fix.

11.9 Conclusion

Neuroscience is unlikely to tell us anything that will challenge the law's stated assumptions. However, we maintain that advances in neuroscience are likely to change the way people think about human action and criminal responsibility by vividly illustrating lessons that some people appreciated long ago. Free will as we ordinarily understand it is an illusion generated by our cognitive architecture. Retributivist notions of criminal responsibility ultimately depend on this illusion, and, if we are lucky, they will give way to consequentialist ones, thus radically transforming our approach to criminal justice. At this time, the law deals firmly but mercifully with individuals whose behaviour is obviously the product of forces that are ultimately beyond their control. Some day, the law may treat all convicted criminals this way. That is, humanely.

The authors thank Stephen Morse, Andrea Heberlein, Aaron Schurger, Jennifer Kessler and Simon Keller for their input.

Endnotes

1. Of course, scientific respectability is not everyone's first priority. However, the law in most Western states is a public institution designed to function in a society that respects a wide range of religious and otherwise metaphysical beliefs. The law cannot function in this way if it presupposes controversial and unverifiable metaphysical facts about the nature of human action, or anything else. Thus, the law must restrict itself to the class of intersubjectively verifiable facts, i.e. the facts recognized by science, broadly construed. This practice need not derive from a conviction that the scientifically verifiable facts are necessarily the only facts, but merely from a recognition that verifiable or scientific facts are the only facts upon which public institutions in a pluralistic society can effectively rely.
2. There are some forms of dualism according to which the mind and body, although distinct, do not interact, making it impossible for the mind to have any observable effects on the brain or anything else in the physical world. These versions of dualism do not concern us here. For the purposes of this paper, we are happy to allow the metaphysical claim that souls or aspects of minds may exist independently of the physical body. Our concern is specifically with interactionist versions of dualism according to which non-physical mental entities have observable physical effects. We believe that science has rendered such views untenable and that the law, insofar as it is a public institution designed to serve a pluralistic society, must not rely on beliefs that are scientifically suspect (see previous endnote).
3. It is conceivable that rationality could someday be redefined in neurocognitive rather than behavioural terms, much as water has been redefined in terms of its chemical composition. Were that to happen, neuroscientific evidence could then be construed as more direct than behavioural evidence. But Steinberg and Scott's argument appears to make use of a conventional, behavioural definition of rationality and not a neurocognitive redefinition.
4. This is not to say that we could not describe Mr Puppet in such a way that our intuitions about him would change. Our point is only that, when the details are laid bare, it is very hard to see him as morally responsible.
5. Compatibilist philosophers such as Daniel Dennett (2003) might object that the story of Mr Puppet is nothing but a misleading 'intuition pump'. Indeed, this is what Dennett says about a similar case of Alfred Mele's (1995). We believe that our case is importantly different from Mele's. Dennett and Mele imagine two women who are psychologically identical: Ann is a typical, good person, whereas Beth has been brainwashed to be just like Ann. Dennett argues, against Mele, that if you take seriously the claim that these two are psychologically identical and properly

imagine that Beth is as rational, open-minded, etc. as Ann, you will come to see that the two are equally free. We agree with Dennett that Ann and Beth are comparable and that Mele's intuition falters when the details are fleshed out. But does the same hold for the intuition provoked by Mr Puppet's story? It seems to us that the more one knows about Mr Puppet and his life the less inclined one is to see him as truly responsible for his actions and our punishing him as a worthy end in itself. We can agree with Dennett that there is a sense in which Mr Puppet is free. Our point is merely that there is a legitimate sense in which he, like all of us, is not free and that this sense matters for the law.

6. We do not wish to imply that neuroscience will inevitably put us in a position to predict any given action based on a neurological examination. Rather, our suggestion is simply that neuroscience will eventually advance to the point at which the mechanistic nature of human decision-making is sufficiently apparent to undermine the force of dualist/libertarian intuitions.

References

Adolphs, R. 1999 Social cognition and the human brain. *Trends Cogn. Sci.* **3**, 469–479.

Baron Cohen, S. 2000 Autism: deficits in folk psychology exist alongside superiority in folk physics. In *Understanding other minds: perspectives from autism and developmental cognitive neuroscience* (ed. S. Baron Cohen, H. Tager Flusberg &D. Cohen), pp. 78–82. New York: Oxford University Press.

Bentham, J. 1982 *An introduction to the principles of morals and legislation.* London: Methuen.

Bowles, S. & Gintis, H. 2004 The evolution of strong reciprocity: cooperation in heterogeneous populations. *Theor. Popul. Biol.* **65**, 17–28.

Boyd, R., Gintis, H., Bowles, S. & Richerson, P. J. 2003 The evolution of altruistic punishment. *Proc. Natl Acad. Sci. USA* **100**, 3531–3535.

Brosnan, S. F. & De Waal, F. B. 2003 Monkeys reject unequal pay. *Nature* **425**, 297–299.

Dennett, D. C. 1984 *Elbow room: the varieties of free will worth wanting.* Cambridge, MA: MIT Press.

Dennett, D. C. 1987 *The intentional stance.* Cambridge, MA: MIT Press.

Dennett, D. C. 1991 *Consciousness explained.* Boston, MA: Little Brown and Co.

Dennett, D. C. 2003 *Freedom evolves.* New York: Viking.

Fehr, E. & Gachter, S. 2002 Altruistic punishment in humans. *Nature* **415**, 137–140.

Fodor, J. A. 1987 *Psychosemantics: the problem of meaning in the philosophy of mind.* Cambridge, MA: MIT Press.

Frankfurt, H. 1966 Alternate possibilities and moral responsibility. *J. Philosophy* **66**, 829–839.

Goldstein, A. M., Morse, S. J. & Shapiro, D. L. 2003 Evaluation of criminal responsibility. In *Forensic psychology.* vol. **11** (ed. A. M. Goldstein), pp. 381–406. New York: Wiley.

Goldstein, A. S. 1967 *The insanity defense.* New Haven, CT: Yale University Press.

Hart, H. L. A. 1968 *Punishment and responsibility.* Oxford Univeristy Press.

Heberlein, A. S. & Adolphs, R. 2004 Impaired spontaneous anthropomorphizing despite intact perception and social knowledge. *Proc. Natl Acad. Sci. USA* **101**, 7487–7491.

Heider, F. & Simmel, M. 1944 An experimental study of apparent behavior. *Am. J. Psychol.* **57**, 243–259.

Hughs, R. I. G. 1992 *The structure and interpretation of quantum mechanics.* Cambridge, MA: Havard University Press.

Kahneman, D. & Tversky, A. (eds) 2000 *Choices, values, and frames.* Cambridge University Press.

Kant, I. 2002 *The philosophy of law: an exposition of the fundamental principles of jurisprudence as the science of right.* Union, NJ: Lawbook Exchange.

Lacey, N. 1988 *State punishment: political principles and community values.* London and New York: Routledge & Kegan Paul.

McCloskey, M., Caramazza, A. & Green, B. 1980 Curvilinear motion in the absence of external forces: naive beliefs about the motion of objects. *Science* **210**, 1139–1141.

Mele, A. 1995 *Autonomous agents: from self-control to autonomy*. Oxford University Press.

Morse, S. J. 2004 New neuroscience, old problems. In *Neuroscience and the law: brain, mind, and the scales of justice* (ed. B. Garland), pp. 157–198. New York: Dana Press.

Pettit, P. 2002 *The capacity to have done otherwise. Rules, reasons, and norms: selected essays*. Oxford University Press.

Pincus, J. H. 2001 *Base instincts: what makes killers kill?* New York: Norton.

Pinker, S. 1997 *How the mind works*. New York: Norton.

Premack, D. & Woodruff, G. 1978 Does the chimpanzee have a theory of mind? *Behav. Brain Sci.* **4**, 515–526.

Rosen, G. 2002 The case for incompatibilism. *Philosophy Phenomenol. Res.* **64**, 699–706.

Sanfey, A. G., Rilling, J. K., Aronson, J. A., Nystrom, L. E. & Cohen, J. D. 2003 The neural basis of economic decision-making in the ultimatum game. *Science* **300**, 1755–1758.

Saxe, R., Carey, S. & Kanwisher, N. 2004 Understanding other minds: liking developmental psychology and functional neuroimaging. *A. Rev. Psychol.* **55**, 87–124.

Scholl, B. J. & Tremoulet, P. D. 2000 Perceptual causality and animacy. *Trends Cogn. Sci.* **4**, 299–309.

Shear, J. (ed.) 1999 *Explaining consciousness: the hard problem*. Cambridge, MA: MIT Press.

Smart, J. J. C. 1961 Free will, praise, and blame. *Mind* **70**, 291–306.

Steinberg, L. & Scott, E. S. 2003 Less guilty by reason of adolescence: developmental immaturity, diminished responsibility, and the juvenile death penalty. *Am. Psychol.* **58**, 1009–1018.

Strawson, P. F. 1962 Freedom and resentment. *Proc. Br. Acad.* **xlviii**, 1–25.

Tonry, M. 2004 *Thinking about crime: sense and sensibility in American penal culture*. New York: Oxford University Press.

Van Inwagen, P. 1982 The incompatibility of free will and determinism. In *Free will* (ed. G. Watson), pp. 46–58. New York: Oxford University Press.

Watson, G. (ed.) 1982 *Free will*. New York: Oxford University Press.

Wegner, D. M. 2002 *The illusion of conscious will*. Cambridge, MA: MIT Press.

Wright, R. 1994 *The moral animal: evolutionary psychology and everyday life*. New York: Pantheon.

12

The frontal cortex and the criminal justice system

Robert M. Sapolsky

In recent decades, the general trend in the criminal justice system in the USA has been to narrow the range of insanity defences available, with an increasing dependence solely on the *M'Naghten* rule. This states that innocence by reason of insanity requires that the perpetrator could not understand the nature of their criminal act, or did not know that the act was wrong, by reason of a mental illness. In this essay, I question the appropriateness of this, in light of contemporary neuroscience. Specifically, I focus on the role of the prefrontal cortex (PFC) in cognition, emotional regulation, control of impulsive behaviour and moral reasoning. I review the consequences of PFC damage on these endpoints, the capacity for factors such as alcohol and stress to transiently impair PFC function, and the remarkably late development of the PFC (in which full myelination may not occur until early adulthood). I also consider how individual variation in PFC function and anatomy, within the normative range, covaries with some of these endpoints. This literature is reviewed because of its relevance to issues of criminal insanity; specifically, damage can produce an individual capable of differentiating right from wrong but who, nonetheless, is organically incapable of appropriately regulating their behaviour.

Keywords: prefrontal cortex; volition; limbic system; frontal disinhibition

12.1 Introduction

It is the duty of every academic to argue for the importance of their field, and to tout the recent advances and expansion that it has undergone. Despite the clichéd ubiquity of this pattern, I believe that neuroscience and our understanding of the functioning of the brain has undergone a particularly dramatic example of this expansion. As one measure of it, the annual meeting of the Society for Neuroscience, arguably the premier general neuroscience conference, attracts some 25 000 attendees and features some 14 000 poster or lecture presentations. Many of these subjects concern deadening minutia (except, of course, to the three people on Earth feverishly taken with that topic), but some findings in neuroscience should seem nothing short of flabbergasting to any intelligent person.

In some instances, these findings must challenge our sense of self. Some examples are listed below.

(i) Huntington's disease is a neurological disorder in which there is extensive damage to the extra-pyramidal motor system in the brain, producing choreic writhing throughout the body, typically starting around the age of 40 years. In a sizeable percentage of patients, these motoric symptoms are preceded a few years earlier by damage to the frontal cortex and associated changes in personality. Such changes typically involve marked social disinhibition, increases in aggressiveness and hypersexuality, patterns of impulsivity and poor social judgement. Because of these features, those with Huntington's disease are often initially diagnosed with a psychiatric disorder (Cummings 1995). Remarkably, Huntington's disease is a result of a single gene mutation. In other words, alter one gene among tens of thousands and, approximately halfway through one's life, there occurs a dramatic transformation of personality.

(ii) Transgendered individuals feel themselves to have been born into a body of the wrong gender, and explanations for this phenomenon have been put forth by various professionals, including endocrinologists, psychoanalysts and developmental biologists. A recent study forces a rethinking of transgenders. There exists a particular nucleus within the hypothalamus of the brain that is sexually dimorphic; there is a pronounced and consistent difference in the size of the nucleus, depending on the gender of the person. Among transgendered individuals, this nucleus has been reported to be the size typical not of the gender of that person, but of the gender they have always felt themselves to be. This is observed whether or not the person actually has undergone a sex change operation and the accompanying hormone treatments. Thus, despite being a particular gender at the level of one's chromosomes, gonads, hormones, phenotype and by one's treatment by society, some individuals, nonetheless, feel themselves to be of the other gender ... and this area of the brain agrees. Thus, the issue with transgenderism may not be that someone feels that they are of the wrong gender: instead, it may be that someone has the body of the wrong gender (Kruijver *et al.* 2000).

(iii) Mammalian species differ as to whether they are monogamous or polygamous (and where genetic, anatomical and ethnographic data in humans suggest that we hover somewhere in between, being neither fish nor fowl). Some recent work has uncovered the neurobiological basis of monogamy in some rodent species. In the males of these species, repeated mating with a female triggers release of the hormone vasopressin. Ample quantities of vasopressin receptors occur in a brain region called the nucleus accumbens of such males (but not in the nucleus accumbens in closely related rodent species that are polygamous). This nucleus plays a central role in mediating pleasure, and the vasopressin activates this pathway, causing the male to associate those pleasurable feelings with that particular female, thereby cementing them into a pair-bond. Remarkably, 'gene therapy' techniques can be used to overexpress vasopressin receptors in that part of the brain in a male rodent of a polygamous species, thereby shifting them to monogamous behaviour (Lim *et al.* 2004).

(iv) Finally, one subtype of epilepsy, centred in the temporal lobe, causes an array of subtle personality changes that are a function of the type of epilepsy itself (rather than of merely suffering from a serious disease). Among these changes is, typically, a preoccupation with religious and philosophical subjects (Waxman & Geschwind 1974).

In other words, neurobiology is beginning to provide the first hints of mechanistic explanations for our personalities, propensities and passions.

These insights can be of extraordinary relevance, in that neurobiology often must inform some of our decision making. Is a loved one, sunk in a depression so severe that she cannot function, a case of a disease whose biochemical basis is as 'real' as is the biochemistry of, say, diabetes, or is she merely indulging herself? Is a child doing poorly at school because he is unmotivated and slow, or because there is a neurobiologically based learning disability? Is a friend, edging towards a serious problem with substance abuse, displaying a simple lack of discipline, or suffering from problems with the neurochemistry of reward?

Issues such as these prompt that chauvinistic sense on my part that a knowledge of neurobiology would make all of us better informed voters, family members and teachers.

Arguably, the most important arena in which a greater knowledge of neuroscience is needed is the criminal justice system. In some cases, the criminal justice system has accommodated well the lessons of neurobiology. If someone with epilepsy, in the course of a seizure, flails and strikes another person, that epileptic would never be considered to have criminally assaulted the person who they struck. But in earlier times, that is exactly what would have been concluded, and epilepsy was often assumed to be a case of retributive demonic possession (Eadie & Bladin 2001). Instead, we are now a century or two into readily dealing with the alternative view of, 'itisnothim, it is his disease'.

However, there are an ever-increasing number of realms in which the legal system has made little headway in incorporating neurobiology. In this paper, I consider some of the greatest incompatibilities between these two realms and some of the most important ways in which modern neurobiology can inform criminology, with an emphasis on the role of impaired volition in the insanity defence. First, two caveats: I write this as a scientist, and thus readily anticipate that some of the representations of the legal realm will be grossly simplified. Second, I write as an American, which means that the criminal justice system that I am most familiar with has some rather unique features to it. This includes a society with extremely high rates of violence, of incarceration and of recidivism, a propensity virtually unmatched in the Judeo–Christian world for executing criminals (coupled with frequent cases of conviction of the wrong person in capital cases (Acker *et al.* 2001)), and well-documented patterns in which the likelihood of conviction and the severity of punishment differ systematically as a function of the ethnicity and socioeconomic status of perpetrators and/or victims.

12.2 The world of science versus the world of law: categories, causality and continua

Before considering the heart of this paper, namely the neurobiology of impulse control and its relevance to issues of criminality, it is important to first consider some cultural differences between the legal world and that of science. The most funda-mental one reflects a luxury available to the basic scientist that is not available to a juror. For the scientist, a world of uncertainty and imperfect evidence is the fuel that drives the next study and the next hypothesis, leading to an ever more nuanced and complex sense of how something works. This is the basis of the quip that science consists of people learning more and more about less and less. By contrast to this luxury of time, for a juror, a world of uncertainty and imperfect evidence must nonetheless still be navigated to pro-duce a decision. Two other contrasts, now discussed, may be less obvious.

(a) Thinking (and judging) in categories versus in continua

A second tension between the legal and scientific worlds concerns the topic of categor-ical thinking. As the joke goes, the world can be divided into two types of people, namely those who divide the world into two types of people and those who do not. There can be an immensely strong cognitive pull to operate in the former way, in terms of labelling, categorizing and dichotomizing, despite the fact that so many phenomena that we are exposed to occur as continua. Labels and boundaries that break continua into cognitively digestible units aid our memory, and many neurons in associational cortical regions respond to stimuli in a categorical manner.

Despite this pull, categorical thinking distorts our ability to view accurately the relationships among facts, in that we tend to underestimate the difference between two facts that happen to be given the same categorical label, while we overestimate the difference between the same two facts if they are given different categorical labels. This was shown in one remarkable study in which 'categorical' neurons were identified in the cortex of monkeys which would respond to the image of a dog or a cat (but not both). The experimenters then presented the test subjects with a computer-generated image of a cat or dog, and then would slowly morph the image so that it was a hybrid of the two (where the image could be, for example, 90% dog and 10% cat, and so on). They found that species-responsive neurons maintained a fairly consistent level of responding as the percentage of the image derived from that animal dropped from 100%, until there was an abrupt transition of responsiveness around the 50% mark. In other words, a neuron 'considered' a 60% dog to have more in common with a 100% dog than with a 40% dog (i.e. neurons themselves underestimate differences within category, and overestimate differences between categories (Freedman *et al.* 2001)).

Good scientists typically struggle to think in continua, a style that is a logical extension of thinking probabilistically. And this awareness of continua permeates all of the life sciences, stretching from determining when life or foetal viability begins to when life ends.

Of necessity, this cognitive style must butt heads with categorical demands in many settings. For example, total cholesterol concentrations of 199 and 200 do not differ in a biologically meaningful way; however, only the latter commands the label of 'elevated'. Scientifically informed clinicians incorporate the irrelevance of such categorical boundaries into their thinking, but insurance companies often do not. This is particularly problematic in the realm of medicine that is most intrinsically built on continua, namely psychiatry. This is seen with genetic aspects of psychiatry where, for example, there is a smooth genetic continuum between schizophrenia, a disorder of wildly disruptive delusional thinking, and schizotypalism, in which there are far milder 'metamagical' delusions. Or consider the obvious continuum between the severity and duration of bereavement grief that counts as 'normal' and that which is categorized as segueing into a major depression. The Diagnostic and Statistical Manual of the American Psychiatric Association is the bible of the field and is structured categorically, partly reflecting the cognitive pull of categorization as well as the exigencies of insurance reimbursement. Currently, its editors are struggling, in preparing the next edition, with converting diagnosis from a categorical structure to one of continua (Helmuth 2003).

Thus, this cultural feature of many types of science must be utterly at odds with the legal world in which continua must be broken into the sharpest and most consequential of dichotomies: guilty versus not guilty.

(b) A cause versus multiple and interactive causes

A belief that it is possible to make categorical judgements can readily lead to having problems with some aspects of causality. One version concerns the difficulty in dealing with the situation in which one agent causes diffuse, statistical harm. This might be the case in a scenario in which some industrial polluter is found to have been illegally dumping a toxin into the water supply. It is not possible to show a single instance in which such dumping could be causally linked to a single case of cancer. However, epidemiologists advise that the cancer risk for a million people has been raised, say, 0.1%. Thus, causality is diffusely distributed.

Conversely, categorical thinking also makes it difficult to deal with the situation in which multiple agents caused a single event. Suppose two men start fires simultaneously, at opposite ends of a property. The fires merge and burn down the property. Who is responsible for the damage? Each of the two arsonist defendants can correctly make the same point: if I had not set the fire, the property would still have burned. So how can I be guilty? For much of American history, both would have gone free. It was only in 1927 that the courts declared for the first time that guilt for a singular burning, a singular injury, a singular killing, could be distributed among contributing parties (Kingston versus Chicago and NW Railroad, concerning two fires of different origins that converged). As an implicit acknowledgement of the legal difficulties in dealing with the idea of multiple causes of a single event, if two men, as a pair, are accused of a killing spree, they will readily be tried separately.

As an extension of this, the legal system has no capacity for contingent judgements. Thus, in considering the two accused murderers, suppose one is barely out of adolescence, the two have something resembling a parent–child relationship, with the older of the pair exerting a great deal of persuasive power over the younger one. While the asymmetry of that relationship may be aired in building the defence for the younger man (as is the case in an ongoing trial in the USA), there is no formal charge that can be given to the jury of 'if and only if A, then B': 'the younger man can be found guilty if and only if the older man is first found guilty by a separate jury'.

The early decades of twentieth century medicine were dominated by single causal and single consequence models: a single virus is the sole cause of polio and does nothing but cause polio; a single different virus is the sole cause of yellow fever and does nothing but cause yellow fever, and so on. But now, medicine predominantly deals with multifactorial diseases, such as heart disease, diabetes and cancer, and lifestyle factors that diffusely increase the risk for a multitude of diseases (e.g. smoking, high fat consumption, sedentary lifestyle). The same is true at the levels of systems physiology and cell biology, where functioning involves considerable amounts of convergence and divergence amid various regulatory pathways. Finally, contingent interactions among causal agents are at the heart of how living systems work. Consider genetics, the discipline that the lay public probably (erroneously) considers to be the best example of single agent causality (genes as the holy grail of life, any given gene 'commanding' the cell/organ/body what to do). In actuality, it is nearly meaningless to ever state what a particular gene 'does'. Far more accurately, it is instead the case of genes having a particular effect only in a particular environment (Moore 2002).

Thus, there are enormous intellectual differences between the worlds of science and of law in the basic premises about causality and certainty. With that as an orientation, we now consider how the concept of volition has played a shifting role in thinking about the insanity defence, and what contemporary neuroscience has to offer on this subject.

12.3 Knowing right from wrong: the growing reliance of the american criminal justice system on *M'Naghten*

In the USA, the core of the insanity defence is a derivation of the *M'Naghten* rule from English case law. This well-known test of insanity requires that the perpetrator, because of some mental disease, was unable to understand the nature or quality of the act that he or she performed, or did not know that the act was wrong. As stated in the most commonly understood sense, this insanity defence revolves around a cognitive disability, namely the inability to know the difference between right and wrong.

The *M'Naghten* rule was criticized on several grounds including, of greatest relevance to this piece, its disregard of mental illnesses that impair volition. Impaired volition has been considered relevant to criminal justice at least beginning with Aristotle (English 1988), and is the idea that it is possible for a person to retain the cognitive capacity to distinguish right from wrong behaviour and, nonetheless, for reasons of mental illness, to be organically incapable of regulating the appropriateness of their behaviour. As a result of this, some states and federal courts expanded upon *M'Naghten* to incorporate the issue of impaired volition. Some rulings introduced throughout the nineteenth century incorporated 'irresistible impulse', a concept that readily proves problematic (i.e. distinguishing between an irresistible impulse and one that is to any extent resistible but which was not resisted). Another test (the American Law Institute Model Penal Code, introduced in 1962) was less absolutist, requiring a 'substantial' rather than complete loss of volition. Another, the *Durham* test, introduced in 1954, stated that a person could be judged innocent by reason of insanity if their criminal act was the 'product' of their mental disease or mental defect (reviewed in Dressler 2001).

By the early 1980s, half the USA and most federal courts were using some sort of insanity test that incorporated elements of loss of volition. This trend abruptly reversed when the potential assassin of Ronald Reagan, John Hinckley, was acquitted on grounds of insanity. This ignited spasms of protests throughout the USA, producing tremendous pressure on courts and legislatures to: (i) narrow the range in which impaired volition could be used as an insanity defence or, more severely; (ii) to retrench back to a sole reliance on *M'Naghten*; or, at the most extreme, (iii) to abandon the insanity defence altogether (Hans 1986). Remarkably, this 'reform' was backed by the American Bar Association, and the American Psychiatric Association (both favouring eliminating impaired volition defences) and the American Medical Association (favouring the complete abandonment of the insanity defence (English 1988)).

This retrenchment was opposed by many legal scholars. In some cases, this was based on constitutional grounds (English 1988), whereas in other instances, the opposition was based on utilitarian thinking: for example, a person with impaired volition who has committed a criminal act is less likely to be rehabilitated if incarcerated in prison than if hospitalized psychiatrically (Arenella 1982). Nonetheless, this retrenchment was widespread throughout the USA. In 1984, the American Congress eliminated impaired volition as an insanity defence at the level of federal courts (the Insanity Defence Reform Act of 1984) and, by 1985, most states within the USA had narrowed or eliminated impaired volitional defences in state courts.

Thus, since that time, the criminal justice system in the USA has been dominated increasingly by a view that an inability to tell right from wrong is the sole basis of an acceptable insanity defence. I will now examine how contemporary neuroscience strongly argues against this trend. Instead, we have come to understand increasingly the organic basis of impaired impulse control.

12.4 The prefrontal cortex: knowing versus controlling

An appreciation of this emerging knowledge requires an exploration of the functioning of one of the most intriguing parts of the brain, namely the PFC. On a certain metaphorical level, the PFC is the closest thing we possess to a superego. Stated in an only slightly more scientific manner, it is the job of the frontal cortex to bias an individual towards doing the harder, rather than the easier thing (Miller & Cohen 2001). Behaviours that are harder to perform are not necessarily ones that are more correct. However, that is often the case, when 'more correct' is used in a behaviourist sense, rather than in a moralistic one. Thus, doing the 'harder' but 'more correct' behaviour implies a circumstance where a rapid reward is available, but where gratification postponement will yield an even larger reward.

I begin by reviewing the workings of the normal PFC. The role of the PFC in doing the 'harder thing' manifests itself in several domains. One is in the realm of cognition. Memory is not a monolithic process; instead, there is a taxonomy of different types of memory. An important distinction is made between explicit, declarative memory, and implicit, procedural memory. The former involves not only knowledge of facts, but conscious awareness of that knowledge. By contrast, implicit, procedural processes are more automatic and non-conscious. Thus, riding a bicycle, shifting the gears on a car, knitting, can all be procedural tasks, once they are mastered. In effect, these are cases where one's hands know the task better than one's head. But procedural tasks are not merely motoric. Instead, they can also include more cerebral tasks that have become over-learned: remembering one's telephone number, singing the national anthem or reciting the alphabet.

Doing a task through an implicit pathway represents the 'easier' version. When we are forced to override an easier, over-learned implicit pathway and perform a related task in a more novel, declarative way the PFC must be engaged, and the more of an implicit pathway that must be over-ridden, the more PFC activation is increased (Jaeggi *et al.* 2003). This has been shown in various brain imaging studies. This is particularly the case when the new task represents a reversal of a previously mastered task (i.e. the transition from the well-learned, 'when X, do Y' to the novel 'when X, do not do Y'). The PFC provides the metaphorical cerebral backbone needed to keep the prior, easier task from intruding. And as the new task becomes easier, and thus more automatic, PFC activity subsides, until a new rule is imposed in the task (Simpson *et al.* 2001). As such, experimental lesions of parts of the PFC in laboratory monkeys, or accidental damage to the homologous region in the human PFC, impairs the capacity of the individual to shift behaviour adaptively in response to changing patterns of reward (Baxter *et al.* 2000).

The PFC also plays a key role in 'executive' cognitive function. Executive function can be thought of as the strategic organizing of facts. This can be shown in a particular neuropsychological task in which a subject hears, with minimal warning, a rapidly read list of 16 disparate items that can be bought in a supermarket, and then is asked to recite the list back. Most subjects can recall only a few of the items, at which the list is read repeatedly, with the subject asked to recall the items after each reading. It is only after a few repetitions that one begins to discern that the 16 items fall into various semantic categories: four are hardware items, four are fruits, and so on. And with that, an executive transition occurs, where the memory strategy shifts from simply remembering the sequences of items to remembering them grouped into their categories. Subjects with damage to the PFC fail to hierarchically organize the list into categories. This executive grouping represents the 'harder' (but eventually, more effective) strategy, insofar as a subject must inhibit and step back from the easier strategy of simply trying to recall items in the sequence they were read (Delis *et al.* 1987). Intrinsic in the ability of the PFC to do such executive strategizing is its ability to organize information both sequentially and categorically. Electro-physiological studies of non-human primates have indicated that there are PFC neurons that respond to sequences or to categories of information (Freedman *et al.* 2001; Fujii & Graybiel 2003).

Of great relevance, the PFC role of 'biasing towards doing the harder thing' pertains to emotional regulation as well. For example, in one study, volunteers are shown a film clip of a graphic and disturbing scene: an amputation. In the 'attend' group, subjects are instructed to do what is easiest, which is to simply be aware of the (typically, strong and negative) feelings evoked by the viewing. In the 'reappraisal' group, subjects are instructed to perform the far harder task of regulating those emotions, 'so that they no longer feel negative responses'. And as shown with functional brain imaging during this task, the harder reappraisal task is associated with activation of regions of the PFC (Ochsner *et al.* 2002). Findings strongly in agreement with ones such as these come from studies of individuals with repressive personalities, individuals who are highly self-regulating in their emotional expressiveness. Such individuals have elevated metabolic rates in the PFC (Tomarken & Davidson 1994).

Research has explored a subtler example, perhaps, of doing the harder thing within an emotional realm. In one session, volunteers undergoing functional brain imaging were given a purely cognitive task to think about. In a second imaging session, they would be read a scenario in which someone did an act that might be considered inappropriate; the subject is then told about some unfortunate circumstance in the life of that person that may mitigate the inappropriate act. Regions of the PFC were consistently activated in the latter scenario, one that called forth contemplating empathy and forgiveness (Farrow *et al.* 2001).

Findings such as these lead to a consideration of the role of the PFC in moral reasoning. Several well-designed studies have required subjects to do some manner of moral reasoning (to decide what behaviour they would choose in a morally ambiguous situation) versus reasoning about the physical world (for example, considering whether one object is heavier than another). Consistently, the moral reasoning scenario preferentially activates parts of the PFC (Greene *et al.* 2001; Schultz *et al.* 2001; Heekeren *et al.* 2003; Moll *et al.* 2003). Moreover, making a *decision* in the face of a moral quandary activates more of the PFC than merely contemplating a moral quandary (Moll *et al.* 2002). Another example links the PFC to moral reasoning. Different types of epilepsies originate—have an epileptic 'focus'—in different parts of the brain, and thoughts, sensations or actions just before a seizure reflect the brain region where the seizure commences. For example, an epileptic with a seizure focus in the olfactory cortex might have an olfactory 'aura' just before a seizure. Remarkably, some epileptics whose foci are in the PFC have a pre-seizure cognition of an unresolved moral quandary (Cohen *et al.* 1999).

A recent paper also implicates the PFC in the sensation of regret. In an elegant experimental design, subjects were allowed to participate in a gambling game. In the control scenario, subjects spun a 'wheel of fortune', producing a rewarding or punishing outcome; the latter would typically provoke a sense of disappointment. In the experimental setting, two wheels of fortune were spun, with subjects having chosen to gamble on only one of them. Thus, in that scenario, subjects not only found out if they were punished or rewarded, but also found out what the outcome would have been had they chosen the other wheel. This could result in the particularly aversive situation in which the subject's choice produced a punishing outcome, whereas the other wheel produced a strongly rewarding one. In normal subjects, this resulted in a constellation of affective, behavioural and physiological changes: (i) a subjective sense of regret (of not having picked the other wheel); (ii) a subsequent shift in behaviour towards choosing the other wheel; and (iii) pronounced arousal of the sympathetic nervous system. By contrast, in a group of patients with extensive damage to the PFC, none of the responses occurred (Camille *et al.* 2004).

Most importantly, the PFC mediates doing the harder thing in the realm of behaviour as well. Stated in terms most pertinent to this essay, the PFC helps to suppress impulsive behaviour. As will be discussed below, this has been amply documented in humans with PFC damage, who fail to carry out the harder, less impulsive behaviour. This can be shown more formally with laboratory rats; upon completing a task such as lever pressing, they can either get a reward (typically food) after some delay, or can opt to get a lesser reward but with no delay. In some testing paradigms, up to 90% of rats can demonstrate 'gratification postponement', in enduring the long delay for the larger reward. However, if the PFC (or some of the sites that project to it, which will be discussed shortly) is lesioned, the rat consistently opts for the more impulsive choice, amid still retaining the cognitive capacity to perform the task (cf. Cardinal *et al.* 2001).

How does the PFC mediate doing the 'harder' thing? One way to gain insight into this is to review the parts of the brain to which the PFC sends projections. Of greatest relevance to the notion of the PFC controlling impulsivity, the structure sends large inhibitory projections into the limbic system, particularly the amgydala, a region heavily implicated in aggressive behaviour. Strikingly, in humans, elevated metabolic rates in parts of the PFC predict low rates of amygdaloid activity (Urry *et al.* 2003). This neuroanatomy is important in trying to understand the biology of violence. There can be striking similarities in the motor output and the associated physiology (i.e. the actual behaviour, the accompanying changes in heart rate, blood pressure, and so on) when a sniper picks off enemy soldiers and when a sniper randomly picks off motorists driving the evening commute. However, one circumstance earns medals and societal acclaim, and the other the death penalty. The limbic system can function in roughly similar ways in both settings. As societies, we do not outlaw violent acts; we outlaw them in the wrong context, and the PFC is centrally involved in learning and imposing context.

The PFC also sends projections to much of the rest of the cortex, and to regions of the brain that initiate movements and behaviour. In this realm, many of those projections are stimulatory. However, those excitatory inputs should not be thought as 'activating' (i.e. in a highly schematic sense, 'causing' a thought to arise in the cortex, or 'causing' an action to arise from these motor pathways). Instead, the excitatory inputs are meant to bias one particular output to occur over another. As a very artificial example, insofar as counting from June forwards to December is the over-learned sequence for reciting the months, the pathway that mediates that sequence is intrinsically a stronger one—has more robust synaptic connections—than the pathway that counts from June backwards to January. Thus, when one is called upon to do the harder reversal task, the 'work' that is required from the PFC takes the form of priming that weaker 'June backwards' pathway sufficiently to tilt the balance in its favour over the overlearned, implicit 'June forwards' route (Miller & Cohen 2001).

Further insights into how the PFC mediates doing the 'harder' thing also come from considering the projections to the structure. Appropriately, the PFC receives information from sites throughout the rest of the cortex, including not only sensory processing regions, but more upstream, associative parts as well. Intriguingly, there are also extensive projections into the PFC from parts of the limbic system, the part of the mammalian brain involved in emotion. Such connections probably go far to explain why strong emotions can adversely impact the quality of executive function, often increasing the likelihood of imprudent or impulsive choices.

Arguably, the most interesting projection into the PFC is a pathway originating in the ventral tegmentum and coursing through the nucleus accumbens before continuing on to the PFC (among other regions). This projection has long been known to be involved in mediating pleasure and reward, being a robust site of 'self-stimulation' (i.e. where rats will work, often to extraordinary extents, to be stimulated in this pathway). Central to this role is the fact that this projection uses the neurotransmitter dopamine, which has long been implicated in pleasure and reward. For example, euphoriant drugs such as cocaine enhance dopamine signalling.

Initially, there was the expectation that this dopaminergic projection would cause the PFC to become active in response to reward. For example, consider a task where a trained monkey would be (i) given a signal (e.g. a light) indicating the beginning of a testing session for a task that it has mastered; this would be followed by (ii), the monkey completing the task, thereby initiating a latency until (iii) delivery of the reward. In a paradigm such as this, dopaminergic neurons themselves would be heavily responsive to period (iii), as would some neurons in the PFC. However, unique to the PFC, there would be substantial numbers of neurons responding instead to periods (i) and (ii) (Schultz *et al.* 2000). Thus, critically, dopamine–PFC interactions are not so much about reward as about the *anticipation* of reward.

The PFC can be quite subtle in this anticipatory function. For example, in one study, rhesus monkeys were trained to perform two different tasks. In both cases, there would be an initial stimulus signalling the start of the task. The monkey would then carry out the task, followed by a signal indicating if the monkey's response was correct. In only one of those two tasks, however, was that 'correct' signal then followed by a food reward. PFC neurons were identified electrophysiologically that would distinguish between anticipating feedback indicating a correct action, and feedback indicating a correct action coupled with a food reward (Matsumoto *et al.* 2003).

The activation of the PFC in anticipation of reward is at the core of its function. Like any other pathway in the nervous system, the strength of the dopaminergic projection into the PFC can change. Such plasticity could take the form of an enhanced capacity to sustain dopamine release as the interval between the onset of a task and its reward increases. This would constitute the neural basis of an increasing capacity for self-discipline and gratification postponement.

12.5 The human prefrontal cortex and its impairments

This very broad (and simplistic) overview of PFC function allows us to appreciate circumstances in which PFC function is compromised in a human. Humans comprise a special case when considering this brain region. Despite evidence that the PFC in rodents and non-human primates regulates cognition and behaviour in ways quite similar to that of the human, we are the most 'frontal' of species, insofar as the frontal cortex is its largest, in both absolute and relative terms, in the human (Rilling & Insel 1999).

The first realm to consider where PFC function is compromised in humans is, quite reasonably, during development. Children show only minimal frontal function, from the standpoints of cognition (for example, in reversal tasks), emotional regulation, control of impulsive behaviour and moral reasoning. One of the myths of child development is that the brain is fully developed at some remarkably early age (the age of 3 years is probably most often cited (Bruer 1999)). Instead, brain development is far more prolonged and, not surprisingly, the PFC is the last region of the brain to fully myelinate. Remarkably, this process extends well beyond adolescence into early adulthood (Paus et al. 1999).

Various transient states can compromise PFC function. Alcohol is long-recognized for its capacity to impair reasoning and impulse control, and surprisingly small quantities of alcohol impair the capacity of the PFC to detect errors of commission or omission, as assessed electrophysiologically (Ridderinkhof et al. 2002). Another example concerns stress. Most individuals have experienced severe and/or prolonged stress as disrupting attention, judgement and other purviews of the PFC, and this has been shown more formally in both humans and animals (Arnsten 2000; Sapolsky 2004). In making sense of this, it should be appreciated that the PFC contains some of the highest levels of receptors in the primate brain for stress hormones (Sanchez et al. 2000). Moreover, stress or stress hormones will dramatically alter the turnover of several classes of neurotransmitters in the PFC (Moghaddam et al. 1994; Arnsten 2000).

PFC function is also compromised in another circumstance experienced by all individuals. With the onset of sleep and the transition to deep, slow wave sleep, there is a characteristic decrease in activity throughout the brain, particularly in the cortex. However, with the transition to paradoxical rapid eye movement sleep, there is increased activity in a variety of brain regions, including associational cortex and limbic systems; strikingly, metabolic rate can even be higher than during wake periods. Amid this shift, there is a virtually complete cessation of activity in the PFC, producing a relatively metabolically active brain that is unconstrained by the regulatory effects of the PFC (Braun et al. 1998). It has been speculated that this, in effect, accounts for why dreams are 'dream-like': characterized by emotional lability, non-sequential thinking and extreme disinhibition (Sapolsky 2001).

PFC function is also often impaired during normative ageing. There is often the misconception that brain ageing involves massive loss of neurons; this mistake is a result of some early and influential studies in which diseases of ageing (specifically dementias) were not viewed as distinct from normal ageing. In actuality, there is only really one brain region in which there is loss of most neurons during normal ageing (the substantia nigra), and only a few additional regions in which there is even moderate neuron loss. The PFC is among these and, commensurate with that, normal ageing involves a mild degree of impairment of frontal function in several realms (Coleman & Flood 1987; Coffey et al. 1992; Tisserand & Jolles 2003).

We now consider the realm of PFC dysfunction most relevant to legal matters, namely, when the frontal cortex is damaged. This literature originates with Phinneas Gage, a man who is arguably the most famous patient in the history of neuropsychology. Gage's PFC was selectively destroyed in an industrial accident some 155 years ago, and it transformed him, virtually overnight, from a taciturn, reliable foreman in a railroad construction crew to a coarse, disinhibited unstable individual who was never able to work again (MacMillan 2000). Since then, an extensive literature links PFC damage with impulse control, antisocial behaviour and criminality (reviewed in Brower & Price 2001; Nyffeler & Regard 2001), as well as more quantifiably 'frontally disinhibited' cognition and behaviour in the context of more formal testing.

There is an increasing appreciation that the age at which the PFC damage occurs can be critical (Damasio 1998; Brower & Price 2001; Moll *et al.* 2003). The general picture is that damage any time after the adolescent years produces an adult who is markedly impulsive in behaviour, and with little capacity for foresight or assessing future consequences when in an emotionally aroused circumstance. Amid that, general intelligence and executive function can remain intact. By contrast, when damage occurs at earlier ages, executive function is impaired and the impulsivity takes on a more global and malign nature that has been termed 'acquired sociopathy', where antisocial behaviours can be markedly premeditated.

The issue of brain development becomes relevant when considering individuals with sociopathic and antisocial behaviour in which there is no obvious history of PFC damage. Despite there being nothing demonstrably, neurologically 'wrong' with such individuals, an abundant literature demonstrates that their PFC, nonetheless, works somewhat differently than most other individuals. Thus, basal metabolic rates in the PFC are decreased in sociopaths (Raine 2002). Moreover, when sociopaths must engage the PFC (i.e. during neuropsychological testing when they are attempting to successfully perform a frontally demanding task), they activate more of the PFC than control individuals to achieve the same level of efficacy (Abbott 2001). In other words, even when these individuals actively attempt to do the 'harder thing', their PFCs are less effective. Importantly, among such sociopathic individuals, the smaller the volume of the PFC (where, again, there is no history of overt PFC damage), the greater the tendency towards aggressive and antisocial behaviour (reviewed in Brower & Price 2001).

Probably the most common cause of major PFC damage in humans is secondary to a stroke. Such 'ischaemic' damage produces an individual who can be highly impaired in cognitive tests of frontal function, and behaviourally and affectively disinhibited (Lezak 1995). The same is seen with fronto-temporal/Pick's dementia, a rare neurodegenerative disorder in which neuron loss is initially concentrated in the PFC (Chow *et al.* 2002). Because strokes and such dementias are situations in which a previously cognitively intact adult loses cortical function (as opposed to the situation of, say, the 3-year-old who has not yet developed full frontal function), this can provide one of the most extraordinary features of PFC damage. During neuropsychological testing, the patient might say, in effect, 'I know, I know how this test works, I am supposed to choose this trickier one because it gets me more of a reward, so that is just what I am going to ...' before impulsively taking the 'easier' route (Lezak 1995). Thus, the frontally damaged patient can verbalize the dissociation between knowing the right from wrong response, and being able to act upon that knowledge.

12.6 Some conclusions: the frontal cortex and the criminal justice system

We have come to recognize numerous realms in which a biological abnormality gives rise to aberrant behaviour. And such recognition has often then given rise to an expectation that people now exert higher-order control over that abnormality. For example, as noted, we would never consider an epileptic violent who strikes someone in the process of a seizure: 'it is not him; it is his disease'. However, we expect that epileptic to not drive a car if their seizures are uncontrolled. Or we are coming to understand the neurochemistry of context-dependence relapse into drug dependency in organisms. Thus, we have come to expect ex-addicts to avoid the settings in which they previously abused drugs.

There is a false dichotomy in this manner of thinking. It is as if we artificially demarcate an area in which biology dominates: yes, there is something organic that gives rise to this person having uncontrolled and synchronous neuronal discharges (i.e. a seizure), or who has certain pathways potentiated that project onto dopamine-releasing 'pleasure' pathways (one theory about the neurochemistry of substance abuse relapse). But it is as if, with that area of organic impairment identified and given credence, we expect it to be bounded, and for the rest of our 'us-ness', replete with free will, to now shoulder the responsibility of keeping that organic impairment within the confines of its boundaries. It cannot possibly work this way. What the literature about the PFC shows is that there is a reductive, materialistic neurobiology to the containment, resulting in the potential for volitional control to be impaired just as unambiguously as any other aspect of brain function. It is possible to know the difference between right and wrong but, for reasons of organic impairment, to not be able to do the right thing.

The most obvious implication of this concerns how individuals with demonstrable PFC damage are treated in the criminal justice system. As the simplest conclusion, everything about this realm of contemporary neurobiology argues against the retrenchment back towards a sole reliance on *M'Naghten* that has gone on in recent decades.

Amid the seeming obviousness of this conclusion, there is always a valid counter-point that can be raised: there are individuals with substantial amounts of PFC damage who, nonetheless, do not commit crimes. At present, knowing that someone has sustained PFC damage does not give much power in predicting whether that person's disinhibition will take the form of serial murder or merely being unable to praise a nearly inedible meal prepared by a host. This seems to weaken the 'volition can be organically impaired, just like any other aspect of brain function' argument; in these interstices of unpredictability seem to dwell free will.

However, we can begin to imagine tree diagrams of variables that, with each new layer, add more predictive power. We can already see two layers in the realm of PFC function. The first layer might query, 'PFC: normal or damaged?' (while recognizing that this is a false dichotomy). The second might then query, 'if damaged: damaged in childhood or later?' This same structure of increasing predictive power was shown in a recent, landmark study concerning clinical depression. Having a particular variant of the gene 5-HTT (which codes for a protein that regulates synaptic levels of the neurotransmitter serotonin) increases the risk of depression. However, '5-HTT: pro-depressive variant or other variant?' gives only a moderate predictive power, but the authors then demonstrated the adding in of a second layer, 'if the pro-depressive variant: major stressors during childhood or not?' now generates an impressive predictive power as to which adults succumb to clinical depression (Caspi *et al.* 2003). If free will lurks in those interstices, those crawl spaces are certainly shrinking.

A second way in which findings about the PFC are relevant to the criminal justice system concerns individuals who have committed grotesquely violent, sociopathic crimes, but who have no demonstrable PFC damage. Initially, it seems a fatuous tautology to say that there must be an organic abnormality in such cases—'it is only an organically abnormal brain that produces abnormal behaviour'—and that we simply lack sufficiently sensitive techniques for demonstrating it. However, it must be emphasized that most of the neuro-biological techniques used to demonstrate PFC abnormalities in humans (predominantly structural and functional brain imaging) did not exist a decade or two ago. It would be the height of hubris to think that we have already learned how to detect the most subtle ways in which PFC damage impairs volitional control. Instead, we probably cannot even imagine yet the ways in which biology can go awry and impair the sorts of volitional control that helps define who we are.

At the most disturbing level, findings about the PFC are relevant to the criminal justice system with respect to those of us with a normal PFC and who have never behaved criminally. It is here that the tendency of science to function in continua comes up against the legal culture of jury decisions. Among sociopaths without overt PFC damage, the smaller the volume of the PFC, the greater the tendency towards aggressive and antisocial behaviour (reviewed in Brower & Price 2001). Similarly, as noted, among humans with no neurological impairments or histories of antisocial behaviour, the greater the level of metabolic activity in parts of the PFC, the lower the activity of the amygdala (Urry *et al.* 2003). There is little support for the idea that over the range of PFC function, there is a discontinuity, a transition that allows one to dichotomize between a healthy PFC in an individual expected to have a complete capacity to regulate behaviour, and a damaged PFC in someone who cannot regulate their behaviour. The dichotomy does not exist.

A conclusion like this makes sense to neurobiologists, but may seem alien to legal scholars. The emphasis on continua seems to hold the danger of a world of criminal justice in which there is no blame and only prior causes. Whereas it is true that, at a logical extreme, a neurobiological framework may indeed eliminate blame, it does not eliminate the need for forceful intervention in the face of violence or antisocial behaviour. To understand is not to forgive or to do nothing; whereas you do not ponder whether to forgive a car that, because of problems with its brakes, has injured someone, you nevertheless protect society from it.

Legal scholars have objected to this type of thinking for a related reason, as well. In this view, it is desirable for a criminal justice system to operate with a presumption of responsibility because, 'to treat persons otherwise is to treat them as less than human' (Morse 1976). There is a certain appealing purity to this. But although it may seem dehumanizing to medicalize people into being broken cars, it can still be vastly more humane than moralizing them into being sinners.

The author acknowledges manuscript assistance from Oliver Goodenough, and discussions with Larry Ainbinder and Daniel Greenwood.

References

Abbott, A. 2001 Into the mind of a killer. *Nature* **410**, 296–298.

Acker, J., Brewer, T., Cunningham, E., Fitzgerald, A., Flexon, J., Lombard, J., Ryn, B. & Stodghill, B. 2001 No appeal from the grave: innocence, capital punishment, and the lessons of history. In *Wrongly convicted: perspectives on failed justice* (ed. S. Westervelt & J. Humphrey), pp. 154–173. New Brunswick, NJ: Rutgers University Press.

Arenella, P. 1982 Reflections on current proposals to abolish or reform the insanity defense. *Am. J. Law Med.* **8**, 271–284.

Arnsten, A. 2000 Stress impairs prefrontal cortical function in rats and monkeys: role of dopamine D1 and norepinephrine 1-a receptor mechanisms. *Prog. Brain Res.* **126**, 183–192.

Baxter, M., Parker, A., Lindner, C., Izquierdo, A. & Murray, E. 2000 Control of response selection by reinforcer value requires interaction of amygdala and orbital prefrontal cortex. *J. Neurosci.* **20**, 4311–4319.

Braun, A., Balkin, T., Wesensten, N., Gwadry, F., Carson, R., Varga, M., Baldwin, P., Belenky, G. & Herscovitch, P. 1998 Dissociated pattern of activity in visual cortices and their projections during human rapid eye movement sleep. *Science* **279**, 91–99.

Brower, M. & Price, B. 2001 Neuropsychiatry of frontal lobe dysfunction in violent and criminal behaviour: a critical review. *J. Neurol. Neursurg. Psychiatry* **71**, 720–726.

Bruer, J. 1999 *The myth of the first three years*. New York: Free Press.

Camille, N., Coricelli, G., Sallet, J., Pradat-Diehl, P., Duhamel, J. & Sirigu, A. 2004 The involvement of the orbitofrontal cortex in the experience of regret. *Science* **304**, 1167–1170.

Cardinal, R., Pennicott, D., Sugathapala, C., Robbins, T. & Everitt, B. 2001 Impulsive choice induced in rats by lesions of the nucleus accumbens core. *Science* **292**, 2499–2501.

Caspi, A. (and 10 others) 2003 Influence of life stress on depression: moderation by a polymorphism in the 5-HTT gene. *Science* **301**, 386–389.

Chow, T., Miller, B., Boone, K., Mishkin, F. & Cummings, J. 2002 Frontotemporal dementia classification and neuropsychiatry. *Neurologist* **8**, 263–269.

Coffey, C., Wilkinson, W. & Parashos, I. 1992 Quantitative cerebral anatomy of the aging human brain: a crosssectional study using magnetic resonance imaging. *Neurology* **42**, 527–536.

Cohen, L., Angladette, L., Benoit, N. & Pierrot-Deseilligny, C. 1999 A man who borrowed cars. *Lancet* **353**, 34.

Coleman, P. & Flood, D. 1987 Neuron numbers and dendritic extent in normal aging and Alzheimer's disease. *Neurobiol. Aging* **8**, 521–545.

Cummings, J. 1995 Behavioral and psychiatric symptoms associated with Huntington's Disease. *Adv. Neurol.* **65**, 179–188.

Damasio, A. 1998 *Descartes' error: emotion, reasoning, and the human brain*. New York: Bard/Avon Books.

Delis, D., Kramer, J., Kaplan, E. & Ober, B. 1987 *California verbal learning test: adult version*. New York: The Psychological Corporation, Harcourt, Brace, Jovanovich, Inc.

Dressler, J. 2001 Insanity. In *Understanding criminal law*, pp. 131–157. New York: Matthew Bender & Co.

Eadie, M. & Bladin, P. 2001 *A disease once sacred: a history of the medical understanding of epilepsy*. New York: Butterworth-Heinemann.

English, J. 1988 The light between twilight and dusk: federal criminal law and the volitional insanity defense. *Hastings Law J.* **40**, 1–33.

Farrow, T. F., Zheng, Y., Wilkinson, I. D., Spence, S. A., Deakin, J. F., Tarrier, N., Griffiths, P. D. & Woodruff, P.W. 2001 Investigating the functional anatomy of empathy and forgiveness. *Neuroreport* **12**, 2433–2438.

Freedman, D. J., Riesenhuber, M., Poggio, T. & Miller, E. K. 2001 Categorical representation of visual stimuli in the primate prefrontal cortex. *Science* **291**, 312–316.

Fujii, N. & Graybiel, A. 2003 Representation of action sequence boundaries by macaque prefrontal cortical neurons. *Science* **301**, 1246–1249.

Greene, J. D., Sommerville, R. B., Nystrom, L. E., Darley, J. M. & Cohen, J. D. 2001 An fMRI investigation of emotional engagement in moral judgment. *Science* **293**, 2105–2108.

Hans, V. 1986 An analysis of public attitudes toward the insanity defense. *Criminology* **24**, 393–411.

Heekeren, H., Wartenburger, I., Schmidt, H., Schwintowski, H. & Villringer, A. 2003 An fMRI study of simple ethical decision-making. *Neuroreport* **14**, 1215–1219.

Helmuth, L. 2003 In sickness or in health? *Science* **302**, 808–810.

Jaeggi, S., Seewer, R., Nirkko, A., Eckstein, D., Schroth, G., Groner, R. & Gutbrod, K. 2003 Does excessive memory load attenuate activation in the prefrontal cortex? Load-dependent processing in single and dual tasks: functional magnetic resonance imaging study. *Neuroimage* **19**, 210–225.

Kruijver, F. P., Zhou, J. N., Pool, C. W., Hofman, M. A., Gooren, L. J. & Swaab, D. F. 2000 Male-to-female transsexuals have female neuron numbers in a limbic nucleus. *J. Clin. Endocrinol. Metab.* **85**, 2034–2041.

Lezak, M. 1995 *Neuropsychological assessment*, 3rd edn. Oxford University Press.

Lim, M., Wang, Z., Olazabal, D., Ren, X., Terwilliger, E. & Young, L. 2004 Enhanced partner preference in a promiscuous species by manipulating the expression of a single gene. *Nature* **429**, 754–757.

MacMillan, M. 2000 *An odd kind of fame: stories of Phinneas Gage*. Cambridge, MA: MIT Press.

Matsumoto, K., Suzuki, W. & Tanaka, K. 2003 Neuronal correlates of goal-based motor selection in the prefrontal cortex. *Science* **301**, 229–232.

Miller, E. K. & Cohen, J. D. 2001 An integrative theory of prefrontal cortex function. *A. Rev. Neurosci.* **24**, 167–202.

Moghaddam, B., Bolinao, M., Stein-Behrens, B. & Sapolsky, R. 1994 Glucocorticoids mediate the stress-induced accumulation of extracellular glutamate. *Brain Res.* **655**, 251–254.

Moll, J., Oliveira-Souza, R., Eslinger, P., Bramati, I., Mourao-Miranda, J., Andreiuolo, P. & Pessoa, L. 2002 The neural correlates of moral senstivitiy: a functional magnetic resonance imaging investigation of basic and moral emotions. *J. Neurosci.* **22**, 2730–2736.

Moll, J., Oliveira-Souza, R. & Eslinger, P. 2003 Morals and the human brain: a working model. *Neuroreport* **14**, 299–305.

Moore, D. 2002 *The dependent gene*. New York: Times Books, Henry Holt.

Morse, S. 1976 The twilight of welfare criminology: a reply to Judge Bazelon. *S. Califormia Law Rev.* **49**, 1247–1253.

Nyffeler, T. & Regard, M. 2001 Kleptomania in a patient with a right frontolimbic lesion. *Neuropsychiatry Neuropsychol. Behav. Neurol.* **14**, 73–76.

Ochsner, K. N., Bunge, S. A., Gross, J. J. & Gabrieli, J. D. 2002 Rethinking feelings: an FMRI study of the cognitive regulation of emotion. *J. Cogn. Neurosci.* **14**, 1215–1229.

Paus, T., Zijdenbos, A., Worsley, K., Collins, D. L., Blumenthal, J., Giedd, J. N., Rapoport, J. L. & Evans, A.C. 1999 Structural maturation of neural pathways in children and adolescents: *in vivo* study. *Science* **283**, 1908–1911.

Raine, A. 2002 Biosocial studies of antisocial and violent behavior in children and adults: a review. *J. Abnorm. Child Psychol.* **30**, 311–326.

Ridderinkhof, K. R., de Vlugt, Y., Bramlage, A., Spaan, M., Elton, M., Snel, J. & Band, G. P. 2002 Alcohol consumption impairs detection of performance errors in mediofrontal cortex. *Science* **298**, 2209–2211.

Rilling, J. & Insel, T. 1999 The primate neocortex in comparative perspective using MRI. *J. Hum. Evol.* **37**, 191–223.

Sanchez, M., Young, L., Plotsky, P. & Insel, T. 2000 Distribution of corticosteroid receptors in the rhesus brain: relative absence of GR in the hippocampal formation. *J. Neurosci.* **20**, 4657–4668.

Sapolsky, R. 2001 Wild dreams. *Discover* **22**, 36–41.

Sapolsky, R. 2004 Stress and cognition. In *The cognitive neurosciences*, 3nd edn (ed. M. Gazzaniga). Cambridge, MA: MIT Press. (In the press.)

Schultz, W., Tremblay, L. & Holerman, J. 2000 Reward processing in primate orbitofrontal cortex and basal ganglia. *Cerebral Cortex* **10**, 272–284.

Schultz, J., Goodenough, O., Frackowiak, R. & Frith, D. 2001 Cortical regions associated with the sense of justice and with legal rules. *Neuroimage* **13** (Suppl.1), S473.

Simpson, J. R. Jr, Drevets, W. C., Snyder, A. Z., Gusnard, D. A. & Raichle, M. E. 2001 Emotion-induced changes in human medial prefrontal cortex. II. During anticipatory anxiety. *Proc. Natl Acad. Sci. USA* **98**, 688–693.

Tisserand, D. & Jolles, J. 2003 On the involvement of prefrontal networks in cognitive ageing. *Cortex* **39**, 1107–1128.

Tomarken, A. & Davidson, R. 1994 Frontal brain activation in repressors and nonrepressors. *J. Abnormal Psychol.* **103**, 339–349.

Urry, H., Van Reekum, C., Johnstone, T., Thurow, M., Burghy, C., Mueller, C. & Davidson, R. 2003 Neural correlates of voluntarily regulating negative affect. *Soc. Neurosci. Abstracts* **725**, 18.

Waxman, S. & Geschwind, N. 1974 Hypergraphia in temporal lobe epilepsy. *Neurology* **24**, 629–637.

Glossary

PFC   prefrontal cortex

13

The emergence of consequential thought: evidence from neuroscience

Abigail A. Baird and *Jonathan A. Fugelsang*

The ability to think counterfactually about the consequence of one's actions represents one of the hallmarks of the development of complex reasoning skills. The legal system places a great emphasis on this type of reasoning ability as it directly relates to the degree to which individuals may be judged liable for their actions. In the present paper, we review both behavioural and neuroscientific data exploring the role that counter-factual thinking plays in reasoning about the consequences of one's actions, especially as it pertains to the developing mind of the adolescent. On the basis of the assimilation of both behavioural and neuroscientific data, we propose a brain-based model that provides a theoretical framework for understanding the emergence of counterfactual reasoning ability in the developing mind.

Keywords: counterfactual; legal; functional magnetic resonance imaging; neuropsychology; reasoning; brain development

13.1 Introduction

One's ability to imagine alternative outcomes and understand the consequences of those outcomes is an essential component of human reasoning. Such *counterfactual thinking* typically involves imagining a set of circumstances leading up to an event that may have had a different outcome *if only* a critical preceding event did not take place. For example, consider the case in which an individual runs over a pedestrian while taking an alternative route home to drop off a coworker. Had the coworker not requested a ride home, the driver might not have taken the alternative route, and thus not struck the pedestrian. Given this set of circumstances, an individual can mutate the events preceding the outcome and judge the degree to which certain mutations could change the outcome (e.g. the consequences of their behaviour).

The legal system places great emphasis on this type of reasoning in that it demands that both judges and jurors use counterfactual thinking when determining the degree to which a particular person or event was responsible for a particular outcome (Spellman & Kincannon 2001). This of course raises several critical issues relating to the extent and efficiency with which people are able to reason counter-factually. These issues are relevant not only to the processes by which judges and jurors engage in counterfactual reasoning, but also relate to the extent to which defendants may be seen as liable for their actions.

In the present paper we will focus on this latter issue, with particular emphasis on its relevance to the developing adolescent. Specifically, we delineate: (i) the role that counter-factual thinking plays in reasoning about the consequences of one's actions; (ii) the neural substrates for counterfactual reasoning; and (iii) the limits that brain maturation

* Author for correspondence (abigail.baird@dartmouth.edu).

places on the ability to successfully reason counterfactually by adolescents. Furthermore, we propose a brain-based model that provides a framework for incorporating the cognitive and neural architecture of counter-factual thought, especially as it pertains to the developing mind. Finally, we suggest possible implications of developmental differences in counterfactual thought as they specifically apply to the juvenile justice system.

13.2 Psychological accounts of counterfactual reasoning

Given the multifaceted nature of counterfactual reasoning, it is not surprising that researchers from numerous disciplines have used a variety of metrics to measure performance on tasks designed to measure counterfactual reasoning processes. For example, cognitive studies of counterfactual reasoning have typically presented participants with story scenarios that involve a chain of events that may have contributed to a specific outcome and ask participants to either (i) generate counterfactual statements that may follow from a specific outcome (e.g. Guajardo & Turley-Ames 2004), (ii) derive ways in which a specific outcome could be undone by mutating the preceding events (e.g. Spellman & Kincannon 2001), or (iii) make forced choice judgements to inference tasks related to the information contained in the antecedent statements (Thompson & Byrne 2002).

Current psychological work on counterfactual thinking can be traced back to the proposal of the *simulation heuristic* by Kahneman & Tversky (1982). They proposed that people may spontaneously run '*if–then*' simulations when they are presented with information that has a negative outcome or is surprising. Specifically, they found that participants would mentally mutate exceptional antecedent events that preceded a fatal car crash. Recent studies have begun to investigate the extent to which this process of mutation through the generation of *if–then* simulations depends on executive and working memory resources.

This relationship between working memory and complex reasoning has now been firmly established in a number of reasoning domains including analogical reasoning (e.g. Morrison *et al.* 2004), deductive reasoning (e.g. Capon *et al.* 2003) and inductive reasoning (e.g. Reverberi *et al.* 2002). In fact, several prominent theories of reasoning rest on the assumption that both the complexity of the reasoning problems and subsequent demands on working memory relate closely to one's ability to generate alternative representations required for successful reasoning performance. Perhaps the most cited reasoning theory that has recently been applied to counterfactual reasoning (see Byrne 2002; Thompson & Byrne 2002) is the theory of mental models (Johnson-Laird 1983; Johnson-Laird & Byrne 1991). As the name implies, mental models are proposed to be internal mental representations of real or imaginary situations that can be derived from something you directly perceive in the environment. The important thing to consider for the present discourse is that mental models are thought to represent a *possibility* for how different events and relationships between events can be described. According to this theory, deductive reasoning occurs in stages whereby reasoners initially represent and then test tentative conclusions that may follow from the circumstances that they encounter. The final stage of reasoning involves the search and testing of *alternative models* that may be consistent or inconsistent with the initial representations of the scenario. Generating alternative representations, however, requires significant working memory resources and is thus rarely accomplished (e.g. Evans *et al*. 1999). Indeed, recent research has found that there are large individual differences in people's ability to generate alternatives, and subsequently reason effectively (Torrens *et al*. 1999; Newstead *et al*. 2002).

For example, Goldinger *et al*. (2003) examined the degree to which performance on a counterfactual reasoning task was influenced by memory load. Participants were given a series of short stories that contained either a prototypical non-surprising decision (control story), or an unusual surprising decision (counterfactual inducing story). Their task was to take the role of a potential juror and make judgements about compensation for a victim. The critical manipulation was the inclusion of a concurrent memory load task that required participants to hold in memory six bisyllabic words while rendering judgement. This concurrent memory load manipulation was intended to tax working memory and thus leave limited cognitive resources available for the primary counterfactual reasoning task. Participants had also been pre-tested on a simple memory span task in order to control for individual differences in basic working memory capacity.

Results demonstrated that participants were more likely to blame the victim when counterfactual thoughts were easily generated. That is, when participants could easily generate an alternative outcome by mutating the antecedent behaviour of the victim, the victim was judged as more liable for the outcome under question. This was true regardless of baseline memory function. Controlling for individual difference in baseline memory function, however, revealed an interesting result. Specifically, participants with relatively lower memory capacity were increasingly likely to blame the victim as a function of memory load. This occurred presumably because reasoning effectively with counterfactuals requires effortful processing and for individuals with a limited working memory capacity at baseline, such processing capacity is significantly diminished by the addition of a concurrent memory task. These latter findings seem counterintuitive when one considers the prior relationship between ease of alternative generation and victim blame and thus highlight the role of additional components of counterfactual thinking. It is important to note that effective counterfactual reasoning requires not only the generation of appropriate alternative courses of action, but also the ability to sort through and decide which behaviours would result in the appropriate outcome, and which would not. These capacities, as well as their integration, rely heavily on cognitive resources; resources that were not available under the memory load condition for participants with a low capacity at baseline.

13.3 Neural substrates of counterfactual reasoning

As described above, the ability to reason counterfactually is highly intertwined with executive function more generally. Because of the paucity of studies directly addressing the brain bases of counterfactual reasoning, it is helpful to interpret the few studies carried out within the context of what is known about the neural substrates of executive function. The term executive function has been used to define complex cognitive processing requiring the flexible coordination of several subprocesses to achieve a particular goal (Funahashi 2001). When these systems break down, behaviour becomes poorly controlled, disjointed and disinhibited (see Elliot (2003) for a review). The structure and function of the frontal lobes are intimately tied to executive processes. Data from both healthy and brain-damaged individuals have provided consistent evidence underscoring the central role that the frontal lobes play in executive function.

Patients with damage to the prefrontal cortex show impaired judgement, organization, planning and decision-making (Stuss & Benson 1984), as well as behavioural disinhibition and impaired intellectual abilities (Luria 2002). Despite the fact that selective aspects of executive function may appear intact in patients with frontal lobe damage, when coordination of a number of functions is required, either in a testing or real life situation, patients with frontal damage are often unable to perform the task (Stuss & Alexander 2000; Elliot 2003). Again, this underscores the significance of the frontal cortex in the generation and coordination of multiple processes that result in appropriate, goal-driven behaviour.

There is a growing body of literature that suggests that one way in which the frontal cortex may enable executive function is by flexibly coordinating with other cortical and subcortical regions. This is not surprising given the fact that the prefrontal cortex has been demonstrated to have reciprocal connections with nearly every part of the brain (see Petrides & Pandya (2002) for a review). In a clever meta-analysis, Duncan & Owen (2000) compared a variety of tasks posited to tap executive function and identified three areas that were reliably active across tasks. The studies examined in the meta-analysis manipulated a particular task demand: response conflict, task novelty, working memory load, memory delay or perceptual difficulty. For each of these demands, five or more studies had assessed the effects of manipulating that demand. Three main clusters were distinguished: dorsal anterior cingulate, a middorsolateral frontal region, and a mid-ventrolateral frontal region. The authors concluded that a common network, involving these three regions, is recruited by diverse cognitive demands. However, they did not rule out the possibility that there may be finer specializations within this network. The investigators suggest that it is possible that the three regions do subserve different functions, but that these functions are sufficiently abstract to be involved in many different complex cognitive tasks.

Similar to the workings of a car, no one would argue that an engine, tyres and steering wheel all serve the same function; however, their most common function is an interdependent and synergistic one, where together they provide transportation. Now, without taking the analogy too far, transportation can be useful to achieve many goals, as can executive function. It is thought that the three regions described above are domain general, but work seamlessly with more domain-specific networks, as is illustrated by tasks requiring semantic memory. Semantic memory is generally considered to be memory for facts, or declarative information. It has been established in the literature that the rich memories that we possess for factual information invoke a distributed network involving both ventral and dorsal streams of processing upon memory retrieval (Thompson-Schill 2003). Here, the degree to which visual, verbal, spatial or sensorimotor networks are recruited during semantic retrieval depends on the degree to which the original encoding episode evoked specialized neural circuitry devoted to domain-specific sensory processing. However, in concert with the recruitment of domain-specific neural circuitry associated with the sensory components of semantic memory, domain general processes in the form of controlled direct memory retrieval act to constrain and deliberate over the outcome of the lower-level sensory processes. This too is the realm of the DLPFC. Succinctly, successful performance on this type of task depends on a minimum of two distinct processes, the ability to generate the information itself and the ability to organize the output in terms of task relevance (i.e. making sure the generated fact fits the imposed category, keeping track of what items have already been said). In summary, the emerging view suggests that multiple brain regions combine with each other in vast numbers of ways, depending on the task requirements and, more generally, on the types of skills that a person, within a specific context, develops (Carpenter *et al.* 2000). Few complex behaviours illustrate executive function better than reasoning.

Consistent with the cognitive demands of everyday reasoning, lesion studies implicate the DLPFC as being essential for everyday reasoning (Shallice & Burgess 1991; Stuss & Alexander 2000). In addition, research by a number of cognitive neuroscientists examining both inductive reasoning (Goel & Dolan 2000; Seger *et al.* 2000) and deductive reasoning (Goel *et al.* 1998; Osherson *et al.* 1998; Parsons & Osherson 2001) using fMRI and positron emission tomography (PET) have pointed to the dominant role of the DLPFC in tasks that demand high-level reasoning. More recently, Goel & Dolan (2004) demonstrated preferential DLPFC activity during an inductive reasoning task (relative to a task that required deductive reasoning). Inductive reasoning is more sensitive to background knowledge rather than logical form, and is essential for knowing which ideas generalize and which do not. The increased activity in DLPFC may thus be because of use of world knowledge in the generation and evaluation of hypotheses (Grafman 2002), which is the basis of inductive reasoning.

Although it is abundantly clear that the prefrontal regions described at length above are involved in many types of reasoning, the additional components required for counterfactual reasoning have remained unclear. In terms of searching for a neural substrate for this type of reasoning, the fronto-striatal system is a likely candidate. There are several convergent lines of evidence that support this notion. In spite of the many functional imaging studies that have examinedmanytypes of reasoning, as well as itssub-components, no studies to date have used functional neuroimaging to examine the neural substrates of counterfactual reasoning. Given this, the scarce amount of lesion data becomes increasingly important. Parkinson's disease presents a unique case of a functional lesion. Recently, McNamara *et al.* (2003) have shown reliable deficits in counterfactual reasoning associated with Parkinson's disease.

Parkinson's disease is characterized by rigidity, bradykinesia, gait disorders, and sometimes tremors. The primary pathology involves loss of dopaminergic cells in the substantia nigra and the ventral tegmental area. These two subcortical dopaminergic sites give rise to two projection systems important for motor, affective and cognitive functioning. The nigrostriatal system, primarily implicated in motor functions, originates in the substantia nigra and terminates in the striatum. The meso-limbic–cortical system contributes to cognitive and affective functioning. It originates in the ventral tegmental area and terminates in the ventral striatum, amygdala and frontal lobes, as well as other basal forbrain areas. The degree of nigrostriatal impairment correlates with the degree of motor impairment, while ventral–tegmental–mesocortical impairment correlates positively with the degree of affective and intellectual impairment. The mesocortical dysfunction most probably has a negative impact on prefrontal function.

Previous neuropsychological investigations have consistently reported evidence of prefrontal dysfunction in Parkinson's patients (see McNamara *et al.* (2003) for a review of these findings). In addition to the observed cognitive deficits, the Parkinsonian personality is said to be rigid, stoic and characterized by low novelty seeking. Many patients in the mid to late stages of the disorder are perseverative both on tests of executive function and in their daily tendency to do counterproductive or even dangerous things (for example driving a car, working with power tools, taking on complex construction projects), despite warnings to avoid these dangers. We suggest that impairments in counterfactual reasoning might help explain why these patients fail to learn from past mistakes and thus why they persist in maladaptive or dangerous behaviour.

McNamara *et al.* (2003) asked both Parkinson's patients and age-matched controls to recall an autobiographical event that they perceived as having been negative. Following recall of the event, they were asked if they had any thoughts of how things might have gone differently (e.g. 'what if ' or 'only if ' type statements). All responses were recorded and the number of distinct counterfactual thoughts were tabulated. The investigators reported that relative to age-matched control subjects Parkinson's patients sponta-neously generated fewer counterfactuals than controls, despite showing no differences from controls on a semantic fluency test. Although the authors attribute the reduction in counterfactual generation to frontal dys-function, it is equally plausible that the deficits arise from the disruption of communication between the basal ganglia and frontal cortices. If the deficits were solely attributable to prefrontal deficits, one might have expected to see more impairment on the semantic fluency task, a task known to rely, in great part, on frontal function. Additional evidence for the role of the basal ganglia in response generation comes from a recent report of deep brain stimulation in Parkinson's patients. Witt *et al.* (2004) surgically stimulated a portion of the basal ganglia (the subthalamic nucleus) in 23 Parkinson's patients, and found that this treatment improved performance on the 'random number generation task', while performance on digit span and verbal fluency tasks were unchanged following treatment. Another group of individuals who show deficits in counter-factual reasoning, but possess a much better prognosis than those with Parkinson's disease, are adolescents.

13.4 Adolescent cognition

Adolescence is the period of life between puberty and adulthood. Adolescence begins at the onset of puberty, which technically refers to the time at which an individual is capa-ble of reproduction. Although estimates vary, pubertal onset generally occurs between the ages of 10 and 12 years for girls, and between 13 and 15 years for boys. Once a child is of reproductive age, they have entered adolescence, but are still far from adulthood. Adolescence describes this transitional time, where the individual undergoes major changes in physiological, social, emotional and cognitive functioning that over a period of years enable them to become an adult member of society.

The hallmark of adolescent cognition is the qualitative change that adolescent think-ing undergoes. Their thought becomes more abstract, logical and idealistic. Adolescents are more capable of examining their own thoughts, others' thoughts, and what others are thinking about them, and are more likely to interpret and monitor the world around them. What this suggests is that the primary change in adolescent cognition is a dramatic improvement in the ability to think and reason in the abstract. Piaget (1954) believed that adolescents are no longer limited to actual, concrete experiences as anchors for thought. They can create make-believe situations, events that are entirely hypothetical possibilities, or strictly abstract propositions. The primary gain in adolescent cognition is that in addition to being able to generate abstract thought, they are able to reason about the products of their cognition.

There are phases to the emergence of adolescent thought. In the first phase, the increased ability to think hypothetically produces unconstrained thoughts with unlimited possibilities. This early adolescent thought submerges reality (Broughton 1978). During the later phases, the adolescent learns to better regulate their thoughts, measuring the products of their reasoning against experience and imposing monitoring or inhibitory cognitions when appropriate. By late adolescence, many individuals are able to reason in ways that resemble those of adults; however, it is clear that the emergence of this ability depends in great part on experience, and therefore does not appear across all situational domains simultaneously. Simply, adult-like thought is more likely to be used in areas where adolescents have the most experience and knowledge (Carey 1988). During development, adolescents acquire elaborate knowledge through extensive experience and practice in multiple settings (e.g. home, school, sports). The development of expertise in different domains of life bolsters high-level, developmentally mature-looking thought. Experience, and the ability to generalize about it, gives older adolescents two important improvements in reasoning ability. Greater experience, and an improved system for organizing and retrieving the memories of experience, enables the adolescent to recall and apply a greater number of previous experiences to new situations. Additionally, an increased ability to abstract and generalize may allow an adolescent to reason about a situation that they have not directly experienced. Improvements in executive function are largely the result of the synergistic maturation in working memory capacity, selective attention, error detection and inhibition, all of which have been shown to improve with maturational changes in brain structure and function.

13.5 Adolescent brain maturation

It is now well established that the overall volume of the human brain does not change dramatically after the age of *ca.* 3 years old (see Thompson *et al.* 2000). Brain maturation, therefore, can be almost entirely attributed to the reorganization and refinement of this relatively fixed space. This process occurs in two distinct ways, myelination and synaptic pruning, each of which directly affects brain functioning. Myelination is the process by which the 'wires' of the brain become insulated. Myelin is a fatty substance that increases the speed with which signals can travel in the brain. It also serves as an index of connectivity within the brain (see Baird *et al.* 2004). Myelinated fibers connect regions of grey matter and enable their communication. Grey matter, or cortex, is where the brain's 'work' is done, it is the light that is lit by the signal delivered via the white matter; it is also where changes in blood oxygenation are measured by fMRI to make inferences about brain function. Synaptic pruning is the process by which the connections within the grey matter are refined, it is believed that the brain follows a strict 'use or lose' policy with regard to grey matter. This process results in a more efficient cortex, and in conjunction with myelination, a more extensively connected cortex.

Perhaps the most consistently reported finding associated with adolescent brain development is the decrease of grey matter and the increase of white matter throughout the cortex, but most significantly within the frontal cortex (see Giedd *et al.* (1999) and Sowell *et al.* (1999) for reviews). The prefrontal cortex is of paramount interest in adolescent development largely because of its well-understood function with regard to cognitive, social and emotional processes in adulthood. The converging evidence of prolonged development and organization of the prefrontal cortex throughout childhood and adolescence (Huttenlocher 1979; Chugani *et al*. 1987; Diamond 1988, 1996) may suggest an important parallel between brain development and cognitive development.

One striking difference regarding the development of the prefrontal cortex relative to other cortical areas is the continuation of synaptic pruning into young adulthood. This decrease in synaptic density during adolescence coincides with the emergence of newly entwined cognitive and emotional phenomena. The secondary process that is likely to be taking place during this time is the fortification of synaptic connections that will remain into adulthood. There has been further speculation that this 'use it or lose it' process may represent the behavioural, and ultimately, the physiological suppressing of immature behaviours that have become obsolete because of the novel demands of adulthood (Casey *et al*. 2000). One can imagine that a response to a particular event in the environment will be potentiated by repeated exposure and subsequent strengthening of the relationship between that event and the generation of the appropriate response. The delayed maturation of this brain region allows the individual to adapt to the particular demands of their unique environment.

Evidence of age-related decreases in grey matter, as a result of synaptic pruning, is borne out in the work of Casey *et al*. (2000) that consistently demonstrated increased volume of cortical activity in younger adolescents who perform less well on tasks of cognitive control and attentional modulation. This pattern of greater brain activity in children relative to adults is suggestive of a gradual decrease in the brain tissue required to perform the task. This observed decrease parallels the observed decrease in frontal grey matter volume, and may result from the elimination of redundant or superfluous synapses (Sowell *et al*. 1999). Many researchers have documented that while there are age-related decreases in grey matter in the pre-frontal cortex, the overall cortical volume does not change significantly. Not surprisingly, the cortical volume remains stable because of simultaneous expansion of white matter that may be equally important in terms of functionality (Klingberg *et al*. 1999). The greater volume of frontal white matter observed during adolescence is probably the result of greater axonal myelination. Increases in the speed with which information is processed in the mature brain may reflect this important structural change. Specifically, maturational improvements in frontal connectivity, both within the frontal cortex and with more distal regions (specifically the parietal cortex and basal ganglia, respectively), tracks closely with age-related behavioural improvements in working memory (Olesen *et al*. 2004), as well as response selection and inhibition (Durston *et al*. 2002).

Another consistent set of findings in the neurodevelopmental literature describes changes in basal ganglia structure and connectivity. Sowell *et al*. (1999) reported reductions in the grey matter volume of the basal ganglia, while a number of investigators have reported age-related increases in white matter integrity in the internal capsule, the band of fibres responsible for communication between the thalamus, basal ganglia and cortex (for a review see Schmithorst *et al*. 2002). The structural and functional maturation of the fronto-striatal circuit has been directly related to improvements in performance on the Stroop task (Blumberg *et al*. 2003) and inhibitory control (Durston *et al*. 2002).

In addition to the frontal and basal ganglia, the parietal cortex also undergoes a great deal of developmental change during adolescence. Similar to what has been described above, there have been numerous accounts of parietal grey matter reduction during adolescence (Giedd *et al*. 1999; Sowell *et al*. 1999; Thompson *et al*. 2000). These changes in the parietal cortex track closely with similar reductions observed in the

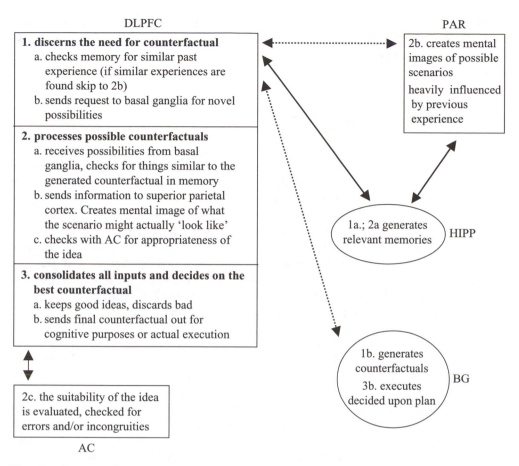

Fig. 13.1 A proposed brain-based model for the generation of counterfactual reasoning. AC, anterior cingulate; BG, basal ganglia; HIPP, hippocampus; PAR, parietal cortex. The dashed lines indicate projections that mature during adolescence.

frontal cortex (Sowell *et al*. 2003). Additionally, the white matter tracks connecting frontal and parietal cortices become increasingly embellished during adolescence as evidenced by both magnetic resonance (MR) studies (Olesen *et al*. 2004) and electro-encephalogram (EEG) studies (Thatcher 1994). Finally, the maturation of fronto-parietal connectivity has been found to be highly correlated with improvements in working memory (Olesen *et al*. 2004). In addition to working memory, the observed refinements in the parietal cortex are also likely to contribute to improvements in mental imagery as well as representations of one's body in space. It is conceivable that one role that the mature parietal cortex plays is allowing an individual to 'try on' a particular experience (i.e. envision themselves engaging in an imagined activity). In the case of counter-factual reasoning, it is plausible that the 'what ifs' generated by the basal ganglia are sent to the prefrontal cortex for logical approval, and following initial approval are forwarded to the parietal cortex to 'see what it might look like', to check the feasibility of the behaviour for the individual. For example, this has become a rather common practice for individuals using mental imagery to improve their golf swing, a method that has recently been shown to produce activity in both pre-frontal and parietal cortex (Ross *et al.* 2003). A hypothesized graphical depiction of the brain-based networks subserving counterfactual thought, their interrelations and developmental trajectory is depicted in figure 13.1.

13.6 Implications for legal thought

What does the development of counterfactual reasoning mean for the justice system? One direct implication of this model is that young adolescents may lack the neural hardware to generate behavioural alternatives in situations demanding a response. For example, adolescents are more likely than most adults to engage in risk-taking behaviour. While there are a myriad of theories about why this is the case (see Spear (2002) for an extensive review), one reason for increased risk taking in adolescents might be their inability to generate alternatives and potential outcomes prior to the initiation of behaviour. More specifically, a great number of adults think about driving their cars at excessive speeds, and while some adults do engage in this behaviour, adults are more likely to also envision a number of counterfactual scenarios that vary in their desirability. This is an important component of appreciating potential consequences of actions.

As stated in § 1, the legal system places great emphasis on the ability to appreciate the consequences of one's actions. Additionally, jurors are more likely to assign greater levels of culpability if they believe that a specific outcome under deliberation would not have occurred 'if only' the action carried out by an individual or organization ensued an alternative action preceding the outcome. As previously stated, adolescents are much more likely to reason abstractly about situations where they have had some previous experience; however, it is the interaction of continued experience and refinements in the adolescent brain that enable the emergence of counterfactual reasoning, as well as the appreciation of consequences, in the absence of actual experience. What the evidence presented in this review suggests is that it may be physically impossible for adolescents to engage in counterfactual reasoning, and as a result of this are often unable to effectively foresee the possible consequences of their actions.

On 19 July 2004, a large number of organizations including the leading American medical, religious and legal institutions, child and victim advocate groups and representatives from nearly 50 countries, along with prominent individuals, including Nobel Peace Prize Laureates and former US Diplomats, filed amicus curiae briefs calling for an end to the juvenile death penalty. 'In their friend-of-the-court briefs, the groups state that the juvenile death penalty violates evolving standards of decency, that it serves no legitimate purpose and is excessive in light of emerging evidence showing the limited capabilities of juveniles, and that the practice is almost universally rejected by the international community' (see http://www.deathpenaltyinfo.org).

Both the American Medical Association and the American Psychological Association have submitted briefs to the United States Supreme Court, reviewing deficiencies in brain structure, function and concomitant behaviour in adolescents relative to adults. Accordingly, these deficiencies warrant exclusion from the death penalty and violate the Eighth Amendment of the United States Constitution, which states that 'excessive bail shall not be required, nor excessive fines imposed, nor cruel and unusual punishments inflicted'. The spirit of this logic is captured in the case of Thompson versus Oklahoma, where the Supreme Court prohibited the execution of juveniles whose crimes were committed prior to their sixteenth birthday. Justice Stevens emphasized the relative immaturity of adolescent cognition:

> Less culpability should attach to a crime committed by a juvenile than to a comparable crime committed by an adult. The basis of this conclusion is too obvious to require extensive explanation. Inexperience, less intelligence and less education make a teenager less able to evaluate the consequences of his or her conduct while at the same time he or she is more apt to be motivated by mere emotion or peer pressure than is an adult. The reasons that juveniles are not trusted with the privileges and responsibilities of an adult also explain why their irresponsible conduct is not as morally reprehensible as that of an adult.
>
> (Thompson versus Oklahoma 1998,487, U.S. 815, p. 835).

The final sentence of Justice Steven's remarks provides the most irony with regard to juvenile justice. In the state of Texas, where more than half of all executions for crimes committed as juveniles have occurred, one cannot attend an R-rated movie unless they are 17 years old. Additionally, an individual cannot purchase a lottery ticket, and perhaps most importantly, serve on a jury, until the age of 18. For juvenile defendants, a jury made up of 15, 16 and 17 year olds is clearly called for by the sixth amendment of the United States Constitution, which guarantees a defendant the right to a trial by a jury of their peers. The idea of a teenage jury violates not only common sense, but also the laws that mandate individuals be a minimum of 18 years old to serve on a jury. Therein lies a bewildering conflict.

While an infant is learning to walk, there may be days when they pull themselves up on the furniture or their parents, they may also balance on their feet without holding onto anything. As anyone who has witnessed an infant learning to walk can report, the first few steps are usually followed by a tumble and sporadic reattempts. They may take their first steps one day, and then not walk again for several days following this initial foray. We acknowledge that this process is nonlinear and a result of the interaction of both an immature brain and lack of experience. Within the developing adolescent, the emergence of adult levels of reasoning is no different. An adolescent may demonstrate an adult-like ability to reason abstractly, and act in accordance with this advanced cognition on Monday, but behave impulsively and irrationally on Thursday. What these two examples have in common is the idea that the appearance of a behaviour does not indicate its permanence. Adolescence is an awkward time, both in terms of movement and thinking, during which the individual becomes increasingly coordinated.

Developmental neuroscience has yet to conclusively offer a chronological age at which we can be absolutely certain that an individual's brain structure and function have become fully mature. A great deal of work remains to be carried out to answer this question convincingly. Until such time, it is of paramount importance that researchers, practitioners and members of the legal community continue to work together to ensure the well being of both our society and its children.

References

Baird, A. A., Colvin, M. K., VanHorn, J., Inati, S. & Gazzaniga, M. S. 2004 Functional connectivity: integrating behavioral, DTI and fMRI datasets. *J. Cogn. Neurosci.* (In the press.)

Blumberg, H. P., Kaufman, J., Martin, A., Whiteman, R., Zhang, J. H., Gore, J. C., Charney, D. S., Krystal, J. H. & Peterson, B. S. 2003 Amygdala and hippocampal volumes in adolescents and adults with bipolar disorder. *Arch. Gen. Psychiatry* **60**, 1201–1208.

Broughton, J. M. 1978 Development of concepts of self, mind, reality, and knowledge. In *Social cognition* (ed. W. Damon), pp. 75–100. San Francisco, CA: Josey-Bass.

Byrne, R. M. J. 2002 Mental models and counterfactual thinking. *Trends Cogn. Sci.* **6**, 405–445.

Capon, A., Handley, S. & Dennis, I. 2003 Working memory and reasoning: an individual differences perspective. *Thinking Reasoning* **9**, 203–244.

Carey, S. 1988 Are children fundamentally different kinds of thinkers and learners than adults? In *Cognitive development to adolescence* (ed. K. Richardson & S. Sheldon), pp. 105–138. Hillsdale, NJ: Earlbaum.

Carpenter, P. A., Just, M. A. & Reichle, E. D. 2000 Memory and executive function: evidence from neuroimaging. *Curr. Opin. Neurobiol.* **10**, 195–199.

Casey, B. J., Giedd, J. N. & Thomas, K. M. 2000 Structural and functional brain development and its relation to cognitive development. *Biol. Psychol.* **54**, 241–257.

Chugani, H. T., Phelps, M. E. & Mazziotta, J. C. 1987 Positron emission tomography study of human brain functional development. *Ann. Neurol.* **22**, 487–497.

Diamond, A. 1988 Abilities and neural mechanisms underlying AB performance. *Child Dev.* **59**, 523–527.

Diamond, A. 1996 Evidence for the importance of dopamine for prefrontal cortex functions early in life. *Phil. Trans. R. Soc. B* **351**, 1483–1493.

Duncan, J. & Owen, A. M. 2000 Common regions of the human frontal lobes recruited by diverse cognitive demands. *Trends Neurosci.* **23**, 475–483.

Durston, S., Thomas, K. M., Worden, M. S., Yang, Y. & Casey, B. J. 2002 The effect of preceding context on inhibition: an event-related fMRI study. *Neuroimage* **16**, 449–453.

Elliot, R. 2003 Executive functions and their disorders. *Br. Med. Bull.* **65**, 49–55.

Evans, J. S. B. T., Handley, S. J., Harper, C. N. J. & Johnson-Laird, P. N. 1999 Reasoning about necessity and possibility: a test of the mental model theory of deduction. *J. Exp. Psychol. Learn.* **25**, 1495–1513.

Funahashi, S. 2001 Neuronal mechanisms of executive control by the prefrontal cortex. *Neurosci. Res.* **39**, 147–165.

Giedd, J. N., Blumenthal, J., Jeffries, N. O., Castellanos, F. X., Liu, H., Zijdenbos, A., Paus, T., Evans, A. C. & Rapoport, J. L. 1999 Brain development during childhood and adolescence: a longitudinal MRI study. *Nature Neurosci.* **10**, 861–863.

Goel, V. & Dolan, R. J. 2000 Anatomical segregation of component processes in an inductive inference task. *J. Cogn. Neurosci.* **12**, 110–119.

Goel, V. & Dolan, R. J. 2004 Differential involvement of left prefrontal cortex in inductive and deductive reasoning. *Cognition* **93**, B109–B121.

Goel, V., Gold, B., Kapur, S. & Houle, S. 1998 Neuroanatomical correlates of human reasoning. *J. Cogn. Neurosci.* **10**, 293–302.

Goldinger, S. D., Kleider, H. M., Azuma, T. & Beike, D. R. 2003 Blaming the victim under memory load. *Psychol. Sci.* **14**, 81–85.

Grafman, J. 2002 The structured event complex and the human prefrontal cortex. In *The frontal lobes* (ed. D. T. Stuss & R. T. Knight), pp. 292–310. Oxford University Press.

Guajardo, N. R. & Turley-Ames, K. J. 2004 Pre-schoolers' generation of different types of counterfactual statements and theory of mind understanding. *Cogn. Dev.* **19**, 53–80.

Huttenlocher, P. R. 1979 Synaptic density in human frontal cortex: developmental changes and effects of aging. *Brain Res.* **163**, 195–205.

Johnson-Laird, P. N. 1983 *Mental models*. Cambridge University Press.

Johnson-Laird, P. N. & Byrne, R. M. J. 1991 *Deduction*. Hillsdale, NJ: Lawrence Erlbaum Associates.

Kahneman, D. & Tversky, A. 1982 The simulation heuristic. In *Judgement under uncertainty: heuristics and biases* (ed. D. Kahneman, P. Slovic & A. Tversky), pp. 201–210. Cambridge University Press.

Klingberg, T., Vaidya, C. J., Gabrieli, J. D., Moseley, M. E. & Hedehus, M. 1999 Myelination and organization of the frontal white matter in children: a diffusion tensor MRI study. *Neuroreport* **10**, 2817–2821.

Luria, A. R. 2002 Frontal lobe syndromes. In *Handbook of clinical neurology*, vol. **2** (ed. P. J. Pinken & G. W. Bruyn), pp. 725–757. Amsterdam: North Holland.

McNamara, P., Durso, R., Brown, A. & Lynch, A. 2003 Counterfactual cognitive deficit in persons with Parkinson's disease. *J. Neurol. Neurosurg. Psychiatry* **74**, 1065–1070.

Morrison, R. G., Krawczyk, D. C., Holyoak, K. J., Hummel, J. E., Chow, T. W., Miller, B. L. & Knowlton, B. J. 2004 A neurocomputational model of analogical reasoning and its breakdown in frontotemporal lobar degeneration. *J. Cogn. Neurosci.* **16**, 260–271.

Newstead, S. E., Thompson, V. A. & Handley, S. J. 2002 Generating alternatives: a key component in human reasoning? *Mem. Cogn.* **30**, 129–137.

Olesen, P. J., Westerberg, H. & Klingberg, T. 2004 Increased prefrontal and parietal activity after training of working memory. *Nature Neurosci.* **7**, 75–79.

Osherson, D., Perani, D., Cappa, S., Schnur, T., Grassi, F. & Fazio, F. 1998 Distinct brain loci in deductive versus probabilistic reasoning. *Neuropsychologia* **36**, 369–376.

Parsons, L. M. & Osherson, D. 2001 New evidence for distinct right and left brain systems for deductive versus probabilistic reasoning. *Cereb. Cortex* **11**, 954–965.

Petrides, M. & Pandya, D. N. 2002 Association pathways of the prefrontal cortex and functional observations. In *Principles of frontal lobe function* (ed. D. T. Stuss & R. T. Knight), pp. 31–51. Oxford University Press.

Piaget, J. 1954 The construction of reality in the child. (Translated by M. Cook.) New York: Basic Books.

Reverberi, C., Lavaroni, A., Gigli, G. L., Skrap, M. & Shallice, T. 2002 Inductive inferences and the frontal lobes. *Cortex* **38**, 899–902.

Ross, J. S., Tkach, J., Ruggieri, P. M., Lieber, M. & Lapresto, E. 2003 The mind's eye: functional MR imaging evaluation of golf motor imagery. *Am. J. Neuroradiol.* **24**, 1036–1044.

Schmithorst, V. J., Wilke, M., Dardzinski, B. J. & Holland, S. K. 2002 Correlation of white matter diffusivity and anisotropy with age during childhood and adolescence: a cross-sectional diffusion-tensor MR imaging study. *Radiology* **222**, 212–218.

Seger, C., Poldrack, R., Prabhakaran, V., Zhao, M., Glover, G. & Gabrieli, J. 2000 Hemispheric asymmetries and individual differences in visual concept learning as measured by functional MRI. *Neuropsychologia* **38**, 1316–1324.

Shallice, T. & Burgess, P. W. 1991 Deficits in strategy application following frontal lobe damage in man. *Brain* **114**, 727–741.

Sowell, E. R., Thompson, P. M., Holmes, C. J., Jernigan, T. L. & Toga, A. W. 1999 *In vivo* evidence for post-adolescent brain maturation in frontal and striatal regions. *Nature Neurosci.* **2**, 859–860.

Sowell, E. R., Peterson, B. S., Thompson, P. M., Welcome, S. E., Henkenius, A. L. & Toga, A. W. 2003 Mapping cortical change across the human life span. *Nature Neurosci.* **6**, 309–315.

Spear, L. P. 2002 The adolescent brain and age-related behavioral manifestations. *Neurosci. Behav. Rev.* **24**, 417–463.

Spellman, B. A. & Kincannon, A. 2001 The relation between counterfactual ('but for') and causal reasoning: experimental findings and implications for jurors' decisions. *Law Contemp. Probl.* **64**, 241–264.

Stuss, D. T. & Alexander, M. P. 2000 Executive functions and the frontal lobes: a conceptual view. *Psychol. Res.* **63**, 289–298.

Stuss, D. T. & Benson, D. F. 1984 Neuropsychological studies of the frontal lobes. *Psychol. Bull.* **95**, 3–28.

Thatcher, R. W. 1994 Cyclic cortical reorganization: origins of human cortical development. In *Human behavior and the developing brain* (ed. G. Dawson & K. Fischer), pp. 232–266. New York: Guilford Press.

Thompson, P. M., Giedd, J. N., Woods, R. P., MacDonald, D., Evans, A. C. & Toga, A. W. 2000 Growth patterns in the developing brain detected by using continuum mechanical tensor maps. *Nature* **404**, 190–193.

Thompson, V. A. & Byrne, R. M. J. 2002 Reasoning counter-factually: making inferences about things that didn't happen. *J. Exp. Psychol. Learn.* **28**, 1154–1170.

Thompson-Schill, S. L. 2003 Neuroimaging studies of semantic memory: inferring 'how' from 'where'. *Neuropsychologia* **41**, 280–292.

Torrens, D., Thompson, V. A. & Cramer, K. M. 1999 Individual differences and the belief bias effect: mental models, logical necessity, and abstract reasoning. *Thinking Reasoning* **5**, 1–28.

Witt, K., Pulkowski, U., Herzog, J., Lorenz, D., Hamel, W., Deuschl, G. & Krack, P. 2004 Deep brain stimulation of the subthalamic nucleus improves cognitive flexibility but impairs response inhibition in Parkinson disease. *Arch. Neurol.* **61**, 697–700.

Glossary

DLPFC   dorsolateral prefrontal cortex
fMRI   functional magnetic resonance imaging

14

Responsibility and punishment: whose mind?
A response

Oliver R. Goodenough

Cognitive neuroscience is challenging the Anglo-American approach to criminal responsibility. Critiques, in this issue and elsewhere, are pointing out the deeply flawed psychological assumptions underlying the legal tests for mental incapacity. The critiques themselves, however, may be flawed in looking, as the tests do, at the psychology of the offender. Introducing the strategic structure of punishment into the analysis leads us to consider the psychology of the punisher as the critical locus of cognition informing the responsibility rules. Such an approach both helps to make sense of the counterfactual assumptions about offender psychology embodied in the law and provides a possible explanation for the human conviction of the existence of free will, at least in others.

Keywords: punishment; insanity defence; criminal law; neuroscience; game theory

14.1 Introduction

The essays collected in this issue demonstrate how the discoveries of cognitive neuroscience are rapidly expanding our understanding of the workings of the human brain. As our models of human mental processes improve, they are beginning to inform debates in other fields. In the law, the rules for assessing criminal responsibility have become the object of such an examination, both in essays within this issue (Baird & Fugelsang 2004; Greene & Cohen 2004; Jones 2004; Sapolsky 2004) and elsewhere (e.g. Lewis 1998; Reider 1998; Winslade 2002; see also Morse 2004).

Although these critiques are persuasive in discrediting their target, i.e. the psychological model of 'free will' that informs the legal tests for responsibility, they are directed at the wrong locus of cognition. Although the legal tests are phrased in terms of the psychology of the person to be punished, I believe that the critical psychology is that of the punisher. The law of responsibility makes much more sense if it is looked at from the strategic position of an agent assessing whether to inflict punishment on a transgressor in a context of social interaction. In this brief essay I will sketch an alternative frame of analysis based on this starting point. In my view, to be optimally effective, a potential punisher will take a committed position, that the agent standing in threat of punishment has a capacity for choice about action that we might well describe as 'free will'. The potential punisher will be persuaded out of this position only in the face of overwhelming evidence. The results of such an approach may be subject to criticism, but they are not illogical. Furthermore, this approach provides a possible explanation for the human conviction that free will exists. Finally, for those who make the distinction between a 'positive' analysis and a 'normative' one, this essay may be viewed as a positive account of the psychology underlying commonly held normative views. It must leave to another occasion a discussion of the useful scope of that distinction itself.

14.2 The law of responsibility

In the Anglo-American legal tradition, one of the predicates for criminal punishment is a showing that the accused meets a test for being able to act responsibly. The failure to meet that requirement is a possible defence to a criminal prosecution. In the United States, this test has come in five principal 'flavours': the *M'Naghten* rule, the 'irresistible impulse' test, the *Durham* standard, the American Law Institute Model Penal Code definition and the federal statutory definition of insanity (Reider 1998; Dressler 2001; Sapolsky 2004). There are two basic components to the test: a cognitive requirement and a volitional requirement. The cognitive component focuses on whether the offender had the capacity to understand the wrongful and/or unlawful nature of the criminal act. The volitional component asks whether or not the offender had the ability to control whether or not he committed the criminal act. The variations in the five flavours revolve largely around the degree to which each of the two requirements is taken into account and the severity of the deficit necessary to provide a legal excuse.

No matter which test is invoked, the US courts have taken a relatively parsimonious approach to accepting the defence, although there have been, over the years, a few widely publicized exceptions to this parsimony; exceptions that often lead to a backlash and a return to even greater parsimony (Reider 1998; Dressler 2001). Generally, only people suffering from extreme and obvious deficits are able successfully to invoke the defence; and often not even them (Lewis 1998). Even success is not a 'get-out-of-jail free' card— the alternative is often a long period of civil commitment for mental illness.

14.3 Critiquing the law of responsibility: a personal addition

The psychology of transgression underlying these tests is subject to challenge, and the picture of human thought emerging from the new neuroscience is strengthening these objections. In this issue, Greene & Cohen (2004) argue that the ideas of 'free will' and blame that bolster the traditional approach are fundamentally untenable, and that the law should shift from a retributive model of punishment to a forward-looking, consequentialist one, more interested in effective prevention than in assessing blame. Consequentialists, they argue, will 'hold people responsible for crimes simply because doing so has, on balance, beneficial effects through deterrence, containment, etc.' (Greene & Cohen 2004). Sapolsky (2004) takes a similar view, reinforcing it with a detailed examination of the role of the prefrontal cortex in decision-making. In particular, he focuses on problems with the *M'Naghten* test, which makes a lack of cognitive awareness of the nature of the action the critical point and largely devalues the volitional aspect. Baird & Fugelsang (2004) look at limitations in the ability of adolescents to fully consider the consequences of their actions, limitations based both in experience and developmental neurobiology. Reider (1998) called for a new test for the insanity defence, promoting an approach that would incorporate the discoveries of neuroscience into moral and legal theory.

In her book *Guilty by reason of insanity*, Lewis (1998) has offered a particularly telling critique of the law of responsibility and insanity, told with a passion and power born of a direct involvement with specific cases. Focusing on death-row inmates, she identifies a widely shared profile of organic brain injury, abuse as a child, and the denial of a loving, nurturing relationship with a parent or other care-giver. The cumulative effect of all of these insults is to remove layer after layer in the systems of desire, control and inhibition that keep most of us from committing capital crimes.

I say most of us, but I have only good luck and the fast reactions of my best friend in high school to thank for not being a statistic of conviction myself. Loss of control is not something that happens only to some distinguishable other. As an 18-year-old, I came close to injuring my best friend seriously, maybe even killing him, in a brief moment of furious rage. We were walking back from a squash game; we often played together. He had beaten me, and was not letting me forget it. I had had a bad day in other contexts, although nothing extraordinary. For some reason his teasing was too much for me. I just 'lost it'. I turned, raised my racquet, and swung it down at his head with all my strength. Luckily, his reactions were quicker than mine, here as well as on the court. He got his racquet up just in time to block my attack. My rage passed almost instantaneously. He swore at me and asked what I thought I was doing. I was unable to really answer; I had not been 'thinking' in any sense that he meant. After calling me an idiot, he kept on walking with me. We stayed friends; the experience has remained vivid in my memory.

As a subjective matter, I do not think any exercise of will would have stopped me from making that attack on my friend. I am not normally homicidal or violent; this person was my best friend at school; I was fully aware of the penalties for intentionally maiming or killing someone. For whatever reason, at that short moment, I was essentially undeterable. Some form of very hard determinism was at work. In Sapolsky's analysis, my prefrontal cortex had disappeared of the picture. I was, briefly, in the state of volitional free fall that must afflict Lewis' subjects every day.

Suppose I had connected with my friend's skull and killed him? Should I have been punished by the law? I have described my experience and posed this question to a variety of academic listeners, most of whom, responding with good intuitive promptness, say yes, of course. A few of the more thoughtful apply the legal tests and agree. Only a very few say no, you had no responsibility. What is going on?

14.4 Turning the perspective inside-out: the brain of a punisher

The law of criminal responsibility begins to make sense if we turn it inside out. Although the legal test for incapacity is phrased in terms of the psychology of the transgressor (and in terms that fall apart under the sophisticated scrutiny suggested in this issue by Sapolsky (2004) and Greene & Cohen (2004)), it is really a proxy for a theory of mind test by the punisher: does the transgressor fall within the class of agents on whom the strategic threat of punishment might have an effect? If so, then the punisher will maximize the effectiveness of the threat of punishment by making both a personal and a public commitment to the strategic presumption that the transgressor is free to choose a course of behaviour in the face of such a threat—i.e. has a form of free will. To understand the law, and its arguably counter-factual psychology of responsibility, we need to look at different brains—the brains of the punishers.

Humans can be viewed as relatively competent strategic actors. In game theory, a strategic actor is one who can take the probable actions and reactions of a different actor into account as he/she plans his/her own course of conduct. Game theory describes what happens when two or more strategic actors are paired in an interaction under a variety of conditions and constraints (see, for example, von Neumann & Morgenstern 1944;

Camerer 2003, 2004; Dixit & Skeath 2004). A key prerequisite to success in strategic thinking is to know what you are dealing with—another strategic actor with whom a strategic game can be played and whose mind and intentions can be 'read' according to the experience available to the strategic actor, or, alternatively, some kind of mechanistic object or process. The nature of the response may vary depending on this knowledge (Sanfey *et al.* 2003).

The ability to distinguish another mentally competent actor is often called a 'theory of mind' (e.g. Baron-Cohen *et al.* 1993; Frith & Frith 2003), and it has been suggested that theory of mind capacities are linked to the function of recognizing a strategic partner (Coricelli *et al.* 2000). History, anecdote and science suggest that the capacity may be over-applied, and that humans may err on the side of attributing strategic agency to non-strategic phenomena. The ancient Greeks saw lightning, heard thunder, and postulated Zeus as an explanation. Most of us have felt the urge to slap a computer that has frozen with a key document unsaved, or to kick a recalcitrant soda machine that has eaten our money and dispensed nothing; many of us have succumbed. Researchers both note the tendency for computer users to personify their machines (Reeves & Nass 1996) and work with that tendency to create psychologically effective interfaces (e.g. Dryer 1999). This apparent over-application suggests that the costs of a false attribution of strategic agency have been less onerous than those related to missing a strategic agent that in fact exists.

Punishment is a well-examined strategic move (Binmore 1998; Dixit & Skeath 2004), and one that is a deeply human trait. Whatever our longing for a utopia where the lion and the lamb lie down together in non-coerced peace and harmony, punishment for the transgression of norms is an important element in maintaining relatively cooperative human societies. Its effectiveness, and in some cases necessity, has been demonstrated both theoretically and as a matter of experimental study (Binmore 1998; Fehr & Gächter 2002; Fehr & Fischbacher 2004*a*). Punishment by a third party is particularly effective at stabilizing cooperative social structures (Bendor & Swistak 2001; Fehr & Fischbacher 2004*b*). The apparent ubiquity of punishment as an element in normative systems gives 'common sense' support to the importance of its role.

To be effective, threats of punishment must involve commitment. 'Tying yourself to a rule, which you would not want to follow if you were completely free to act at a later time, is an essential part of this process' (Dixit & Skeath 2004, p. 231). As parents discover, an empty threat is no threat at all. (A corollary of this is that threats need to be chosen carefully.) At its most extreme, this commitment can be assured by creating a mechanistic 'doomsday' device (a 'grim reaper' strategy), where a terrible consequence is simply unavoidable if the targeted default occurs (id). The adolescent game of 'chicken' involving driving two cars at each other and seeing who turns away first can often be won by the person who observably ties the wheel straight ahead and jumps into the back seat. Of course, if both jump, there is no winner. A possible corollary of this is that an actor will benefit strategically by forcefully and publicly committing him/herself to the proposition that the other driver cannot make the jump, and therefore will always be at the wheel. The convinced projection of a 'free will' model of choice on a potential offender as part of a punishment rule can be seen as a similar move to maximize the effect of a punishment threat.

Punishment by a third party is typically not without cost, however; it often requires the 'altruistic' bearing of a cost without any direct material gain (Fehr & Gächter 2002). It will be to the punisher's advantage not to waste punishment on those for whom it could never act as a deterrent.[1] This utilitarian logic is recognized in legal scholarship as one of the justifications for the insanity defence (Dressler 2001). In this, as in other strategic contexts where the outcome for an actor is influenced by the behaviour and choices of another and vice versa, it is costly to waste punishment on the truly un-influencible. In trust and ultimatum game experiments, the differential neurological and behavioural reactions to defections by a known computer as opposed to by a perceived human agent (Coricelli *et al.* 2000; Sanfey *et al.* 2003) suggest that human brains sort the world on precisely this kind of basis.

As discussed above in the context of the game of chicken, there appears to be a psychological tilt toward imputing 'free will' agency in doubtful cases; the countervailing costs of mistaken punishment, however, should constrain the extent of the tilt. This constraint can be gamed in return by a competent actor *faking* incapacity. Whereas most defendants claiming lack of mental capacity probably have at least some basis for their claim, Mafia don Vincent 'The Chin' Gigante notoriously wandered around New York's Greenwich Village in his pyjamas, muttering to himself, in what a federal court determined to be a calculated attempt to forestall prosecution (Tyre 1997). Furthermore, it is a rare defendant who is not at least somewhat intimidated by threats of legal punishment; almost anyone, in fact, walking the streets has some kind of partial control over impulsive, illegal actions (the psychology of the transgressor is of interest in this context). In a cooperative game where both sides play within these expectations, an agent threatening punishment will seek to avoid being deceived about incapacity and will work to make the other agent as suggestible as possible.

I believe that these goals lead to a commitment and to a bias in human psychology. *The commitment* is to treating the other agent as if he/she had the capacity to fully integrate the threat of punishment into its decision-making calculus, and to act accordingly, i.e. as if he/she had a kind of free will. Declaring this committed position both neutralizes attempts at deception by the transgressor and to some degree forces the role of a considering agent on the other player. However counterfactual the free will proposition may be in a deterministic world (Greene & Cohen 2004), it is a strategic fiction that underlies the productivity of a punishment rule, and is a fiction that may be deeply lodged in human cognitive and emotional psychology.[2] Our free will intuitions may be false in the world of deterministic science and yet nonetheless effective in the world of strategic interaction.

The bias will be against surrendering this commitment, even in the face of evidence to the contrary. The transgressor will seek to invoke the 'don't-waste-punishment' proposition, claiming, in the often-repeated words of children to their parents, 'I couldn't help it'. In fact, in many instances where punishment is inflicted, the transgressor indeed cannot help it—exactly the point made by Greene and Cohen, by Sapolsky, and by my own lapse into attempted manslaughter. Even in a fully accurate criminal system, those being punished will be either the inattentive or the undeterred, and many of the undeterred will be those who, for whatever reason, were, at the time of the criminal action, effectively the undeterable. Relaxing the bias against being persuaded of this fact, however, appears likely to lead to an increase in deception and to a decrease in attention to consequence, i.e. a decrease in deterability. In either case, the effectiveness of the punishment scheme would begin to unravel, a consequence described by Dixit & Skeath (2004) for a professor willing to listen to student excuses about paper deadlines. Only in the clearest, most common-sense recognized cases of near-total incapacity will the bias be overridden.

Holmes adopted this conclusion in his treatment of responsibility in criminal law:

> [The tests for liability] take no account of incapacities, unless the weakness is so marked as to fall into well known exceptions, such as infancy or madness. They assume that every man is as able as every other to behave as they command.
>
> (Holmes 1963)

Sadly, the efficacy of a punishment system may rest on a willingness to punish many people who really could not help it. For better or for worse, the Anglo-American approach to the law of responsibility, parsimonious in definition and in application, is consistent with both the commitment and the bias suggested here.

14.5 Possibilities for reform?

What do we make of a system like this? From an individual fairness standpoint, it does cry out for reform. Holmes, with his customary moral coolness (Alschuler 2000; Hoffman 2004), suggested that the convicted awaiting capital punishment should be viewed as dying for the good of society, not unlike soldiers on the battlefield (Holmes 1963). I am sceptical as to whether such an approach would provide much comfort to those on death row, and it is intuitively disturbing for society when honestly faced. This may be an issue where judgement at a macro-level sometimes reverses at the micro-level. Perhaps the insights of neuroscience about the development of reasoning in adolescents (Baird & Fugelsang 2004) will help to reinforce and reinstate rules prescribing less harsh treatment for offenders who are minors. Youth is a marker, which folk psychology, popular acceptance and the law have all recognized, at various points and in various degrees, as a reliable, unlikely to be faked, impairment of competence (Robinson & Darley 1995). Perhaps the increased understanding that neuroscience can provide about profound, but nonobvious, mental illness (Lewis 1998; Sapolsky 2004) will come to replace the common-sense estimations of mental illness that are rooted in our shared theory of mind capabilities. Greene and Cohen foresee such a change. However, any such reforms will face resistance from deeply rooted human psychology, based in the strategic logic of punishment: the psychology of the punisher.

14.6 Conclusions

The critiques in this issue and elsewhere, based in cognitive neuroscience, of the Anglo-American approach to criminal responsibility are correct in pointing out the deeply flawed psychological assumptions underlying the legal tests. The critiques themselves, however, may be flawed in looking, as the tests do, at the psychology of the offender. Introducing the strategic structure of the punishment decision into the analysis leads us to consider the psychology of the punisher as the critical locus of cognition informing the rule. Such an approach both helps make sense of the counterfactual assumptions about offender psychology embodied in the law and provides a possible explanation for the human conviction of the existence of free will, at least in others.

The author is grateful to the Gruter Institute for Law and Behavioral Research and to the Vermont Law School for support in this research, to Paul Zak, Morris Hoffman and Semir Zeki for comments in the draft stage, and to Sarah Sun Beale and the International Society for the Reform of Criminal Law for the opportunity and impetus to develop the approach described here.

Endnotes

1. Binmore (1998) suggests that there is also an incentive for the participants in a social order to seek light punishments, growing out of the possibility that each may end up, if only through inattention, on the wrong side of the law.
2. Fehr & Gächter (2002) have argued that emotional engagement is an important proximate mechanism for initiating altruistic punishment. See also Sanfey *et al.* (2003).

References

Alschuler, A. W. 2000 *Law without values: the life, work and legacy of Justice Holmes*. University of Chicago Press.

Baird, A. A. & Fugelsang, J. A. 2004 The emergence of consequential thought: evidence from neuroscience. *Phil. Trans. R. Soc. B* **359**, 1797–1804. (doi:10.1098/rstb.2004. 1549)

Baron-Cohen, S., Tager-Flusberg, H. & Cohen, D. J. 1993 *Understanding other minds*. Oxford University Press.

Bendor, J. & Swistak, P. 2001 The evolution of norms. *Am. J. Sociol.* **106**, 1493–1547.

Binmore, K. 1998 *Just playing: game theory and the social contract*. Cambridge, MA: MIT Press.

Camerer, C. F. 2003 Behavioral studies of strategic thinking in games. *Trends Cogn. Sci.* **7**, 225–231.

Camerer, C. F. 2004 Behavioral game theory: prediction human behavior in strategic situations. In *Advances in behavioral economics* (ed. C. F. Camerer, G. Loewnestein & M. Rabin), pp. 374–392. Princeton University Press.

Coricelli, G., McCabe, K. & Smith, V. 2000 Theory-of-mind mechanism in personal exchange. In *Affective minds* (ed. G. Hatano, N. Okada & H. Tanabe), pp. 249–259. Amsterdam: Elsevier.

Dixit, A. & Skeath, S. 2004 *Games of strategy*, 2nd edn. New York: W. W. Norton.

Dressler, J. 2001 *Understanding criminal law*. New York: Lexis.

Dryer, D. C. 1999 Getting personal with computers: how to design personality for agents. *Appli. Artif. Intell.* **13**, 273–295.

Fehr, E. & Fischbacher, U. 2004*a* Social norms and human cooperation *Trends Cogn. Sci.* **8**, 185–190.

Fehr, E. & Fischbacher, U. 2004*b* Third party punishment and social norms. *Evol. Hum. Behav.* **25**, 63–87. Available at www.iew.unizh.ch/wp/iewwp106.pdf.

Fehr, E. & Gächter, S. 2002 Altruistic punishment in humans. *Nature* **415**, 137–140.

Frith, U. & Frith, C. D. 2003 Development and neurophysiology of mentality. *Phil. Trans. R. Soc. B* **358**, 459–473. (doi:10.1098/rstb.2002.1218)

Greene, J. & Cohen, J. 2004 For the law, neuroscience changes nothing and everything. *Phil. Trans. R. Soc. B* **359**, 1775–1785. (doi:10.1098/rstb.2004.1546)

Hoffman, M. B. 2004 The neuroeconomic path of the law. *Phil. Trans. R. Soc. B* **359**, 1667–1676. (doi:10.1098/ rstb.2004.1540)

Holmes, O. W. 1963 *The Common law*. Boston: Little Brown & Co. [Re-edited edition published 1963, original edition published 1881.]

Jones, O. D. 2004 Law, evolution and the brain: applications and open questions. *Phil. Trans. R. Soc. B* **359**, 1697–1707. (doi:10.1098/rstb.2004.1543)

Lewis, D. O. 1998 *Guilty by reason of insanity: a psychiatrist explores the minds of killers*. New York: Fawcett.

Morse, S. J. 2004 New neuroscience, old problems. In *Neuroscience and the law: brain, mind and the scales of justice* (ed. B. Garland), pp. 157–198. New York: Dana Press.

Reeves, B. & Nass, C. 1996 *The media equation: how people treat computers, television, and new media like real people and places*. New York: Cambridge University Press.

Reider, L. 1998 Toward a new test for the insanity defense: incorporating the discoveries of neuroscience into moral and legal theories. *UCLA Law Rev.* **46**, 289–342.

Robinson, P. H. & Darley, J. M. 1995 *Justice, liability, and blame*. Boulder, CO: Westview Press.

Sanfey, A. G., Rilling, J. K., Aronson, J. A., Nystrom, L. E. & Cohen, J. D. 2003 The neural basis of economic decision-making in the ultimatum game. *Science* **300**, 1755–1758.

Sapolsky, R. M. 2004 The frontal cortex and the criminal justice system. *Phil. Trans. R. Soc. B* **359**, 1787–1796. (doi:10.1098/rstb.2004.1547)

Tyre, P. 1997 Mob bosses took a beating last year. *CNN Interactive U.S. News Story Page*, 3 January 1997, available at www.cnn.com/US/9701/03/mobster.wrap.

von Neumann, J. & Morgenstern, O. 1944 *Theory of games and economic behavior*. Princeton University Press.

Winslade, W. J. 2002 Traumatic brain injury and legal responsibility. In *Neuroethics: mapping the field* (ed. S. Marcus), pp. 74–82. New York: Dana Press.

Index

abandonment 191
Abnormal Conditions Focus models 159
accuracy 68–9
actor–observer paradox 87
adolescents 148, 214–16, 250–5
adoption 41
adverse possession 191, 192
agency 27–8
aggression 9, 235
alcohol 237
alienation 186
altruism 7–10
ambiguity 143–4
amygdala 30, 138, 141, 143, 145, 220, 235
analogical reasoning 161, 246
angular gyrus 149
anteroventral striatum 146
anticipation 236
antisocial behaviour 238, 240
association areas 12
attachments 190–2
autism 148, 220
automation 122–4
autonomic nervous system 138

basal ganglia 250, 252
behaviour
  biology 114
  cognitive 10
  complex 11
  evolution 6–7
  integrated models 62
  losing control 30, 261
  models 60–2
  proximate causes 59, 134
  simple 11
  three central rules 10–11
  ultimate causes 59, 134
behavioural biology 23, 25–6
behavioural data 89
behavioural economics 134
behavioural genetics 60
beliefs 159, 160–2, 163
bioassays 140
bioeconomics 134
biology
  behaviour 114
  law and 3–4, 60–1
  misuse xii, 63
  morality xv
bird warning cries 8
'bourgeois' strategy 190

Boys from Brazil problem 215–16
brain
  activity measurement xi, 89–90, 138–40
  association areas 12
  automation 122–4
  basic facts and terminology 136–40
  bottleneck 218
  Brodmann's areas 116, 136–7
  depth electrodes 140
  distributed function 116
  evolution xiii
  fingerprinting 27, 59
  grey matter 136, 251, 252
  gross anatomy 136–7
  imaging xiii, 58–9, 89–90, 93–4
  integration 86
  intervention technologies 58
  lesion studies 89–90, 93
  lie detection 27, 59, 179–80
  localized function 116
  location terminology 137–8
  maturation 251–4
  mind and 214
  modularity 86, 115
  multiplicity of information sources 87–8
  myelination 251
  neurochemistry 90
  neurons 136
  ownership 189–90
  plasticity 27
  primitives 86
  probabilistic model 13
  recruitment 86, 95–6
  specialization 86
  synaptic pruning 251, 252
  white matter 136, 252, 253

Cartesian dualism 11–12
Cataglyphis 57–8
categorical thinking 229–30
caudate nucleus 122, 142, 162, 176
causal reasoning 68, 157–66, 230–1
  Abnormal Conditions Focus models 159
  beliefs 159, 160–2, 163
  brain 161–2
  covariation principle 158–9
  enabling conditions 159–60
  expectations 159, 160–2, 163
  instructions 163
  legal decision-making 158–60
  models 158–60
  Power PC theory 158–9